Artificial Intelligence and Mobile Robots

Artificial Intelligence and Mobile Robots

Case Studies of
Successful Robot Systems

Edited by David Kortenkamp,
R. Peter Bonasso, and Robin Murphy

AAAI Press / The MIT Press

Menlo Park, California, Cambridge, Massachusetts, London, England

Copublished and distributed by The MIT Press, Massachusetts Institute of Technology, Cambridge, Massachusetts and London, England.

Library of Congress Cataloging-in-Publication Data

Artificial intelligence and mobile robots : case studies of successful
   robot systems / edited by David Kortenkamp, R. Peter Bonasso, and
   Robin Murphy.
       p.   cm.
   Includes bibliographical references and index.
   ISBN 0-262-61137-6 (pbk. : alk. paper)
   1. Mobile robots—Case studies. 2. Artificial intelligence
—Case studies. I. Kortenkamp, David, 1965– . II. Bonasso,
R. Peter (Russell Peter), 1947– . III. Murphy, Robin, 1957– .
TJ211.415.A78 1998
629.8'92—dc21   97-49701
                                                                CIP

Printed on acid-free paper in the United States of America.

10 9 8 7 6 5 4 3 2

Contents

Preface

Mobile robots pose a unique challenge to artificial intelligence researchers. They are inherently autonomous and they force the researcher to deal with key issues such as uncertainty (in both sensing and action), reliability, and real-time response. Mobile robots also require the integration of sensing, acting and planning within a single system. These are all hard problems, but ones that must be solved if we are to have truly autonomous, intelligent systems. Even those readers that do not use mobile robots can learn from the experiences of those researchers who do.

This book contains thirteen case studies of successful mobile robot systems. These robot systems were carefully chosen; they represent the best available implementations by leading universities and research laboratories. Many of the robots have distinguished themselves (usually with first or second place finishes) at various indoor and outdoor mobile robot competitions. These are not robots that simply work in the laboratory under constrained conditions. They have left the lab and been tested in natural and unknown environments. They have all demonstrated their robustness many times over.

The robot systems in this book perform many different tasks, from giving tours to collecting trash. However, many common themes are apparent throughout the book. Navigation and mapping are crucial to all robots systems. This includes sonar sensor interpretation, collision avoidance, localization and path planning. In many cases there are competing approaches to the same problem and the reader is encouraged to compare and contrast these approaches. Another theme common to many robots is computer vision. While some of the case studies describe robots that accomplish their tasks without vision, the majority use vision in many important ways. As yet, no robot performs complete scene recognition, instead vision is used selectively and tailored to a specific task or problem. A final common theme across the robot systems is architecture. James Albus states that architecture is "a description of how a system is constructed from basic components and how those components fit together to form the whole." Indeed, every robot has an architecture, even if implicitly. However, some researchers emphasize the role of architecture as a central component in their approach to robotics while others do not. Many architectures are described in this book and, again, the reader is encouraged to compare architectures across the case studies.

Each case study is self-contained and describes a complete robot system. As such, the reader will have thirteen complete mobile robot systems from which they can pick and choose the technologies that they might want to try on their mobile robot. Each case study includes detailed descriptions of important algorithms, including pseudo-code. Thus, this book serves as a "recipe book" for designing successful mobile robot applications.

We hope this book will encourage artificial intelligence researchers to apply their ideas to mobile robots. We believe that there is no better testbed for both researching and teaching AI than real-world, autonomous systems. The robots described in this book demonstrate the progress that has been made in the field of artificial intelligence and robotics. However, the field of mobile robots is still in its infancy with real-world, everyday applications few and far between. By leveraging the work described in this book, the community can move forward and tackle the important research issues that remain.

We wish to thank all of the chapter editors whose efforts made this book possible. We would also like to thank Kenneth Ford of AAAI Press for his advice on preparing the book, and his editorial comments. In addition, David Mike Hamilton of The Live Oak Press was instrumental in helping us produce a high-quality book on a short schedule. Finally, we gratefully acknowledge the use of computers and network facilities of the Robotics, Automation, and Simulation Division of NASA Johnson Space Center in the preparation of this book.

— David Kortenkamp, R. Peter Bonasso, Robin Murphy

Artificial Intelligence and Mobile Robots

Mobile Robots

A Proving Ground for Artificial Intelligence

R. Peter Bonasso, David Kortenkamp, and Robin Murphy

This book is about artificial intelligence (AI) as applied to *mobots*—mobile robots that perform tasks useful to people in an intelligent way. Within these pages, you will find reports on intelligent robots in office environments, outdoors on land and under water, alone or in concert, and in and among people or in remote locations.

Why is this book relevant today? The impetus has come from the success of the American Association for Artificial Intelligence (AAAI) Robot Competition and Exhibition held over the past five years. Since the first show in 1992 in San Jose, California, 30 different teams have competed, and almost that many more have exhibited intelligent robots. Participant teams and exhibitors have come from as far away as Korea and as near as the host city itself; they have included universities, companies, and ad hoc garage-based teams; they have been composed of undergraduates, young entrepreneurs, and senior professors alike. All the teams, however, have been unified in their purpose—to realize robotic agents that, on their own, can serve and work with humans in natural environments. That is their passion. This passion has a rather straightforward technical explanation: to integrate software and hardware to get the robot to act intelligently and autonomously in a given task and environment. The true breadth and depth of this undertaking, however, can only be sensed when you watch one or more of these creatures running unattended in the competition arena. Actor Alan Alda—leaping with excitement at the 1996 competition when one robot, after making little headway in its task, finally succeeded with but scant seconds left on the clock—remarked that only then could he understand why the competitors undertook such a tedious, yet ultimately rewarding, task.

However, the competition is really only a focused reflection of the broader progress that AI researchers have made toward building an artificial person. Research in the field of mobile robots is critical to the AI community because it forces researchers to connect perception to action to support intelligent behavior. This connection can take many forms, as is shown in the chapters of this book, and it lies at the heart of what it means to be an intelligent system. Indeed, the revolution in practical, intelligent robots has been fomented in large measure by AI researchers trying to bring their work to bear on mobile robots. This progress crept along at a snail's pace until a fundamental paradigm shift took place around 1985.

The Sense-Plan-Act Paradigm

The link between mobile robotics and AI was probably first forged with SHAKEY the robot, developed at the Stanford Research Institute in the late 1960s (Nilsson 1969). After the dormant 1970s, the Defense Advanced Research Projects Agency (DARPA) Strategic Computing Program generated renewed research in the 1980s with its autonomous land vehicle (for example, Andresen et al. [1985]). By this time (largely as a result of the funding support from the government), AI research was beginning to produce, among other things, useful automated planning systems. Such large software systems could take a goal, a starting situation, and a desired situation and generate an ordered, finite set of actions—actions for human agents for the most part—that would bring about the desired situation. Written largely in Lisp, such planning systems admitted the intractability of solving general problems by incorporating large amounts of domain knowledge, including domain-specific analytic functions used to predict the future implications of actions. It seemed only reasonable then to apply these systems to robot platforms as a first step in realizing an autonomous artificial agent. The general approach taken, overly simplified, is shown in figure 1.

Sensors from the robot would populate the lower regions of a large structure, usually a complex semantic net, that served as a model of the world. This action could be time consuming—even with simple sensors. Data had to be conditioned to present to the world model as definitive a signal as possible. When the sensor was a camera, all visual data in each frame (typically, 512 x 512 x 8 bits a frame) went through preprocessing, known as *early vision*, to yield the image structures that the world model could process. The world model would interpret the sensor data by percolating the implications up through the network until logical propositions about the state of the world were produced. These propositional accounts of the world state then served as input, along with the goal and possibly some user preferences, to the planning process, which would churn through the possibilities to produce a set of actions that would provably bring about the desired situation. Each step of this plan would then be passed to the control level of the robot for execution, which meant that the plan had to include actions down to the actuator level. For example, if the first part of a plan to search for and retrieve an item was to move to a location, the first two

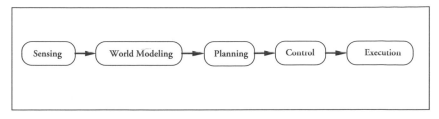

Figure 1. The sense-plan-act (SPA) paradigm.
The world model interpreted the sensor data such that a plan could be generated.
Each step of the plan was then executed using the robot control system.

commands might be "turn 0.56 radians" and then "move 122.25 centimeters."

Now the robot is moving. In a few seconds, its cameras detect in its path a large pothole that is not predicted by the world model. The sensor information is processed; the world model is populated; and at some point while the world model is trying to assert that the large black blob on the ground is a depression, not a shadow, the robot falls into the pothole. Even if downward-looking sonars are used, the crash might occur during one of the levels of plan operator decomposition. The point is that the sense-plan-act (SPA) cycle could not run fast enough to keep up with the state of the robot or the world. Much of the early work in applying AI to robots involved making the SPA cycle faster—faster central processing units, more memory, finer-tuned search algorithms—or making the robot run more slowly, indeed, so slowly that it hardly appeared to be moving at all.

From the standpoint of building an artificial person, or *android*, figure 2 (Bonasso and Dean 1996) describes this situation more generally. The robot's view of the world was transmitted directly to the brain using a general sensing apparatus. The amount of data moving from the sensors to the centralized computing resources was significant; therefore, the communication was slow and expensive. In the brain, the world was reconstructed into a form that the reasoning could process. The robots relied on building and maintaining these complex representations of the environment. These representations were motivated not by the task at hand but by a particular technology concerned with general representations of the world, physically resulting in much off-board computing or very large robots.

Even ignoring the computational overhead, it was difficult to keep the complex representations in sync with the real world. These baroque representations turned out to be impractical and unnecessary. Not only was the representation difficult, if not impossible, to maintain, but the associated planning systems attempted to use similarly rich representations for planning and prediction. Uncertainty made the underlying dynamics difficult to model and the representations of dubious value for most tasks.

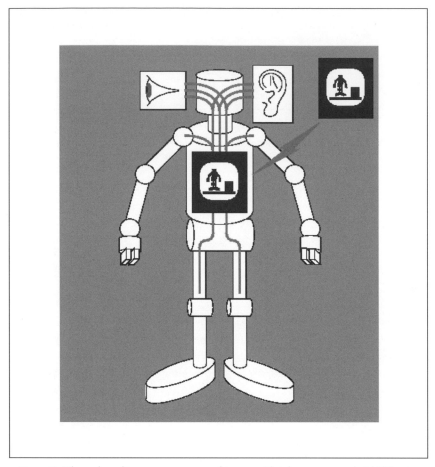

*Figure 2. The early architecture as represented in an artificial person, or android (following
the early Asimov novels, we depict the brains as being in the robot's belly).
Most of the computing was centralized, with the main processing concerned with the reconstruction of the world and with deliberative reasoning such as planning.*

The Paradigm Shift

In 1986, Rod Brooks published a landmark paper on the *subsumption architecture,* which heralded a fundamentally different approach to getting robots to
come alive. Brooks, a veteran of the computer vision community and its atten-
dant frustrations, began thinking about how animals seemed to bring fast, specific behaviors to bear to survive in the world. Brooks was not to the first to use
the findings of ethological research (for example, Arbib [1981]), but he was the

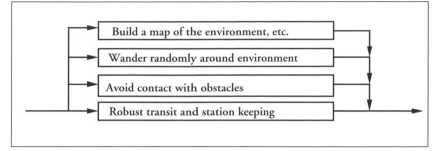

Figure 3. The new control paradigm.
Behaviors are run in parallel with arbitration at the robot actuators.

first to bring those findings to fruition with real mobile robots. He developed the subsumption language that would allow one to model something analogous to animal behaviors in tight sense-act loops using asynchronous finite-state machines. The first set of behaviors for a robot might simply be used to avoid letting anything come too close by running a little ways away but otherwise standing still. Another higher-level behavior might be to move in a given direction. This behavior would dominate the obstacle-avoidance behavior by suppressing its output to the actuators unless an object got too close. The higher levels subsumed the lower levels, hence the name of the architecture. The result was a robot that could wander around a laboratory for hours without colliding into objects or moving people, using only simple sonar or infrared sensors.

In short order, Brooks and his students were developing highly mobile robots—mobots, both wheeled and legged—that could chase moving objects or people; run to, or hide from, light or sound; or negotiate a cluttered landscape such as might be found in a rugged outdoor environment. In addition, they grew in sophistication. There was HERBERT, a soda-can–collecting robot (Connell 1990); GENGHIS, a robot that learned to walk (Maes and Brooks 1990; Brooks 1989); TOTO, a hallway-navigating robot (Mataric 1992); and POLLY, a tour-guide robot (Horswill 1993).

The AI community was alternately fascinated and frustrated by these "creatures." They were frustrated because they did not want to give up the expected power of formal systems or computer vision, but they did want the robots to survive and perform at the natural pace of humans and their environments, much as Brooks's mobots were demonstrating. However, there was hope because essentially Brooks was advocating not so much insect intelligence but a complete rearrangement of the SPA cycle, as shown in figure 3.

The idea was to build up capability in the robot through behaviors that ran in parallel, accomplishing possibly competing goals. These behaviors could execute well within the cycle times of most natural environments, yet with a reasonably simple arbitration among goals based on priorities, useful tasks could be accomplished. The world model was now distributed among the behaviors, with only the relevant part of the model being processed for each behavior. Simple plan generation, mostly for path planning, and the compilation of the resulting network of actions were done before run time. Returning to our previous example, the robot under the new control paradigm would detect the pothole with one of its low-level behaviors, merge an avoidance vector with the current direction vector, and smoothly veer from the danger on its way to its goal.

This paradigm shift in terms of our android architecture is shown in figure 4. It is characterized by simpler representations computed closer to the sensing apparatus and tailored to the particular tasks at hand. This change in representation resulted in smaller computational requirements. Coupled with improved technology in computers and batteries, on-board computing thus became practical, and the robots became smaller. This shift to reactive kinds of control also marked the first steps toward using distributed computing. In particular, robot manufacturers were marketing sensor systems with self-contained processing and standard communication buses. Thus, the practicality of plug-and-play behaviors increased the number of researchers who could develop reactive robots.

Intelligent Robots: The New Wave

Following Brooks's success, several research groups, some new and some not so new, began readvocating or exploiting this shift to increased emphasis on sensing and acting and reduced emphasis on planning. Arbib and Arkin (Arkin 1987) pioneered the new paradigm from a cognitive science perspective within the robotics community, calling it *action-oriented perception*. This approach has proven useful for manipulation (Iberall and Lyons 1984), navigation (Arkin et al. 1987), and sensor fusion (Murphy 1996). Efforts by Khatib (1985) and Payton (1986) illustrate the reactive movement originating in engineering fields.

Formalizing the Reactions

For the AI formalists, the work of Stan Rosenschein and Leslie Kaelbling (1986) stands out. They proved that if one could represent robot goals of state achievement and maintenance in the form of an electronic circuit, a consistent semantics could be maintained between the memory states of the circuit and the states of the world represented by these states. The REX language compiled propositional goal states and robot actions for achieving these states into circuits (actually C-based simulations of circuits) that executed in bounded time and usually on the order of 10 hertz. Thus, the programmer was allowed to use a propositional language to specify desired goals, yet the robot was able to execute the required resulting actions in real time. To deal with multiple goals that would

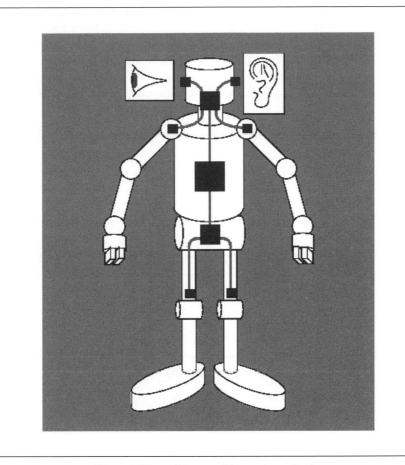

Figure 4. The architecture of the reactive android.
Most of the computing is distributed in sense-act behaviors running
close to the robot's sensors. These robots were fast and reactive, but
few were considered useful for normal human endeavors.

contend for the robot's sensors or actuators (the REX compiler would flag conflicting commands to the robot), REX programs typically included a scheme to arbitrate among active circuits.

Animate Vision

What of the use of cameras for robots? Human and animal vision are the most powerful perception systems. However, we have seen how the processing of the low-level data alone, much less the addition of rapid control of a pan-tilt head, seemed to have little chance of fitting into the new paradigm. Fortunately, in the late 1980s, an analogous paradigm shift was taking place in the way researchers were approaching vision for agents.

Again using ethology, several researchers began using animal visual behaviors as models for computational counterparts. For example, a frog primarily used its motion detection to catching flying food. Other animals keyed on specific aspects of the color spectrum for certain tasks. Indeed, psychophysical studies showed the human visual system to be, not surprisingly, even more adept. The human retina is arranged in such a manner as to have a higher concentration of receptors in the center and decreasing numbers radiating outward. Thus, humans don't process square arrays of data, for example, 512 x 512 x 8 bits, in a time step; rather, they use lower-resolution peripheral vision to watch for indications of motion or looming objects while they concentrate the higher-resolution center of the retina—the *fovea*—to reason about a specific object or part of an object in great detail. Humans don't take in everything at once in all its color and motion dimensions; instead, they concentrate on a narrow portion of their visual field.

Moreover, humans move this portion rapidly about the environment in patterns dictated by the task at hand and the last time step of visual information that was produced. For example, when looking at a picture of a group of people, if one is asked what the ages of the people are, one's eyes move in a pattern that concentrates on the faces of the people, with a few scans to determine the height of the people. To determine where a cup is in the picture, the eyes dart quickly about the picture for a table, then move to the objects on the table. Only when told that they must remember as many objects in the picture as possible will the eye-scanning machinery move in a pattern resembling the scan of a full image as found in the classic algorithms of computer vision (Ballard 1991).

Now computer vision paradigms were being recast into small, quick behaviors that not only dealt with a given field of view more efficiently but also where to next point the pan-tilt head of the camera. These well-defined, compact routines, such as tracking a given color or attending to peripheral motion, were much like the behaviors being developed by the nouveau planning community and could now be incorporated as another part of the paradigm shift in programming robots.

A New Kind of Mapping

Just as AI had much to learn from the attempts to make robots intelligent, so did the robotics community stand to gain from the same endeavor. A good example was the use of maps for robot navigation. Early maps in the robotics community were geometric in nature, often as grids with each cell representing some amount of space in the real world. The grid had a single-coordinate system in which elements were represented. These maps became sophisticated at representing the spatial structure of the world (Moravec and Elfes 1985). It also was easy to do path planning and obstacle avoidance with geometric maps (for example, Lozano-Perez and Wesley [1979] and Brooks [1982]). However, geometric maps, as a part of the traditional world model of the robot, can require vast amounts of memory for large areas; in addition, the robot must know precisely where it is so that it can reason from the map or add to it. Just as with computer vision, trying to maintain accurate geometric maps was computationally intensive and extremely difficult in real-world situations.

The solution, in keeping with the paradigm shift in vision, was the use of topological maps (Kuipers and Byun 1987; Brooks 1985). Patterned after how humans represent space, topological maps represent the world as a graph of places connected by arcs, thus using no metric or geometric information, only the notions of proximity and order. With a topological map, the robot navigates locally from place to place, minimizing movement errors. Moreover, topological maps are clearly much more compact in their representation of space.

This notion was rapidly adopted by the AI and robotics communities. Kuipers and Byun (1991) continued their work on topological maps, producing a representation of space called the *spatial semantic hierarchy*. Another implementation of topological maps, by Kortenkamp and Weymouth (1994), used both sonar and vision to determine places in a topological representation. The first part of this book introduces several other topological-based map representations and also some initial attempts at integrating topological and grid-based map representations.

Return to Planning

Although the movement away from general representations was considered healthy, the resulting degree of specialization was viewed with some alarm. As Chuck Thorpe of Carnegie Mellon University once remarked about Brooks's robots: "I wouldn't want one to be my chauffeur." In point of fact, many researchers exploring the new paradigm had no intention of throwing out the classic planning baby with the bath water. However, it was clear that planning in both its form and its function had to be rethought.

Two researchers involved in this rethinking by looking at the psychophysical aspects of human activity were Phil Agre and David Chapman (1987). Their research pointed to evidence that humans somehow put together plans for action based on the set of routine behaviors they can carry out. Moreover, logical decomposition planning is rarely invoked in the course of human affairs, and when it is, it serves primarily as a guide to the general direction in which one should head rather than a production of rigid sets of action.

During the late 1980s and early 1990s, several approaches along these lines were being pursued at once for intelligent robots. There were attempts to expand on the mobot approach (Maes 1990); others went further in the direction of enumerating all possible actions using planning prior to run time (for example, Kaelbling [1988] and Schoppers [1987]). Still others tried a combination of these approaches (for example, Bonasso [1991]).

One of the most important of these efforts was the work by Jim Firby (1989) on reactive action packages (RAPs). In his dissertation, Firby described a three-layered architecture with classic planning at the top, a reactive layer of behaviors at the bottom, and a middle layer with the goals of the resulting plan executed as dynamic sequences of these behaviors (that is, RAPs). When this framework was significantly expanded (Bonasso et al. 1995; Gat 1992), it became possible to program a large variety of robots—or any group of computer-controlled machines for that matter—to carry out a variety of tasks over long duration in the vicinity of, and in concert with, human counterparts. Erann Gat's chapter in this book on the three-layered approach explains why it has become a popular approach for the design and implementation of intelligent robots.

Figure 5 shows the current approach to intelligent robotics in our android form. We might call this approach P-SA; that is, the robot plans based on initial conditions and common knowledge (P) and then executes this plan using sense-act (SA) behaviors, replanning only when the reactive behaviors run out of routine solutions. In this architecture, simple representations are tailored to specific tasks. Layered software allows behaviors such as obstacle avoidance to coordinate smoothly with behaviors such as path following. A new level of routines—cached plans—execute between the reactive behaviors and the central brain, and planning and other deliberate reasoning guide the procedures and behaviors in accomplishing the primary task and interacting with humans. In addition, there have been some remarkable advances in hardware. Plug-and-play subsystems that combine sensors and effectors are much more common.

The AAAI Mobile Robot Competition and Exhibition

By 1992, AAAI had decided that there was enough interest in AI as applied to mobile robots that it held a Robot Competition and Exhibition at its Tenth National Conference on Artificial Intelligence (AAAI-92) in San Jose. Ten teams competed in three events (Dean and Bonasso 1993). The events consisted of finding tall poles in a large arena while avoiding stationary obstacles.

The disadvantages of the SPA approach were fairly well acknowledged at the first competition, but we still saw a mixed bag of generalists and specialists, and the advantages and disadvantages were illustrated in a fairly dramatic way. One

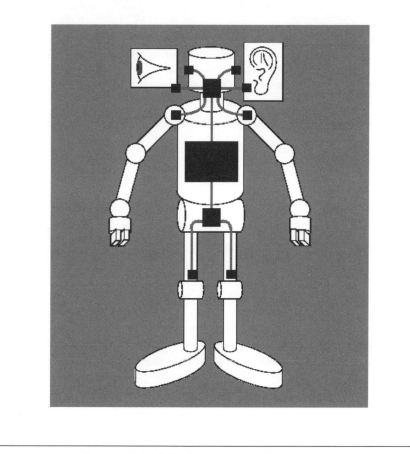

Figure 5. Today's hybrid approach to intelligent robotics.
Reactive behaviors close to the sensors are orchestrated by cached plans operating between the behaviors and the central processor. Deliberative reasoning takes place at the central brain and serves to guide the functioning of the rest of the system.

robot builder took the P-SA idea to the extreme. A robot called SCARECROW, built by Dave Miller and his son Jacob (Yeaple 1992), had no computer and instead utilized simple electromechanical feedback loops to generate relatively simple but remarkably effective behavior given the task at hand—locating and identifying tall poles in a cluttered arena. SCARECROW did not use a systematic method for exploring its environment; instead, it performed what was essentially a random walk. SCARECROW offered a dramatic illustration of a theoretical result—a short random walk in an undirected graph will visit every location in the graph with high probability. What SCARECROW lacked in intelligence (like its namesake in the *Wizard of Oz*, SCARECROW had no brains), it made up for in raw speed; as a result, it was still a contender going into the final event and finished fourth overall, beating many more traditionally intelligent robots.

Nonetheless, the winner of the 1992 competition was a robot strong on reactive behaviors (in particular, a fast sonar activation and response scheme) and lean on deliberative algorithms. David Kortenkamp's chapter in this book recounts the design of this winning robot, CARMEL.

The event was an unqualified success and led to a second competition and exhibition at AAAI-93 in Washington, D.C. The tasks were more complicated, including pushing boxes into a pattern, escaping from an office with real furniture, and navigating in an office building (Konolige 1994; Nourbakhsh et al. 1993). This step up in complexity proved to be difficult for the robots, and the next competition, at AAAI-94 in Seattle, again focused on office navigation as well as on trash cleanup (Simmons 1995). The following year, the competition moved to the Fourteenth International Joint Conference on Artificial Intelligence (IJCAI-95) in Montreal, Canada, with a slightly harder set of tasks built on the previous competition (Hinkle et al. 1996). The tasks involved giving the robots navigation directions in an office building and picking up and sorting trash. At the AAAI-96 in Portland, Oregon competition, (Kortenkamp et al. 1997), there was another incremental increase in the difficulty of the tasks, including having robots detect the occupancy of a room and having robots catch moving balls. By AAAI-97, held in Providence, Rhode Island, the state of the art was sufficiently advanced for the organizers to stage four competitions at once. "Find Life on Mars" combined the open space navigation of the first competition with vision-based search and small article manipulation. "Where's the Remote" required the recognition and fetching of everyday objects in a home, without engineering the environment. The "Home Vacuum" contest involved keeping several rooms of a house cleaned, while not disturbing the human occupants. In a break from the technical direction of all previous competitions, "Hors d'Oeuvres Anyone?" required the robots to move about a crowded reception area while serving hors d'oeuvres and being entertaining as well—an event that was, by far, the most popular of the contests.

The robot competitions provide a good yardstick with which to measure progress in the field (although certainly not the only measure). The first competition involved finding tall poles rising above small static obstacles. Teams could mark the poles in any way they wanted. The object was simply to visit the poles. In the most recent competition, one task was to use a sparse map to visit two conference rooms in an office building and determine if they were occupied. Along the way, people could be walking in the corridors, and hallways and doorways could be blocked. The robots also had to estimate how long it would take them to finish the task. The second task involved picking up tennis balls, as well as a moving "squiggle" ball, and placing them in a pen. This is a significant amount of progress in five years, and many of the case studies in this book document the different robots that have performed exceptionally in the competition as well as robots that have performed well in a separate competition for outdoor mobile robots patterned after the ARPA Unmanned Ground Vehicle Initiative.

About This Book

This book consists of thirteen case studies of AI techniques applied to mobile robots. These case studies were largely taken from competitors in the AAAI robot competitions, allowing the reader to compare and contrast the different approaches to tasks that require sensing, acting, and planning. Here, we give a brief overview of each case study and explain why it has been included in this volume. The case studies in this book are divided into three parts: navigation and mapping, vision for mobile robots, and mobile robot architectures.

Navigation and Mapping

The chapters in this section concentrate on the issue of getting around in the world. Substantial progress has been made in this area in the last five years, and there are many excellent solutions to the problems of obstacle avoidance, pose (position and orientation) estimation, and global path planning. The following chapters offer tried-and-true methods for mobile robot navigation and mapping:

Sebastian Thrun and his colleagues Arno Bücken, Wolfram Burgard, Dieter Fox, Thorsten Fröhlinghaus, Daniel Hennig, Thomas Hofmann, Micheal Krell, and Timo Schmidt describe a mobile robot called RHINO in their chapter on map learning and high-speed navigation. They present an innovative technique for constructing topological maps from grid maps. They also give algorithms for performing localization within maps and doing path planning with both grid maps and topological maps. Finally, they discuss vision-based approaches to building maps.

David Kortenkamp and his colleagues Marcus Huber, Charles Cohen, Ulrich Raschke, Frank Koss, and Clare Congdon describe CARMEL, the robot that won the first AAAI Mobile Robot Competition and Exhibition in 1992. This robot integrated a high-speed obstacle-avoidance technique called *vector field histogramming* (VFH) with a simple, yet effective, object-recognition technique. Algorithms for VFH, path planning, vision-based localization, and object recognition are described in detail.

Illah Nourbakhsh describes a robot called DERVISH that won the 1994 AAAI Mobile Robot Competition and Exhibition in Seattle, Washington. It was the first mobile robot to use probabilistic state progression to navigate reliably with little explicit map information. DERVISH also used a unique sonar configuration to perform robust obstacle avoidance.

Sven Koenig and Reid Simmons show how to use partially observable Markov decision process models (POMDPs) to build a navigation architecture that allows for localization, pose estimation, path planning, and learning. They present results using their robot XAVIER, which wanders the hallways of Carnegie Mellon University for hours at a time while it responds to requests made over the internet.

Vision for Mobile Robots

In the second section, we begin to look closely at the specific uses of computer vision in mobile robotics. Although vision is not necessary to perform many mobile robot tasks, it is desirable for many reasons, including its long-range high resolution and its passive sensor (that is, it doesn't emit energy). Thus, it is ideal for outdoor mobile robots, and several of the chapters in this part specifically address this domain.

Ian Horswill's chapter describes the design of a robot that uses real-time vision as its sole sensing modality and performs complicated navigation tasks that included giving tours of parts of the Massachusetts Institute of Technology Artificial Intelligence Laboratory. POLLY takes a minimalist approach based on Brooks's subsumption architecture. POLLY provides proof that relatively simple algorithms and components, specialized to task requirements, can create robust systems.

Robin Murphy describes the Colorado School of Mines entries in the 1994 and 1995 Autonomous Unmanned Vehicle Systems (AUVS) International Unmanned Ground Vehicle Competitions. She presents architectural paradigms for coordination and control of perception, with a special emphasis on how sensing is interfaced with acting. She describes a simplified version of Dickmanns's road-following algorithm and explains how it was implemented on two outdoor mobile robots.

Bill Schiller and his colleagues Yu-Feng Du, Don Krantz, Craig Shankwitz, and Max Donath also look at mobile robots that operate in outdoor road-following environments. Their autonomous land experimental vehicle (ALX) uses vision for road following and sonar sensors for obstacle detection and collision avoidance. A real-time control strategy arbitrates between processes for visual perception, path tracking, obstacle detection, and collision avoidance.

Mobile Robot Architectures

A mobile robot architecture reflects the overall design principles of its designers, which have been learned from many years of trial and error. At the 1995 AAAI Spring Symposium, James Albus (1995) stated that "an architecture is a description of how a system is constructed from basic components and how those components fit together to form the whole" The case studies in this section look closely at the issues of architecture and how it influences mobile robot design and performance.

Erann Gat's chapter on three-layer architectures, discusses the approach alluded to in the previous section, Return to Planning, that has been used successfully on a variety of robots as well as to control life-support systems. Gat shows how three different groups of researchers arrived at the same architectural conclusion and gives us an example of how he used a three-layer architecture to win an event in the second national AI robot competition.

Kurt Konolige and Karen Myers describe the SAPHIRA architecture for autonomous mobile robots in their chapter. This architecture emphasizes coordination of behavior, coherence modeling, and communication with other agents. Konolige and Myers show how this architecture was used to perform a complicated task that involved attending to a human agent, taking advice about the environment using natural language, and recognizing gestures. Their robot, FLAKEY, placed second in the 1992 AAAI Mobile Robot Competition and Exhibition. Successors to FLAKEY, using the same architecture, placed second in the 1994 robot competition and first in the 1996 competition.

Jim Firby, Peter Prokopowicz, and Michael Swain present an animate agent architecture, which integrates reactive plan execution, behavioral control, and active vision within a single software framework. This framework includes reactive skills and the RAP reactive planning system. Their robot—CHIP—is one of the few discussed in this book that performs manipulation tasks. CHIP placed second at the 1995 AAAI Mobile Robot Competition in trash pickup and sorting.

Ron Arkin and Tucker Balch explore the exciting research area of cooperating mobile robots. They present two applications: an outdoor task in which teams of high mobility multipurpose wheeled vehicles (HMMWVs) must coordinate their actions and an indoor trash-collection task (for which they placed first in the 1994 AAAI competition). Their approach to multirobot coordination is centered on a reactive schema-based control architecture that has its roots in neuroscience and psychology.

Housheng Hu and Michael Brady describe a series of mobile robots that use a distributed architecture called the *locally intelligent control agent* (LICA). LICA encourages a modular approach to building complex control systems. The authors show how path planning and localization can be done on robots using their architecture. In particular, they give detailed algorithms for global path planning and dynamic localization using artificial beacons.

Finally, Don Brutzman describes the difficulties unique to underwater robots in his chapter about PHOENIX, an autonomous underwater vehicle (AUV). Most vision sensors are useless underwater, and unlike land vehicles, the very medium in which the autonomous underwater vehicle travels generates forces that must be reckoned with in even the simplest of behaviors. Brutzman describes a particularly successful approach to AUV development using simulations and distributed computer graphics.

The Future

Already the technical successes we have seen in the robot competitions over the years are finding their way into practical applications. Today unattended mobots fetch and carry in semistructured hospital environments. Vacuum mobots are used regularly in North American industry to clean large storage and staging spaces during off-work hours. Mobots are also used to semiautonomously explore uninhabitable venues such as Terran volcanoes and Martian landscapes. The case studies in this book are ample proof that mobots have technically evolved to a point where, today, they are poised to help humankind in broad ranging tasks from mapping the ocean floor and long-term nursing home care to planetary colonization.

For mobots to move to the next level of competence necessary to complete such tasks, however, they need a broader base of technical support. It is our hope that, from this book, AI researchers will be inspired to expend additional effort in mobile robot research. One of the editors is fond of saying that "acting and sensing are still the hardest parts." So naturally, new developments in robot perception and low-level control will always be necessary to advance the state of the art and meet the challenge of applications in difficult environments such as under water or outer space.

Mobots can benefit from all artificial intelligence disciplines, however, and, as we have previously explained, the robot architectures that support more traditional AI research are already in place. Mobots need to reason about their acts, both for feasibility and for rationality. Thus they can benefit from advances in planning and logical theories of sensing and acting. Most future robot tasks will involve working with humans. Consequently, spoken language generation and understanding must be developed for them to be effective team members. For missions of long duration—such as those involving deep sea or planetary exploration—mobots must adapt their behavior, and even their preferences over time. This requirement involves machine learning at all levels of competency.

The time has thus come, and the technology is here, for artificial intelligence and robotics to more closely join forces in improving the quality of life on earth and in establishing new civilizations in the cosmos.

Acknowledgements

The authors wish to acknowledge Tom Dean's insights into the evolving architectural issues of the AAAI robot competitions and his android graphical depictions. These first appeared in an invited talk for AAAI 96 entitled "A Retrospective of the AAAI Robot Competitions."

Mapping and Navigation

This is a book about mobile robots. While it is possible for a robot to be mobile and not do mapping and navigation, sophisticated tasks require that a mobile robot build maps and use them to move around. Levitt and Lawton (1990) posit three basic questions that define mobile robot mapping and navigation:

- Where am I?
- How do I get to other places from here?
- Where are other places relative to me?

Each of the case studies in part one of this book address one or more of these questions. Each uses a different approach to representing and using spatial information. As such, they span the spectrum of options for mapping and navigation.

On one side of the spectrum are purely metric maps. In these representations, the robot's environment is defined by a single, global coordinate system in which all mapping and navigation takes place. Typically, the map is a grid with each cell of the grid representing some amount of space in the real world. These grids became quite sophisticated at representing the spatial structure of the world (see, for example, Moravec and Elfes [1985]). The case study of CARMEL by Kortenkamp and his colleagues describes a mobile robot that uses a grid-based approach to mapping and navigation. These approaches typically work well in bounded environments, with little consistent structure and where the robot has opportunities to realign itself with the global coordinate system using external markers.

On the other side of the spectrum are qualitative maps, in which the robot's environment is represented as places and connections between places. Indeed, the idea of a map that contains no metric or geometric information, but only the notions of proximity and order, is enticing because such an approach eliminates the inevitable problems of dealing with movement uncertainty in mobile robots. Movement errors do not accumulate globally in qualitative maps as they do in maps with a global coordinate system since the robot only navigates locally, between places. Qualitative maps can also be more compact in their representation of space, in that they represent only interesting places and not the entire environment. Qualitative maps (also referred to as topological maps) have become increasingly popular in mobile robotics (see, for example, Brooks 1985; Kuipers and Byun 1991; and Kortenkamp and Weymouth 1994). The case studies by Nourbakhsh and by Koenig and Simmons describe the current state-of-the-art in qualitative mapping. These techniques work well in structured environments (i.e., office buildings) where there are distinctive places that are goals for the robot.

There have been efforts to combine metric and qualitative maps so that the strengths of both representations can be used (Asada et al. 1988; Kuipers and Levitt, 1988). The first case study in this part, by Thrun and his colleagues, gives an overview of both metric and topological mapping and describes their approach to integrating these two representations.

David Kortenkamp

CHAPTER ONE

Map Learning and High-Speed Navigation in RHINO

Sebastian Thrun, Arno Bücken, Wolfram Burgard, Dieter Fox,
Thorsten Fröhlinghaus, Daniel Hennig, Thomas Hofmann,
Michael Krell, and Timo Schmidt

Building autonomous mobile robots has been a primary goal of robotics and artificial intelligence. This chapter surveys some of the best methods for indoor mobile robot navigation that have been developed in our lab over the past few years. The central objective of our research is to construct reliable mobile robots, with a special emphasis on autonomy, learning, and human interaction.

In the last few years, we have built a mobile robot system, RHINO, which is capable of exploring and navigating in unknown indoor office environments with a speed of approximately 90 centimeters per seconds. While doing so, it can learn metric and topological maps and, based on these, perform all kinds of missions. In addition, RHINO is capable of locating and retrieving objects, delivering them to specific locations or dumping them into trash bins without human intervention, and giving tours to visitors.

The purpose of this chapter is to present the key ideas and algorithms underlying our research in a coherent and accessible form in order to share our experiences and, if possible, provide some guidance for building autonomous mobile robots. The following list summarizes the primary software design principles underlying our approach.

- Distributed and decentralized processing. Control is distributed and decentralized. Several on-board and off-board machines are dedicated to several subproblems of modeling and control. All communication between modules is asynchronous. There is no central clock, and no central process controls all other processes.

- Any-time algorithms. Any-time algorithms are able to make decisions regardless of the time spent for computation (Dean and Boddy 1988). Whenever possible, any-time algorithms are employed to ensure that the robot operates in real-time.

Figure 1. The robot RHINO.

- Hybrid architecture. Fast, reactive mechanisms are integrated with computationally intense, deliberative modules.
- Models. Models, such as the two-dimensional maps described below, are used at all levels of the architecture. Whenever possible, models are learned from data.
- Learning. Machine learning algorithms are employed to increase the flexibility and the robustness of the system. Thus far, learning has proven most useful close to the sensory side of the system, where algorithms such as artificial neural networks interpret the robot's sensors.
- Modularity. The software is modular. A plug-and-play architecture allows us to quickly reconfigure the system, depending on the particular configuration and application.
- Sensor fusion. Different sensors have different perceptual characteristics. To maximize the robustness of the approach, most of the techniques described here rely on more than just a single type of sensor.

These principles are important, since robots and their environments are complex physical systems. Robot environments are dynamic and inherently unpredictable, and robot hardware often fails or malfunctions, as do our computers and our communication networks. To control a robot reliably, the software must react adequately and timely to sudden changes, failures, delays, or other unforeseen events—which requires special care when designing robot control software.

This chapter focuses exclusively on robot navigation. In particular, it describes our current best approaches for mapping indoor environments, and for high-speed exploration and navigation in dynamic environments. It is organized into sections on mapping, localization, and navigation.

The mapping section describes our method for constructing two-dimensional occupancy grids using sonar sensors and the cameras. Artificial neural networks are used to interpret sonar measurements. On top of the grid-based maps, more compact topological maps are constructed that facilitate fast planning.

Localization is the problem of aligning the robot's coordinate system with the global world coordinates. The localization section describes algorithms for self-localization and position tracking.

Approaches to global path planning, exploration, and reactive collision avoidance are described in the section on navigation.

Most of the software has been developed using a B21 mobile robot manufactured by Real World Interface Inc. The robot, shown in figure 1, is a synchro-drive robot equipped with a stereo camera system and 24 ultrasonic transducers (in short, sonars). Its maximum velocity is 90 centimeters per second. Our robot is equipped with two on-board 486 personal computers that are connected via a radio Ethernet link to several SUN Sparc stations. Currently some of the processing is done off-board. For robots equipped with Pentium computers, the entire software is run locally on the robot (except for the stereo vision system). A second radio link communicates video images to a Datacube, a special-purpose machine for processing images in real-time. The robot is also equipped with active infrared proximity sensors and tactile sensors, which are currently being incorporated into our map-building and collision-avoidance routines.

Mapping

Mapping refers to the process of constructing a model of the environment based on sensor measurements. This section describes an approach that integrates grid-based and topological representations. Grid-based approaches, such as those proposed by Moravec and Elfes (1988) and Borenstein and Koren (1991) and many others, represent environments by evenly-spaced grids. Each grid cell contains a value which indicates the presence or absence of an obstacle in the corresponding region of the environment. Topological approaches, such as those described in Engelson and McDermott (1992), Kortenkamp and Weymouth (1994), Kuipers and Byun (1990), Mataric (1994), Pierce and Kuipers (1994), and Torrance (1994), represent robot environments by graphs. Nodes in such graphs correspond to distinct situations, places, or landmarks (such as doorways). They are connected by arcs if there exists a direct path between them.

As argued in more detail elsewhere (Thrun [forthcoming]), both grid-based and topological representations exhibit orthogonal strengths and weaknesses:

Grid-based maps are considerably easier to learn, partially because they facilitate accurate localization, partially because they are easy to maintain. Topological maps, on the other hand, are more compact and thus facilitate fast planning.

Grid-Based Maps

The metric maps considered here are two-dimensional, discrete occupancy grids, as originally proposed by Elfes (1987) and Moravec (1988) and since implemented successfully in various systems. Each grid-cell $<x, y>$ in the map has an occupancy value attached—denoted by $Prob(occ_{x,y})$—which measures the robot's subjective belief whether or not its center can be moved to the center of that cell (the occupancy map models the configuration space of the robot; see for example, Latombe 1991). This section describes the two major steps in building grid-based maps (see also Thrun 1993): sensor interpretation and integration. Examples of metric maps are shown in various places in this chapter.

Sonar Sensor Interpretation

Sonar sensors measure approximate echo distances to nearby obstacles, along with noise. To build metric maps, sensor reading must be "translated" into occupancy values $Prob(occ_{x, y})$ for each grid cell $<x, y>$. The idea here is to train an artificial neural network using Back-Propagation (Rumelhart, Hinton, and Williams 1986) to map sonar measurements to occupancy values (Thrun 1993; van Dam, Kröse, and Groen 1996). The input to the network consists of the four sensor readings closest to $<x, y>$, along with two values that encode $<x, y>$ in polar coordinates relative to the robot (angle to the first of the four sensors, and distance). The output target for the network is 1, if $<x, y>$ is occupied, and 0 otherwise. Training examples can be obtained by operating a robot in a known environment and recording and labeling its sensor readings; note that each sonar scan can be used to construct many training examples for different x-y coordinates. In our implementation, training examples are generated with a mobile robot simulator.

Once trained, the network generates values that can be interpreted as probability for occupancy. Figure 2 shows three examples of sonar scans (top row, bird's eye view) along with their neural network interpretation (bottom row). The darker a value in the circular region around the robot, the larger the occupancy value computed by the network. Figures 2a and b show situations in a corridor. Here the network predicts the walls correctly. Notice the interpretation of the erroneous long reading in the left side of figure 2a and the erroneous short reading in 2b. For the area covered by those readings, the network outputs roughly 0.5, which indicates its uncertainty. Figure 2c shows a different situation in which the interpretation of the sensor values is less straightforward. This example illustrates that the network interprets sensors in the context of neigh-

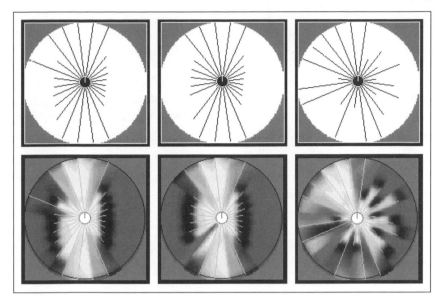

Figure 2. Sonar sensor interpretation.
Three example sonar scans (top row) and local occupancy maps (bottom row),
generated by the neural network. Bright regions indicate free space, and
dark regions indicate walls and obstacles (enlarged by a robot radius).

boring sensors. Long readings are interpreted as free space only if the neighboring sensors agree. Otherwise, the network returns values close to 0.5, which again indicates uncertainty. Situations such as the one shown in figure 2c—that defy simple interpretation—are typical for cluttered indoor environments.

Training a neural network to interpret sonar sensors has two key advantages over hand-crafted approaches to sensor interpretation. First, since neural networks are trained based on examples, they can easily be adapted to new circumstances. For example, the walls in the competition ring of the 1994 AAAI robot competition (Simmons 1995) were much smoother than the walls in the building in which the software was originally developed. Even though time was short, the neural network could quickly be retrained to accommodate this new situation. Secondly, multiple sensor readings are interpreted simultaneously. Most existing approaches interpret each sensor reading individually, one-by-one, which can be problematic in practice. For example, the reflection properties of most surfaces depend strongly on the angle of the surface to the sonar beam, which can only be detected by interpreting multiple sonar sensors simultaneously.

Stereo Camera Interpretation

A second source of occupancy information is the stereo camera system, which provides pairs of images recorded simultaneously from different spatial view-points. Stereo images are transmitted via a radio link to a Datacube, a special-purpose computer for image processing. Like the human visual apparatus, stereo images can be used to compute depth information (i.e., proximity). Put shortly, our approach (Fröhlinghaus and Buhmann 1996a, Fröhlinghaus and Buhmann 1996b) analyzes stereo images for co-occurrences of vertical edges. By analyzing the disparity of vertical edges found in both images, the proximity of obstacles projects the obstacle onto a two-dimensional occupancy grid.

Figure 3 illustrates the stereo image analysis. Images are first preprocessed (sep-arately for both channels) using a set of three horizontal Gabor filters (Sanger 1988). Gabor filters, which are similar to local Fourier transforms, basically band-filter images to obtain two local coefficients: The amplitude of a certain fil-ter-specific frequency, and its phase. Vertical edges characterized by a sharp hori-zontal brightness difference yield large amplitudes; their precise location in the image is determined with subpixel accuracy based on the phase. Figure 3a depicts one of the images, and figure 3b shows the vertical edges extracted from this im-age using Gabor filters. To establish correspondence between the left and the right image, both amplitude and phase information is used to identify the projec-tion of the same real-world edge in both images. Once such a vertical edge has been identified in both images, its disparity (spatial shift between both images) is used to estimate its proximity to the cameras (depth). A simple geometric projec-tion yields the x-y location of the edge relative to the robot. Figure 3c shows the projected location (bird's eye view) of the edges found in figure 3b; notice that the information concerning the height of an edge is lost when projecting the edge information onto the two-dimensional plane. To construct the final occu-pancy grid (like the one shown in figure 3d), edges are enlarged by a robot ra-dius, and the area between the edge projections and the robot is marked as free space. The last step relies on the assumption that vertical edges correspond to corners of obstacles; since occupancy maps represent configuration space, these edges are increased by a robot radius. To compensate for some of the uncertainty in depth estimation, corners of obstacles are smoothed with a Gaussian, and the free-space between obstacles and the robot is smoothed with a logistic function ($f(x) = (1 + e^{-x})^{-1}$). Notice in our implementation, the Datacube preprocesses im-ages at about 4 Hertz. The entire generation of occupancy maps, most of which is done on a SUN Sparc station, requires currently less than a second.

When the original image is compared (figure 3a) with the resulting map (fig-ure 3b), the door posts and two of the posters can clearly be identified in the fi-nal map (large dark areas in the map). The region close to the white poster does not contain clear vertical edges; thus the robot fails to identify the white wall. This example illustrates that strictly speaking, occupancy maps derived from stereo vision contain only edges of obstacles—large unstructured obstacles such as walls are "invisible" and hence will not be mapped. Consequently, stereo vi-sion alone would not be sufficient for building accurate maps. On the other

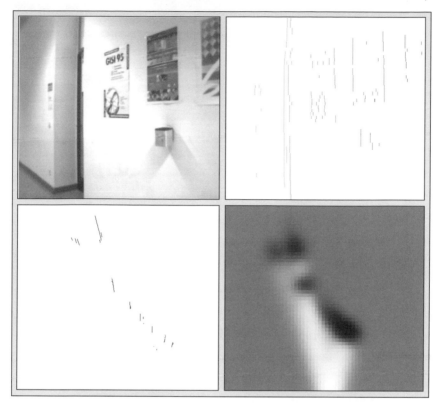

Figure 3. Estimation of occupancy maps using stereo vision.
Top left(a): Left camera image. Top right (b): Sparse disparity map.
Bottom left (c): Two-dimensional edge projections.
Bottom right (d): Local occupancy map.

hand, stereo vision gives more accurate obstacle information than sonar sensors do, due to the higher resolution of cameras. It also frequently detects obstacles that are "invisible" to sonar sensors, such as objects that absorb sound. As we will demonstrate later, stereo vision is well-suited to augment sonar information.

Integration Over Time

Sensor interpretations must be integrated over time to yield a single, consistent map. To do so, it is convenient to interpret the interpretation of the t-th sensor reading (denoted by $s^{(t)}$) as the probability that a grid cell $<x, y>$ is occupied, conditioned on the sensor reading $s^{(t)}$:

$$Prob(occ_{x, y} \mid s^{(t)})$$

A map is obtained by integrating these probabilities for all available sensor

*Figure 4. Grid-based map, constructed at the 1994 AAAI
autonomous mobile robot competition with the techniques described here.
(Height is 23.1 meters. Width is 32.2 meters.)*

readings, denoted by $s^{(1)}$, $s^{(2)}$, ..., $s^{(T)}$. In other words, the desired occupancy value for each grid cell $<x, y>$ can be written as the probability

$Prob(occ_{x,y} | s^{(1)}, s^{(2)}, ..., s^{(T)})$,

which is conditioned on all sensor readings. A straightforward approach to estimating this quantity is to apply Bayes' rule. To do so, one has to assume independence of the noise in different readings. More specifically, given the true occupancy of a grid cell $<x, y>$, the conditional probability $Prob(s^{(t)}|occ_{x, y})$ must be assumed to be independent of $Prob(s^{(t')}|occ_{x,y})$ if $t \neq t'$. This Markov assumption (Chung 1960) is commonly made in approaches to building occupancy grids. The desired probability can now be computed as follows:

$$Prob(occ_{x,y} | s^{(1)}, s^{(2)}, ..., s^{(T)})$$
$$= 1 - \left(1 + \frac{Prob(occ_{x,y})}{1 - Prob(occ_{x,y})} \prod_{\tau=1}^{T} \frac{Prob(occ_{x,y} | s^{(\tau)})}{1 - Prob(occ_{x,y} | s^{(\tau)})} \frac{1 - Prob(occ_{x,y})}{Prob(occ_{x,y})}\right)^{-1}$$

(1)

Here $Prob(occ_{x,y})$ denotes the prior probability for occupancy (which, if set to 0.5, can be omitted in this equation). The derivation of this formula is straightforward and can be found in Moravec (1988) and Pearl (1988). Notice that this formula can be used to update occupancy values incrementally.

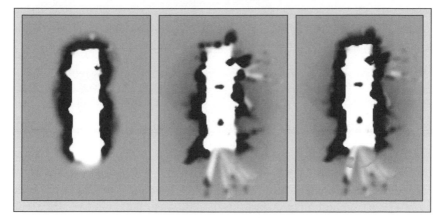

*Figure 5. Maps built in a single run. Left (a): Using only sonar sensors.
Center (b): Using only stereo information. Right (c): Integrating both.
Notice that sonar models the world more consistently but misses the
two sonar-absorbing chairs which are found using stereo vision.*

An example map of a competition ring constructed at the 1994 AAAI autonomous mobile robot competition is shown in figure 4. This map has been constructed exclusively from sonar information. Figure 5 illustrates the advantage of integrating sonar and stereo vision. All three maps shown there show the same experiment. The map shown in figure 5a has been constructed purely on sonar information. While sonar models walls well, it misses the two sound-absorbing chairs in the middle of the hallway. Stereo vision (figure 5b) detects these chairs, but fails to detect a glass door at the top of the diagram. The map in figure 5c, which is superior to both single-sensor maps since is contains the chairs and models the walls consistently, is obtained by integrating both maps. Notice that both maps were integrated by taking the maximum occupancy value at each grid cell. Taking the maximum is the most conservative way to integrate maps, since all obstacles are preserved. In principle, the maps could also have been integrated by (1); however, then the result is influenced by the relative frequency of sonar and camera measurements, which in this example makes the obstacles disappear.

Topological Maps

Topological maps represent robot environments as graphs, where nodes correspond to distinct places, and arcs represent adjacency. A key advantage of topological representations is their compactness. In our approach, topological maps are built on top of the grid-based maps. The basic idea is simple but very effective: The free-space of a grid-based map is partitioned into a small number of regions, separated by critical lines. Critical lines correspond to narrow passages such as doorways. The partitioned map is then mapped into an isomorphic graph. The precise algorithm works as described in the following paragraphs:

Thresholding. Initially, each occupancy value in the occupancy grid is thresholded. Cells whose occupancy value is below the threshold are considered freespace (denoted by C). All other points are considered occupied (denoted by $\bar{C}$).

Voronoi Diagram. Consider an arbitrary point $<x, y> \in C$ in free-space. The basis points of $<x, y>$ are the closest point(s) $<x', y'>$ in the occupied space $\bar{C}$, i.e., all points $<x', y'> \in \bar{C}$ that minimize the Euclidean distance to x, y. We will call these points $<x', y'>$ the basis points of $<x, y>$, and the distance between $<x, y>$ and its basis points the clearance of $<x, y>$. The Voronoi diagram, which is a form of skeletonization (Latombe 1991), is the set of points in free space that have at least two different (equidistant) basis points. Figure 6a sketches the Voronoi diagram for the map shown in figure 4.

Critical Points. The key idea for partitioning the free-space is to find "critical points." Critical points $<x, y>$ are points on the Voronoi diagram that minimize clearance locally. In other words, each critical point $<x, y>$ has the following two properties: (a) it is part of the Voronoi diagram, and (b) there exists an $\varepsilon > 0$ for which the clearance of all points in an ε-neighborhood of $<x, y>$ is not smaller.

Critical Lines. Critical lines are obtained by connecting each critical point with its basis points (cf. figure 6b). Critical points have exactly two basis points (otherwise they would not be local minima of the clearance function). Critical lines partition the free space into disjoint regions (see also figure 6c).

Topological Graph. The partitioning is mapped into an isomorphic graph. Each region corresponds to a node in the topological graph, and each critical line to an arc.

Figure 6d shows an example of a topological graph. The compression is enormous: The topological graph has 67 nodes, whereas the original map contains 27,280 occupied cells. Notice that critical lines are useful for decomposing metric maps primarily for two reasons. First, when passing through a critical line, the robot is forced to move in a considerably smaller region. Hence, the loss in performance inferred by planning using the topological map (as opposed to the grid-based map) is rather small. Secondly, narrow regions are more likely blocked by obstacles (such as doors, which can be open or closed).

Localization

Localization is the process of aligning the robot's local coordinate system with the global coordinate system of the map. Localization is particularly important

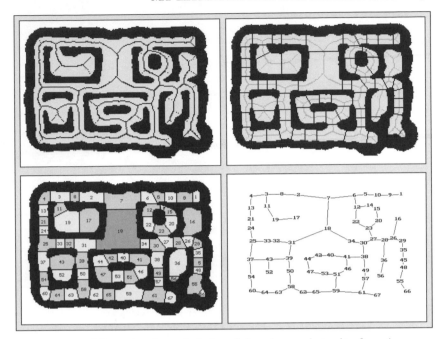

Figure 6. Extracting the topological graph from the map depicted in figure 4.
Top left (a): Voronoi diagram. Top right (b): Critical points and lines.
Bottom left (c): Regions. Bottom right (d): The final graph.

(and particularly difficult) for map-based approaches that learn their maps, since the accuracy of a metric map depends crucially on the alignment of the robot with its map (Feng, Borenstein, and Everett 1994; Rencken 1993). Figure 7 gives an example that illustrates the importance of localization in robot mapping. In figure 7a, the position is determined based solely on dead-reckoning. After approximately fifteen minutes of robot operation, the position error is approximately eleven and one-half meters. Obviously, the resulting map is too erroneous to be of practical use. Figure 7b is the result of applying the position tracking method described below. In fact, none of the maps presented in the previous section would have been possible without our methods for localizing the robot based on sensor input. Identifying and correcting for slippage and drift is thus a most important issue in map building.

An excellent overview of different approaches to localization can be found in Feng, Borenstein, and Everett (1994). Traditionally, localization addresses two subproblems, which are often attacked separately: position tracking and global localization.

Position Tracking. Position tracking refers to the problem of estimating the location of the robot while it is moving. Drift and slippage impose limits on the

*Figure 7: Map constructed without (a)(left) and with (b)(right) the
position estimation mechanism described in this chapter.
In (a), only the wheel encoders are used to determine the robot's position.
The positional error accumulates to more than eleven meters, and the
resulting map is clearly unusable. This illustrates the importance
of sensor-based position estimation for map building.*

ability to estimate the location of the robot within its global map. As figure 7 demonstrates, even the smallest errors in the robot's odometry can have devastating effects. The problem of position tracking is particularly difficult to solve if mapping is interleaved with localization.

Global Localization. Global localization is the problem of determining the position of the robot under global uncertainty. This problem arises, for example, when a robot uses a map that has been generated in a previous run, and when it is not informed about its initial location within the map.

Global localization and position tracking are two sides of the same coin: localization under uncertainty. In our current implementation, different computational mechanisms are used for localization within a previously learned map (global localization and position tracking), and position tracking when interleaved with exploration and mapping. Each of these approaches exploits the specific properties of the two problems.

Probabilistic Model

The problem of localization is most generally described in probabilistic terms.

Let $l^{(t)}$ denote the location of the robot at time t. For mobile robots, l is usually three-dimensional (x-y location and heading direction). l is not directly accessible; i.e., the robot does not know where it is. Instead, it maintains an internal belief as to where it might be and uses its sensors periodically to update this belief. It is convenient to denote the belief as a probability density $Prob^{(t)}(l)$ over locations l. The problem of localization is then to estimate $Prob^{(t)}(l)$ so that it matches as closely as possible the true location, $l^{(t)}$. Initially, at time $t = 0$, $Prob^{(0)}(l)$ may be distributed uniformly, assuming that the robot does not know its initial location, or, alternatively, $Prob^{(0)}(l)$ may contain a single peak at $l^{(0)}$ if the robot happens to know its location. $Prob(l)$ is updated whenever the robot senses, using mostly ad hoc approaches to determine the conditional probability $Prob(s^{(t)} \mid l)$:

$$Prob^{(t)}(l) \leftarrow \alpha \, Prob^{(t-1)}(l) \cdot Prob(s^{(t)} \mid l) \tag{2}$$

Here α is a normalizer, $s^{(t)}$ is the sensor input at time t, and $Prob(s^{(t)} \mid l)$ is the probability of observing $s^{(t)}$ when at l. Strictly speaking, the update formula (2) is only valid under a conditional independence (Markov) assumption: Given the true location of the robot and the true model of the environment, subsequent sensor readings must be conditionally independent. In practice, we have found this approach to be fairly robust to various kinds of violations of this assumption (dependencies are due to nonstationary environments model errors, crude representations of the space of locations, or unmodeled robot dynamics). However, the key thing to note here is that the problem of localization requires (a) sensors (to obtain $s^{(t)}$) and (b) knowledge about $Prob(s^{(t)} \mid l)$, i.e., the probability of observing $s^{(t)}$ at l. We currently employ and integrate a variety of different sensor modalities: wheel encoders, map matching, sonar modeling, maneuverability, wall orientation, and landmarks.

Wheel Encoders. Wheel encoders measure the revolution of the robot's wheels. Based on their measurements, odometry yields an estimate of the robot's location $l^{(t)}$ which, when expressed relative to the robot's previous location, $l^{(t-1)}$, is impressively accurate. To model errors in odometry, we assume that the position at time t is distributed normally around the very location measured by odometry. The probability $Prob(s^{(t)} \mid l)$, thus, is normally distributed.

Map Matching. As described above, every sensor reading is converted into a "local" map (such as the ones shown in figures 2 and 3). The robot can localize itself by comparing the global with the local map. More specifically, the pixel-wise correlation of the local and the global map—which is a function of the robot's location—is a measure of their correspondence (Schiele and Crowley 1994). The more correlated the maps are, the more likely is the corresponding location of the robot. Thus, the probability $Prob(s^{(t)} \mid l)$ is assumed to be proportional to the correlation of both maps if the robot were at l. See Thrun (forthcoming) for details.

Sonar Modeling. Another source of information for localization, which we have begun to explore more recently (Burgard et al. 1996a), is obtained using a simplistic model of sonar sensors. In essence, it is assumed that each grid cell in the global map possesses a certain probability of being detected by a sonar sensor. More specifically, our model assumes that with probability $Prob(detect_{i, x, y})$ the i-th sonar sensor detects an obstacle at $<x, y>$ (where $Prob(detect_{i, x, y})$ is a monotonic function of $Prob(occ_{x, y})$, which is 0 if $<x, y>$ does not lie in the perceptual field of the i-th sensor, see Burgard, Fox, Hennig, and Schmidt (1996a). For simplicity, we also assume that the detection probability is independent for different values of i, x, and y.

Sonar sensors return the distance to the nearest obstacle. Thus, the probability that an obstacle is detected at distance d is given by the probability that one or more cells at distance d respond, times the probability that no obstacle at distance smaller than d is detected. Put mathematically, let $d(i, <x, y>)$ denote the distance of $<x, y>$ to the i-th sonar sensor. Then the probability of measuring a specific distance, say s_i, is given by

$$Prob(s_i) = \beta\left(1 - \prod_{d(i,\langle x,y\rangle)=s_i}(1 - Prob(detect_{i,x,y}))\right) \prod_{d(i,\langle x,y\rangle)<s_i}(1 - Prob(detect_{i,x,y}))$$

where β is a normalization factor that ensures that the probabilities for different measurements s_i sum up to 1. Here only cells that are in the primary perceptive field of the i-th sonar sensor are considered (a fifteen degree cone). Notice that the distribution of $Prob(s_i)$ bears close resemblance to a geometric distribution.

The probability of observing the entire sonar scan $s^{(t)}$ at l, $Prob(s^{(t)} \mid l)$, is the product of the individual sensor probabilities:

$$Prob(s^{(t)} \mid l) = \prod_{i=1}^{24} Prob(s_i^{(t)}) \tag{3}$$

Notice that the model of sonar sensors is extremely simplistic, partially because it considers only the main cone of sonar sensors (ignoring the side cones), and partially because it assumes independence between different grid cells, ignoring cumulative effects in the reflection of sound. However, it can be computed very efficiently, which is important if the location of the robot shall be estimated in real-time.

Maneuverability. Assuming the map is correct, the mere fact that a robot moves to a location $<x, y>$ makes it unlikely that this location is occupied. Thus, the global map can be used to derive further probabilistic constraints on the robot location. Our approach assumes that the probability of being at $<x, y>$ is proportional to the probability of this grid cell being unoccupied:

$$Prob(<x, y>) = \gamma(1 - Prob(occ_{x, y}))$$

where γ is an appropriate normalization factor.

Wall Orientation. A final source of information, which can be used to correct rotational errors, is the global wall orientation (Crowley 1989, Hinkel and Knieriemen 1988). This approach rests on the restrictive assumption that walls are either parallel or orthogonal to each other, or differ by more than fifteen degrees from these canonical wall directions. In the beginning of robot operation, the global orientation of walls is estimated by searching straight line segments in consecutive sonar measurements (cf. figure 8). Once the global wall orientation has been estimated, it is used to readjust the robot's orientation based on future sonar measurements. See Thrun (forthcoming) for more details.

Landmarks. Landmarks are used in various approaches to mobile robot localization (see, for example, Betke and Gurvits 1993, Kortenkamp and Weymouth 1994, Neven and Schöner 1995 and references in Thrun 1996). We recently have begun to explore mechanisms that enable a robot to select its own landmarks, based on sonar and camera input. The key idea underlying this approach is to train artificial neural networks to recognize landmarks by minimizing the average localization error (assuming that update rule (2) is applied in localization). As a result, our robot successfully "discovered" a variety of useful visual landmarks, such as doors, wall color, ceiling lights and so on. Details of the algorithm and performance results are surveyed in Thrun (1996).

This list of sources for estimating l has been developed over the last few years. Some of these methods make strong assumptions on the correctness of the global map (such as the maneuverability method), and hence cannot be interleaved with map learning. These approaches differ significantly in computational complexity. For example, the map-matching approach, as it is currently implemented, requires extensive comparisons of maps, whereas wall orientations can be determined very efficiently.

Global Localization

Global localization addresses the problem of mobile robot localization under global uncertainty. To localize the robot globally, the entire density $Prob(l)$ for arbitrary locations l is computed. In our current implementation, $Prob(l)$ is approximated using a grid representation, just like the occupancy grids described in the nest section. The orientation of the robot is represented with 1° resolution. Currently, only the wheel encoders, sonar modeling and maneuverability are used to localize the robot. To update $Prob(l)$ in real-time while the robot is in motion, only a subset of sonar readings is currently considered in global positioning, since the process of updating $Prob(l)$ is computationally expensive. From the previous list of sensor modalities, the global localization approach utilizes wheel encoders and sonar sensors, using the sonar modeling and maneuverability approach.

Figure 9a shows a path taken by the robot in the arena depicted in figure 4 (same arena, different run). As shown in that figure, twelve sonar sweeps were

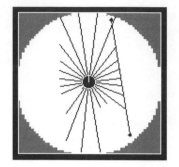

Figure 8. Wall, detected by considering five adjacent sonar measurements. Wall orientations are used to correct for dead-reckoning errors in the robot orientation.

used for the global position estimation, each of which consisted of eight sensor readings. Figure 9b shows the logarithm of the density $Prob(l)$ (maximized over all orientations) after evaluating six of these twelve sensor scans. Although those six readings appear to be insufficient for uniquely localizing the robot, the density indicates that the robot is most likely in a corridor. After evaluating all twelve sensor readings (figure 9c), the position of the robot is uniquely determined. Notice that the probability of the "correct" grid cell in figure 9c is approximately 0.96, while the value of the second largest peak is less than $8 \cdot 10^{-6}$. Notice the approach deals adequately with uncertainty and ambiguities, as demonstrated by the empirical examples. The global localization approach has also given very reliable results for real-time position tracking (Burgard et al. 1996b). However, since this approach estimates the robot's location in a previously learned map, it is not applicable during exploration and map learning.

Position Tracking When Learning Maps

When learning maps, the robot knows initial location by definition (i.e., is defined to be origin of the global coordinate system). Thus, during exploration, position control seeks to compensate for short-term localization errors such as slippage and drift. The key assumption here is that the position of the robot is known except for some small error, so that instead of estimating an entire probability distribution, it suffices to keep track of the most likely location of the robot. Our current best approach for position tracking differs from the above approach to localization in two aspects (cf. Thrun 1993, Thrun [forthcoming]):

First, the approach estimates only the point l that maximizes $Prob(l)$, instead of the entire density. The advantage of tracking only one value is twofold: the space of localization does not have to be represented discretely (or by parametric densities), and the approach is computationally much more efficient. It comes at the obvious disadvantage that complex distributions, such as multimodal distri-

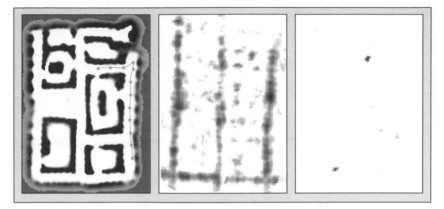

*Figure 9. Initial self-localization. Left (a): Path of the robot.
Center (b): Prob(l) after evaluating six sonar readings.
Right (c): Prob(l) after evaluating twelve sonar readings,
both plotted logarithmically.*

butions, cannot be represented. Thus, once the position is lost, this approach is unable to recover. However, if the initial location is known, we almost never observed that the location was estimated inaccurately.

Second, primarily for historical reasons, our approach to position tracking relies only on wheel encoders, map matching, and wall orientation to estimate location. Position control based on wheel encoders and map matching alone works well if the robot travels through mapped terrain, but ceases to function if the robot explores and maps unknown terrain. The third mechanism, which arguably relies on a restrictive assumption concerning the nature of indoor environments, has proven extremely valuable when autonomously exploring and mapping large-scale indoor environments.

Position tracking is implemented in an any-time fashion, using gradient descent to estimate the location that maximizes *Prob(l)*. When a new sonar reading arrives, the previous gradient search is terminated and its result is incorporated into the current position estimation. In practice, we have found this approach to be fast enough to accurately track the robot position even if the robot is mapping unknown terrain with maximum velocity. Notice that all maps shown in this chapter (with the exception of the map shown in figure 7a) have been generated using this position-tracking approach.

Navigation

This section is concerned with robot motion. RHINO's navigation system consists of two modules: A global planner (Thrun 1993) and a reactive collision avoidance module (Fox, Burgard, and Thrun 1995; Fox, Burgard, and Thrun 1997). Control is generated hierarchically: The global path planner generates minimum-cost paths to the goal(s) using the map. As a result, it communicates intermediate subgoals to the collision avoidance routine, which controls the velocity and the exact motion direction of the robot reactively, based on the most recent sensor measurements only. Both modules adjust their plans and controls continuously in response to the current situation.

Both approaches—the global path planner and the reactive collision avoidance approach—are characterized by orthogonal strengths and weaknesses: The collision avoidance approach is easily trapped in local minima, such as U-shaped obstacle configurations (Latombe 1991). However, it reacts in real-time to unforeseen obstacles such as humans and is capable of changing the motion direction while the robot is moving. The global planner, in contrast, does not suffer from the local minimum problem, since it plans globally. It alone, however, is not sufficient to control the robot, since it does not take robot dynamics into account and since learned maps are incapable of capturing moving obstacles. Thus, global planning alone would simply not avoid collisions with humans and other rapidly moving obstacles.

Path Planning with Grid-Based Maps

The idea for path planning is to let the robot always move on a minimum-cost path to the goal (or the nearest goal, if multiple goals exist); The cost for traversing a grid cell is determined by its occupancy value. The minimum-cost path is computed using a modified version of value iteration, a popular dynamic programming algorithm (Bellman 1957; Howard 1960):

Initialization. The grid cell that contains the target location is initialized with 0, all others with ∞.

$$V_{x,y} \leftarrow \begin{cases} 0, & \text{if} \langle x,y \rangle \text{ target cell} \\ \infty, & \text{otherwise} \end{cases}$$

Update Loop. For all nontarget grid cells $<x, y>$ do:

$$V_{x,y} \leftarrow \min_{\substack{\xi=-1,0,1 \\ \varsigma=-1,0,1}} \left\{ V_{x+\xi,y+\varsigma} + Prob\left(occ_{x+\xi,y+\varsigma}\right) \right\}$$

Value iteration updates the value of all grid cells by the value of their best neighbors plus the costs of moving to this neighbor (just like A^*) (Nilsson 1982). Cost is here equivalent to the probability $Prob(occ_{x,y})$ that a grid cell $<x, y>$ is occupied. The update rule is iterated. When the update converges, each value $V_{x,y}$ measures the cumulative cost for moving to the nearest goal. However, control can be generated at any time, long before value iteration converges.

Determine Motion Direction. To determine where to move, the robot generates a minimum-cost path to the goal. This is done by steepest descent in V, starting at the actual robot position. The steepest descent path is then postprocessed to maintain a minimum clearance to the walls and, if possible, to move parallel to walls, using the global wall orientation described in the previous section. Determining the motion direction is done in regular time intervals and is fully interleaved with updating V.

Figure 10 shows V after convergence with one and two goals, respectively, using the map shown in figure 4. The gray level indicates the cumulative costs V for moving toward the nearest goal point. Notice that every local minimum in the value function corresponds to a goal. Thus, for every point $<x, y>$, steepest descent in V leads to the nearest goal point.

Unfortunately, plain value iteration is too inefficient to allow the robot to navigate and learn maps in real-time. Strictly speaking, the basic value iteration algorithm can only be applied if the cost function does not increase (which frequently happens when the map is modified). This is because when the cost function increases, previously adjusted values V might become too small. While value iteration quickly decreases values that are too large, increasing too small a value can be arbitrarily slow (Thrun 1993). Consequently, the basic value iteration algorithm requires that the value function be initialized completely (initialization step) whenever the map—and thus the cost function—is updated. This is very inefficient, since the map is updated almost constantly. To avoid complete reinitializations, and to further increase the efficiency of the approach, the basic paradigm was extended in the following way:

Selective Reset Phase. Every time the map is updated, values $V_{x, y}$ that are too small are identified and reset. This is achieved by the following loop, which is iterated:

For all nongoal $<x, y>$ do:

$$V_{x,y} \leftarrow \infty \text{ if } V_{x,y} < \min_{\substack{\xi=-1,0,1 \\ \varsigma=-1,0,1}} \left\{ V_{x+\xi,y+\varsigma} + Prob\left(occ_{x+\xi,y+\varsigma}\right) \right\}$$

Notice that the remaining $V_{x, y}$-values are not affected. Resetting the value table is a version of value iteration.

Bounding Box. To focus value iteration, a rectangular bounding box $[x_{min}, x_{max}] \times [y_{min}, y_{max}]$ is maintained that contains all grid cells in which $V_{x,y}$ may change. This box is easily maintained in the value iteration update. As a result, value iteration focuses on a small fraction of the grid only and hence converges much faster. Notice that the bounding box bears similarity to prioritized sweeping (Moore and Atkeson 1993).

Value iteration is a very general procedure which has several properties that make it attractive for real-time mobile robot navigation:

Any-time Algorithm. As previously mentioned, value iteration can be under-

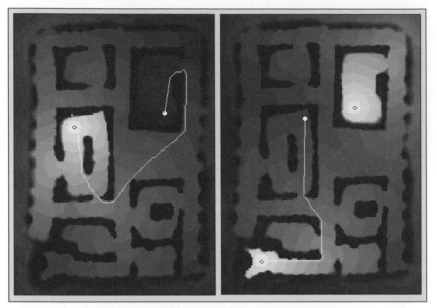

*Figure 10: Path planning with dynamic programming.
Value functions V, computed by value iteration for (a)(left) one goal
and (b)(right) two goals (goals are marked by "0").
By following the gray-scale gradient, the robot moves to the
next unexplored area on a minimum-cost path.*

stood as an any-time planner (Dean and Boddy 1988). Consequently, value iteration allows the robot to move in real-time, even though some of its motion commands might be suboptimal.

Full Exception Handling. Value iteration preplans for arbitrary robot locations. This is because V is computed for every location in the map, not just the current location of the robot. Consequently, the robot can quickly react if it finds itself in an unexpected location, and generate appropriate motion directions without any additional computational effort. This is particularly important in our approach, since the robot uses a fast routine for avoiding collisions (described below) which adjusts the motion direction commanded by the planner based on sensor readings.

Exploration. To autonomously acquire a map, the robot has to explore. For exploration, the same value iteration algorithm is employed, with the only exception being that goals correspond to unexplored grid cells. Figure 11a shows an autonomous exploration run. At the current point, the robot has already explored the major hallways and is about to continue to explore an interior room. Circular motion, such as found in the bottom of this plot, occurs when two unexplored regions are about equally far away (= same costs). Notice that the complete exploration run shown here took less than fifteen minutes. The robot moved constantly and frequently reached a velocity of 80 to 90 centimeters per second (see also Buhmann et al. 1995; Fox, Burgard, and Thrun 1995).

Figure 11b shows the exploration value function. All white regions are unexplored, and the gray level indicates the cumulative costs V for moving toward the nearest unexplored point. The value function indicates the robot would continue exploration by moving straight ahead.

Multiagent Exploration. Since value iteration generates values for all grid-cells, it can easily be used for collaborative multiagent exploration.

In grid maps of size thirty by thirty meters, optimized value iteration done from scratch requires approximately two to ten seconds on a SUN Sparc station. In cases where the selective reset step does not reset large fractions of the map (which is the common situation), value iteration converges in less than a second. For example, the planning time in the map shown in figure 4 lies generally under two seconds, and most of the time under a tenth of a second. In light of these results, one might be inclined to think that grid-based maps are sufficient for autonomous robot navigation. However, value iteration (and similar planning approaches) requires time quadratic in the number of grid cells, imposing intrinsic scaling limitations that prohibit efficient planning in large-scale domains. Due to their compactness, topological maps scale much better to large environments. In what follows we will describe our approach to path planning with topological maps.

Path Planning with Topological Maps

The enormous compactness of topological maps—when compared to the underlying grid-based map—increases the efficiency of planning. To replace the grid-based planner by a topological planner, the planning problem is split into three subproblems, all of which can be tackled separately and very efficiently.

Topological Planning. First, paths are planned using the abstract topological map. Shortest paths in the topological maps can easily be found using one of the standard graph search algorithms, such as Dijkstra's or Floyd and Warshal's shortest path algorithm, A^*, or dynamic programming. In our implementation, we used the value iteration approach described in the path planning with grid-based maps section.

Triplet Planning. To translate topological plans into motion commands, a so-called "triplet planner" generates (metric) paths for each set of three adjacent topological regions in the topological plan. Specifically, let T_1, T_2, ..., T_n denote the plan generated by the topological planner, where each T_i corresponds to a region

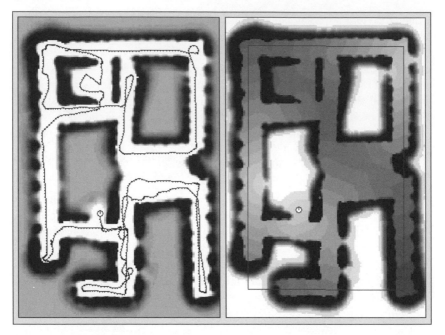

Figure 11: Autonomous exploration. Left (a):Exploration path.
Right (b): Value function during exploration. Notice that the large
black rectangle in (b) indicates the global wall orientation.

in the map. Then, for each triplet $<T_i, T_{i+1}, T_{i+2}>$ ($i = 1, ..., n - 1$ and $T_{n+1} := T_n$), and each grid cell in T_i, the triplet planner generates shortest paths to the cost-nearest point in T_{i+2} in the grid-based map, under the constraint that the robot exclusively moves through T_i and T_{i+1}. For each triplet, all shortest paths can be generated in a single value iteration run: Each point in T_{i+2} is marked as a (potential) goal point, and value iteration is used to propagate costs through T_{i+1} to T_i just as described in the path planning with grid-based maps section. Triplet plans are used to "translate" the topological plan into concrete motion commands: When the robot is in T_i, it moves according to the triplet plan obtained for $<T_i, T_{i+1}, T_{i+2}>$. When the robot crosses the boundary of two topological regions, the next triplet plan $<T_{i+1}, T_{i+2}, T_{i+3}>$ is activated. Notice that the triplet planner can be used to move the robot to the region that contains the goal location.

Final Goal Planning. The final step involves moving to the actual goal location, which again is done with value iteration. Notice that the computational cost for this final planning step does not depend on the size of the map. Instead, it depends on the size and the shape of the final topological region T_n, and the location of the goal.

The key advantage of this decomposition is that all the expensive computation required for path planning can be done off-line, for all path planning problems. As documented in Thrun (forthcoming), planning using the topological map is between three and four orders of magnitude more efficient than planning with the grid-based map, for maps similar to those shown in this chapter. On the other hand, plans generated with the topological map are typically between one and four percent longer than plans generated using the grid-based map, numbers that are considerably small given the huge computational savings.

Collision Avoidance

The task of the collision avoidance routine is to navigate the robot to subgoals generated by the planner while avoiding collisions with obstacles. It adjusts the actual velocity of the robot and chooses the concrete motion direction. For obvious reasons, the collision avoidance module must operate in real-time. When the robot moves as fast as 90 centimeters per second, it is imperative that the robot dynamics (inertia, torque limits) be taken into account, particularly because the path planner considers only robot kinematics. The remainder of this section describes the "dynamic window approach" to collision avoidance (Fox, Burgard, and Thrun 1995; Fox, Burgard, and Thrun 1997), currently our best collision avoidance routine.

The key idea of the dynamic window approach is to choose control in the velocity space of the robot. Figure 12 shows an example of the robot traveling down a hallway with a certain velocity, and figure 13 shows the corresponding velocity space. The velocity space is a projection of the configuration space (with a fixed kinematic configuration). The horizontal axis in figure 13 measures the rotational velocity, denoted by ω, and the vertical axis depicts the translational velocity, denoted by v. The actual velocity of the robot is a single point in this diagram (in the center of the white region). The robot sets its velocities in regular time intervals (in our current implementation every 0.25 seconds). To ensure that the robot travels safely and makes progress toward the goal, it has to obey a variety of constraints, which are described in turn.

Hard Constraints. Hard constraints are imposed by the requirement to not to collide with obstacles and by the dynamics of the robot.

Torque Limits. Torque limits impose bounds as to how the robot might change its velocity in the immediate next decision interval. In the example shown in figure 13, these bounds are visualized by the rectangle V_d.

Safety. Obstacles impose additional constraints on the velocity. Velocities with which the robot would inevitably collide, even if decelerated maximally after the decision interval, are not admissible. The dark regions in figure 13 illustrate such regions in the velocity space. Notice that obstacles such as walls are directly mapped into the velocity space.

These constraints are hard constraints, i.e., for obvious reasons the robot

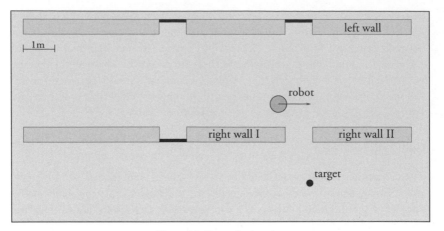

Figure 12. Example situation.

must obey them. In figure 13, the space of admissible velocities under these constraints is depicted in white color. These constraints do not specify preferences, nor do they contain goal-related information.

Soft Constraints. Soft constraints impose preferences on the motion direction and velocity of the robot. Currently, three soft constraints are used:

1. Target heading. The target heading, denoted *heading*(v, ω), is defined as the absolute angle of the target (subgoal) relative to the robot's heading direction after 0.25 seconds of robot motion. The target point is usually set by the path planner. If *heading*(v, ω) = 0, the target would be right in front of the robot at the beginning of the next time interval. To make progress toward its target, it is desired that the robot move towards it, i.e., the target heading be as close as possible to zero.

2. Clearance. The clearance, denoted by *dist*(v, ω), is defined as the free distance in front of the robot, assuming that the robots sets its velocity once and does not change it thereafter. By maximizing clearance, the robot avoids being close to obstacles.

3. Translational velocity. The translational velocity v is also maximized, which causes the robot to always move as fast as permitted by the other constraints.

Notice that all three soft constraints, *heading*(v, ω), *dist*(v, ω), and v, are functions of v and ω. The actual velocity, denoted by $<v^*, \omega^*>$, is obtained by maximizing a linear combination of these constraints:

$$\left\langle v^*, \omega^* \right\rangle = \operatorname*{arg\,max}_{v, \omega} \left(-\alpha_1 \cdot \left| heading(v, \omega) \right| + \alpha_2 \cdot dist(v, \omega) + \alpha_3 \cdot v \right) \qquad (4)$$

Here α_1, α_2, and α_3 are constants which trade off the three different soft constraints, thus determining the overall behavior of the robot. In our approach, (4) is optimized by discrete grid search.

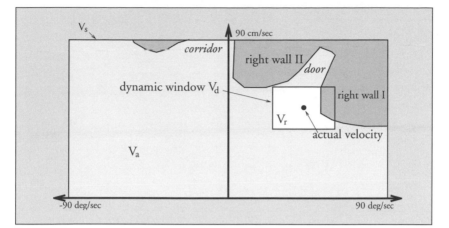

Figure 13. Velocity space.

Figure 14 depicts the value (argument of the "argmax") corresponding to the situation depicted in figure 12, as a function of the velocities v and ω. Values that would violate the safety constraint are set to zero. The shape of the remaining function indicates that higher translational velocities are generally preferable and that the rotational velocity possesses an "optimal" value, which is dictated by the target heading (ridge toward the right in figure 14). The global maximum, marked by the vertical line in figure 14, corresponds to a sharp right turn for moving directly through the door (see figure 12). Notice that the dynamic window (torque limits) is not shown in figure 14. If the dynamics of the robot do not permit such a turn, the robot would instead move straight, decelerate and eventually backup. Notice that taking the robot dynamics into account is important if the robot travels at more than 30 centimeters per second—if the dynamics were ignored, an attempt to turn at high speed could easily result in a collision.

Using Sensors. While the constraints are sufficient to generate collision-free robot control if the model of the environment is correct, sensors are erroneous and models err. Thus, our approach employs a variety of additional strategies to recover from errors in perception.

Sensor Data. In reality, exact locations of obstacles are unknown. Maps react very slowly to changes in the environment, they are incapable of modeling fast-moving obstacles, and they typically lag behind because of the computational costs involved in sensor interpretation and localization. Thus, the dynamic window approach works with raw proximity data, as obtained by sonar sensors or computer vision (see below). Every sensor reading can potentially constrain the motion of the robot; however, sensor readings are only memorized for approximately three seconds. Such an approach is maximally conservative in the sense

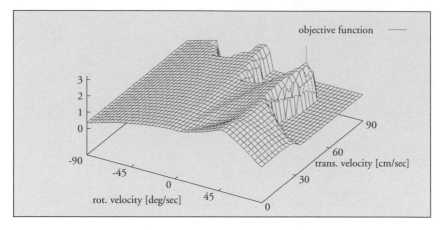

Figure 14. Example of an objective function. The vertical axis depicts value.

that no sensor reading is ignored. Nevertheless, the relatively short temporal window makes it adapt quickly to moving obstacles.

Smoothing. The objective function is smoothed to increase the side-clearance of the robot and to decrease the sensitivity to noise in the sensor readings.

Safety Margin. To travel safely at high speed, the robot is enlarged by a safety margin. This safety margin increases with the forward velocity. As a result, the robot keeps safe distances from obstacles when traveling at high speed, while still being able to move through narrow doors with low speed.

Rotate Away Mode. Because of sensor noise and changes in the environment, it can happen that every nonzero velocity violates a hard constraint. In such cases, which are rare in practice, the robot turns completely away from the nearest obstacle, from which point on it resumes normal operation.

Figure 15 shows an example of the robot traveling through a cluttered environment, based purely on sonar information. All obstacles in the corridor are smoothly circumvented with a maximal speed of 90 centimeters per second. Although in this experiment the robot decelerated to approximately 20 centimeters per second when passing through the narrowest passage, it still maintained an average speed of 65 centimeters per second. In extensive experiments, we found that the dynamic window approach controls the robot very reliably even in populated environments with obstacles that are hard to detect for sonar sensors.

Real-Time Vision

Sonars are convenient sensors in that they directly generate proximity information. However, they fail to detect obstacles outside their perceptual range, e.g., small objects on the floor, and they also frequently fail to detect obstacles with

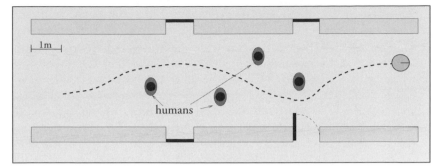

Figure 15. Trajectory through a cluttered corridor.

sound-absorbing surfaces. To supplement the sonar information, a real-time vision module for obstacle detection is integrated into collision avoidance. Our monocular vision module is able to robustly detect and locate obstacles on the floor, based on image segmentation and discriminant analysis. The main processing stages are as follows.

1. *Preprocessing.* The color image is low-pass filtered and subsampled, typically to 150x120 pixels.

2. *Edge Detection.* The subsampled image is convolved with a gradient operator to detect vertically and horizontally oriented edges.

3. *Presegmentation.* A fast, pixel-based image segmentation evaluates the local contrast between pixels and links them together if the contrast is below a certain threshold θ_0(Ballard and Brown, 1982). This presegmentation usually results in an over-segmented image with many small region patches.

4. *Segmentation.* Neighboring regions are merged (Zucker 1976) if the mean contrast along their common border is below a threshold θ_t, and if their average color differs by less than a second threshold, σ_t. Both thresholds are iteratively increased $(\theta_{t+1}, \sigma_{t+1}) = (\theta_t, \sigma_t) + (\Delta\theta, \Delta\sigma)$ to a final threshold tuple (θ_T, σ_T).

5. *Interpretation.* The segmented image is interpreted to identify the major floor region and to detect regions that possibly correspond to obstacles. Based on knowledge about the height and the tilting angle of the camera, the robot first locates the horizon within its camera image. It then identifies floor patches using size and location relative to the robot and the horizon as the major criteria. The remaining nonfloor regions are obstacle candidates, given that they touch the floor and given that they fit certain size constraints.

6. *Feature extraction.* For each region of interest, the following features are extracted: (1) the height, (2) the width and (3) the total area, (4/5) two color components (the "U" and "V" channel of the NTSC signal), (6) average brightness and (7) brightness variance; the latter feature provides texture in-

formation. Height, width and area are expressed in world-coordinates, computed under the assumption that obstacles extend all the way to the floor.

7. *Recognition.* Finally, regions are classified by a Bayesian classifier. In the "training phase," the feature mean and covariance of typical obstacles that may block the robot's path are estimated from 50 to 100 examples. During recognition, a region is considered an obstacle—and passed to the collision avoidance module—if its Mahalanobis distance to one of the pre-trained obstacle models exceeds a certain threshold. The Mahalanobis distance corresponds to the probability of observing a feature vector assuming normal distribution (Duda and Hart 1973).

Once a region has been classified as obstacle, its world coordinates are passed to the collision avoidance, to supplement the sonar information. The vision module evaluates images with a frequency of more than 1 Hz on a Pentium computer. Obstacles of the size of a bottle are usually detected at a maximal range of five meters, which is sufficient for real-time collision avoidance even if our robot is operated at its maximum speed. Figure 16 shows two typical images together with random color representations of the segmentation result. In various experiments, we found this algorithm to reliably detect small, can-sized obstacles in our university building.

The reader may notice that this algorithm has been successfully used for detecting and grasping free-standing objects on the floor (Buhmann et al. 1995), as demonstrated at the 1994 AAAI mobile robot competition (Simmons 1995).

Example Application

The RHINO-software described in this chapter has served as a low-level platform for various indoor mobile robot applications. A complete coverage of our current applications is beyond the scope of this chapter. One of the most recent and most interesting applications, however, is that of a robotic "tour guide" (similar to the one proposed in Horswill 1994). The tour guide offers tours to visitors and explains rooms, locations, and their relation to each other. For this purpose, RHINO is equipped with a CD ROM for storing and replaying music and text.

Figure 17 depicts one of the maps the robot used when giving tours through our university building in Bonn. Maps are recorded by teleoperating (joy-sticking) the robot through the building, using some of the techniques described in this chapter. Each location or object of interest (such as an office) is taught by moving toward it and pressing a button when the robot is facing the object or location at the distance of one meter. The gray shaded numbers in figure 17 depict eleven target locations, and the corresponding numbers with white background show the positions at which the robot was taught. The entire teach-in requires

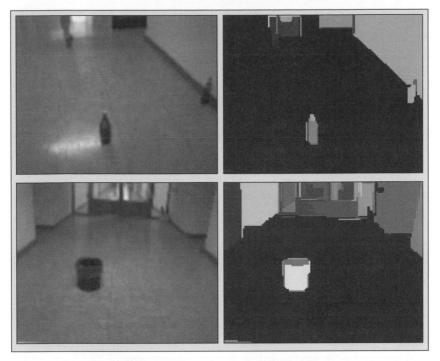

*Figure 16: Two indoor scenes with obstacles
and the corresponding image segmentation.*

less than ten minutes, not counting the time required for recording the verbal explanations of the different tour items. When the robot gives a tour, its localization routines quickly align its position with its previously constructed map. It then sequentially navigates to the target locations and replays previously recoded text for each of them (with user-controlled levels of granularity). The duration of the complete tour depends on the amount of information the user wants to obtain and is typically in the order of five minutes. If the visitor loses interest, the tour can be terminated at any time. In approximately thirty testing runs in different buildings, we never observed a failure of the navigation routines, even in populated hallways. We found that the integration of speech, sound, interaction, and fast motion contributes significantly to the interestingness of the guide.

Conclusion

This chapter presents our currently best approaches to autonomous mobile robot navigation. Our current approaches are map-based. In particular, integrated metric-topological maps are learned autonomously using sonar and camera information. Bayesian analysis permits the robot to track its position accurately during navigation and mapping and to localize itself in cases where it is globally ignorant about its position. Path planning is performed by a fast dynamic programming routine, and collisions are avoided by a module that is capable of reacting to unforeseen obstacles by adjusting the motion direction and the velocity of the robot.

The software has been tested thoroughly using various mobile robots at different sites and is now distributed and regularly exhibited by a major mobile robot manufacturer (Real World Interface) along with their robots. The software provides the "low-level" control that allows several AI researchers inside and outside our university to perform high-level AI experiments without having to pay much attention to the low-level navigation.

Certainly, there are a variety of limitations and desiderata that warrant future research. The following list addresses some of the most significant and challenging ones:

- Dynamic environments. Maps, as presented in this chapter, are generally incapable of modeling moving obstacles. In a recent thesis (Schneider 1994), Schneider extended our approach to model semidynamic obstacles such as doors. Such obstacles are dynamic but appear only at fixed locations and thus can be detected by analyzing long-term dependencies in the occupancy grid. Modeling moving objects such as humans is a significant open problem in map-based navigation.

- Three-dimensional maps. Our current maps are two-dimensional, and our planning algorithms are tailored toward navigation of a circular robot. This chapter does not address manipulation. To facilitate manipulation, three-dimensional representations are clearly advantageous. Extending our current approach to 3D representations is an open problem that clearly warrants further research. Planning using such representations is necessarily more complex, and more sophisticated approaches are probably required if the robot is to plan and act in real-time.

- Self-tuning sensor interpretation. Currently, our sensor models are adjusted once and frozen thereafter. It is generally desirable to adjust sensor models while the robot is operating, to compensate for sensor defects and drift.

- A unified approach to localization. Our present approach relies on two quite different methods for localization, one of which is specialized to global position estimation, the other of which is dedicated to position tracking during map learning. Since both attack the same general problem—sensor-based localization under uncertainty—it is desirable to find a single, unified mechanism.

- Unknown state spaces. At various occasions throughout this chapter, we made the assumption that the robot environment is Markov and partially observable. In particular, all our probabilistic approaches, such as our methods

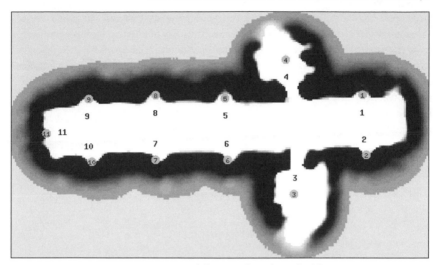

Figure 17: Map used for tours through our building.
The numbers in gray circles indicate the different target objects, and the numbers
with white background mark the positions at which these targets were taught.

for mapping and localization, make strong assumptions as to what the non-observable quantities (state) of the environment are that make the environment Markov. Since in general it is difficult to specify what constitutes the "state" of the environment, methods that can discover hidden state and model it from data are clearly desirable (see for example, Chrisman [1992], McCallum [1995], Rabiner [1990]).

- Other sensors. Integrating sensors other than sonar and cameras into mobile robot navigation is an important problem, since different sensors have different perceptual characteristics. In principle, the general mechanisms for mapping, localization, and navigation are not specialized to a particular type of sensor. However, incorporating other sensors is not trivial, and we believe many interesting research opportunities will come up from actually trying it.

- Scaling up. The largest cycle-free map that has been generated with this approach was approximately one hundred meters long; the largest single cycle measured approximately fifty-eight by twenty meters. What happens if the environment is an order of magnitude larger? Clearly, there are intrinsic limits as to how well a robot can localize itself incrementally without a global positioning system. We believe that by localizing the robot backwards in time, we can increase the size of the environments that can be mapped reliably. However, the general problem will never disappear, and the best we can hope for are incremental improvements in the size of environments that our software can manage reliably.

As this chapter documents, we have found the map-based paradigm to be surprisingly powerful and reliable. While to date, there exists a variety of successful architecture for mobile robot navigation (such as Brooks's (1989) subsumption architecture, each of which is characterized by different advantages and disadvantages, we believe that the map-based paradigm is particularly well-suited for fully autonomous robots that are to perform a multitude of tasks in large indoor environments. Maps are well understood, and it is easy to specify new navigation tasks using a map. We also believe that probabilistic models, such as the maps described in this chapter, are powerful concepts in robot navigation, as long as they compile percepts into compact representations that capture relevant details and are easy to access.

Acknowledgment

We thank the other members of the RHINO team and the XAVIER mobile robot team at CMU for insightful discussion, help and advice. The low-level process communication software TCX (Fedor 1993) was provided by CMU, which is gratefully acknowledged.

Sebastian Thrun's work on this project was sponsored in part by the National Science Foundation under award IRI-9313367, and by the Wright Laboratory, Aeronautical Systems Center, Air Force Materiel Command, USAF, and the Defense Advanced Research Projects Agency (DARPA) under grant number F33615-93-1-1330 (T. Mitchell, principal investigator). The views and conclusions contained in this document are those of the author and should not be interpreted as necessarily representing official policies or endorsements, either expressed or implied, of NSF, Wright Laboratory or the United States Government. Thorsten Fröhlinghaus acknowledges financial support by the European Community under grant CORMORANT 8503 (J. Buhmann, principal investigator).

CHAPTER TWO

Integrating High-Speed Obstacle Avoidance, Global Path Planning, and Vision Sensing on a Mobile Robot

David Kortenkamp, Marcus Huber, Charles Cohen,
Ulrich Raschke, Frank Koss, and Clare Congdon

The first Mobile Robot Competition was held by AAAI in 1992, where a total of ten robots competed in a series of events (Dean and Bonasso 1993). The robot described in this chapter, CARMEL, won this inaugural competition. It did so by combining high-speed sonar-based obstacle avoidance with task-directed vision. In this case study, we will give a detailed description of the robot and the algorithms that led it to victory.

The competition consisted of three stages. The first stage required roaming a 22 meter by 22 meter (70 foot by 70 foot.) arena while avoiding static and dynamic obstacles. The second stage involved searching for ten distinctive objects in the same arena and visiting each of the objects. Visiting was defined as moving to within two robot diameters of the object. The last stage was a timed race to visit three of the objects located in the second stage and return home. Since the first stage is primarily a subset of the second stage requirements and the third stage implementation is very similar to the second stage implementation, this case study will focus on the second stage of the competition.

The arena boundaries were defined by three-foot high walls and three-foot high cardboard boxes were used as obstacles. The objects to be found were ten-foot tall three-inch diameter poles. To each pole we attached an omnidirectional barcode tag, which allowed our computer vision system to distinguish one pole from another (see the section on vision sensing). The objects could be seen above the obstacles, while the clearance between obstacles was a minimum of 1.5 meters.

CARMEL (computer-aided robotics for maintenance, emergency, and life support) is based on a commercially available Cybermotion K2A mobile robot platform. It is a cylindrical robot about a meter in diameter, standing a bit less than a meter high when equipped with a large hollow shell (for holding electronics and other equipment) on top (see figure 1). It has a top speed of approximately

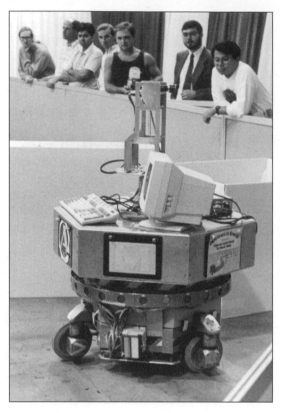

Figure 1. CARMEL at the AAAI robot competition.

800 millimeters per second and is driven by three synchronously driven wheels. CARMEL's hexagonal top is decoupled from these wheels, so that the orientation of the top is unchanged when the robot itself turns. Wheel encoders calculate the robot's displacement from a homed position; this calculation is called dead-reckoning. Errors accumulate in the dead-reckoned position because of wheel slippage; dealing with these errors is a major concern.

CARMEL is equipped with a ring of twenty-four ultrasonic sonar sensors evenly distributed around the robot's torso, each with a two-meter range and a sensing cone of about thirty degrees. A grayscale CCD (charge-coupled device) camera was added to CARMEL to give it visual capabilities. The camera is mounted on a rotating tower, allowing it to turn 360 degrees independent of the robot's orientation.

CARMEL has three computers working cooperatively while the robot is running. A motor control processor (Z80) receives motor and steering commands from the top-level computer and controls the robot's wheel speed and direction.

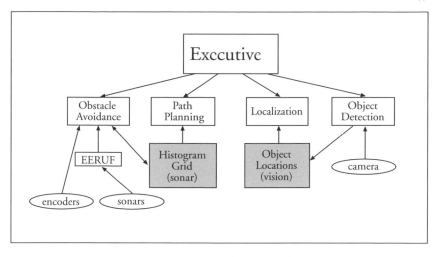

Figure 2. Major components of CARMEL's *software system.*
Gray rectangles are maps, white rectangles are processes, ovals are sensors.

This processor also maintains the robot's dead-reckoning information. An IBM PC XT clone is dedicated to the sonar ring, controlling the firing sequence and filtering sonar crosstalk and external noise from the sonar data. Finally, an IBM PC clone running a 33-MHz, 80486-based processor performs the top-level functions of the robot, including obstacle avoidance, vision processing, planning, and localization. This computer communicates with the sonar and motor control processors via RS-232 (9600 baud).

CARMEL has a hierarchical software structure. At the top level is a planning system that decides when to call subordinate modules for movement, vision or recalibration of the robot's position. Each of the subordinate modules is responsible for doing low-level error handling and must return control to the planner at the end of a set period of time, perhaps reporting failure. Figure 2 shows the major components of CARMEL's software system. Obstacle avoidance, path planning, vision sensing, and localization are described in the following four sections. Then we discuss the top-level planner.

Obstacle Avoidance

A key to CARMEL's success was its ability to deal with sonar sensor noise. CARMEL used a novel algorithm called EERUF (error-eliminating ultrasonic firing) to allow for rapid firing and sampling of ultrasonic sonar sensors, which means faster obstacle avoidance. EERUF allows the robot to detect and reject ultrasonic noise, including crosstalk. The sources of ultrasonic noise may be classified as external

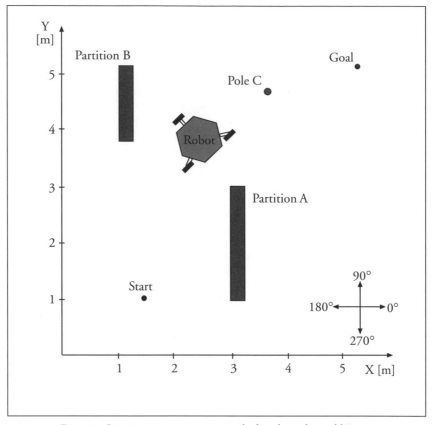

Figure 3. CARMEL *in its environment with obstacles and a goal location.*

sources, such as ultrasonic sensors used on another mobile robot operating in the same environment; or internal sources, such as stray echoes from other on-board ultrasonic sensors. The latter phenomenon, known as crosstalk, is the reason for the slow firing rates in many conventional mobile robot applications: most mobile robots are designed to avoid crosstalk by waiting long enough between firing individual sensors to allow each echo to dissipate before the next sensor is fired. EERUF, on the other hand, is able to detect and reject about ninety-seven percent of all erroneous readings caused by external or internal noise.

In general, external noise is random and can be detected simply by comparison of consecutive readings. Crosstalk, however, is mostly a systematic error, which may cause similar (albeit erroneous) consecutive errors. EERUF overcomes this problem by firing each sensor after individual, alternating delays that disrupt the repetitiveness of crosstalk errors, rendering these errors detectable by the method of comparison of consecutive readings. Because EERUF practically

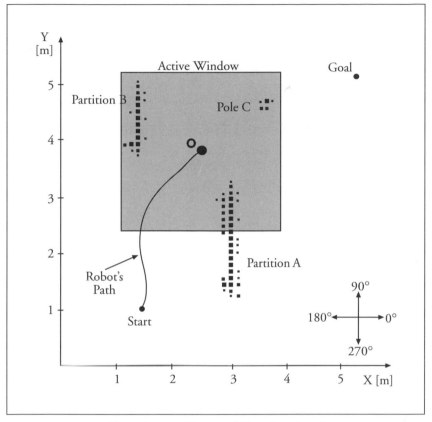

Figure 4. CARMEL has moved along the path and created a histogram grid showing object locations.

eliminates the problem of crosstalk, it allows for very fast firing rates. See Borenstein and Koren (1992) for more details on EERUF.

Vector Field Histogram

To map the obstacles in the environment, CARMEL uses another innovative approach called a vector field histogram (VFH). The VFH method uses a two-dimensional Cartesian grid, called the histogram grid, to represent data from ultrasonic range sensors. Each cell in the histogram grid holds a certainty value that represents the confidence of the algorithm in the existence of an obstacle at that location. Figure 3 shows CARMEL in a sample environment with obstacles and a goal location. Figure 4 shows the map that CARMEL creates as it moves towards the goal. This representation was derived from the certainty grid concept originally presented in Moravec and Elfes (1985).

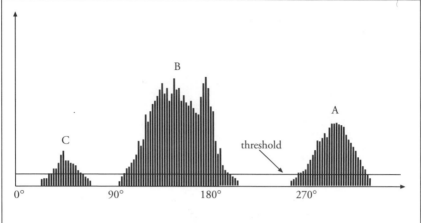

Figure 5. VFH's polar histogram has "mountains" in the direction of obstacles. CARMEL is steered toward a "valley"in the direction of the goal location.

The central idea behind a certainty grid is to fuse sonar readings over time to eliminate errors in individual sonar readings. In CARMEL's case, each cell of the grid array represents a ten centimeter square, and the array covers the entire environment space. As the robot (CARMEL) travels through the environment, its sonar sensors are continuously being fired and returning range readings to objects. Since the approximate location of the robot at any time is known through odometry and the direction of each sonar sensor is known, the location of objects in the grid array can be estimated. Each time an object is detected at a particular cell location, the value of the cell is increased and the values of all the cells between the robot and this cell are decremented (since they must be empty). The cells have minimum and maximum values, which have been chosen arbitrarily for computational convenience. Greater detail of the histogram method can be found in Borenstein and Koren (1991).

To perform the actual obstacle avoidance using the histogram grid, CARMEL creates an intermediate data representation called the polar histogram. The purpose of the polar histogram is to reduce the amount of data that needs to be handled for real-time analysis while at the same time retaining the statistical information of the histogram grid, which compensates for the inaccuracies of the ultrasonic sensors. In this way, the VFH algorithm produces a sufficiently detailed spatial representation of the robot's environment for travel among densely cluttered obstacles, without compromising the system's real-time performance. The spatial representation in the polar histogram can be visualized as a mountainous panorama around the robot, where the height and size of the peaks represent the proximity of obstacles, and the valleys represent possible travel directions (see figure 5). The VFH algorithm steers the robot in the direction of one of the valleys, based on the direction of the target location. The details of CARMEL's algorithm for creating and using the polar histogram is detailed in Borenstein and Koren (1991b). A high-level description of the algorithm follows:

1. Collect current sonar sensor readings.

2. Create the histogram grid. For each sonar reading do the following:
   a) Given the direction of the sensor, the distance returned, and the robot's current location, determine the cell in the histogram grid in which the obstacle lies. If the sonar did not detect an obstacle, then determine the cell that lies at the maximum range of the sonar and skip the next step.
   b) Increment the value in that cell by a fixed amount (we use three in our implementation) up to some maximum (we use fifteen).
   c) For each cell lying on a straight line between the robot and the cell determined in (a) above, decrement its value by a fixed amount (we use one) down to a minimum of zero.

3. Calculate the polar histogram as follows:
   a) Define an active window surrounding the center of the robot (we use a window of size 33 x 33).
   b) For each direction around the robot, in five-degree increments, total the value in all cells in that direction within the active window.
   c) Smooth the histogram by averaging neighboring directions.

4. Set a threshold such that a polar histogram value below that threshold means that direction is "free," while a polar histogram value above that threshold means that direction is "occupied." This threshold can vary greatly between robots and even between environments.

5. Search the polar histogram for a free direction of travel as follows:
   a) If the direction to the target is free and enough neighboring histogram directions are free (to assure that the path is wide enough for the robot), then the target direction is the free direction.
   b) Otherwise, begin checking to the left and right of the target direction (alternating) for a free segment of the histogram that is wide enough for the robot to pass. The last direction in such a free segment can be returned as the free direction.
   c) If no free segment is found, the robot is trapped (i.e., surrounded on all sides by obstacles).

The combination of EERUF and VFH is uniquely suited to high-speed obstacle avoidance; it has been demonstrated to perform obstacle avoidance in the most difficult obstacle courses at speeds of up to 1.0 meters per second. All of CARMEL's experimental runs were at speeds of 780 millimeters per second or less. At the actual competition, CARMEL's maximum speed was 500 millimeters per second although it would run more slowly when in tight spaces or when approaching an object. CARMEL was distinguished by a graceful motion around obstacles in open terrain.

Global Path Planning

In addition to VFH, CARMEL uses a global path planner that searches the histogram grid created during obstacle avoidance and creates a list of via points (intermediary goal points) that represent the shortest path to the goal. The algorithm was developed at the Oak Ridge National Laboratory (Andersen et al., 1992) and reimplemented on CARMEL. The algorithm is simple and fast:

1. Initialize a planning grid of the same size and granularity as the histogram grid.
2. Threshold the histogram grid to determine occupied cells for planning purposes. Mark these cells as occupied in the planning grid.
3. Expand each occupied cell by the radius of the robot in the planning grid.
4. If the start or target locations fall inside an obstacle, move them to the nearest edge of the obstacle.
5. Create a linked list of structures of the type:

```
struct NODE {
    int x,y;              /* coordinates of grid cell */
    int distance;         /* distance from the target */
    struct NODE *next;    /* forward link */
};
```

6. Initialize the head of the linked list to the coordinates of the target cell and initialize the distance to zero.
7. While there is something in the list and the start cell has not yet been processed:
   a) Pop the head of the list.
   b) Place the distance of that item into its corresponding cell (x,y) in the planning grid.
   c) Put all neighboring cells that are still 0 and are not obstacles at the end of the linked list with a distance equal to one plus the distance of the popped item.
8. Starting at the start cell, follow the minimum path (including diagonal elements) to the target cell. If all the neighbors of the start cell are zero then there is no path.
9. Select those cells where the slope of the path changes and store their coordinates as via points that the robot should try to follow.

If a path is not found, it is possible to iterate the path planner using higher and higher thresholds for occupied cells. This algorithm is very quick, taking less than one second to run on a grid size of 256 by 256 cells (each cell represents 20 centimeters in the environment). The speed of the algorithm lets it run on the fly to extract CARMEL from potential trap situations. With an appropriate threshold, the algorithm rarely fails to find a path—in cases where a path is not found CARMEL is simply instructed to head in the direction of the goal. One characteristic of this algorithm is that the path is not always the shortest path; however, VFH will cut corners while following via points along the way to a goal, allowing a path to be straightened out.

Grid-based systems have many limitations, including the amount of memory they require and the need to always know very precisely the location of the robot. In the competition, a grid representation was sufficient, as the arena was of a fixed (and known) size and we had mechanisms for determining the location of the robot. Given a larger environment, or an environment of unknown extent, a different representation scheme might be better.

Vision Sensing

The ability to accurately detect and identify objects in the world was important for earning the maximum number of points, as well as for keeping position and orientation errors within tolerable limits. The competition rules allowed the objects (tall poles) to be tagged to allow for easier recognition. Various tagging schemes were considered, but a vision-based system had an important advantage in its potential for long-range sensing. A major concern was the inherently heavy computation generally required for image processing. By intelligently designing the object tags, we greatly reduced the required computation.

Tag Design

The object tag design used for CARMEL consists of a black and white stripe pattern placed on 4 inch PVC tubing. Examples of the object tags that were used are shown in figure 6. The basic stripe pattern is six evenly spaced horizontal black bands (which we refer to as separator bands) of 100 millimeters height, with the top of the top band and the bottom of the bottom band spaced 1,100 millimeters apart. The size of the object tag is not important for the detection of objects. It is important, however, that the algorithm know the physical size of the object so that it can estimate its distance.

The white gaps between the black separator bands correspond to bit positions in a five-bit word, and are also 100 millimeters high. A white space between two black separator bands corresponds to an OFF bit, while a black space corresponds to an ON bit. The five bits between the six bands can then represent thirty-two unique objects. Although we needed to identify only ten objects, we utilized a five-bit code so that we could select bit patterns that did not have consecutive ON bits. Consecutive ON bits create long segments of black, reducing the number of black and white bands in the object tag and, therefore, reducing the number of constraints that an object has to satisfy before being accepted. By using

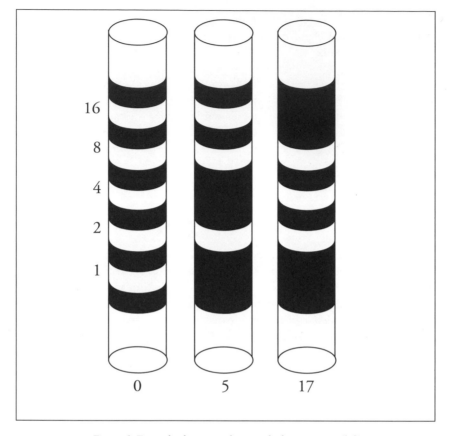

*Figure 6: Example object tags showing the basic pattern (left)
and the patterns for some of the objects used.*

only those patterns that had sparse bit patterns, we greatly reduced the risk of identifying false objects in the environment.

One of the most significant aspects of the striped PVC tags is that they are omnidirectional, appearing the same from all directions. This had a great impact on the exploration algorithm used, as the robot did not have to approach objects from a particular direction. Rather, CARMEL had only to get within visual range of an object to perform identification. See Huber et al. (1992) for a comparison of CARMEL's object recognition system with that of other teams at the competition.

Image Acquisition

Images were acquired using the on-board 486-based computer while the robot was motionless. This computer was equipped with an Imaging Technologies fg100 framegrabber with an image resolution of 640 by 480 pixels. Low-level C routines were written to move a single column of the image from the framegrabber's memory to the CPU's memory, where it was processed using the algorithm given below. Our black and white CCD camera had a lens with an 8.5 millimeter focal length and the focus set at infinity. The resulting field of view was approximately 48 degrees. The camera was fixed onto a rotating table mounted on top of CARMEL and was positioned slightly off center from CARMEL's axis. This table could turn independently of CARMEL.

The Algorithm

The vision algorithm is composed primarily of three routines: scanning a column of an image for objects, merging these objects with those objects found in previous columns, and heuristics for eliminating invalid tags and merging multiply identified objects. The algorithm works on the raw image. We do not perform any filtering or preprocessing on the images before running the algorithm.

The algorithm works by scanning an image column by column, from the left side of the image to the right side. In each column, the algorithm looks for sharp intensity changes that mark the edges of the black and white bands. Because all object tags start with a black band, the algorithm identifies a potential object whenever it detects a transition from white to black. As the algorithm continues scanning the column, it calculates the height of the black and white bands for each potential object. The relative sizes of each potential object's black and white bands must comply with the tag design (for example, white bands are the same size as separator bands, and black bands representing an ON bit are three times the height of either of these). A potential object is then eliminated from further consideration if any of the tag design's constraints are violated.

Once an object with all five bits is detected, it is merged with the same object found in previous columns, resulting in objects that "grow" in width from left to right until the right edge of the object is found. Once the entire image has been scanned, the completed object list is then pruned of illegal bit patterns. When objects are extremely close—less than two meters—the object may be detected as several adjacent thin objects with the same bit pattern. A heuristic process merges these separate objects into a single object.

The distance between the top of the top band and the bottom of the bottom band, in terms of the number of pixels in the image, is then used to estimate the distance from the camera to the object. Distance estimation is possible with a single image since the actual size of the object is known beforehand and the object's size in the image is simply a function of how far away it is from the camera. The horizontal location of the object on the image plane is then used to calculate the orientation of the object from the camera's axis. These two values, the distance and orientation, are then transformed from the camera's coordinate system to the robot's coordinate system.

Once objects were located, their locations were recorded so that the robot could visit them. A global map, distinct from the sonar-based VFH map, was created to record object locations. This map used the same coordinate system as the VFH map, however, to simplify path planning.

Discussion

The algorithm described above is very quick, running on a 486-based PC clone in under two seconds in most cases. This is primarily because it is a single pass algorithm and there is no preprocessing of the image. In the final version, the algorithm could identify objects up to nineteen meters distant, with a minimum detection distance of slightly less than one meter. Localization of the object also proved to be quite accurate and reliable. The algorithm proved to be very robust, very seldom detecting false objects even in visually cluttered environments.

We anticipate that we will be able to use the vision system in a great number of future robotics tasks. Until a general computer vision system is perfected, there will necessarily be engineering of the environment in which the robots operate in order to simplify the computer vision portion of tasks. General purpose robots will most likely operate in an environment similar to that in which humans operate, where a large number of landmarks, such as signs and markers, will exist to assist them. While the vision system is an object recognition system very specific to a particular type of object, its use is not limited to the robot competition. The object tags, perhaps in various sizes, may be used to identify landmarks (e.g. doorways, intersections, road signs), distinguish between objects in the world, and act as road signs, among a great number of other uses.

Localization

A robot's internal (dead-reckoned) knowledge of where it is accumulates errors during movement due to wheel slippage, etc. Therefore, triangulation from known landmark positions was studied. The intention was to update CARMEL's position and orientation using landmarks whose positions were recorded early in the navigation process, before dead-reckoning errors had accumulated. A number of papers describe methods for triangulating a robot's position from three known landmarks, including Levitt and Lawton (1990); Sugihara (1988); and Krotkov (1989). We implemented and experimented with our own landmark triangulation algorithm. This method is based on the geometric circle method, which is widely used in literature.

In this section we present an overview of the developed three-object triangulation algorithm. Referring to figure 7, landmark 1, landmark 2, and the robot form one circle (circle A). Even though the robot's location is not known, there

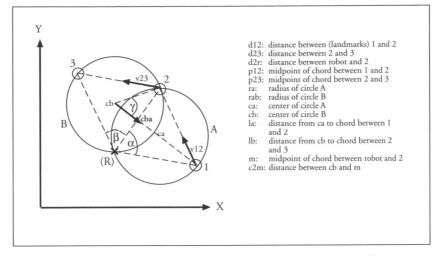

d12:	distance between (landmarks) 1 and 2
d23:	distance between 2 and 3
d2r:	distance between robot and 2
p12:	midpoint of chord between 1 and 2
p23:	midpoint of chord between 2 and 3
ra:	radius of circle A
rab:	radius of circle B
ca:	center of circle A
cb:	center of circle B
la:	distance from ca to chord between 1 and 2
lb:	distance from cb to chord between 2 and 3
m:	midpoint of chord between robot and 2
c2m:	distance between cb and m

Figure 7. Using angles to three known objects to calculate the robot's position and orientation.

are only two possible circles because the angle between landmarks as viewed by the robot is known. Landmark 2, landmark 3, and the robot also form another unique circle (B). From the information available (landmark locations and the angles α and β) the equations of the circles can be determined. The two circles intersect at landmark 2 and the robot's location. Landmark 2's location is already known and the robot's location is the other intersection point. The algorithm is as follows (refer to figure 7):

1. Properly order landmarks:

   a) For this algorithm to work properly, both α and β must be less than 180 degrees. When this condition holds we say that the landmarks are "ordered" properly. Properly ordered landmarks assure that the desired solution (out of the two solutions possible) is found. Properly ordered landmarks have the following two features (see figure 8): First, they are labeled consecutively (1, 2, 3) in a counterclockwise fashion; and second, the angle between landmarks 1 and 2 (β) and the angle between landmarks 1 and 3 (α) must be less than 180 degrees.

2. $\alpha = Lo2 - Lo1$. If α is too small or equals 90 degrees or 270 degrees, return with error because division by 0 will occur.

3. $\beta = Lo3 - Lo2$. If β is too small or equals 90 degrees or 270 degrees, return with error because division by 0 will occur.

4. $ra = d12 / 2 \sin(\alpha)$

5. $rb = d23 / 2 \sin(\beta)$

6. $la = d12 / 2 \tan(\alpha)$

7. $lb = d12 / 2 \tan(\beta)$

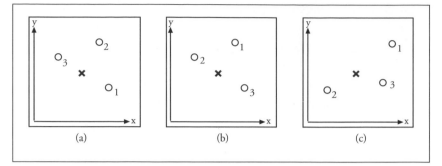

Figure 8. *Landmarks must be properly ordered for the geometric circle algorithm to work correctly. Only (a) shows properly ordered landmarks. In (b) the landmarks are not labeled in a counterclockwise fashion. In (c) the angle between landmark 1 and landmark 2 is greater than 180 degrees.*

8. Let $v12x$ and $v12y$ be the unit vector from landmark 1 to landmark 2.

9. Let $v23x$ and $v23y$ be the unit vector from landmark 2 to landmark 3.

10. $cax = p12x - la(v12y)$

11. $cay = p12y + la(v12x)$

12. $cbx = p23x - lb(v23y)$

13. $cby = p23y + lb(v23x)$

14. Return an error if the centers of the two circles are too close (we use 10 units).

15. If γ is very large, then return error.

16. Let $cbax$ and $cbay$ be the unit vector from the center of circle B to the center of circle A.

17. $d2r = 2rb \sin(\gamma)$

18. $c2m = rb\cos(\gamma)$

19. Robot x position = $Rx = 2mx - Lx2 + 0.5$

20. Robot y position = $Ry = 2my - Ly2 + 0.5$

21. $\phi = \arctan(Ly1 - Ry / Lx1 - Rx)$, the heading of landmark 1 from the true robot position.

22. If $\phi > 0.0$ then robot orientation error $= - (Lo1 - \phi)$ else robot orientation error 360 degrees $+ \phi - Lo1$

23. Return with solution

In the geometric circle intersection algorithm, the errors occur when circle A and circle B overlap; i.e., landmarks 1, 2, and 3, and the robot all lie on or close to the same circle. When this happens, the method cannot be used. This algorithm is fast, because of the simple vector manipulations used to find the solution, and failure detection is easy.

As a result of a large number of experiments the actual implementation of the geometric circle intersection method was discovered to require the headings of at least two of the landmarks to be greater than 90 degrees and the angular separation between any pair of landmarks to be greater than 45 degrees. If this was not the case, the robot is moved to a location in which the landmarks fit these restrictions. With these restrictions, the algorithm proved very robust with respect to uncertainty in object headings and locations. Additionally, the result from triangulation can be compared with the current dead-reckoned position, and if the two are widely different then the triangulated value can be discarded. For a detailed analysis and complete algorithm of the geometric circle intersection method, and a comparison with three other triangulation methods, see Cohen and Koss (1992).

The Supervising Execution System

The design of our execution system was motivated by several goals. First, and most importantly, we wanted to keep the executive very simple. The hierarchical design eliminated many problems, such as contention for resources between submodules and lack of coordination between submodules. All scheduling was done through the top-level planner. Second, we wanted the overall system to be extremely robust. Because the competition rules prohibited outside interference with the robots after they had started the task, the executive needed to handle even catastrophic errors during run-time. Third, we wanted to use existing research as submodules. For example, the obstacle avoidance routines we used had been developed over many years as stand-alone processes. We wanted to integrate them within the framework of the task without substantial modifications. Finally, we wanted to develop and test each submodule independently of the others. This allowed several groups to work in parallel in developing the software system.

What emerged from these design goals was a strict hierarchy of modules with calls to each submodule and information exchange between each submodule being completely controlled by a supervising executive. No submodule was allowed to run by itself, and all submodules were guaranteed to return, even if they returned an error condition.

Overview

The executive has three primary tasks: First, it has to decide what to do (i.e., which submodule to call). Second, it has to decide when to do it; and finally, it has to decide where to do it. The basic strategy for performing the task previously described in the task description is for the executive to: (1) tell the obstacle avoidance submodule to move the robot to a particular location where objects might be seen. (2) tell the object detection submodule to find all objects within a certain sweep area (e.g., the 180 degrees in front of the robot). (3) tell the obstacle avoidance submodule to approach the nearest object or item and tell the object detection submodule to verify the location of the object. (4) tell the obstacle avoidance submodule to approach nearer to the object if the robot is still too far away from it.

These steps are repeated until all of the objects have been visited. In some environments (such as the competition), steps (1) and (2) are repeated before the robot begins to visit objects. This allows many objects to be placed in the map before dead-reckoning errors accumulate.

At any time during this cycle, the planner can decide that CARMEL has moved far enough that its dead reckoning is probably in error. The executive then interrupts the cycle and directs the obstacle avoidance submodule to move the robot to a location from which it can see at least three objects in the proper configuration (as was previously described in the section on localization). The executive then points the camera at each of the three objects and asks the object detection submodule to determine new headings to the three objects. These headings are passed to the localization submodule. That submodule returns the new position and orientation of CARMEL, which the executive uses to update CARMEL's internal position and orientation.

Error Recovery

There are two major causes of errors that the executive has to deal with. First, there are errors in movement, whereby the obstacle avoidance submodule cannot move the robot to the position requested by the executive. The second major cause of errors are errors in object location, whereby the object detection submodule cannot verify that the robot has moved to an object. Recovery from these two types of errors is discussed in the following subsections.

Errors in Movement

The obstacle avoidance submodule can detect two types of movement errors: trap situations, such as U-shaped obstacles, and failures to attain the goal location. Traps are detected automatically by the obstacle avoidance algorithm. The executive's solution to this error is to call the path planning submodule to plot a set of via points that will lead the robot out of the trap and to the goal location. The obstacle avoidance submodule is then called with this list of via points instead of a single goal location. The obstacle avoidance submodule guides the robot through each via point.

Failure to attain the goal location is not detected automatically by the obstacle avoidance algorithm. The algorithm was designed to attempt to reach its goal location, running forever if necessary. Obviously, this was not desirable, since the goal location could be located inside an obstacle or behind a long wall. The *obstacle avoidance* submodule guarantees termination by estimating how long it should take the robot to reach the goal location and stopping the robot and returning to the executive when this time limit is exceeded (or it has reached the goal location).

When the executive is informed of a failure to attain the goal location, it first determines if CARMEL is close enough to the goal location so that no further action is necessary. "Close enough" varies depending on the situation. For example, when CARMEL is just trying to take an image, a few meters away may be close enough. But when CARMEL is approaching within two robot diameters of an object, fractions of a meter are important. If the executive determines that CARMEL is not close enough, the executive asks the obstacle avoidance submodule to try again. After repeated failures, the executive chooses a new goal location that will also be suitable (such as the other side of the object) and starts the process all over.

Errors in Object Location

In the course of visiting an object, the planner will move CARMEL to a spot approximately three meters from the object. At this point, the executive will request another image to verify the location of the object. It is this new heading and distance that is used to make the final approach to within two robot diameters of the object; using this new, robot-relative information reduces the reliance on dead reckoning. However, there may be situations when the object cannot be seen from the verification location. In this case, the executive rotates the camera left and right in an ever-widening arc, searching for the object. If this fails, the executive assumes that CARMEL is too close to the object to detect it (the vision system has a minimum range of one meter) and so it backs CARMEL up. If this fails, the object is assumed to be occluded and the executive chooses a new goal location on the opposite side of the object and starts the verification process over again.

Analysis

An integrated system to perform a specific task has been described. In practice, this system performed above expectations. The decision to dedicate specific submodules to different tasks paid off handsomely at execution time. Since sub modules are encapsulated and guaranteed to return, they can have the entire resources of the computer at their disposal, without needing to sacrifice CPU time for the top-level planner. For the obstacle avoidance submodule, this results in movement that is fast and continuous, displaying none of the move-stop-move behavior of many other robots at the competition. For the object detection submodule, this results in analysis of images that takes only a few seconds.

It also became apparent during the course of implementing the system that the performance of each submodule affected the design of the supervising executive. In particular, the object detection submodule evolved over time and became much more accurate and could extract objects at much greater ranges. This reduced the need for dealing with uncertainty and error.

The system was tested over many runs in three different environments, with the largest being 22 meters by 22 meters. Error recovery routines for movement errors were tested by forcing CARMEL into traps. Error recovery routines for object location errors were tested by manually moving objects after their positions had been recorded by the planner. In practice, the error recovery routines for visiting objects allowed us to be less concerned with the precise position of the robot, so that we didn't need to perform landmark triangulation as often. Since landmark triangulation is time consuming, requiring a movement and three images, the less often that it needs to be performed, the better.

In the actual competition, CARMEL found and visited all ten objects in just over nine minutes. This far out-paced the competition, none of whom could complete the task in the allotted twenty minutes. For the competition run, CARMEL used two hard-coded view points from which it hoped to see all ten objects; it went immediately to these two points, storing objects that it found in its map. Should CARMEL not have found all ten objects at these first two view points, there were other view points to which it could have gone. Because CARMEL was able to find all ten objects at the first two view points, its global object map was very accurate. CARMEL then proceeded to visit each object in turn, going to the nearest unvisited object first.

Conclusion

The CARMEL project teaches several important lessons in the design of actual mobile robot systems. The first is that a significant advantage is gained by keeping all computation on-board. Second, engineering the environment with simple tags can greatly simplify many robot tasks—much as hanging street signs greatly simplifies many human navigation tasks (see Miller 1994 for further discussion of this point). Third, the CARMEL project gives a blueprint for developing modular robot systems by encapsulating existing submodules and integrating them with a simple planner.

Finally, CARMEL demonstrates that in order to have a successful robot, much attention needs to be devoted to sensing. Fully forty percent of CARMEL's C code was dedicated to vision or sonar processing, with only thirty-five percent of the code devoted to higher-level tasks such as planning or triangulation (the rest of the code was devoted to user interface, communication, or other, low-level, processes). In the case of CARMEL's vision algorithm, we found that fast, reliable, long-range sensing can have a simplifying effect on task execution. If CARMEL had not been able to see as far, we would have had to design much more complicated exploration patterns to assure that the entire arena was explored.

Acknowledgments

The authors wish to thank the other members of the CARMEL team, including Johann Borenstein, Doug Baker, Chris Conley, Roy Feague, LiQuang Feng, Rob Giles, Scott Huffman, Kevin Mangis, Alex Woolf, Annie Wu, and Cigdem Yasar. Support for the CARMEL team was provided by The University of Michigan College of Engineering, The University of Michigan Rackham School of Graduate Studies, the American Association for Artificial Intelligence, ABB Robotics Inc., and ABB Graco Robotics Inc. Support for development of many of the algorithms used on CARMEL was supplied by Department of Energy grant no. DE-FG0286NE37969.

CHAPTER THREE

Dervish: An Office-Navigating Robot

Illah Nourbakhsh

The judges are ready and Dervish knows its mission: to exit the room in which it has been placed, navigate down the artificial hallways to one of the goal room's two doors, and enter the room. Dervish begins by exiting the room. Turning to align itself with the hallway, it begins to move toward the near door of the goal room, which is just a few feet in front. This should be an easy run, or so the robot thinks. Oops! Dervish sees a hallway on its left and knows that the hallway is opposite the door: Dervish must have missed the door. Dervish backs up to where the door must be and searches back and forth a few feet, looking for an opening. Finding none, Dervish decides that this door must be closed, replans to the far door, and begins to move down the hallway again. Uh-oh! There is a large object in front blocking the robot's path. Dervish searches to find a way around the object, but to no avail; it must be a blockade, so Dervish plans to use another hallway. After successfully traveling to the other side of the office building, Dervish reaches the final hallway, slowly but surely approaching the far door. Dervish reaches the door and keeps going—the audience gasps in despair, thinking that Dervish has missed the door. But Dervish stops, backs up to the door, enters the room, and the crowd cheers. And so Dervish won the "Office Delivery" event of the 1994 AAAI National Robot Contest, being the only robot to successfully complete this fourth and final trial.

The 1994 AAAI Robot Contest required Dervish to navigate through a static, artificial office environment. But the contest organizers had a more ambitious goal in mind: autonomous navigation in real-world office buildings. The Stanford University team, of which I was a part, entered the robot contest with this more ambitious goal in mind; the result was a robot architecture that navigates with minimal domain information in actual office buildings.

Dervish has demonstrated competent navigation as well as competent obstacle avoidance in three office buildings at Stanford University and at the American Association for Artificial Intelligence's robot contest in Seattle, Washington. It was the first mobile robot to use probabilistic state set progression, demonstrating that AI techniques can enable a robot to navigate reliably with far less domain information than would otherwise be necessary.

Dervish also demonstrated reliable obstacle avoidance using sonar range sensors. Its secret was a radically redesigned sonar configuration that provides far more reliable freespace coverage than the traditional sonar ring.

In this chapter, I will give a tour of Dervish's architecture, beginning with a hardware description and ending with the interleaving planning and execution strategy Dervish employed. The hardware section describes the basic hardware, including the unusual sonar configuration. The low-level control section presents Dervish's control architecture at an abstract level, describing obstacle avoidance in detail. The localization section introduces the state set representation and elements of localization, including feature recognition and state set progression. The assumptive planning section describes the planning and execution architecture used by Dervish. Finally, the results section describes the environments in which Dervish was developed and tested in preparation for the national robot contest.

Hardware

Dervish's hardware was born out of the modification of a four-year old Nomad 100 mobile robot, Vagabond (Dugan and Nourbakhsh 1993). Our Stanford team stripped Vagabond of its infrared range sensors, bumpers, and its name. The result was a robot with only sonars, which are inexpensive indicators of directional freespace information.

Vagabond's sonars, however, were arranged in the traditional 16-sonar planar ring. The problem with planar sensor rings is that robots and office buildings are not planar. Therefore any robot with such a sensor configuration is subject to both tripping over short objects below the ring and to decapitation by tall objects (such as ledges, shelves, and tables) above the ring.

Surprisingly, sonar placement has been largely ignored by the research community and by almost every commercially available research robot. One exception is TRC's HelpMate robot which is used for delivery tasks in several hospitals.

The challenge was to design a new sonar geometry that would allow the robot to see all relevant objects in real office buildings. The sonars would also have to provide sufficient coverage to allow the robot to recognize features of the world to enable navigation—features such as closed doors and hallway intersections.

Figures 1 and 2 show different views of the final sonar geometry. The most unusual sonars are the pair that point diagonally upward, their paths crossing somewhere in front of the robot's head. These are crucial sonars because they break the plane of a traditional sonar array. The upward-pointing sonar pair detects ledges and tables well before the robot either beheads itself or wanders under a desk.

Straight ahead is the most important direction for a reliable obstacle sensor. Our team's solution has the lion's share of sonars—five in all—pointed in approximately the straight-ahead direction. Two forward sonars near the base of

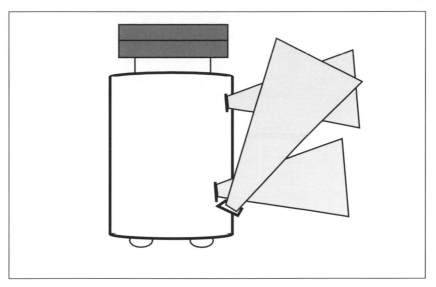

Figure 1. Side view of Dervish's sonar coverage.

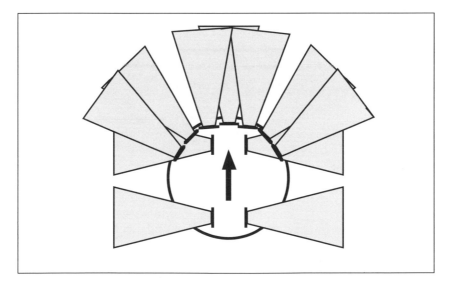

Figure 2. Top view of Dervish's sonar coverage. Note the redundancy in each basic direction. The redundant units form a "cluster."

the robot detect styrofoam cups, wads of paper, and pop cans. Three forward sonars at the middle of the robot provide a redundant view of taller objects.

One important trick the team incorporated was varying the angle of the sonars within each sonar cluster by up to five degrees. This variation makes the

*Figure 3: The complete Dervish robot, including its two
head-mounted powerbooks (one for navigation; one for commentary).*

sonar redundancy more effective by enabling one sonar to detect smooth surfaces that are invisible to another sonar due to the particular reflection angle.
This sonic problem is akin to the problem one faces in a house of mirrors, not
knowing which object is just a picture of a mirror farther away and which object
is the real mirror to be avoided. Sometimes, a slight change in the angle of the
eyes to the mirror allows one to see the mirror itself more clearly and avoid being fooled by the reflection.

There are four remaining sonar clusters in the robot's solution geometry. Two
sonar pairs point 45 degrees left and right of the direction of motion. These

clusters provide excellent information about the sizes of openings, obstacles and doorways. The third and fourth pair of sonars point left and right 90 degrees from the direction of motion. Each of these sonar pairs consists of two parallel, widely-spaced sonars. Side clusters can detect both the robot's distance from nearby walls and the robot's angle to these walls, using the difference in distances registered by the two sonars.

This new robot, however, has no backward-pointing sonars. Our team's basic philosophy was that humans clearly don't need eyes in the back of their heads to navigate office buildings; so, neither should a robot.

When all modifications were made, the sonars had been repositioned and reattached using wire and balsa wood (to absorb enery and protect the sonar transducers in case of impact), the whirling robot that rose out of the ashes of Vagabond was named Dervish.

Dervish is controlled by an on-board Macintosh Powerbook running Lisp. The Macintosh communicates with a 6811 processor by means of a serial link. This 6811, in turn, communicates with a second 6811 controlling the sonars as well as an off-the-shelf motor controller in charge of motion. A second Powerbook, also on-board, is dedicated to providing verbal commentary with regard to Dervish's actions and discoveries. The complete robot is shown in figure 3.

Our team has found that exclusively on-board computation has at least two key advantages: commands to the robot are never lost to due radio interference; and the robot's range of motion is unlimited.

Low-Level Control

Dervish's control architecture is a simple two-part system, consisting of a high-level planning module and a plan execution module, shown in figure 4. Dervish interleaves planning and execution at a very high rate, and so these modules communicate frequently. The planner invokes execution, and the execution module returns control to the planner with termination condition information.

I will describe the details of the modules and their interaction in a bottom-up fashion. The next subsection describes the obstacle avoidance strategy implemented, as well as its relationship to navigation-based goals. The localization section introduces state-set progression and feature recognition, crucial ingredients in the strategy Dervish uses for localization and navigation. Finally, the assumptive planning section describes empirical results of robot navigation tests as well as theoretical results pertaining to search space and computational cost.

Obstacle Avoidance

Obstacle avoidance must moderate navigation, resulting in a system that reacts

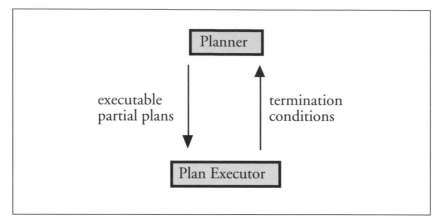

*Figure 4. Our control architecture is a simple two-level one in which the
planner provides executable plans in real-time and the plan executor
executes some portion of the plan and returns a termination condition.*

to unexpected obstacles, yet achieves goal positions whenever there is a path to
the goal. Therefore, a reliable obstacle avoidance system is an important ingredi-
ent of the plan execution module.

In our team's efforts to design an obstacle avoidance system for Dervish, one
serious challenge involved the limited range of the sonars, which return depth
readings no closer than 17 inches (the team was unfamiliar with the process of
changing the sonar's blanking interval to decrease this lower limit). A rational
conclusion was that Dervish must stay at least 17 inches away from all objects to
be safe. If the robot were closer than that to a wall, the sonar unit would not
necessarily be listening for an echo in time to hear it. Even if the sonar did pick
up the wall, it would at best return 17.

After experimenting with two general approaches to obstacle avoidance using
Dervish's forward and 45-degree sonar clusters, the team eventually settled on
the second approach.

The initial approach was an instance of a common method used by roboticists
for reactive obstacle avoidance: the weighted sum. The basic idea behind the
weighted sum is that the robot multiplies each sonar's return value by a weight
based on the significance of that sonar's position to obstacle avoidance. The
weights for sonars on the left side and right side of the robot are given opposite
signs. When the sum is computed, its sign determines the direction in which the
robot should turn. The magnitude of the sum determines how hard the robot
should turn and how slowly the robot should move forward while turning.

The primary advantage of the weighted sum approach is the continuous behavior of the sum as objects move gradually closer to the robot. As sonar values
change slightly, so too does the resultant sum and, therefore, the behavior of the

```
(setf forward-velocity
      (if (or (< up-sonars 40) (< front-sonars 20)
              (< side-sonars 17))
          0
          (if (or (< front-sonars 40) (< side-sonars 22))
              20
              80)))
```

Figure 5. A simple case-based program for collision avoidance on a one-motor robot.

robot appears to be smooth and intelligent. This method makes particularly good sense with a radial sonar ring, since the forward-facing sonar can be weighted highest and the sonars that are farther away from straight ahead can be weighted correspondingly lower.

The weighted sum has two serious disadvantages that prompted an alternative. First, it is extremely difficult to rationalize the proper weights for Dervish because our three-dimensional sonar geometry is so complex. Something more discrete makes sense in Dervish's case. For instance, Dervish should ignore the upward-pointing sonar cluster whenever the range values are greater than Dervish's height. But as soon as this cluster registers 25 inches or less, obstacle avoidance becomes an immediate issue.

The second disadvantage of weighted sums is that humans have a difficult time adjusting (or fine tuning) a weighted sum effectively. The operation tends to become one of trial and error, with no real intuition about how to modify the obstacle avoidance behavior of the robot *slightly* by making minor changes to the weighted sum. Changes to the weights, however small, can potentially affect the robot's behavior in general. This is undesirable if the robot performs well in all but one or two specific cases. This unpredictability, combined with nonintuitive sonar geometry, makes the weighted sum approach unusable on Dervish.

The approach Dervish uses is based on the intuition that one can tune a robot's obstacle avoidance behavior case by case. A case-based system divides up the robot's possible responses based on sets of sonar values. This results in different responses for separate *categories* of sonar values. For example, one categorical division is between all cases in which the upward-pointing sonars are short and all cases in which they are long. By creating tens of categories, the robot's response becomes extremely discrete and easy to analyze.

Figure 5 demonstrates a simple case-based "program" to move a robot straight ahead only when the path is clear. The example is extremely simple; however, the same approach is used to identify and deal with every complex environmental case that Dervish may encounter.

The major advantage of this approach is that undesirable robot behavior is much easier to correct. Simply trace out the bad behavior to the category corresponding to the corresponding sonar inputs. The human can then modify the control algorithm for this one case with the confidence that the robot's behavior in all other cases will be unaffected.

The case-based obstacle avoidance strategy proved extremely reliable. During the entire 1994 Robot Contest, Dervish never collided with an obstacle. Combining this competence with goal-directed behavior was quite simple, involving a further case-based analysis in which the obstacle avoidance system commands the robot's motion only when it detects an obstacle. Otherwise, the robot velocity is based on the position of the robot, laterally and longitudinally, in the hallway.

The only complication to this architecture involved explicit navigation around unexpected obstacles using left and right wall-following modules. The plan executor was thus a simple state machine, switching between several navigation modes as well as several obstacle exploration modes that are used to determine if an obstacle is impassable.

Localization

The choice of a localization strategy depends heavily on the type of representation used in the national robot contest. I describe the three key components of the navigation system in this section: the representation of state, the feature recognition system, and state set progression.

Representation

According to the contest rules, the robot would be given a topological map of the environment; that is, purely nonmetric information about the connectivity of rooms and hallways. Figure 6 geometrically depicts a segment of an office environment (left) and the corresponding topological map (right).

The robot would start in a known initial room and was required to travel to a goal room specified at the beginning of the run. The challenge was to reach the goal room reliably in spite of obstacles that render the supplied topological map inaccurate.

The real-world is so fine-grained that any attempt to plan using a highly detailed model of reality to solve this problem is doomed because of the enormous computational complexity. Furthermore, the topological map supplied to Dervish would be extremely abstract, communicating only very high-level connectivity without specifying geometric distances between those features at all.

For both of these reasons, Dervish was designed to reason about an abstraction of the real world based on a discretization of the world into states, with each state corresponding to a node on the topological map or a hallway segment between two nodes. Figure 7 depicts the discretization of a hallway fragment.

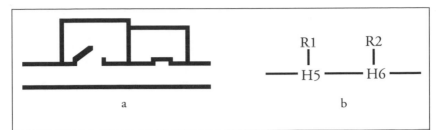

Figure 6. A geometric map (left) consistent with a topological map (right) of an office environment.

The area encompassing a topological node is labeled with a number, whereas the area between two topological nodes is labeled with a dashed number. Note that each abstract state in fact captures a whole set of possible robot positions, expressing the concept that the actual position of the robot is not important, as long as it is within the bounds of a particular state.

For Dervish, localization therefore does not mean geometric x, y coordinate computation. Instead, localization involves identifying the topological node that Dervish occupies. Each such topological node is part of a *state descriptor*.

Of course, Dervish may have uncertainty regarding its position; and there is no guarantee that the uncertainty will be limited to a single state. The *state set* is introduced, representing Dervish's positional uncertainty because it captures all of the actual positions at which the robot believes it could be located. (No uncertainty as to Dervish's orientation once it has left the initial room is assumed.) Associated with each state is a certainty factor which represents the relative likelihood of the robot being in the corresponding state.

Note that the robot's notion of state consists only of information about its own location. For instance, the state does not contain information about whether particular doors are open or closed. Including more information would help reduce positional uncertainty over time but would also greatly increase the size of the set of possible states. Experimentally, Dervish has been found to perform well without this additional information.

Feature Recognition

The next step was to design a feature recognition system for Dervish that matched the level of abstraction at which Dervish's map and, therefore, its own planning process would operate. The solution was a feature recognition system that detected precisely the items that defined points of connectivity in the topological map: doorways and hallways.

Our team's strategy for feature detection is a two-tiered one that filters away

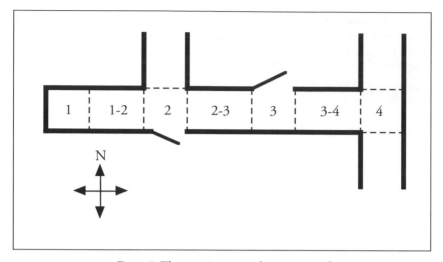

Figure 7. The quantization, or discretization, of geometric space based on topological connectivity.

most false sonar data. The first step is to ignore the feature recognizer altogether when the robot's angle to the hallway centerline is greater than some preset threshold. As the robot becomes less aligned with the hallway, the angle between the side sonars and the walls becomes more acute and the sound waves begin to bounce off coherently instead of returning an echo back to the robot. Of course the angle at which this sonar problem occurs depends on the smoothness of the walls (the smoother the wall, the earlier this specular reflection occurs).

When our team arrived at the AAAI convention in Seattle, we saw to our horror that the simulated walls were made of smooth sheet plastic. This drastically reduces the amount of misalignment necessary to produce specular reflection, from about 35 degrees at Stanford to 9 degrees. The smooth Seattle walls confused many of the sonar-based robots, causing them to veer into the walls and also to pick up large numbers of false features. Consider the fate of a sonar ring in such an environment. Only one or two sonars in a ring would be within 9 degrees of the wall. Consequently, all the other sonars would essentially see through the wall. Fortunately, Dervish's behavior was successfully adjusted simply by lowering the threshold value for this alignment filter.

The second step for feature detection is to compare the measured hallway width to the expected hallway width. If the alignment filter says that the sonar values are reliable and the measured hallway width is much larger than the expected hallway width (by more than 60 inches), then the robot is passing some type of opening— either a doorway or a hallway. If the difference between measured and expected hallway widths is three to seven inches, then the robot may be passing a closed door. Surprisingly, this three- to seven-inch range has been effective in three separate office buildings at Stanford and at the AAAI contest.

Of course, a single positive reading does not convince Dervish that it has found a feature. In the case of closed doors, Dervish must see the three- to seven-inch indentation for at least one second continuously. In the case of doorway and hallway openings, Dervish looks for a continuous opening that then terminates when Dervish passes the far end of the opening. Using the distance it has traveled while seeing the opening, Dervish computes the width of the opening. Based on this opening width, the feature detector can choose to categorize the feature as an open hallway or an open door.

State Set Progression

Was Dervish's feature detection system totally reliable? Actually, it wasn't. In fact, the closed door detector was less than 70% reliable, because of false positives and false negatives. The false positives and negatives have a great deal to do with the inherent unreliability of sonar sensors in smooth-walled worlds and with the limitations of this feature detection method in hallways filled with obstacles. But the point of our team's research was to develop a robot that is reliable as a whole despite unreliable sensors. Consequently, *state set progression* was introduced as a high-level reasoning system that solves the problem of low-level inaccuracy.

As the robot moves down a hall, whenever it discerns a percept-pair (a feature on one or both sides of the robot), it updates the state set by progressing each state based upon the percept-pair and the current direction of travel. Progression of a state involves removing it from the state set and replacing it with all possible subsequent states.

For example, consider a robot with perfect sensors facing east with the initial state set {1-2, 2-3} (see figure 7). If this robot were to detect a hallway on its left and a door on its right, the percept-pair would uniquely determine its position; i.e., its state set would become the singleton set, {2}. Possible state 1-2 would progress to {2} while 2-3 would progress to the empty set (i.e., the percept-pair is impossible if the world state were 2-3).

Of course, Dervish does not have perfect sensors; so state set progression is augmented with certainty factors that are computed using a certainty matrix and the probability of doors being closed. For each of the five world features that the robot can encounter (wall, closed door, open door, open hallway, foyer), the certainty matrix assigns a likelihood that each of the three possible percepts (or nothing) will be detected.

For example, using the certainty matrix below, if Dervish is next to an open hallway, the likelihood of mistakenly recognizing it as an open door is 0.10. For each new environment, a certainty matrix is empirically generated and the closed door probability is determined. Not surprisingly, the success of state set

	Wall	Closed Door	Open Door	Open Hallway	Foyer
Nothing detected	0.70	0.40	0.05	0.001	0.30
Closed door detected	0.30	0.60	0	0	0.05
Open door detected	0	0	0.90	0.10	0.15
Open hallway detected	0	0	0.001	0.90	0.50

Table 1. The certainty matrix for Margaret Jacks Hall, the former Computer Science Department at Stanford University.

progression is not dependent on precise values in the certainty matrix.

Table 1 contains the certainty matrix for Margaret Jacks Hall, the former Computer Science Department building at Stanford, where the probability of any particular door being closed is 0.6. Entries in the matrix can be zero, allowing the state set to collapse when certain percepts are discerned; however, this limits robustness since, in the real world, anything may be possible.

Now I can reexamine the earlier example with a more realistic robot using this certainty matrix. Once again, assume that the original state set is {1-2, 2-3}. But now, the states have certainty factors of 1.0 and 0.2, respectively. (Only the relative magnitudes of certainty factors are important). How will the state-set progress if the robot simultaneously detects an open hallway on its left and an open door on its right?

State 2-3 will progress potentially to states 3, 3-4, and 4. But states 3 and 3-4 can be eliminated since the likelihood is zero of detecting an open door when the actual feature is a wall. The likelihood of being in state 4 is the product of the initial certainty factor for state 2-3, 0.2, the likelihood of not detecting anything at node 3, (a), and the likelihood of detecting a hallway on the left and a door on the right at node 4, (b).

(a) occurs only if Dervish fails to detect the door on its left at node 3 (either closed or open), [(0.6)(.4) + (1-0.6)(.05)], and correctly detects nothing on its right, .70.

(b) occurs if Dervish correctly identifies the open hallway on its left at node 4, .90, and mistakes the right hallway for an open door, .10.

The final formula, (0.2)[(0.6)(0.4)+(0.4)(0.05)](0.7)[(0.9)(0.1)], yields a certainty factor of 0.003276 for state 4.

State 1-2 will potentially progress to states 2, 2-3, 3, 3-4, and 4. Again, states 2-3, 3 and 3-4 can all be eliminated since the likelihood is zero of detecting an open door when a wall is present. The likelihood for state 2 is the product of the initial certainty, (1.0), the likelihood of detecting the door on its right as an open door, [(0.6)(0) + (0.4)(0.9)], and the likelihood of correctly detecting an open hallway on its left, 0.9. The certainty factor for being at state 2 is then $(1.0)(0.4)(0.9)(0.9) = 0.324$. In addition, 1-2 will progress to state 4 with a certainty factor of 4.259×10^{-6}, which is added to the certainty factor in the preceding paragraph to bring the total for state 4 to 0.00328. Dervish would therefore compute the state set {2, 4}, believing strongly that it is in state 2 while retaining the remote possibility that it is in state 4.

Assumptive Planning: An Interleaving Architecture

Given the state set representation, a traditional approach to planning would be to conduct an exhaustive search in the state set transition diagram. The result would be a full conditional plan that would prescribe action sequences for every possible series of perceptual inputs. Unfortunately, the cost of complete conditional planning is prohibitive for real-world robot navigation.

Some roboticists bypass this problem by foregoing planning altogether, using reactive or functional architectures (Slack 1993; Brooks 1986). Still others plan rarely and then execute the plan steps using reactive components (Nilsson 1992; Gat 1992). Our team's solution addresses uncertainty by allowing for large numbers of planning instances, effectively interleaving planning and execution (Hsu 1990; Dean et al. 1990; Ambros-Ingerson and Steel 1988; Olawsky et al. 1993; Genesereth and Nourbakhsh 1993). I present the assumptive approach in the next subsection, then compare its computational cost to that of full conditional planning in the subsection on the cost of making assumptions.

Assumptive Planning

In the *assumptive* planning strategy, Dervish plans by assuming that its current state is the most likely state in the state set and finding a sequential solution to the goal. Then, Dervish executes the plan while progressing its state set using features detected at run-time until the current most likely state is either at the goal or is inconsistent with the intended path.

Because the robot knows its initial and final locations and has a map of the world, it constructs only one path to the goal and begins to traverse that path. Whenever Dervish detects a percept, it employs state set progression to determine its most likely position. As long as the most likely state corresponds to a node along the planned path, it continues execution without interruption, even if it has missed some earlier expected percepts. Dervish stops and replans when it is no longer on the intended path, either because it has overshot the turn or has localized to an entirely different hallway.

Dervish is extremely robust, in part because state set progression prevents the robot from becoming lost because of false percepts. A false or missing percept

	Conditional	Assumptive	Savings?
double whammy	$|P|^k|A|^k$	$|P|^{l2^j}|A|^{l2^j}$	$l2^j < k$
ceiling distance	$|P|^k|A|^k$	$|P|^{cl}|A|^{cl}$	$cl < k$
kind world	$|P|^k|A|^k$	$\dfrac{k}{l}|P|^l|A|^l$	$l < k$

Table 2: A comparison of the planning cost of advance planning versus assumptive planning for three domain classes. P is the set of robot percept-pairs; A is the set of robot actions (4 in the case of Dervish); k is the length of the resultant plan.

may cause Dervish to temporarily assume the wrong state, but the correct state is retained in the state set and becomes the most likely state after one or more correctly detected percepts.

In practice, Dervish can be off by one or two nodes while moving down the hallway because of sensory unreliability. Then why does this method work so well? The robot's positional uncertainty is almost always limited to one hallway. Therefore, the current action, which is to move forward, usually moves the robot toward the goal. This action normally terminates in one of two situations: when the robot reaches an intersection or when the robot believes it is just outside of the goal room. The first situation rarely results in an incorrect subsequent plan because the reliability of the open hallway detector tends to condense the state set at intersections. In the other situation, the robot examines the state set to see if the second most probable state is also highly likely. If so, the robot proceeds to the end of the hallway in order to collapse its state set and then return to the goal door.

The Cost of Making Assumptions

This discussion would not be complete without a comparison of the computational cost of full state-set conditional planning and the assumptive architecture (table 2).

For the analysis of planning complexity I introduce two variables: l represents the search depth for the first assumptive planning episode; and j refers to the total number of incorrect assumptive planning episodes. Note that j is identical to the *counterexample* measure defined by Rivest and Shapire (1993).

I have looked at the relative costs of conditional and assumptive planners in three classes of problem domains.

Double whammy represents a problem domain that is so unforgiving that every step executed under an incorrect assumption puts the robot two more steps away from the goal. Furthermore, double whammy assumes that assumption errors are not detected until the very last step of the conditional plan being executed. Under these extreme conditions, the assumptive approach is at a clear disadvantage because of the exponential backtracking cost.

Ceiling distance captures what may appear to lie at the other extreme: domains in which the robot cannot get further than a certain ceiling, c, from the goal. In this case, l turns out to dominate the total assumptive planning cost. A further intuition behind this domain lies in the possibility that actions taken under incorrect assumptions can still be benign and even useful.

In real-world domains, our team's research has discovered that both of these analyses can overestimate the assumptive planning cost. One reason is that the probability distribution over the states in I is usually not uniform. Therefore, the assumption tends to be correct. In addition, execution under an invalid assumption often results in progress toward the goal. In the *kind world* case, the assumption is that every l actions executed by the robot place it l steps closer to the goal.

There are, of course, disadvantages to assumptive planning. First, if the world is dangerous (for example, if it contains staircases), the assumptive approach can be deadly. In fact, assumptive planning is dangerous any time the robot can take an irreversible action before realizing that its assumption is wrong: one partial solution is to modify the planner to avoid irreversibilities.

Another serious disadvantage is that an assumptive system usually cannot guarantee an upper bound on the execution path length. Of course, in a real world with imperfect sensors and effectors, full conditional planning is usually unable to make any reachability guarantees either. In practice, assumptive planning produces near-optimal execution lengths if the initial assumption is correct and replanning is rare (i.e., if the sensors operate reasonably well). Soundness and completenes results for the assumptive system have been proven under well-defined conditions. For details, see Nourbakhsh and Genesereth (1996).

Results

Table 3 compares Dervish's assumptive performance in the actual AAAI contest finals maze with the theoretical performance of a conditional state set planner. The first column lists the size of the search space, in terms of the number of possible states. Note that the conditional advance-planning approach is prohibitively costly in this domain where the robot has no geometric information because the search can be extremely deep. Furthermore, the assumptive system attenuates the perceptual branching factor of the search space by assuming more complete knowledge than is actually available.

In its final contest run, Dervish actually encountered one closed door to the

	|S|	perceptual branching factor	action branching factor	plan length	number of planning episodes
conditional	2,592	15	3	>84	1
assumptive		1	3	10-28	6

Table 3: A comparison of the conditional and assumptive search spaces for the final contest at the AAAI 1994 National Robot Competition.

goal room, a blocked hallway and three false positive percepts, nevertheless executing correctly for approximately 15 minutes to reach the goal room through another entrance.

Even though Dervish replanned frequently, its planning time was insignificant compared to its execution time. Yet Dervish's behavior in the final run was (coincidentally) identical to the optimal behavior one would expect from a complete conditional plan produced off-line. The "office building" of the robot contest, like most real-world domains, is a *kind world*: incorrect assumptions are generally discovered at execution time before invalid assumptions leads to suboptimal execution behavior.

Dervish has also been tested in three unmodified office buildings on Stanford University's campus: the history building, the psychology building, and the former computer science building. Abbreviated topological maps of example floors from these three buildings are given in figure 8.

In all three environments, Dervish was again able to navigate reliably using the same code. Modifications made between buildings consisted only of changing Dervish's assumptions concerning the approximate hallway width and the likelihood that doors would be closed (as appropriate for the department). The psychology basement posed an especially difficult challenge in that there is a very long hallway with a large number of doorways. Dervish needed to localize almost exclusively using doorways that were almost always closed.

The fact that Dervish can navigate in such varied circumstances with no geometric knowledge (i.e., no knowledge about the distance between features) is an important result. Equally important is the fact that Dervish does not collide with obstacles or people in any of these environments. This demonstrates the power of intelligent sensor placement, even when using somewhat antique sensor technology.

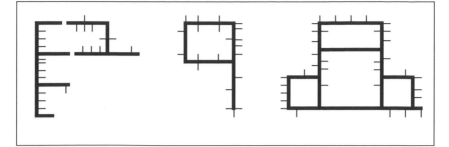

Figure 8. Topological maps corresponding to the psychology department basement (left), the history department 3rd floor (center), and MJH 2nd floor (right). The thick lines denote hallway connections; the thin line segments denote hallway-office connections. Note that Dervish navigates all of these environments reliably with no information regarding the distances between topological intersections!

Conclusion

Dervish's implementation of state set progression is essentially heuristic, although entirely adequate for reliable navigation. Recent work has offered improvements, formalizing the problem in terms of discrete Bayesian models and applying solution techniques from the domain of partially observable Markov decision processes (Simmons and Koenig 1995; Gutierrez-Osuna and Luo 1996; Cassandra et al. 1996).

These more recent methods have offered formally thorough treatments of probabilistic state set progression, which is often called belief-state update. However, surprisingly, in most cases the resultant mobile robot systems have been given geometrically accurate maps.

Although state set progression is an excellent tool for high-level AI planning, it is not an enabling mechanism for robot navigation per se. Indeed, in real-world mobile robot tasks *with* geometric information, discrete state sets are demonstrably unnecessary so long as the robot uses localization techniques that have less error than the motor encoders.

State set progression on Dervish was implemented because of contest rules that allowed Dervish only a topological map, not because of physical limitations of our mobile robot navigation systems.

In that light, I believe the most important lesson learned from the Dervish project is the value of interleaving planning and execution. Interleaving has been an area of fruitful research in the planning and robotics communities, with several recent works concentrating on assumptive systems that replan when assumptions are violated, such as Olawsky et al. (1993); Erdmann (1990); Stentz

(1995); Ambros-Ingerson and Steel (1988); Dean et al. (1990); Donald (1989); Genesereth and Nourbakhsh (1993). See Rivest and Shapire (1993); Shen (1993); and McCallum (1995) for discussions of assumptive systems as they relate to the domain of discovering finite automata.

Interleaving systems, and especially assumptive systems, have been demonstrated to attenuate the cost of explicit goal planning sufficiently as to make it practical, resulting in more goal-directed robots that respond deliberately to changing world conditions. This is the point at which AI will impact mobile robotics most strongly, as it affects the full range of higher-level planning issues faced by productive, real-world robots.

CHAPTER FOUR

Xavier: A Robot Navigation Architecture Based on Partially Observable Markov Decision Process Models

Sven Koenig and Reid G. Simmons

We are interested in autonomous mobile robots that perform delivery tasks in office environments. It is crucial that such robots be able to navigate corridors robustly in order to reach their destinations reliably. While the state of the art in autonomous office navigation is fairly advanced, it is not generally good enough to permit robots to traverse corridors for long periods of time without eventually getting lost.

Our approach to this problem involves using partially observable Markov decision process models (POMDPs). POMDPs explicitly account for various forms of uncertainty: uncertainty in actuation, sensing, and sensor data interpretation; uncertainty in the initial *pose* (position and orientation) of the robot; and uncertainty about the environment, such as corridor distances and blockages (including closed doors). Instead of maintaining a single estimate of its current pose, the robot uses a POMDP to maintain a probability distribution over its current pose at all times. Thus, while it rarely knows exactly where it is, the robot always has some belief as to what its true pose is, and thus is never completely lost. To update the belief in its current pose, the robot can use all available sensor information, including landmarks sensed and distance traveled.

We use the POMDP-based navigation architecture on a daily basis on our robot, Xavier. Our experiments show that the architecture leads to robust long-term autonomous navigation in office environments (with corridors, foyers, and rooms) for an actual indoor mobile robot, significantly outperforming the landmark-based navigation technique that we used previously (Simmons 1994a).

The POMDP-based navigation architecture uses a compiler that automatically produces POMDPs from topological maps, actuator and sensor models, and uncertain knowledge of the environment. The resulting POMDPs seamlessly integrate topological and metric information and enable the robots to use as much, or as little, metric information as they have available. Pose estimation easily deals with metric map uncertainty and deteriorates gracefully with the quality of the models. Finally, learning algorithms can be used to improve the models while the robots are carrying out their delivery tasks.

We show how to use POMDPs to build a complete architecture for mobile robot navigation that provides a uniform framework with an established theoretical foundation for pose estimation, path planning (including planning when, where, and what to sense), control during navigation, and learning. In addition, both the POMDP and the generated information (such as the pose information and the plans) can be used by higher-level planning modules, such as task planners.

The POMDP-based navigation architecture is one layer of our office delivery system (figure 1) (Simmons, Goodwin, Haigh, Koenig, and O'Sullivan 1997). Besides the navigation layer described here, the layers of the system include a servo-control layer that controls the motors of the robot, an obstacle avoidance layer that keeps the robot moving smoothly in a goal direction while avoiding static and dynamic obstacles (Simmons 1996), a path planning layer that reasons about uncertainty to choose paths that have high expected utility (Koenig, Goodwin and Simmons 1996), and a multiple-task planning layer that uses PRODIGY, a symbolic, nonlinear planner, to integrate and schedule delivery requests that arrive asynchronously (Haigh and Veloso 1996). The layers, which are implemented as a number of distributed, concurrent processes operating on several processors, are integrated using the Task Control Architecture. This architecture provides facilities for interprocess communication, task decomposition and sequencing, execution monitoring and exception handling, and resource management (Simmons 1994b). Finally, interaction with the robot is by means of the World Wide Web, which provides pages for both commanding the robot and monitoring its progress.

In the following section, we contrast our POMDP-based navigation architecture with more traditional approaches to robot navigation. We then discuss POMDPs and algorithms for pose estimation, planning, and learning in the abstract. In the POMDP-based navigation architecture section, we apply the models and algorithms to our navigation problem. Finally, we present experiments that we performed with both our robot simulator and the actual robot.

Traditional Approaches to Robot Navigation

Two common approaches to robot navigation are metric-based and landmark-based navigation:

Metric-based navigation relies on metric maps of the environment, resulting in navigation plans such as move forward ten meters, turn right ninety degrees, move forward another ten meters, and stop. Metric-based navigation methods are able to take advantage of information about the motion of the robot, which

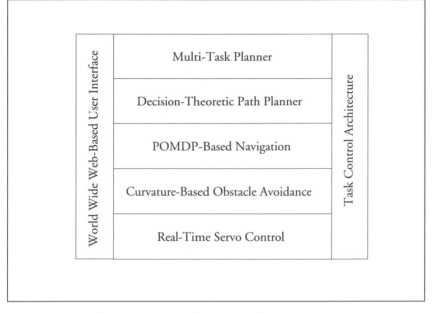

Figure 1. A layered architecture for office delivery robots.

we call *motion reports*, such as the translation and rotation derived from the wheel encoders. They are, however, vulnerable to inaccuracies in both the map making and dead-reckoning abilities of the robot. Such approaches are often used where the robot has good absolute position estimates, such as for outdoor robots using the global positioning system (GPS).

Landmark-based navigation, on the other hand, relies on topological maps whose nodes correspond to *landmarks* (locally distinctive places), such as corridor junctions or doors. Map edges indicate how the landmarks connect and how the robot should navigate between them. A typical landmark-based navigation plan might be to move forward to the second corridor on the right, turn into that corridor, move to its end, and stop. Landmark-based approaches are attractive because they are able to take advantage of information about the sensed features of the environment, which we term *sensor reports*, such as data from the sonar sensors that indicate whether the robot is in a corridor junction. Thus they do not depend on geometric accuracy. They suffer, however, from problems of unreliable sensors occasionally not detecting landmarks, and problems of *sensor aliasing* (sensors not being able to distinguish between similar landmarks, such as different doorways of the same size). This can lead to both inefficiencies and mistakes. For example, it takes the robot longer to notice that it overshot its destination when it does not use metric information, and it might even turn into the wrong one of two adjacent corridors.

To maximize reliability in navigation, it makes sense to use all information that is available to the robot (that is, both motion and sensor reports). While some landmark-based approaches use motion reports, mostly to resolve topological ambiguities, and some metric-based approaches use sensor reports to continuously realign the robot with the map (Kuipers and Byun 1988; Mataric 1990), the two sources of information are treated differently. We want an approach that seamlessly integrates both sources of information, and is amenable to adding new sources such as a priori information about which doorways are likely to be open or closed. We also do not want to assume that the distances are known precisely.

Another problem with the metric- and landmark-based approaches is that they typically represent only a single pose that is believed to be the current pose of the robot. If this pose proves to be incorrect, the robot is lost and has to relocalize itself, an expensive operation. This can be avoided by representing all possible poses of the robot. Since some poses will be more likely than others, this suggests explicitly maintaining a probability distribution over possible poses. Then, Bayes's rule can be used to update this pose distribution after each motion and sensor report. To achieve this task, we have to explicitly represent the various forms of uncertainty present in the navigation task:

- *Actuator uncertainty.* For example, motion commands are not always carried out perfectly because of wheel slippage and mechanical tolerances, resulting in *dead-reckoning error.*

- *Sensor uncertainty.* Unreliable sensors produce *false positives* (features that are not present) or *false negatives.* For example, sonar can bounce around several surfaces before returning to the robot and therefore does not necessarily give correct information on the distance to the closest surface.

- *Uncertainty in the interpretation of the sensor data.* For example, sonar sensor data often do not allow the robot to clearly distinguish between walls, closed doors, and lines of people blocking a corridor junction.

- *Map uncertainty.* For example, the lengths of corridors might not be known exactly.

- *Uncertainty about the initial pose of the robot.*

- *Uncertainty about the dynamic state of the environment.* For example, blockages can change over time as people open and close doors and block and unblock corridors.

Previously reported approaches that maintain pose distributions often use either Kalman filters (Kosaka and Kak 1992; Smith and Cheeseman 1986) or temporal Bayesian networks (Dean, Kaelbling, Kirman, and Nicholson 1993). Both approaches can use motion and sensor reports to update the pose distribution.

Kalman filters model only restricted pose distributions in continuous pose space. In the simplest case, these are Gaussians. While Gaussians are efficient to encode and update, they are not ideally suited for office navigation. In particular, because of sensor aliasing, one often wants to encode the belief that the robot might be in one of a number of noncontiguous (but similar looking) locations, such as at either of two adjacent doorways. In this case, because Gaussians are unimodal, the Kalman filter would estimate that the most likely location is right in between the two doorways—precisely the wrong result. Although Kalman filters can be used to represent more complex pose distributions than Gaussians (at the cost of an increased complexity), they cannot be used to model arbitrary pose distributions.

Temporal Bayesian networks unwind time. With such methods, the size of the models grows linearly with the amount of temporal lookahead, which limits their use for planning to rather small lookaheads. They usually tessellate the possible poses into discrete states, which allows them to represent arbitrary pose distributions.

To summarize, temporal Bayesian networks are typically able to represent arbitrary pose distributions, but discretize the pose space. Kalman filters, on the other hand, do not discretize the pose space, but cannot represent arbitrary pose distributions. Consequently, there is a tradeoff between the precision and expressiveness of the models. We contend that, for office navigation, the added expressiveness of being able to model arbitrary pose distributions outweighs the decrease in precision from discretization, especially since a coarse-grained representation of uncertainty is often sufficient. When a more fine-grained representation is required, one can use low-level control routines to overcome the discretization problem. For example, we use such control routines to keep the robot centered in corridors and aligned along the main corridor axis. Similarly, we use vision and a neural network to align the robot exactly with doorways when it has reached its destination.

POMDPs compare to the traditional robot navigation approaches as follows: They seamlessly integrate topological information and approximate metric information and therefore use both motion and sensor reports to determine the pose distribution. They are similar to many Bayesian networks in that they discretize the possible poses, and thus allow one to represent arbitrary pose distributions, but do not suffer from the limited horizon problem for planning, because their lookahead is unlimited.

There have been several other approaches that use Markov models for robot navigation: Dean, Basye, Chekaluk, Hyun, Lejter, and Randazza (1994) use Markov models, but, different from our approach, assume that the location of the robot is always known precisely. Nourbakhsh, Powers, and Birchfield (1995) use Markov models that do not assume that the location of the robot is known with certainty, but do not use any metric information (the states of the robot are either at a topological node or somewhere in a connecting corridor). Cassandra, Kaelbing, and Kurien (1996) build on our work, and consequently use Markov models similar to ours, including modeling distance information, but assume that the distances are known with certainty. Similarly, Burgard, Fox, Hennig, and Schmidt (1996a) use a fine-grained discretization of both location and orientation to track the robot's position with great precision.

An Introduction to POMDPs

This section provides a general high-level overview of POMDPs and common algorithms that operate on such models. These models and algorithms form the basis of our POMDP-based navigation architecture, which is described in the POMDP-based navigation architecture section.

POMDPs consist of a finite set of states S; a finite set of observations O; and an initial state distribution π (a probability distribution over S), where $\pi(s)$ denotes the probability that the initial state of the POMDP process is s. Each state $s \in S$ has a finite set of actions $A(s)$ that can be executed in s. The POMDP further consists of a transition function p (a function from $S \times A$ to probability distributions over S), where $p(s'|s, a)$ denotes the probability ("transition probability") that the system transitions from state s to state s' when action a is executed; an observation function q (a function from S to probability distributions over O), where $q(o|s)$ denotes the probability ("observation probability") of making observation o in state s; and an immediate reward function r (a function from $S \times A$ to the real numbers), where $r(s, a)$ denotes the finite immediate reward resulting from the execution of action a in state s.

A POMDP *process* is a stream of (state, observation, action, immediate reward) quadruples: The process is always in exactly one state and makes state transitions at discrete time steps. Assume that at time t, the POMDP process is in state $s_t \in S$. Initially, $p(s_1 = s) = \pi(s)$. Then, an observation $o_t \in O$ is generated according to the probabilities $p(o_t = o) = q(o|s_t)$. Next, a decision maker chooses an action a_t from $A(s_t)$ for execution. This results in the decision maker receiving immediate reward $r_t = r(s_t, a_t)$ and the process changing state. The successor state $s_{t+1} \in S$ is selected according to the probabilities $p(s_{t+1} = s) = p(s|s_t, a_t)$. This process repeats forever. Note that the probabilities with which the observation (and successor state) are generated depend only on s_t (and a_t) but not, for example, on how the current state s_t was reached. This is called the *Markov property*.

An *observer* of the POMDP process is someone who knows the specification of the POMDP (as stated above) and observes the actions $a_1 \ldots a_{T-1}$ and observations $o_1 \ldots o_T$, but not the current states $s_1 \ldots s_T$ or immediate rewards $r_1 \ldots r_{T-1}$. A *decision maker* is an observer who also determines which actions to execute. Consequently, observers and decision makers usually cannot be sure exactly which state the POMDP process is in. This is the main difference between a POMDP and a completely observable Markov decision process model, where observers and decision makers always know exactly which state the process is in, although they will usually not be able to predict in advance the state that results from an action execution, since actions can have nondeterministic effects.

Properties of POMDPs have been studied extensively in operations research. In artificial intelligence and robotics, POMDPs have been applied to speech and handwriting recognition (Huang, Ariki and Jack 1990) and the interpretation of tele-operation commands (Hannaford and Lee 1991; Yang, Xu, and Chen 1994). They have also gained popularity in the artificial intelligence community as a formal model for planning under uncertainty (Cassandra, Kaelbling, and Littman 1994; Koenig 1991). Consequently, standard algorithms are available to solve tasks that are typically encountered by observers and decision makers. In the following subsections, we describe some of these algorithms.

State Estimation: Determining the Current State

Assume that an observer wants to determine the current state of a POMDP process. This corresponds to estimating where the robot currently is. Observers do not have access to this information but can maintain a belief in the form of a *state distribution* (a probability distribution α over S) since they know which actions have been executed and which observations resulted. We write $\alpha(s)$ to denote the probability that the current state is s. Under the Markov property, α summarizes everything known about the current state. This probability distribution can be computed incrementally using Bayes's rule. To begin, the probability of the initial state of the POMDP process is $\alpha(s) = \pi(s)$. Subsequently, if the current state distribution is α_{prior}, the state distribution after the execution of action a is α_{post}:

$$\alpha_{post}(s) = \frac{1}{scale} \sum_{s' \in S | a \in A(s')} p(s \mid s', a) \alpha_{prior}(s'), \tag{1}$$

where *scale* is a normalization constant that ensures that $\sum_{s \in S} \alpha_{post}(s) = 1$. This normalization is necessary only if not every action is defined in every state.

Updating the state distribution after an observation is even simpler. If the current state distribution is α_{prior}, then the state distribution after observing o is α_{post}:

$$\alpha_{post}(s) = \frac{1}{scale} q(o \mid s) \alpha_{prior}(s), \tag{2}$$

where *scale*, again, is a normalization constant that ensures that $\sum_{s \in S} \alpha_{post}(s) = 1$.

POMDP Planning: Determining which Actions to Execute

Assume that a decision maker wants to select actions so as to maximize the expected total reward received over an infinite planning horizon, which is defined as $E(\sum_{t=1}^{\infty} \gamma^{t-1} r_t)$, where $\gamma \in (0, 1]$ is the discount factor. This corresponds to navigating the robot to its destination in a way that minimizes its expected travel time. The *discount factor* specifies the relative value of an immediate reward received after t action executions compared to the same reward received one action execution earlier. If $\gamma = 1$, the total reward is called undiscounted. To simplify mathematics, we assume here that $\gamma < 1$, because this ensures that the expected total reward is finite, no matter which actions are chosen.

Consider a completely observable Markov decision process model. A fundamental result of operations research is that, in this case, there always exists a *policy* (a mapping from states to actions) so that the decision maker maximizes the expected total reward by always executing the action that the policy assigns to the current state of the process. Such an *optimal policy* can be determined by solving the following system of $|S|$ equations for the variables $v(s)$, that is known as Bellman's equation (Bellman 1957):

$$v(s) = \max_{a \in A(s)}\left[r(s,a) + \gamma \sum_{s' \in S} p(s' \mid s,a) v(s') \right] \qquad \text{for all } s \in S. \qquad (3)$$

$v(s)$ is the expected total reward if the process starts in state s and the decision maker acts optimally. The optimal action to execute in state s is $a(s) = \text{argmax}_{a \in A(s)} [r(s, a) + \gamma \sum_{s' \in S} p(s'|s, a) v(s')]$. The system of equations can be solved in polynomial time using dynamic programming methods such as linear programming (Littman, Dean, and Kaelbling 1995). Another popular dynamic programming method is value iteration (Bellman 1957) (we leave the termination criterion unspecified):

1. Set $v_1(s) := 0$ for all $s \in S$. Set $t := 1$.
2. Set $v_{t+1}(s) := \max_{a \in A(s)} [r(s, a) + \gamma \sum_{s' \in S} p(s'|s, a) v_t(s')]$ for all $s \in S$. Set $t := t + 1$.
3. Go to 2.

Then, for all $s \in S$, $v(s) = \lim_{t \to \infty} v_t(s)$.

The POMDP planning problem can be transformed into a planning problem for a completely observable Markov decision process model. First, since the decision maker can never be sure which state the POMDP process is in, the set of executable actions A must be the same for every state s, that is, $A(s) = A$ for all $s \in S$. The completely observable Markov decision process model can then be constructed as follows: The states of the model are the state distributions α ("belief states"), with the initial state being α_o with probability $\sum_{s \in S} q(o|s)\pi(s)$ for all $o \in O$, where $\alpha_o(s) = q(o|s)\pi(s)/\sum_{s \in S} q(o|s)\pi(s)$ for all $s \in S$. Its actions are the same as the actions of the POMDP. The execution of action a in belief state α results in an immediate reward of $\sum_{s \in S} \alpha(s) r(s, a)$ and the Markov process changing state. There are at most $|O|$ possible successor states, one for each $o \in O$. The successor state α'_o is characterized by:

$$\alpha'_o(s) = \frac{q(o \mid s)\sum_{s' \in S} p(s \mid s',a)\alpha(s')}{\sum_{s \in S} q(o \mid s)\sum_{s' \in S} p(s \mid s',a)\alpha(s')} \qquad \text{for all } s \in S.$$

The transition probabilities are:

$$p(\alpha'_o \mid \alpha,a) = \sum_{s \in S} q(o \mid s) \sum_{s' \in S} p(s \mid s',a)\alpha(s') \; .$$

Any mapping from states to actions that is optimal for this completely observable Markov decision process model is also optimal for the POMDP and characterizes a POMDP policy (a mapping from state distributions to actions). Unfortunately, the number of belief states α is infinite. Thus, the completely observable Markov decision process model is infinite. This has two consequences. First, one has to make (reasonable) assumptions to ensure that there exists a POMDP policy that maximizes the expected total reward (Sondik 1978). This POMDP policy can be precomputed. During action selection, the decision maker only needs to calculate the current state distribution α and can then look up which action to execute. Second, an optimal POMDP policy cannot be found efficiently. In fact, the POMDP planning problem is PSPACE-complete in general (Papadimitriou and Tsitsiklis 1987). However, there are POMDP planning algorithms that trade off solution quality for speed, but that usually do not provide quality guarantees (Littman, Cassandra, and Kaebling 1995; Cassandra 1997; Hauskrecht 1997). The SPOVA-RL algorithm (Parr and Russell 1995), for example, can determine approximate POMDP policies with about a hundred states in a reasonable amount of time. Further performance improvements are anticipated, since POMDP planning algorithms are the object of current research (Littman 1996) and researchers are starting to investigate, for example, how to exploit the restricted topology of some POMDPs (Boutilier, Dean, and Hanks 1995).

We describe here three greedy POMDP planning approaches that can find POMDP policies for large POMDPs fast, but still yield reasonable robot navigation behavior. These three approaches share the property that they pretend that the POMDP is completely observable and, under this assumption, use equation (3) to determine an optimal policy. Then, they transform this policy into a POMDP policy. We call this transformation "completing" the policy because the mapping from states to actions is completed to a mapping from state *distributions* to actions. Given the current state distribution α, the approaches greedily complete the policy as follows:

- The *"most likely state"* strategy (Nourbakhsh, Powers, and Birchfield 1995) executes the action that is assigned to the most likely state, that is, the action $a(\arg \max_{s \in S} \alpha(s))$.

- The *"voting"* strategy (Simmons and Koenig 1995) executes the action with the highest probability mass according to α, that is, the action

  $\mathrm{argmax}_{a \in A} \sum_{s \in S \mid a(s) = a} \alpha(s)$.

- The *"completely observable after the first step"* strategy (Chrisman 1992; Tenenberg, Karlsson, and Whitehead 1992) executes the action

  $\arg \max_{a \in A} \sum_{s \in S} \alpha(s) \, (r(s, a) + \gamma \sum_{s' \in S} p(s' \mid s, a) \, v(s'))$.

This approach allows one, for example, to choose the second best action if all states disagree on the best action, but agree on the second best action. The selected action is optimal if the POMDP becomes completely observable after the action execution.

POMDP Learning: Determining the POMDP from Observations

Assume that an observer wants to determine the POMDP that maximizes the probability of generating the observations for the given actions. This POMDP is the one that best fits the empirical data. In our application, this corresponds to fine-tuning the navigation model from experience, including the map, actuator, and sensor models. While there is no known technique for doing this efficiently, there exist efficient algorithms that approximate the optimal POMDP (Chrisman 1992; McCallum 1995; Stolcke and Omohundro 1993). The Baum-Welch algorithm (Rabiner 1986) is one such algorithm. This iterative expectation-maximization algorithm does not require control of the POMDP process and thus can be used by an observer to learn the POMDP. It overcomes the problem that observers can never be sure about the current state of the POMDP process because they cannot observe the current state directly and are not allowed to execute actions to reduce their uncertainty. Given an initial POMDP and a training trace (a sequence of actions and observations), the Baum-Welch algorithm generates a POMDP that better fits the trace, in the sense that it increases the probability with which observations are generated, given the actions, times the probability that the action sequence can be executed (the Baum-Welch algorithm changes only the transition and observation probabilities, but not the number of states or the possible transitions between them). By repeating this procedure with the same training trace and the improved POMDP, we get a hill-climbing algorithm that eventually converges to a POMDP which locally, but not necessarily globally, best fits the trace.

The Baum-Welch algorithm estimates the improved POMDP in three steps. First Step: A dynamic programming approach ("forward-backward algorithm") is used that applies Bayes's rule repeatedly (Devijver 1985). The forward phase calculates scaling factors $scale_t$ and alpha values $\alpha_t(s) = p(s_t = s | o_{1\ldots t}, a_{1\ldots t-1})$, for all $s \in S$ and $t = 1 \ldots T$. The alpha values are the state distributions calculated in the subsection on state estimation.

A1. Set $scale_1 := \sum_{s \in S} q(o_1|s) \pi(s)$.

A2. Set $\alpha_1(s) := q(o_1|s) \pi(s)/scale_1$ for all $s \in S$.

A3. For $t := 1$ to $T - 1$

(a) Set $scale_{t+1} := \sum_{s \in S} q(o_{t+1}|s) \sum_{s' \in S | a_t \in A(s')} p(s | s'a_t) \alpha_t(s')$.

(b) Set $\alpha_{t+1}(s) := q(o_{t+1}|s) \sum_{s' \in S | a_t \in A(s')} p(s | s'a_t) \alpha_t(s') /scale_{t+1}$ for all $s \in S$.

The backward phase of the forward-backward algorithm calculates beta values $\beta_t(s)$, for all $s \in S$ and $t = 1 \ldots T$:

A4. Set $\beta_T(s) := 1 \,/\, scale_T$ for all $s \in S$.

A5. For $t := T-1$ downto 1

(a) Set $\beta_t(s) := \begin{cases} \sum_{s' \in S} p(s' \mid s, a_t) q(o_{t+1} \mid s') \beta_{t+1}(s') \,/\, scale_t & \text{for all } s \in S \text{ with } a_t \in A(s) \\ 0 & \text{for all } s \in S \text{ with } a_t \notin A(s) \end{cases}$

Second Step: The Baum-Welch algorithm calculates the gamma values $\gamma_t(s, s') = p(s_t = s, s_{t+1} = s' \mid o_{1 \ldots T}, a_{1 \ldots T-1})$ for all $t = 1 \ldots T-1$ and $s, s' \in S$ with $a_t \in A(s)$, and $\gamma_t(s) = p(s_t = s \mid o_{1 \ldots T}, a_{1 \ldots T-1})$ for all $t = 1 \ldots T$ and $s \in S$. The gamma values $\gamma_t(s)$ are more precise estimates of the state at time t than the alpha values $\alpha_t(s)$, because they also use information (represented by the beta values) that became available only after time t.

A6. Set $\gamma_t(s, s') := \alpha_t(s) p(s' \mid s, a_t) q(o_{t+1} \mid s') \beta_{t+1}(s')$ for all $t = 1 \ldots T-1$ and $s, s' \in S$ with $a_t \in A(s)$.

A7. Set $\gamma_t(s) := scale_t \alpha_t(s) \beta_t(s)$ for all $t = 1 \ldots T$ and $s \in S$.

Third Step: The Baum-Welch algorithm uses the following frequency-counting re-estimation formulae to calculate the improved initial state distribution, transition probabilities, and observation probabilities (the asterisked symbols represent the probabilities that constitute the improved POMDP):

A8. Set $\pi^*(s) := \gamma_1(s)$.

A9. Set $p^*(s' \mid s, a) := \sum_{t = 1 \ldots T-1 \mid a_t = a} \gamma_t(s, s') \,/\, \sum_{t = 1 \ldots T-1 \mid a_t = a} \gamma_t(s)$ for all $s, s' \in S$ and $a \in A(s)$.

A10. Set $q^*(o \mid s) := \sum_{t=1 \ldots T \mid o_t = o} \gamma_t(s) \,/\, \sum_{t=1 \ldots T} \gamma_t(s)$ for all $s \in S$ and all $o \in O$.

To apply the Baum-Welch algorithm to real-world problems, there exist standard techniques for dealing with the following issues (Koenig and Simmons 1996b): when to stop iterating the algorithm, with which initial POMDP to start the algorithm and how often to apply it to different initial POMDPs, how to handle transition or observation probabilities that are zero or one (the Baum-Welch algorithm does not change these probabilities), and how to deal with short training traces. In addition, we have extended the Baum-Welch algorithm to address issues of limited memory and the cost of collecting training data (Koenig and Simmons 1996b) and augmented it so that it is able to change the structure of the POMDP (Koenig and Simmons 1996a).

Most Likely Path: Determining the State Sequence from Observations

Assume that an observer wants to determine the most likely sequence of states that the POMDP process was in. This corresponds to determining the path that the robot most likely took to get to its destination. While the techniques from the POMDP learning subsection can determine the most likely state of the POMDP process at each point in time, merely connecting these states might not result in a continuous path. The Viterbi algorithm uses dynamic programming to compute the most likely path efficiently (Viterbi 1967). Its first three steps are steps A1 to A3 in the POMDP learning subsection, except that the summations on lines A3(a) and A3(b) are replaced by maximizations:

B1. Set $scale'_1 := \sum_{s \in S} q(o_1|s)\pi(s)$.

B2. Set $\alpha'_1(s) := q(o_1|s)\pi(s) \,/\, scale'_1$ for all $s \in S$.

B3. For $t := 1$ to $T - 1$

    (a) Set $scale'_{t+1} := \sum_{s \in S} q(o_{t+1}|s) \max_{s' \in S|a_t \in A(s')} p(s|s'a_t)\,\alpha'_t(s')$.

    (b) Set $\alpha'_{t+1}(s) := q(o_{t+1}|s) \max_{s' \in S|a_t \in A(s')} p(s|s'a_t)\,\alpha'_t(s') \,/\, scale'_{t+1}$ for all $s \in S$.

B4. Set $s^*_T := \max_{s \in S} \alpha'_T(s)$.

B5. For $t := T - 1$ to 1

    (a) Set $s^*_t := \arg\max_{s' \in S|a_t \in A(s')} p(s^*_{t+1}|s',a_t)\alpha'_t(s')$.

s^*_t is the state at time t that is part of the most likely state sequence.

The POMDP-Based Navigation Architecture

This section describes the architecture of a navigation system that applies the general models and algorithms presented in the previous section to the corridor navigation problem. The POMDP-based navigation architecture is one layer of our autonomous mobile robot system for office delivery (figure 1). Given a goal location for the robot, the role of the navigation layer is to send directives to the obstacle avoidance layer that move the robot toward its goal, where a *directive* is either a change in desired heading or a "stop" command. The obstacle avoidance layer then heads in that direction while using sensor information to avoid obstacles.

The POMDP-based navigation architecture consists of several components (figure 2). The *sensor interpretation* component converts the continual motion of the robot into discrete *motion reports* (heading changes and distance traveled) and uses the raw sonar sensor data to produce *sensor reports* of high-level features, such as walls and openings of various sizes, observed in front of the robot and to its immediate left and right. The *pose estimation* component uses the motion and sensor reports to maintain a belief about the current pose of the robot by updating the state distribution of the POMDP.

The *policy generation* component, in conjunction with the path planning layer, generates a POMDP *policy* that maps state distributions to directives. Whenever the pose estimation component generates a new belief in the current pose of the robot, the *directive selection* component uses this state distribution to index

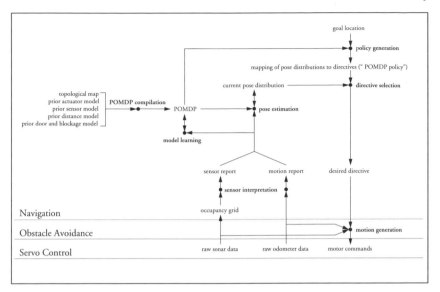

Figure 2. The POMDP-based navigation architecture.

the POMDP policy and sends the resulting directive to the obstacle avoidance layer, which then generates the robot motion commands. Thus, directive selection is fast and very reactive to the motion and sensor reports received.

The initial POMDP is generated once for each environment by the *POMDP compilation* component. It uses a topological map, initial approximate actuator and sensor models, and uncertain knowledge of the environment. As the robot gains more experience while it performs its tasks, the unsupervised and passive *model learning* component uses the Baum-Welch algorithm to automatically adapt the initial POMDP to the environment of the robot, which improves the accuracy of the actuator and sensor models and reduces the uncertainty about the environment. This increases the precision of the pose estimation component, which ultimately leads to improved navigation performance.

In the following paragraphs, we first describe the interface between the POMDP-based navigation architecture and the obstacle avoidance layer, including the sensor interpretation component. Then, we describe the POMDP and the POMDP compilation component in detail. Finally, we explain how the POMDP is used by the pose estimation, policy generation, and directive selection components. The model learning component is described in Koenig and Simmons (1996a and 1996b).

Interface to the Obstacle Avoidance Layer

An advantage of our layered robot architecture is that the navigation layer is insulated from many details of the actuators, sensors, and the environment (such as stationary and moving obstacles). The navigation layer itself provides further abstractions in the form of discrete motion and sensor reports that further insulate the POMDP from details of the robot control.

This abstraction also has the advantage of enabling us to discretize the possible poses of the robot into a finite, relatively small number of states, and keep the number of possible motion and sensor reports small. In particular, we discretize the location with a precision of one meter and discretize the orientation into the four compass directions. While more fine-grained discretizations yield more precise models (Burgard, Fox, Hennig, and Schmidt 1996), they also result in larger POMDPs and more time-consuming computations.

Directives

The main role of the obstacle avoidance layer is to make the robot head in a given direction while avoiding obstacles. The task of the navigation layer is to supply a series of changes in desired headings, which we call *directives*, to the obstacle avoidance layer to make the robot reach its goal location.

The directives issued by the navigation layer are to change the desired heading by ninety degrees (turn right), minus ninety degrees (turn left), zero degrees (go forward), and stop. Directives are cumulative, so that, for example, two successive "right turn" directives result in a smooth 180 degree turn. If the robot is already moving, a new directive does not cause it to stop and turn, but merely to change the desired heading, which the obstacle avoidance layer then tries to follow. This results in the robot making smooth turns at corridor junctions.

The robot uses the curvature velocity method (Simmons 1996) to do local obstacle avoidance. The curvature velocity method formulates the problem as one of constrained optimization in velocity space. Constraints are placed on the translational and rotational velocities of the robot that stem from physical limitations (velocities and accelerations) and the environment (the configuration of obstacles). The robot chooses velocity commands that satisfy all the constraints and maximize an objective function that trades off speed, safety, and goal directedness. These commands are then sent to the motors and, if necessary, change the actual heading of the robot.

The obstacle avoidance layer also keeps the robot centered along the main corridor axis by correcting for angular dead-reckoning error. It tries to fit lines to the sonar data and, if the fit is good enough, uses the angle between the line (for example, a wall) and the desired heading to compensate for angular drift.

Sensor Interpretation: Motion and Sensor Reports

The sensor interpretation component asynchronously generates discrete motion and sensor reports that are abstractions of the continuous stream of information provided by the sensors onboard the robot (wheel encoders for the motion reports and sonar sensors for the sensor reports).

Sensor	Features that the Sensor Reports On
front	unknown, wall
left	unknown, wall, small_opening, medium_opening, large_opening
right	unknown, wall, small_opening, medium_opening, large_opening

Table 1. Sensors and their features.

Motion reports are generated relative to the desired heading. They are discretized in accordance with the resolution of the POMDP (ninety degrees, one meter). Thus, there are motion reports for when the robot has turned left or right by ninety degrees, gone forward or backward one meter (in a direction parallel to the desired heading), and slid left or right one meter (orthogonal to the desired heading). Slide motions often occur in open spaces (such as foyers) where the robot can move a significant distance orthogonally to the desired heading during obstacle avoidance.

The motion reports are derived by discretizing the smooth motion of the robot. The sensor interpretation component periodically receives reports from the odometer onboard the robot. It combines this information with the robot's commanded heading to produce a virtual odometer that keeps track of the distance traveled along, and orthogonal to, that heading. This ensures that the distance the robot travels in avoiding obstacles is not counted in determining how far it has traveled along a corridor. The odometer reports are integrated over time. A "forward" motion report is generated after each meter of cumulative travel in the desired heading. Similarly, the sensor interpretation component reports when the heading of the robot has changed relative to the desired heading, and this is reported in units of ninety degree turns. This assumes that corridors are straight and perpendicular to each other.

Sensor reports are generated for three virtual (high-level) sensors that report features in front, to the left of, and to the right of the robot. New sensors (such as vision-based sensors) are easily added by specifying their observation probabilities. Table 1 lists the sensors that we currently use, together with the features that they report on. The sensor reports are derived from the raw sensor data by using a small, local occupancy grid (Elfes 1989) in the coordinates of the robot that is centered around the robot (figure 3). The occupancy grid combines the raw data from all sonar sensors and integrates them over the recent past. The occupancy grid is then processed by projecting a sequence of rays perpendicular to the robot heading until they intersect an occupied grid cell. If the end points of the rays can be fit to a line with a small chi-squared statistic, a wall has been de-

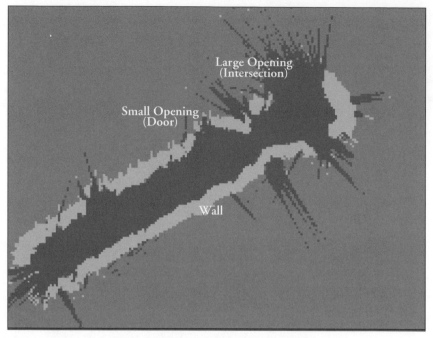

Figure 3. Occupancy grid with corridor features.

tected with high probability. Similarly, a contiguous sequence of long rays indicates an opening.

The occupancy grid filters some noise out of the raw sensor data by integrating them over time and over different raw sensors. Raw data from sonar sensors, for example, can be very noisy because of specular reflections. The sensor reports also approximate the Markov property better than do the raw sensor data. Two sonar sensors, for example, that point in approximately the same direction produce highly correlated data. By bundling sets of features into one virtual sensor, we attempt to make sensor reports more independent of each other, given the current pose of the robot.

POMDP Compilation

A POMDP is defined by its states and its initial state distribution, its observations and observation probabilities, and its actions, transition probabilities, and immediate rewards. In our POMDP-based navigation architecture, the states of the POMDP encode the pose of the robot. The initial state distribution encodes the available knowledge about the initial pose. The observations correspond to the features, one for each virtual sensor, and the observation probabilities encode the sensor model. The actions are the motion reports (for pose estimation) and

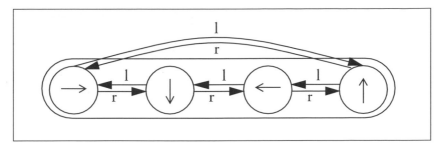

Figure 4. Group of four states modeling one location.

the directives (for policy generation), and the transition probabilities encode the topological map, the map uncertainty, and the actuator model. Finally, the immediate rewards (here, costs) express the expected travel times needed to complete the actions, and the objective is to minimize the expected total cost.

The map information is initially encoded as a *topological map*, a graph that contains information about the connectivity of the environment. Nodes represent junctions between corridors, doorways, or foyers. They are connected by edges, which are augmented with approximate length information (in the form of probability distributions over the possible lengths of the edges). We assume that the topological map of the environment can easily be obtained. The approximate corridor lengths can then be obtained from either rough measurements, general knowledge, or the model learning component. The rest of this section describes how this information is used to create the POMDP automatically.

States and Initial State Distribution

Since we discretize the orientation of the robot into the four compass directions, a group of four states, together with "left turn" (l) and "right turn" (r) actions, is necessary to fully represent the possible robot poses at each spatial location (figure 4). Since we discretize space with a resolution of one meter, each group of four nodes represents one square meter of free space. The initial state distribution of the POMDP process then encodes the, possibly uncertain, knowledge of the initial robot pose.

Observations and Observation Probabilities

We denote the set of virtual sensors by I and the set of features that sensor $i \in I$ reports on by $F(i)$ (table 1). The sensor model is then specified by the probabilities $q_i(f|s)$ for all $i \in I, f \in F(i)$, and $s \in S$, which encode the sensor uncertainty. $q_i(f|s)$ is the probability with which sensor i reports feature f in state s. An observation of the POMDP is the aggregate of one report from each sensor. We do not represent it explicitly, but calculate only its observation probability: If sensor i

Class	Explanation
wall	a wall about one meter away
near-wall	a wall about two meters away
open	no wall for at least three meters (for example, a corridor opening)
closed-door	a closed door
open-door	an open door
door	a door with unknown door state (open or closed)

Table 2. Classes of states.

reports feature f_i, then $q(o|s) = \prod_{i \in I} q_i(f_i|s)$. This formula assumes that the sensor reports of different sensors are independent, given the state.

A sensor that has not issued a report (for example, because the sensor interpretation component has made no determination which feature is present or was not able to issue a report in time) is assumed to have reported the feature "unknown." The probabilities $q_i(\text{unknown}|s)$ are chosen so that the state distribution remains unaffected in this case, that is, $q_i(\text{unknown}|s) = q_i(\text{unknown}|s')$ for all $i \in I$ and $s, s' \in S$. Learning can change these probabilities later because even the sensor report "unknown" can carry information.

To simplify the specification of the sensor model, rather than characterizing $q_i(f|s)$ for each state individually, we characterize classes of states (table 2). New classes can easily be added: for example, for walls adjacent to openings so that a sensor could pick up some of the opening (an example is the wall marked X in figure 6). The sensor model is then specified by the probabilities that a sensor reports a given feature when the robot is in that particular class of states. For example, the "left" sensor is partially characterized by:

$q_{\text{left sensor}}(\text{wall}|\text{open})$ $= 0.05$
$q_{\text{left sensor}}(\text{small\_opening}|\text{open})$ $= 0.20$
$q_{\text{left sensor}}(\text{medium\_opening}|\text{open})$ $= 0.40$
$q_{\text{left sensor}}(\text{large\_opening}|\text{open})$ $= 0.30$
$q_{\text{left sensor}}(\text{unknown}|\text{open})$ $= 0.05$

These probabilities indicate that corridor openings are most commonly detected as medium-sized openings but can often be seen as either large or small openings, although they are hardly ever confused for walls.

Modeling Actions

The actions of the POMDP encode the motion reports (for pose estimation) and the directives (for policy generation). For the most part, the transition probabilities of a motion report and its corresponding directive are identical. A motion report "turned left" and a directive "turn left," for example, both lead with high probability to a state at the same location whose orientation is ninety degrees counterclockwise. The transition probabilities of actions encode the actuator uncertainty, and their immediate costs encode how long it takes to complete them.

Only the semantics of "forward" motion reports and "forward" directives differ slightly. If the robot is able to move forward one meter, it is unlikely that it was facing a wall. Thus, for dealing with motion reports, the self-transition probability of "forward" actions are set very low in states that face walls. On the other hand, for planning purposes, the same self-transition probabilities are set high, since we know that low-level control routines prevent the robot from moving into walls.

In general, all actions have their intended effect with high probability. However, there is a small chance that the robot ends up in an unintended pose, such as an unintended orientation (not shown in the figures). Exactly which poses these are is determined by the actuator model. Dead-reckoning uncertainty, for example, usually results in the robot overestimating its travel distance in corridors (because of wheel slippage). This can be modeled with self transitions (that is, modeling a small probability that "forward" actions do not change the state).

There is a trade-off in which possible transitions to model and which ones to leave out. Fewer transitions result in smaller POMDPs and thus in smaller memory requirements and less time consuming computations. On the other hand, if one does not model all possible action outcomes, the pose estimates can become inconsistent (every possible pose is ruled out). This is undesirable, because the robot can only recover from an inconsistency by relocalizing itself. Therefore, while we found that most actions have fairly deterministic outcomes, we introduce probabilistic outcomes where appropriate. This also benefits the Baum-Welch algorithm used by the model-learning component, which never inserts missing transitions.

Modeling Corridors

The representation of topological edges is a key to our approach. If the edge lengths are known exactly, it is simple to model the ability to traverse a corridor with a Markov chain that has "forward" (f) actions between those states whose orientations are parallel to the main corridor axis (figure 5a).

When only approximate edge lengths are known, an edge is modeled as a set of parallel Markov chains, each corresponding to one of the possible lengths of the edge (figure 5b). The transition probabilities into the first state of each chain model the map uncertainty. They are the same as the probability distribution over the possible edge lengths. Each "forward" transition after that is deterministic (modulo actuator uncertainty). While this representation best captures the actual structure of the environment, it is relatively inefficient: The number of states is quadratic in the difference between the maximum and minimum lengths to consider.

As a compromise between fidelity and efficiency, one can model edges by col-

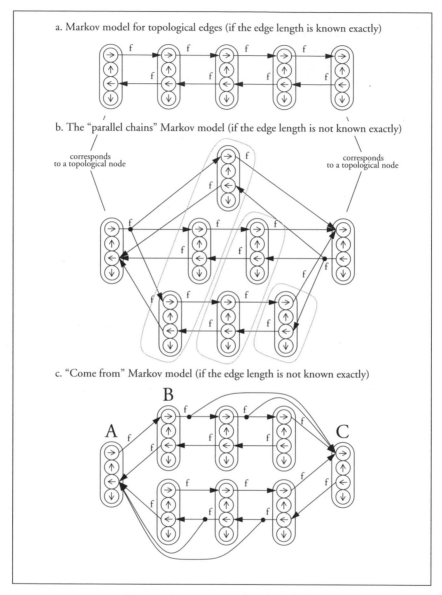

Figure 5. Representation of topological edges.

lapsing the parallel chains in a way that we call the "come from" semantics (figure 5c). The groups of four states that we collapse into one are framed in figure 5b. Each topological edge is then represented using two chains, one for each of the corridor directions. In the "come from" semantics, the spatial location of a state is known relative to the topological node from which the robot comes, but

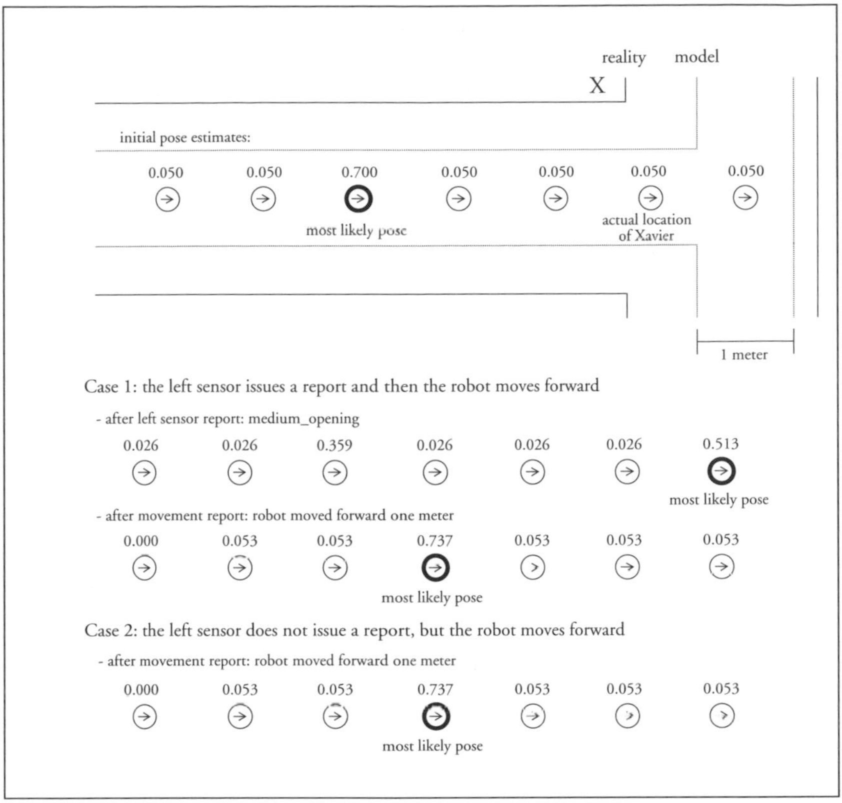

Figure 6. The effect of pretending that corridors are one meter wide.

its location relative to the end of the chain is uncertain (for example, state B is one meter away from A, but is between one and three meters away from C). An alternative representation is the "go to" semantics, in which the location of a state is specified relative to the topological node toward which the robot is heading, but the distance from the start node is uncertain.

When the length uncertainty is large, the "come from" and "go to" semantics can save significant space over the "parallel chains" representation. For example, for a topological edge between two and ten meters long, they need only eighty states to encode the edge, compared to one hundred eighty-eight for the "parallel chains." Since the length uncertainty in our maps is not that large, we actually use the "parallel chains" representation in the POMDP-based navigation architecture that is implemented on Xavier.

Modeling Junctions, Doorways, Rooms, and Foyers

While we could represent corridor junctions simply with a single group of four states, our experience with the real robot has shown this representation to be inadequate, since the spatial resolution of a state is one meter, but our corridors are two meters wide. To understand why this can lead to problems, consider the scenario shown in figure 6: The robot is one state away from the center of a T-junction (facing the wall), but because of map uncertainty still believes itself to be farther away from the junction. The "left" sensor picks up the opening and reports it. This increases the belief that the robot is already in the junction. Now assume that, because of communication delays, the robot continues to move forward, which is possible because the junction is two meters wide. According to the model, however, this rules out the robot's being in the junction (the robot cannot move forward in a junction that is one meter wide, except for a small probability of self-transitioning), and the most likely state jumps back into the corridor. The resulting state distribution is approximately the same as if the "left" sensor had not issued its report. Thus, the sensor report contributes little to the current pose estimate, and its information is essentially lost. Figure 6 illustrates this effect under the simplifying assumptions that there is no map uncertainty, the actuator model is completely deterministic, and the "left" sensor is characterized by $q_{\text{left sensor}}(\text{medium\_opening}|\text{open}) = 0.40$ and $q_{\text{left sensor}}(\text{medium\_opening}|\text{wall}) = 0.02$. However, the effect is independent of the sensor model or the initial state distribution.

While one remedy is to represent junctions using four (that is, two by two) groups of four states each, we achieve nearly the same result with four groups of two states each, which both saves space and makes the model simpler (figure 7). The basic idea is that turns within a junction are nondeterministic, and transition with equal probability to one of the two states of the appropriate orientation in the junction. For example, in entering the junction of figure 7 from the south, the robot would first encounter state A, then state B if it continued to move forward. If it then turned left, it would be facing west and would transition to either of state C or D with equal probability. This model agrees with how the robot actually behaves in junctions. In particular, it corresponds to the fact that it is very difficult to pin down the robot's location exactly while it is turning in the middle of an intersection.

Doorways can be modeled more simply, since the width of our doors is approximately the resolution of the POMDP. A single exact-length edge, as in figure 5a, leads through a door into a room. The state of a door (open or closed) can typically change and thus is often not known in advance. We therefore associate with doorways a probability p that the door is open. This probability encodes the uncertainty about the dynamic state of the environment. The observation probabilities associated with seeing a doorway are

$q(o|\text{door}) = p \times q(o|\text{open-door}) + (1 - p) \times q(o|\text{closed-door})$.

While we model corridors as one-dimensional chains of states, we represent foyers and rooms by tessellating two-dimensional space into a matrix of locations. From each location, the "forward" action has some probability of transi-

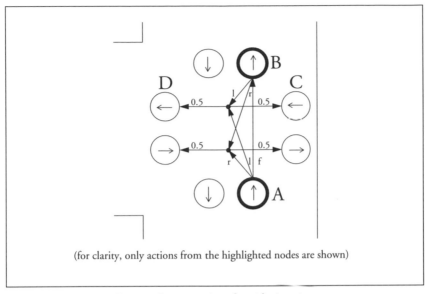

(for clarity, only actions from the highlighted nodes are shown)

Figure 7. Representation of corridor junctions.

tioning straight ahead, but also some probability of self-transitioning and moving to diagonally adjacent states, which represents the robot drifting sideways without noticing it (figure 8). Currently, we do not have a good method for efficiently representing map uncertainty in rooms and foyers.

Using the POMDP

In this section, we explain how our navigation architecture uses POMDP algorithms for estimating the robot's pose and for directing its behavior.

Pose Estimation

The pose estimation component uses the motion and sensor reports to update the state distribution (that is, the belief in the current pose of the robot) using equations (1) and (2) from the state estimation subsection. The updates are fast, since they require only one iteration over all states, plus an additional iteration for the subsequent normalization. While the amount of computation can be decreased by performing the normalization only once in a while (to prevent rounding errors from dominating), it is fast enough that we actually do it every time.

Since reports by the same sensor at the same location are clearly dependent (they depend on the same cells of the occupancy grid), aggregating multiple reports without a motion report in between would violate the Markov assumption. The pose estimation component therefore uses only the latest report from

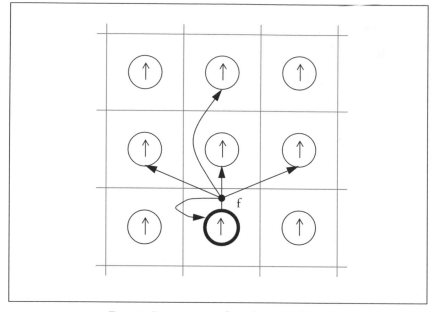

Figure 8. Representation of two-dimensional space.

each sensor between motion reports to update the state distribution.

Motion reports tend to increase the pose uncertainty because of nondeterministic transitions (actuator and map uncertainty), while sensor reports tend to decrease it. An exception is "forward" motion reports that can decrease uncertainty if some of the states with nonzero probability are "wall facing." In practice, this effect can be seen when the robot turns at an intersection: Before the turn, there is often some probability that the robot has not yet reached the intersection. After the robot has turned and successfully moved forward a bit, the probability that it is still in the original corridor quickly drops. This is a major factor in keeping the positional uncertainty low, even when the robot travels long distances.

Policy Generation and Directive Selection

The policy generation component has to compute a POMDP policy that minimizes the expected travel time of the robot. The directive selection component then simply indexes this POMDP policy repeatedly with the current state distribution to determine which directives to execute.

For policy generation, we need to handle "stop" directives. This is done by adding a "stop" action to the set $A(s)$ of each state s. The immediate cost of the "stop" action is zero in states that correspond to the goal location, and is high otherwise. In all cases, the "stop" action leads with certainty to a distinguished

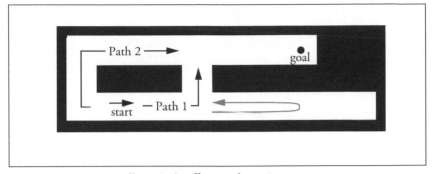

Figure 9. An office corridor environment.

POMDP state from which no future immediate costs are possible. The policy generation component then has to determine a POMDP policy that minimizes the expected total cost received, since the immediate costs of all actions reflect their execution times.

Since our POMDPs typically have thousands of states, we need to use the greedy POMDP planning approaches from the POMDP planning subsection. These approaches pretend that the POMDP is completely observable. Under this assumption, they determine an optimal mapping from states to directives (a policy) and then transform it into a mapping from state *distributions* to directives (a POMDP policy). This, however, can lead to very suboptimal results. In figure 9, for example, path 1 is shorter than path 2 and thus requires less travel time if the states are completely observable. Because of sensing uncertainty, however, a robot can miss the first turn on path 1 and overshoot. It then has to turn around and look for the corridor opening again, which increases its travel time along path 1. On the other hand, when the robot follows path 2 it cannot miss turns. Thus, it might actually be faster to follow path 2 than path 1, but the greedy POMDP planning approaches would always recommend path 1.

We address this problem by using a different approach for generating the policy, but continue to use the approaches from the POMDP planning subsection to complete it. To generate the policy, we use the decision-theoretic path planning layer of our robot system, which takes into account that the robot can miss turns and that corridors can be blocked. It uses a generate, evaluate, and refine strategy to determine a path in the topological map that minimizes the expected travel time of the robot (Koenig, Goodwin, and Simmons 1996). The navigation layer then converts this path to a complete policy. For states corresponding to a topological node on the path, directives are assigned to head the robot toward the next node (except for the states corresponding to the last node on the path, which are assigned "stop" directives). Similarly, for all states corresponding to the topological edges between two nodes on the path, directives are assigned to head the robot toward the next node. Finally, for states not on the path, directives are assigned that move the robot back toward the planned path. This way, if the robot strays from the nominal (optimal) path, it will automatically execute corrective directives once it realizes its mistake. Thus, replanning is only necessary when the robot detects that the nominal path is blocked. While this planning method is still suboptimal, it is a reasonable compromise between planning efficiency and plan quality.

As described in the POMDP planning subsection, there are several greedy approaches for choosing which directive to issue, given a policy and the current state distribution. It turns out that the "most likely state" strategy does not work well with our models, because topological entities are encoded in multiple states. For example, since corridor junctions are modeled using several states for each orientation, it is reasonable to consider all of their recommendations when deciding which directive to issue. The "voting" and "completely observable after the first step" strategies both work well in our environment if the initial positional uncertainty is not overly large. Both strategies are relatively immune to the limited positional uncertainty that arises during navigation.

These greedy approaches also have disadvantages. Since they operate on a policy and account for positional uncertainty only greedily, they make the assumption that the robot collects sensor data on the fly as it moves closer to its destination. As opposed to other POMDP planning methods, they do not plan when, where, and what to sense. This property fits sonar sensors well, since sonar sensors produce a continuous stream of data and do not need to be pointed. A disadvantage of this property, however, is that the robot does not handle well situations in which localization is necessary, and we thus recommend using more sophisticated POMDP planning techniques as they become more efficient. For example, it is often more effective to actively gather information that helps the robot to reduce its pose uncertainty, even if this requires the robot to move away from the goal temporarily.

On the other hand, the greedy approaches often lead to an optimal behavior of the robot. For example, even if the robot does not know for certain which of two parallel corridors it is traversing, it does not need to stop and replan, as long as the directives associated with both corridors are the same. In this way, the robot can continue making progress toward its desired goal, while at the same time collecting evidence, in the form of sensor readings, that can help to disambiguate its true location. This behavior takes advantage of the fact that buildings are usually constructed in ways that allow people to obtain sufficient clues about their current location from their past experience and local environment — otherwise they would easily become confused (of course, some landmarks that can be observed by people, such as signs or door labels, cannot be detected by sonar sensors).

Experiments

The POMDP-based navigation architecture described in this chapter is implemented in C and runs on-board the robot on Intel 486 computers under the Linux operating system. The navigation layer is a separate, concurrent process that communicates with the other layers of the robot system via message passing, supported by the Task Control Architecture (Simmons 1994).

In this section, we report on experiments that we performed in two environments for which the Markov property is only an approximation: an actual mobile robot navigating in our building, and a realistic simulation of the robot. The experiments show that the Markov property is satisfied well enough for the POMDP-based navigation architecture to yield reliable navigation performance. We use the same navigation code for both sets of experiments, since the robot and its simulator have the exact same interfaces, down to the level of the servo control layer (figure 1).

In all experiments, we modeled the length uncertainty of each topological edge as a uniform distribution over the interval ranging from 80 to 150 percent of its true length and kept the initial positional uncertainty minimal: The initial probability for the robot's actual location was about 70 percent. The remaining probability mass was distributed in the vicinity of the actual location.

We report results for the "voting strategy" of policy generation and directive selection. The experiments demonstrate that for the office navigation problems considered here, the efficient voting strategy performs very well. For an empirical comparison of several greedy policy generation and directive selection strategies in more complex environments, but using simpler POMDPs than we use here, see (Cassandra, Kaelbling, and Kurien 1996).

Experiments with the Robot

The robot experiments were performed on Xavier (figure 10). Xavier, which was designed and built by our group at Carnegie Mellon University, is built on top of a 24 inch diameter RWI B24 base, which is a four-wheeled synchro-drive mechanism that allows for independent control of the translational and rotational velocities. The sensors on Xavier include bump panels, wheel encoders, a Denning sonar ring with twenty-four ultrasonic sensors, a front-pointing Nomadics laser light striper with a thirty-degree field of view, and a Sony color camera that is mounted on a pan-tilt head from Directed Perception (the current navigation system does not use the laser light striper, and the camera is used only for fine positioning at the destination).

Control, perception, and planning are carried out on two on-board 66 megahertz Intel 486 computers. An on-board color Intel 486 lap-top computer is used to monitor Xavier's status with a graphical interface, a screen shot of which

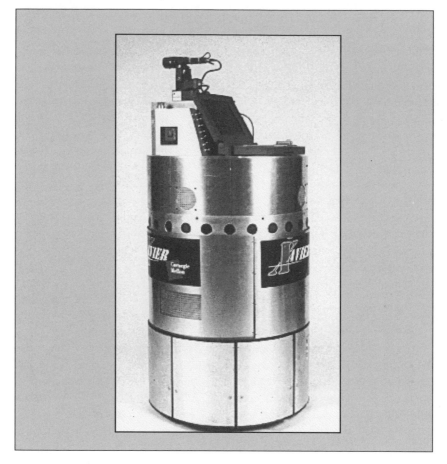

Figure 10. Xavier.

is shown in figure 11 (the sizes of the small circles in the right corridor are proportional to the probability mass in each corridor segment; the amount of positional uncertainty shown is typical). The computers are connected to each other via Ethernet and to the outside world via a Wavelan radio connection.

Xavier is controlled via a World Wide Web interface (www.cs.cmu.edu/~Xavier) that allows users worldwide to specify goal locations for Xavier on one floor of our building, half of which is shown in figure 11. The part shown has 95 nodes and 360 directed edges, and the POMDP has 3, 348 states. In the period from December 1, 1995, to May 31, 1996, Xavier attempted 1,571 navigation requests and reached its intended destination in 1,467 cases, where each job required it to move 40 meters on average (see table 3 and Simmons, Goodwin, Haigh, Koenig, and O'Sullivan [1997] for more details). Most failures are

Month	Days in Use	Jobs Attempted	Jobs Completed	Completion Rate	Distance Traveled
December 1995	13	262	250	95%	7.7 km
January 1996	16	344	310	90%	11.4 km
February 1996	15	245	229	93%	11.6 km
March 1996	13	209	194	93%	10.0 km
April 1996	18	319	304	95%	14.1 km
May 1996	12	192	180	94%	7.9 km
Total	87	1,571	1,467	93%	62.7 km

Table 3. Performance data (all numbers are approximate).

due to problems with our hardware (boards shaking loose) and the wireless communication between the on-board robot system and the off-board user interface (which includes the statistics-gathering software), and thus are unrelated to the POMDP-based navigation architecture. This success rate of 93 percent compares favorably with the 80 percent success rate that we obtained when using a landmark-based navigation technique in place of the POMDP-based navigation layer on the same robot with an otherwise unchanged robot system (Simmons 1994a). Thus, the difference in performance can be directly attributed to the different navigation techniques.

Experiments with the Simulator

To show the performance of the POMDP-based navigation architecture in an environment that is more complex than what we have available in our building, we also performed two navigation experiments with the Xavier simulator in the office corridor environment shown in figure 12. Its topological map has 17 nodes and 36 directed edges, and the POMDP has 1,184 states.

In experiment 1, the task was to navigate from $start_1$ to $goal_1$. The preferred headings are shown with solid arrows. Note that the preferred heading between B and C is toward C because this way the robot does not need to turn around if it overshoots B (which minimizes its travel time, even though the goal distance is a bit longer). We ran a total of fifteen trials (table 4), all of which were completed successfully. The robot has to travel a rather long distance from $start_1$ before its first turn. Since this distance is uncertain and corridor openings are occasionally missed, the robot occasionally overshoots B and then becomes uncertain whether it is really at C or B. However, since the same directive is as-

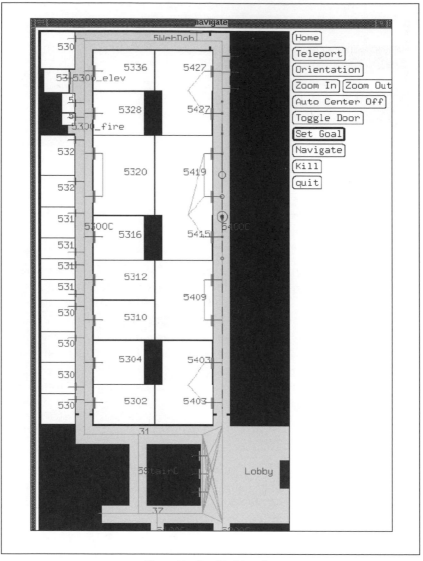

Figure 11. Graphical interface.

signed to both nodes, this ambiguity does not need to be resolved; the robot turns left in both cases and then goes straight. The same thing happens when it gets to *D*, since it thinks it may be at either *D* or *E*. The robot eventually corrects its beliefs when, after turning left and traveling forward, it detects an opening to its left. At this point, the robot becomes fairly certain that it is at *E*. A purely landmark-based navigation technique can easily get confused in this situ-

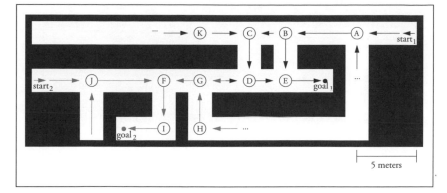

Figure 12. Another office corridor environment.

Path	Frequency	Time	Speed
ABE	12	68.2 s	25.7 cm/s
ABCDE	3	79.7 s	29.5 cm/s

Table 4. Experiment 1.

ation, since it has no expectations about seeing this opening and can only attribute it to sensor error (which, in this case, is incorrect).

In experiment 2, the robot had to navigate from *start*$_2$ to *goal*$_2$. The preferred headings for this task are shown with dashed arrows. Again, we ran 15 trials (table 5). For reasons that are similar to those in the first experiment, the robot can confuse G with F. If it is at G but thinks it is probably at F, it turns right and goes forward. However, when it detects the end of the corridor but does not detect a right corridor opening, it realizes that it must be at H rather than I. Since the probability mass has now shifted, it turns around and goes over G, F, and I to the goal. This shows that our navigation technique can gracefully recover from misjudgments based on wrong sensor reports — even if it takes some time to correct its beliefs. It is important to realize that this behavior is not triggered by any explicit exception mechanism, but results automatically from the way the pose estimation and directive selection components interact.

Path	Frequency	Time	Speed
JFI	11	60.6 s	28.9 cm/s
JFGFI	2	91.5 s	25.7 cm/s
JFGHGFI	1	116.0 s	23.7 cm/s
JFGFGFI	1	133.0 s	22.2 cm/s

Table 5. Experiment 2.

Conclusions

This chapter has presented a navigation architecture that uses partially observable Markov decision process models (POMDPs) for autonomous indoor navigation. The navigation architecture, which is one layer in a larger autonomous mobile robot system, provides for reliable and efficient navigation in office environments.

The implemented POMDP-based navigation architecture has demonstrated its reliability, even in the presence of unreliable actuators and sensors, as well as uncertainty in the metric map information. Robot control is fast and reactive during navigation (Xavier averages fifty centimeters per second), and robust, as demonstrated by experiments that required the robot to navigate over 60 kilometers in total.

We believe that such probabilistic navigation techniques hold great promise for making robots reliable enough to operate unattended for long periods of time in complex and uncertain environments. Applying POMDPs to robot navigation also opens up new application areas for more theoretical results in the area of planning and learning with Markov models.

Acknowledgements

Thanks to Lonnie Chrisman, Richard Goodwin, Karen Haigh, and Joseph O'Sullivan for helping to implement parts of the robot system and for many valuable discussions. Swantje Willms helped to perform some of the experiments with the simulator. This research was supported in part by NASA under contract NAGW-1175 and by the Wright Laboratory and ARPA under grant number F33615-93-1-1330. The views and conclusions contained in this chapter are those of the authors and should not be interpreted as representing the official policies, either expressed or implied, of the sponsoring organizations and agencies.

PART TWO

Vision for Mobile Robots

Vision is the single most powerful sense in the human repertoire, yet for most of the history of mobile robotics, vision has avoided in almost phobic proportions. In the early years of the AAAI competitions, the rules committees couldn't offer enough bonus points to get teams to forsake ultrasonic based solutions to navigational tasks. Certainly, there were good reasons for a roboticist to defer on incorporating vision into the robot's sensor suite. The hardware was prohibitive: vision processing required expensive specialized (and difficult to maintain) hardware and cameras which were often too large to physically reside on a mobile robot. The traditional software processing paradigm was worse yet: visual scenes were completely analyzed to reconstruct the outside world. The most fundamental token of information for navigation, whether a region of space in front of the robot was occupied or empty, could take hours to extract from stereo. Vision was so demanding that researchers could justify putting man-months of effort into fusing data from cheap Polaroid ultrasonics or infra-red sensors.

But now almost every mobile robot has a camera or some sort of image processing. Two competitions, MIROSOT and RoboCup, which require significant visual processing have recently begun, and the AAAI competition is hosting events which simply cannot be done without vision. What happened? Certainly the costs of the hardware have dropped significantly. In the early 1990s Horswill published an inexpensive framegrabber that could be built from parts for under US $1000.00. Shortly there after commercial framegrabbers dropped to the same price, while Sparc 10s became a common budget item in grant proposals.

But another more fundamental reason is because the paradigm shift in behavioral organization towards reactivity propagated to vision. In the mid-1980s, researchers such as Arbib (1981) began examining animal models for both motor control *and* perception. They found that a frog uses primarily used simple visual motion detection to catch flying prey. Bees key on specific aspects of the color spectrum for foraging. Indeed, psychophysical studies showed that the human visual system supported similar simple behaviors. The lower-resolution peripheral vision is used to watch for indications of motion (e.g., collisions with looming objects), while the higher resolution fovea is used to gather information for reasoning about an object. Humans don't take in everything at once in all its color, motion, and temporal dimensions, but rather direct attention to a very narrow portion of their visual field based on the task they're performing.

As a result of these investigations, the paradigm in vision shifted to a philosophy where perception exists to support the behaviors of a robot. Furthermore, the vision processing for each behavior might necessitate radically different representations and algorithms. The division and encapsulation of vision processing into compact, well-defined routines was also extended to pan-tilt control of ameras (see Combs and Brown, 1991, Huber and Kortenkamp, 1995, and Kroktkov, 1989). Behavioral-based vision has arrived!

However, understanding a paradigm shift and implementing a new organizational style are two different beasts. The chapters in this section address how behavior-based vision is being incorporated into programming robots. They concentrate on the architectural issues of integrating vision into behavioral-based robots, providing a mini-tutorial on how to implement vision in behaviorally-based mobile robots. The chapter by Horswill describes a minimalist system in which simple visual processes produce very sophisticated behavior. The chapter by Murphy describes how mobile robots can control multiple sensors in both indoor and outdoor environments. Finally, the chapter by Schiller and colleagues provides a look at how vision can be used on an outdoor mobile robot.

Robin Murphy and David Kortenkamp

CHAPTER FIVE

The Polly System

Ian Horswill

This chapter describes the design and rationale of the Polly system. Although now decommissioned, Polly was unique in the following ways: It performed a complicated task involving navigation in an unmodified environment for extended periods; it used real-time vision as nearly its only sensing modality; and all computation was performed on board by a low-cost off-the-shelf vision system.

Polly was a simple, low-cost robot designed and built between 1992 and 1993 at the MIT Artificial Intelligence Laboratory. It was designed to patrol the seventh floor of the laboratory, find visitors, and give them tours. Polly roamed the hallways of the laboratory looking for visitors. When someone approached the robot, it stopped, introduced itself, and offered visitors a tour, asking them to answer by waving their foot around (the robot could only see the person's legs and feet). If the person agreed, the robot led them around the lab, describing places as it recognized them.

Although primitive in many ways, Polly was unusual for its time in that it performed a relatively complicated task over an extended period of time (up to a period of hours), it only used real-time vision, and it only required on-board power and processing. The robot was built using off-the-shelf commercial hardware for less than $20,000.00, and was capable of running approximately six hours off batteries.

Polly was intended to explore a number of ideas that were prevalent at the time. First, operation in a real environment. Polly was built for and tested in a real environment with real people going about their daily business. Second, it explored the use of minimalism. The aim of the designers was to build the simplest possible system that solved a given task and use its performance to determine what architectural extensions were necessary. Third, Polly used active, purposeful, and task-based vision (Gibson 1966; Ballard 1991, Ikeuchi and Herbert 1990; Aloimonos 1990). Rather than computing a task-independent model of the environment, vision should compute the specific information needed to solve the agent's tasks. Fourth, Polly explored the use of environmental specialization (Gibson 1966). The robot exploited pre-existing environment structure to simplify agent design. Finally, Polly tested the limits of reactivity. It traded

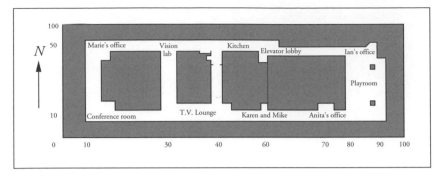

*Figure 1. The approximate layout of Polly's environment
(not to scale) and its coordinate system.*

speed of decision making for sophistication of decision making. Although many of these ideas are now widely accepted, Polly was an early test of how far they could be scaled.

Polly was very fast and simple. Its sensing and control systems ran at 15 hertz, so all percepts and motor commands were updated every 66 milliseconds. It also used very little hardware (an equivalent robot could be built for approximately $10,000.00 today) and consisted of less than a thousand lines of scheme code (not including device drivers and data structures). All computation was done on-board on a low-cost digital signal processor (a TI C30 with 64K of RAM). Polly was among the best tested mobile robots to date, having seen hundreds of hours of service, and still has one of the larger behavior repertoires.

Design Methodology

Given the desire to build a minimalist system and to use task-based vision, the design methodology needed for Polly is straightforward:

- Choose the tasks to be performed.
- For each task, find a set of actions sufficient to perform the task.
- For each action, find a condition under which each action should be taken.
- For each condition, find a set of perceptual measurements that are sufficient to determine the truth of the condition.
- For each measurement, design a custom visual process to compute it.
- If the process is too expensive or unreliable, find a set of environmental (domain) constraints that can be used to simplify it.

The difficulty in building the system comes from the fact that each step underdetermines the next; for example, there are many possible sets of condition and action pairs that can implement a given task. Finding a decomposition that bottoms out in a tractable set of vision primitives is difficult.

Another problem is to find domain constraints that are sufficiently true in practice to yield a robust system. Idealizations such as surface smoothness or the assumption of a slowly changing world are well known to be only approximately true. Oftentimes, they may depart from reality when they are most needed.

Having found a workable decomposition into actions, triggers, and perceptual measurements, we can build a working control program as a network of (simulated) parallel processes in the standard "reactive" or "behavior-based" style (Mataric 1997; Brooks 1986; Rosenschein and Kaelbling 1986). On each clock tick, every perceptual computation recomputes its output, every action trigger recomputes its truth value based on the new perceptual data, and any actions to be taken are fired in parallel. In practice, of course, the system is more complicated than a raw stimulus-response engine: perceptual computations, triggering decisions, and action performance may all require the maintenance of state information. Triggering decisions often share perceptual measurements, and perceptual measurements often share processing steps, so visual processes are only partly specific to actions or tasks.

Computational Properties of Office Environments

Office buildings are actively structured to make navigation easier (Passini 1984). The fact that they are structured as open spaces connected by networks of corridors means that much of the navigation problem can be solved by corridor following. In particular, we can reduce the problem of finding paths in space to finding paths in the graph of corridors. The MIT AI lab is even simpler because the corridor graph has a grid structure, so we can attach coordinates to the verticies of the graph and use difference reduction to get from one pair of coordinates to another.

Determining one's position in the grid is also made easier by special properties of office environments: the lighting of offices is generally controlled; the very narrowness of their corridors constrains the possible viewpoints from which an agent can see a landmark within the corridors. I will refer to this latter property as the *constant viewpoint constraint:* that the configuration space of the robot is restricted so that a landmark can only be viewed from a small number of directions. These properties make the recognition of landmarks in a corridor an easier problem than the fully general recognition problem. Thus very simple mechanisms often suffice.

Another useful property of office buildings is that they are generally carpeted, and their carpets tend to be either regularly textured or not textured at all. The

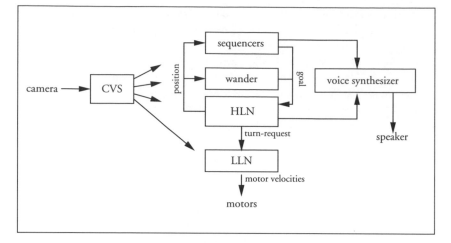

Figure 2. Overall architecture of the control system.

predictability of the texturing of the carpet means that any region of the image which isn't textured like the carpet is likely an object resting on the ground (or an object resting on an object resting on the ground). Thus *obstacle detection* can be reduced to *carpet detection,* which may be a simpler problem admitting simpler solutions. In the case of the MIT AI lab, the carpet has no texture and so a texture detector suffices for finding obstacles. I will refer to this as the *background-texture constraint* (see Horswill 1995b for a more detailed discussion).

Finally, office buildings have a useful property in that they have flat floors, so objects that are farther away will appear higher in the image, provided the objects rest on the floor. This provides a very simple way of determining the rough depth of such an object. I will refer to this as the *ground-plane constraint:* that all obstacles rest on a flat floor (see Horswill 1995b).

Architecture

The components of Polly's control system are seen grouped in figure 2. The "core vision system," or CVS, computes a set of percepts that are used to guide and trigger various behaviors in the system. The low-level navigation system (LLN) consists of a set of reactive behaviors that collectively attempt to move forward while avoiding obstacles and following any corridors or walls that may be visible. The high-level navigation system (HLN) keeps track of the robot's destination and last-recognized location and periodically overrides the LLN by issuing ballistic turns to redirect the robot from one corridor to another or to reverse directions if it determines that it has overshot. The wander system imple-

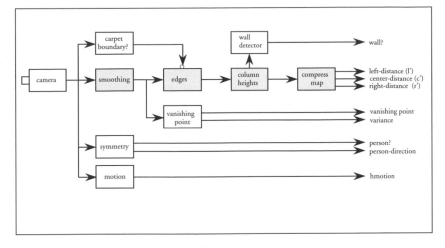

Figure 3. The Core vision system.

ments a patrol pattern by alternately posting opposite corners of the lab as goal locations. Finally, a set of sequencers implements the execution of prespecified action sequences (i.e. plans) that coordinate the overall process of giving a tour or offering a tour.

The actual implementation is a set of scheme procedures, roughly one per parallel process, with variables used to simulate wires. On each clock tick (66 milliseconds), the robot grabs a new image and runs each process in sequence to compute a new motor command that is fed to the base computer.

Physically, the Polly consists of an RWI B12 robot base, which houses the motors and motor control logic, with an added enclosure that houses an extra battery, a VMEbus DSP board (based on the TI TMS320C30 running at 30 MHz), an 8-bit memory mapped VMEbus frame grabber, a 6811 microcontroller for servicing low-speed peripherals, a voice-synthesizer, and an LCD display. All computation is done on board.

Visual System

The visual system processes a 64 x 48 image every 66 milliseconds and generates a large number of "percepts" from it (figure 4). Most of these are related to navigation, although some are devoted to person detection or sanity checking of the image.

The central pipeline in figure 3 ("smoothing" ... "compress map") computes-depth information. The major representation used is a *radial depth map*—that

open-left?	open-region?	person-direction
open-right?	blind?	wall-ahead?
blocked?	light-floor?	wall-far-ahead?
left-turn?	dark-floor?	vanishing-point
right-turn?	person-ahead?	farthest-direction

Figure 4. Partial list of percepts generated by the visual system.

is, a map from direction to distance, similar to the output of a sonar ring. Computing depth is a notoriously difficult problem. As previously discussed, Polly simplified the problem using knowledge of the pre-existing structure of its environment. The fact that obstacles rest on the ground, and satisfy certain technical constraints on their geometry (the "ground-plane constraint"), allows Polly to use the image-plane height of the lowest pixel of an object as a measure of its distance. The fact that the floor has little or no texture (the "background-texture constraint") allows it to perform figure and ground segmentation using an edge detector. The conjunction means that a radial depth map can be computed, modulo monotone deformations, by finding the image plane height of the lowest textured pixel in each image column (see figure 5).

The visual system then compresses the depth map into three values, *left-distance*, *right-distance*, and *center-distance*, which gives the closest distance on the left side of the image, right side, and the center third, respectively. Other values are then derived from these. For example, *open-left?* and *open-right?* are true when the corresponding distance is over a threshold. *Left-turn?* and *right-turn?* are true when the depth map is open on the correct side and the robot is aligned with the corridor. The depth map is also used as input to a simple heuristic wall detector. If all column heights are approximately equal in a wide range of the depth map, the system assumes there is a wall directly ahead.

The visual system also computes the vanishing point of the corridor for use in steering. Bellutta, Collini, Verri, and Torre (1989) describe a system that extracts vanishing points by running an edge finder, extracting straight line segments, and performing two-dimensional clustering on the pairwise intersections of the edge segments. Polly uses a simplified algorithm based on domain constraints such as knowledge of the location of the horizon and the knowledge that the corridor edges are the predominant edges in the image (for details, see Horswill [1993]); however in practice, the vanishing point algorithm adds little over and above the collision avoidance algorithm.

In addition to the depth and vanishing point computations, the CVS implements a gray-level symmetry operator used to find pairs of legs in the image and a very simple motion operator to detect foot gestures.

Figure 5. Computing freespace from texture. The robot computed a depth map by first labeling every pixel as being floor-like or not (middle) and then finding the image plane height of the lowest non-floor pixel in each column. The result was a monotonic measure of depth for each column (right).

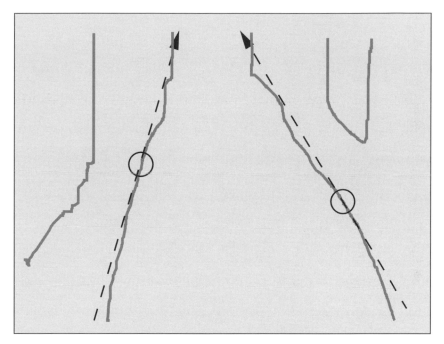

Figure 6. The vanishing point computation. Edge fragments at individual pixels (shown in circles) are extended (dashed lines) and intersected with the top of the image to find the horizontal location of their intersections (arrowheads). The mean of the horizontal locations is used as the vanishing point.

Low-Level Navigation

Polly's motion is controlled by three parallel systems. The speed control system drives forward with a velocity of α(center-distance $- d_{stop}$,), where d_{stop} is the threshold distance for braking and α is a gain parameter. This means it backs

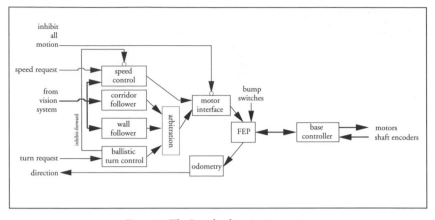

Figure 7. The Low-level navigation system.

up if it overshoots or is herded by an aggressive graduate student.

The corridor follower drives the turning motor to keep the vanishing point in the middle of the screen and keep *left-distance* and *right-distance* equal. An arbiter switches from corridor-following to wall-following mode (keeping the wall at a constant distance) when only one wall is visible. Finally, the turn unit drives the base in open-loop turns when instructed to by higher-level systems. The arbiter overrides both corridor and wall following during open-loop turns. During large turns, the speed control system also inhibits forward motion, which could otherwise lead Polly to suddenly turn into a wall. For a more detailed discussion of the low-level navigation system, see Horswill (1993). Polly's last line of defense against collision is a set of bump switches that immediately limp the motors on contact. The bump switches extend approximately 10 centimeters in front of the robot, so at 1 meter per second, they can predict a collision only 100 milliseconds in advance—an insufficient time for the robot to actively brake. Thus the most the bump switches can do is prevent Polly from continuing to push against the wall once it collides. To insure that the motors are limped as quickly as possible, they are polled not by the DSP (which runs at 15 Hz), but by the front-end processor (FEP), which runs a 1 KHz sense-action loop. The FEP is normally responsible for linking the DSP to the base, control panel, and other low-speed peripherals.

Place Recognition

Polly keeps track of its position by recognizing landmarks and larger-scale "districts," which are given to it in advance. The lab and some of its landmarks are

Kitchen		**Elevator Lobby**	
Position	(50, 40)	Position	(60, 40)
Direction	west	Direction	east
Veer	0	Veer	45
Image	...	Features	right, wall

Figure 8. Example place frames.

shown in figure 1. Since Polly patrols corridors, most landmarks are corridor intersections.

The corridors of the lab provide a great deal of natural constraint on the recognition of landmarks. The corridors form a grid, with each corridor running either north-south (NS) or east-west (EW). The robot's base provides rough rotational odometry which is good enough for the robot to distinguish which of four directions it is moving in and the type of corridor it is in.

Landmarks are represented using a topological map in which nodes are landmarks and arcs are corridors (Kuipers and Byun 1988; Mataric 1992). An unusual feature of the map is that it does not contain explicit representations of edges because the environment is known a-priori to have a grid topology. Instead, landmarks are identified by a pair of "qualitative coordinates" (figure 1) that, although not metrically accurate, preserve the ordering of places along each of the axes. Since the coordinates do not accurately encode real distances, even to within an order of magnitude, they effectively contain only topological information: landmarks are joined by a corridor if they share a coordinate value. Keeping accurate metrical information is unnecessary for this task and would have required more odometric information than was available.

Landmarks are stored in an associative memory that is exhaustively searched on every clock tick (66 milliseconds). The memory consists of a set of framelike structures, one for each possible view of each landmark (figure 8). A frame specifies the expected appearance of a particular landmark view. Frames contain a place name, qualitative coordinates, a compass direction from the viewpoint from which the landmark was viewed, and some specification of the view's appearance: either a 16 X 12 gray-scale image or a set of qualitative features (left-turn, right-turn, wall, dark-floor, light-floor). Frames can also be tagged with a turn (or "veer") to make once a landmark had been reached. This is useful when a corridor jogs to one side or the other. The representation is quite compact; The complete set of frames for the seventh floor require approximately 1 kilobyte of storage.

Matching is performed by finding the landmark view closest to the most recently recognized landmark that is consistent with the current direction of travel

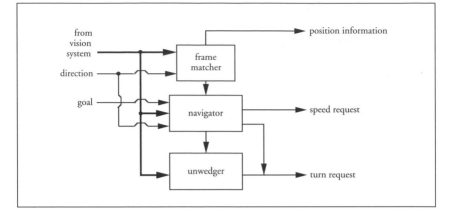

Figure 9. The high-level navigation system.

and the observed visual features. For example, a landmark east of the last recognized landmark can't be matched if the robot is presently traveling west, nor can a north-facing view of a landmark.

The system can also recognize large-scale "districts" and correct its position estimate even if it can't determine exactly where it is. For example, when the robot is driving west and sees a left turn, it can only be in the southern EW corridor, so its y coordinate has to be 10, regardless of its x position. District recognition helps the robot recover more quickly from navigational errors.

High-Level Navigation

By default, the corridor follower is in control of the robot at all times. The corridor follower always attempts to go forward and avoid obstacles until it is overridden. Higher-level navigation is implemented by a set of independent processes that are parasitic upon the corridor follower. These processes control the robot by enabling or disabling motion and by forcing open-loop turns.

The navigator chooses corridors by performing difference reduction between the (qualitative) coordinates of the goal and the last recognized location. When there is a positive error in the y coordinate, it attempts to drive south, or north for a negative error, and so on. This technique is very tolerant of place recognition errors because it effectively replans at every time-step. If a landmark is missed, the system automatically compensated when it relocalizes itself.

Because the LLN implements a potential fieldlike algorithm, it is possible for it to get stuck in local minima. The "unwedger" unit detects this condition and forces open-loop turns to get it out of stuck states. The unwedger fires whenever

```
(define-sequencer (offer-tour :import (...))
   (first  (set! global-mode 3)
           (set! inhibit-all-motion? true))
   (when done-talking?
     (new-say  "Hello. I am Polly. Would you like a tour?
                If so, wave your foot around."))

   (sleep 9)
   (then (if blocked?
             ;; The person's still there.
             (if (> hmotion 30)
               (do! give-tour)
               (begin
                 (new-say "OK. Have a nice day.")
                 (set! global-mode 1)
        (set! inhibit-all-motion? false)))
             ;; The person's gone.
             (begin    (set! global-mode 1)
                       (set! inhibit-all-motion? false)))))
```

Figure 10. Sequencer code for offering a tour.

the corridor follower is blocked for a long period of time (2 seconds). One useful feature of the unwedger is its ability to force a turn in the direction of the goal, rather than in a random direction. This helps keep it on track.

Finally, a set of action-sequencers (roughly plan executives for hand-written plans) is used to implement tour-giving and operations such as docking. The sequencers executed a language of high-level commands such as "go to place," which are implemented by sending commands to lower-level modules such as the navigator.

Performance

Polly ran at 1 meter per second. Its speed was generally limited by mechanical factors rather than by computing power. The robot ran as fast as 1.5 meters per second, but the base had difficulty accelerating past that point. Even at that speed, the robot became mechanically unstable. If, when running at 1.5 meters per second, it tried to stop in less than a meter or so, it tipped over. The update

```
(define-sequencer (give-tour :import (...))
  (first  (new-say "OK. Please stand to one side.")
          (if (= last-y 40)
              (begin  (set! tour-end-x 80)
                      (set! tour-end-y 10))
              (begin  (set! tour-end-x last-x)
                      (set! tour-end-y last-y))))
  (when (not blocked?)
    (new-say "Thank you. Please follow me.")
    (set! inhibit-all-motion? false)
    (set! global-mode 2))
  (wait frame-strobe?)
  (wait (at-place? tour-end-x tour-end-y))
  (sleep 1.0)
  (then
    (new-say  "That's the end of the tour.
               Thank you and have a nice day.")
    (set! global-mode 1)))
```

Figure 11. Sequencer code for giving a tour.

rate of the control system was limited by the I/O performance of the frame grabber, not by computing power. More recent implementations of the algorithm run at video rate.

By the standard of research robotics, Polly was very robust, having seen hundreds of hours of service in multiple environments. Polly's successors have been run in many environments, including conferences and elementary schools.

Low-Level Navigation

Most locomotion problems were obstacle detection problems. The corridor follower performed well on all floors of the MIT AI lab building on which it was tested (floors 3-9) except for the 9th floor, which has very shiny floors; there the system braked for reflections of the overhead lights in the floor.

The system's major failure modes were due to violations of the background-texture constraint. If the environment contained strong illumination gradients, surface markings on the floor, or floor surfaces with high specular reflectivity, the system hallucinated obstacles. Thus, for example, sufficiently strong shadows triggered false positives. This is less of a problem than one would expect, because office buildings typically have area light sources that generate diffuse shadows. Another example was the boundary between two distinct carpets, each with a different color, which could be mistaken for obstacles. Polly dealt with this problem using a hand-crafted recognizer tailored to the particular carpet boundaries of the lab. A better approach would be to verify the presence of the obstacle using a different algorithm or sensor with statistically independent failure modes.

Polly's other locomotion problems were mechanical. Because of the relatively small support polygon of its base and its relative top-heaviness, it was necessary to limit the maximal acceleration of the base to prevent it from tipping. That, in turn, meant limiting the maximum velocity of the robot to insure that it could stop quickly if someone walked in front of it. Thus, although Polly was capable of running at better than 1.5 meters per second, it was necessary to limit it to 1 meter per second to ensure safety.

Place Recognition

Place recognition was the weakest part of the system. While recognition by matching images is quite general, it is also fragile, and particularly sensitive to changes in the world. If a chair is in view when a landmark template is photographed, then it must continue to be in view, and in the same place and orientation forever. If the chair moves, then the landmark becomes unrecognizable until a new view is taken. Another problem was that the robot's camera was pointed at the floor, and there isn't much of interest to see there. For these reasons, place recognition was restricted to corridor intersections represented by feature frames, because they are more stable over time. The one exception was the kitchen, which was recognized using images. In ten trials, the robot recognized the kitchen eight times while going west, and ten times while going east. Westward recognition of the kitchen failed completely when the water bottles in the kitchen doorway were moved, however.

Both methods consistently missed landmarks when there was a person standing in the way. This often led the robot to miss a landmark immediately after picking up a visitor. The methods also failed if the robot was in the process of readjusting its course after driving around an obstacle or if the corridor was very wide and had a large amount of junk in it. Both conditions caused the constant-viewpoint constraint to fail. The former sometimes caused the robot to hallucinate a turn because one of the walls was invisible, although this was rare.

Recognition of districts was very reliable, although it could sometimes become confused if the robot was driven in a cluttered open space rather than a corridor.

High-Level Navigation

High-level navigation performance was limited by the accuracy of place recognition. In general, the system worked flawlessly unless the robot got lost. For example, Polly often ran laps (implemented by alternately giving opposite corners as goals to the navigator) for over an hour without any navigation faults. When the Polly got lost, the navigator generally overshot and turned around. If the robot got severely lost, the navigator flailed around until the place recognition system reoriented. The worst failure mode occurred when the place recognition system thought that it was east of its goal when it was actually at the western edge of the building. In this case, the navigator unit and the unwedger fought each other, making opposite course corrections. The place recognition system should probably have been modified to notice that it was lost in such situations so that the navigator would stop making course corrections until the place recognition system relocked. This has not yet been implemented, however.

Getting lost is a more serious problem for the action sequencers, since they are equivalent to plans but there is no mechanism for replanning when a plan step fails. This absence can be mitigated by using the navigator to execute individual plan steps, which amounts to shifting responsibility from plan-time to run-time.

Polly's Successors

In the last few years, we have built a number of systems based on various aspects of Polly, particularly its collision avoidance system. The Frankie, Wilt, and Gopher systems built at MIT focused on optimizing the hardware designs of the vision system. They are based on a custom-built computer, camera, and active-head system that cost less than $1,000.00 (Horswill and Yamamoto 1994). Because these systems are highly portable, they have been tested in a wide range of environments, including corporate research labs, hotels, grammar school classrooms, and even an auditorium at West Point.

The Pebbles (Lorigo 1996) and Elvis systems, also built at MIT, run on the Cheap Vision Machine, a low-cost, high-performance vision computer designed by Barnhart and Horswill. Lorigo (1996) has extended the collision avoidance system to novel environments, including outdoor environments. Thau (1997) has extended it to fuse multiple views into coherent geometric maps in real-time. I integrated elements of Polly with an implementation of the Ullman visual routine processor theory (Ullman 1984) to build a system that could search for and approach objects in specified configurations on demand (Horswill 1995). This system also ran on the Elvis hardware. At Northwestern, my colleagues and I are developing highly programmable systems that extend this work. Kluge is a robot based on the Cheap Vision Machine that combines search and navigation, and manipulation capabilities to perform relatively high-level tasks such as delivering and playing fetch. One of Northwestern's principal goals is to build a very robust place recognition system for office environments.

Conclusions

Many vision-based mobile robots have been developed in the past (see for example Kosaka and Kak 1992; Kriegman, Triendl, and Binford 1987; Crisman 1992; and Turk, Morgenthaler, Gremban, and Marra 1987). The unusual aspects of Polly were its relatively large behavioral repertoire, simple design, and principled use of special properties of its environment.

Polly's efficiency and reliability were due to a number of factors. Specialization to a task allowed the robot to compute only the information it needed. Specialization to the environment allowed the robot to substitute simple computations for more expensive ones. The use of multiple strategies in parallel reduced the likelihood of catastrophic failure (Horswill and Brooks 1988). Thus, if the vanishing point computation generated bad data, the depth-balancing strategy compensated and the distance control system prevented collisions until the vanishing point was corrected. Finally, the speed of its perception and control loop allowed it to rapidly recover from errors. This relaxed the need for perfect perception and allowed simpler perceptual and control strategies to be used.

The principled use of environmental constraints not only facilitated the design of efficient algorithms, but also helped understand and generalize them. The analysis of the collision avoidance system showed that the background-texture constraint was used to simplify figure and ground separation and nothing else. Thus the system could be ported to environments that satisfied the ground-plane constraint but not the BTC by finding replacement constraints that it did satisfy. As Lorigo (1996) has shown, this can be used to build a relatively general system by adaptively switching between specialized systems.

Specialized systems need not simply be hacks. We can learn things from their design and apply it to the design of other systems.

Polly was an existence proof that a robust system with a large behavioral repertoire could be built using simple components specialized to a task and environment. As with other AI methodologies, it remains to be seen how far this approach can be scaled. Either way, the principled analysis of task requirements and environments will surely play a critical role in any successful methodology for studying action in the world.

CHAPTER SIX

Coordination and Control of Sensing for Mobility Using Action-Oriented Perception

Robin R. Murphy

I n the reactive renaissance of the 1980s, autonomous mobile robots were constructed with one sensor per each active behavior. As a result, coordination and control of sensing for mobility was not an issue. However, the coordination and control of sensing is becoming increasingly more challenging as mobile robots are applied to more difficult tasks, with larger sets of possible behaviors and a small set of general purpose sensors. Now a designer must decide how to select sensors, design representations and algorithms, and organize and share sensing resources to accomplish demanding tasks.

This chapter presents one philosophy of sensing organization, *action-oriented perception*, and discusses how it can be applied to mobile robots, with multiple sensors performing locomotive tasks. According to action-oriented perception, all perceptual processes should be examined in terms of their *perceptual context*: the requirements of the task, the projected condition of the environment for the expected duration of the robot's activities, and the available sensing capabilities. The perceptual context can be viewed as defining the ecological niche of a situated agent. The principles of action-oriented perception have been successfully applied to a number of domains in motor control and sensor fusion for autonomous mobile robots (Arkin 1992; Arkin and Murphy 1990; Murphy and Arkin 1992). This chapter attempts to distill the experiences at the Colorado School of Mines (CSM) in applying this philosophy to one application domain, outdoor road following. The principles of action-oriented perception and the guidelines presented in this article are expected to be relevant for other forms of robotics including industrial manipulators and semi-autonomous teleoperation control systems.

In the next section, I review three current trends in the coordination and control of mobile robots and the associated constraints on the organization of sensing. These architectural paradigms serve as a framework, or "skeleton" of actions, to which sensing, the "muscle," is attached. The skeletal arrangement of the reactive and hybrid styles of architecture is compatible with action-oriented perception. Studies from cognitive psychology on the role of sensing in locomotor activities provide insights in the section on sensing organization in robotic architectures as to how the sensing "muscles" can be analyzed and arranged. Finally, I post a set of guidelines intended to aid the designer in arranging sensing for a specific task. Illustrative examples are taken from the CSM entries in the 1994 and 1995 Association for Unmanned Vehicle Systems (AUVS) International Unmanned Ground Vehicle competitions. The competition and the CSM entries are described in in the section on sensing organization from cognitive psychology. It should be emphasized that this chapter concentrates on the architectural aspect of sensing: *how sensing is interfaced with acting and other sensing demands*. Unfortunately, a discussion of the control and coordination of sensing in general is beyond the scope of a single chapter. Specific aspects, such as multisensor integration and sensing resource allocation, are not addressed. Murphy (1996) provides overview of these issues. The relative merits of different sensors for locomotion (such as laser range finders versus sonar) are also not addressed in this chapter.

Example Domain: UGV Competition

The 1994 and 1995 AUVS International Autonomous Ground Vehicle Competitions serve as motivating examples of realistic outdoor locomotion tasks. The AUVS has sponsored the competitions annually since 1993. The competition is open to teams composed of both graduate and undergraduate students and faculty. The goal of the competition is to have a small autonomous vehicle navigate around an outdoor course in the shortest amount of time. All power, sensing, and computing must be done onboard. In many regards, the competition task is comparable to the road-following demonstrations for the DARPA Autonomous Land Vehicle and Unmanned Ground Vehicle projects.

This section summarizes the competition rules, which delineate the task demands portion of the perceptual context and provides a brief overview of the CSM entries. Each entry was based on the research project for that year's MACS574 graduate course, AI Robotics and Computer Vision. The 1994 team took first place, while the 1995 entry placed fourth. Murphy (1995) and Murphy, Hoff, Blitch, Gough, Hoffman, Hawkins, Krosley, Lyon, Mali, MacMillan, and Warshawsky (1995) provide details of each entry.

Competition

The course boundaries are designated by Department of Transportation white lane lines approximately four inches wide painted on the ground and ten to twelve feet apart. The boundaries were continuous throughout the course for the 1994 competition. In 1995, the majority of the course boundaries were continuously lined; however, one portion was marked with alternating dashed lines. The dashed lines were alternating twenty foot lines with a fifteen foot separation. Obstacles (hay bales covered in plastic) were randomly placed on the course along with a sand pit and, in 1995, a ramp. In practice, the bales never extended more than three feet into the lane, although the rules do permit bales to be placed in the center and almost completely block the course. The teams did not know the metric layout of the course prior to the competition and were expected to compete under late spring weather conditions, such as heavy cloud cover or bright sun. The maximum permissible speed of any entry was five miles per hour. Approximate layouts of the courses are shown in figure 1; both courses were on the order of 800 yards long. The courses were divided into four sections, I-IV, of increasing difficulty (terrain, obstacle density). The course boundaries in 1995 were significantly fainter than in 1994 and offered little contrast with brown grass, confounding the vision processing of almost all entries.

1994 CSM Entry

The 1994 CSM entry used *Omnibot*, a fully autonomous vehicle lent to the team by Omnitech Robotics, Inc., the team's industrial sponsor. The robot is shown in figure 2a. The vehicle base is a Power Wheels battery powered children's jeep. Its maximum drive speed was 1.5 mph. All control was done onboard with a 33 MHz 486 PC using Omnitech CANAMP controllers. The sensor suite consisted of a single panning ultrasonic sensor mounted in front and a video camcorder on a mast near the center. The ultrasonic could sweep 180 degrees and had a reliable range of approximately 10 feet. The video camcorder was a standard consumer electronics model; the output was digitized by a black and white framegrabber board in the PC. All programming was done in C++ with the Lynx UNIX PC operating system.

The pedagogical objectives of the 1994 entry were for the students to become familiar with purely reactive architecture, ecological principles of action-oriented perception, and the use of multiple sensors. The details of sensing and acting will be discussed in later sections, but it is helpful to have an initial overview of the software layout. The design relied on a physical configuration of the robot where both the camera and the ultrasonic sensor were fixed in position, pointing to the right side of the robot (perpendicular to its centerline). The robot viewed only the right course boundary, and the line occupied at least one-fourth of the image area to reduce the signal-to-noise ratio.

The software was divided into two behaviors, *follow-path* and *move-ahead*, coordinated by an *innate releasing mechanism* style of sequencer (Anderson and Donath 1990). The primary behavior was the vision based *follow-path*. *follow-path* exploited the conclusions from an empirical investigation suggesting that the white line was usually represented by the brightest pixels in the image. Highlights on the grass appeared to be randomly distributed. There-

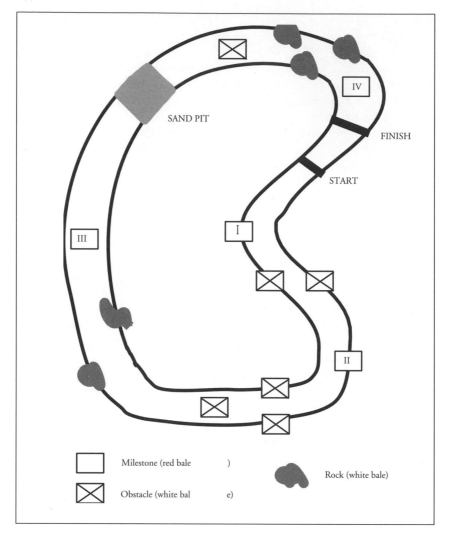

Figure 1: General layout of the competition courses.

fore, the centroid of the brightest pixels in the image generally coincided with the center of the line. Another behavior, *move-ahead*, was needed to navigate past the hay bales on the side lines which confused the vision based *follow-path* behavior. *move-ahead* was activated by the *distraction?* releaser whenever a bale was detected via sonar. *move-ahead* behaved as a no-op, using shaft encoders to maintain the course for the estimated time needed to move out of the viewing range of the bale.

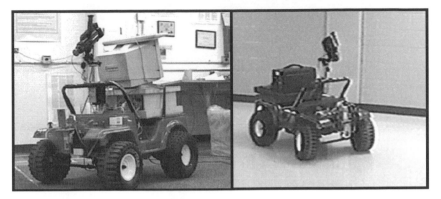

Figure 2: The CSM entries. Left: Omnibot (1994). Right: C2 (1995).

1995 CSM Entry

The 1995 CSM team used *C2* (figure 2). *C2* is the *Omnibot* base and hardware donated to CSM by Omnitech Robotics, Inc. The Lynx-based PC was replaced with a DCI Diamondback field PC using a 100 MHz Pentium Intel microprocessor operating under MS-DOS. The vision system was changed to a ImageNation black and white framegrabber board. The pedagogical objectives of the 1995 entry were for the students to become familiar with the CSM architecture, evaluate existing computer vision based road following techniques, and gain practical experience in using multiple sensing modalities.

The software layout is shown in figure 4. The heart of the entry was the reactive behavior *follow-path,* which used a simplification of the Dickmanns and Graefe vision-based road-following algorithm (Dickmanns and Graefe 1988) called "dynamic vision." Dynamic vision offers several mechanisms for achieving real-time, robust navigation. It interprets only those parts of a road image and image sequence containing features relevant to vehicle navigation. This reduces the amount of computation performed on each image, increasing the update rate of vision to the road model from which the vehicle computes steering commands. This interpretation is facilitated by subdividing the image into regions that can be processed separately in parallel. Again, this increases the update rate of the road model. Finally, the dynamic vision performs error checking by correlating road location information across several images. This prevents the vision system from identifying a shadow or an intersection as an abrupt change in the road.

Dynamic vision requires that the road construction parameters, such as road width, be known in advance in order to focus processing on the relevant regions of the image where the road is likely to be and to provide error checking. The method is particularly attractive in that is does not assume that the road boundaries are homogeneous, that is, that the road and shoulders are uniform color with no shadows, interruptions due to shadows or intersections, etc. One disadvantage

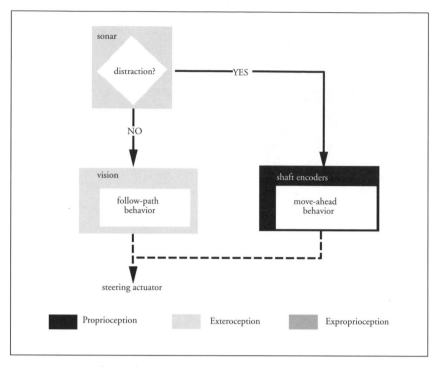

Figure 3: Behavioral control scheme for 1994 with innate releasing mechanism.

of dynamic vision for *follow-path* is its underlying assumption that the camera will always be pointed down the road so that road edges will be within specific regions of the image. This means that the vehicle can only slow down or stop in response to obstacles rather than turn the vehicle and risk not facing the road.

Dynamic vision processing starts by the acquisition of an image from the camera. Using the road model, six regions of interest representing likely locations of the road boundary (three left and three right) are selected. All operations on a region are handled by a dedicated processor in parallel. First, edges are extracted from the regions of interest. Edges that do not match the expected orientation of the road at that distance are rejected. The remaining feasible edges from each region are correlated with each other to refine the road model. Once the road model is updated, new steering commands can be generated, which then lead to new predictions for guiding processing of the next image. It should be noted that the correlation algorithm does not require that the edges in all regions agree; some regions may be affected by local phenomena such as shadows, occlusions of the boundaries by obstacles, or puddles. It is assumed that these phenomena are local and temporary, that as the vehicle moves forward according to the road model, new information without these distortions

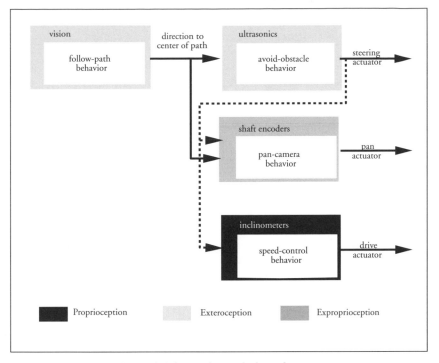

Figure 4. Behavioral control scheme for 1995.

will be acquired and the road model updated. This implies that the update rate must occur fast enough that a few updates can be missed every now and then.

The structure of the CSM implementation follows the dynamic vision hierarchy of edge detection, edge filtering, correlation, and updating of the road model. However, the implementation differed in four major ways. First, the CSM implementation has to run on a single processor and relatively slow framegrabber. Second, a Hough transform (Niblack and Petkovic 1988) is used for the edge detection and filtering since the literature did not report on the specific algorithms used by Graefe. Third, the CSM implementation made use of a panning mast to keep both road boundaries in view at all times. This was used because the CSM robot must go around obstacles rather than stop or slow down. Finally, in order to increase processing speed, there is no check for correlations between images.

Two advantages of using the more complicated algorithm in 1995 were (1) it was expected to work even in the presence of dashed lines, and (2) it could be reused for other applications, including indoor hall following. Essentially, the 1995 approach broadened the ecological niche defined in 1994 from following white lines outdoors to following paths in general. In practice, the simplifications in *follow-path* were too severe, and when combined with other

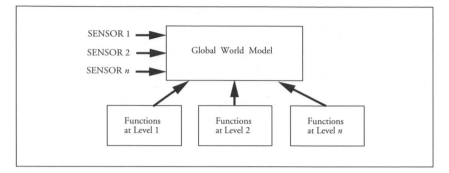

Figure 5. Sensing in the hierarchical paradigm.

hardware and software defects, *C2* placed only fourth in the competition.

The *follow-path* behavior computed the direction to the center of the path. The *avoid-obstacle* behavior was based on the vector field histogram method (Borenstein and Koren 1991) and used ultrasonics to avoid collisions while maintaining progress toward the center of the path. *pan-camera* was intended to keep both course boundaries in view. The *speed-control* behavior was not instantiated at the competition because the robot's speed was not upgraded to five mph. However, it was intended to use inclinometer, steering shaft encoder, and sonar data to slow the robot as it went up ramps, made hairpin turns, and approached obstacles.

Sensing Organization in Robotic Architecture

Robotic motor control systems can be loosely grouped into three categories: hierarchical, reactive, and hybrid reactive-deliberative. The paradigms focus on structuring motor actions. Sensing is largely a secondary issue, although recent efforts have attempted to refine the role of sensing within hybrid architecture. This section describes the architectural paradigms in terms of ramifications for sensing organization and their ability to support action-oriented perception. The overall software design of the 1994 and 1995 entries is also discussed. Both entries used a reactive style of architecture, but with major differences in the perceptual representations at the lowest levels. These entries illustrate the range and flexibility of sensing within an architectural paradigm.

Hierarchical Style

Hierarchical robotic motor control typically views a robotic action as the result of a sequence of operations within a strict hierarchy involving functional de-

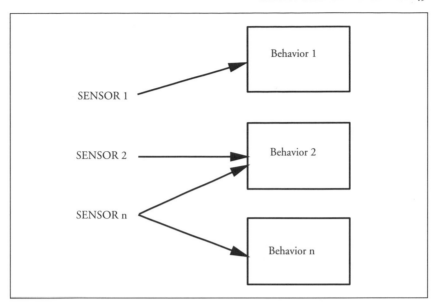

Figure 6. Sensing in the reactive paradigm.

composition, global world models, and fixed levels of sensory processing. Generally speaking, perception exists to update the global world model, and thereby only indirectly influences the robot's actions, as shown in figure 5. These systems can be characterized as following a *sense, plan, act* scenario. The real-time control system (RCS) developed at the National Institute for Standards and Technology (Albus 1990) is an example of a hierarchical system.

The hierarchical style is usually not consistent with the action-oriented perception philosophy. The global world model and rigid levels of sensory processing are independent of the task. The levels within the hierarchy may be considered to be an attempt to couple a motor function with the perceptual context, but the coupling is indirect at best.

Reactive Style

As shown in figure 6, reactive style architecture follows a *sense-act* arrangement, which lends itself to a reflexive, stimulus-response method of linking perception with actions. A behavior can be thought of as a motor action template (act) coupled to dedicated perceptual processing routines (sense). The behavioral paradigm is inherently aligned with the philosophy of action-oriented perception. Behaviors encapsulate the sensing necessary for a particular action in the expected environment.

Reflexive behaviors, popularized by Brooks (1986), exploit the computational simplicity and speed of sensing a "stimulus" which is directly channeled to the motor action "response." More recent implementations of reactive motor control systems do not strictly adhere to a stimulus-response-like relation between sensing and acting. The behavior may use an internal, behavior-specific sensing representation to interpret the sensing data. The distinction between local (internal) representations consistent with a reactive style architecture and the global representations appropriate for a hierarchical system is vague. For the purposes of this chapter, a local sensing representation is defined as being constructed and maintained by only the user behavior. A global world model is intended to be general purpose; it is constructed and maintained by processes not necessarily associated with a behavior (such as map making).

One connotation of the reactive style of architecture is that one behavior is serviced by one sensor. In systems which have more behaviors active at one time than relevant sensors, more than one behavior may take and manipulate a sensor's observations. Since each behavior is acting locally on the sensory output, the other behaviors are unaffected by the concurrent uses of the same data. It is a matter of debate whether a behavior can share or communicate its sensing representation with another behavior in the reactive paradigm. This chapter assumes that if the sensing representation being shared does not require additional processing by functions outside of the behaviors using it, then it is local and the sensing organization is still reactive.

In some situations, one behavior may need to integrate or "fuse" the output of multiple sensors in order to reduce uncertainty or provide complementary information. Murphy and Arkin (1992) describes how evidence from multiple sensors can be fused locally within a reactive behavior (the Sensor Fusion Effects Architecture, SFX), and Murphy and Mali (1996) and Arkin and MacKenzie (1994) describe methods of sequencing perceptual routines.

Another connotation of reactivity is that the perception for a behavior is from the efficacy of early behaviors which were able to rely on stimulus-response methods. A less restrictive interpretation of the reactive paradigm is that the only deciding factor is whether the representation is local or global, not the number of observations or time period for its construction.

Hybrid Style

Hierarchical and reactive motor control, while on the opposite ends of the spectrum, are not necessarily mutually exclusive. Systems such as the Autonomous Robot Architecture (Arkin 1987), Task Control Architecture (Simmons, Lin, and Fedor 1990), and 3T (Bonasso et al. 1997) make use of reactive motor behaviors that are instantiated according to a hierarchical higher cognitive process. This approach can be described as *plan, sense-act*. The hybrid paradigm is also consistent with action-oriented perception, since the reactive

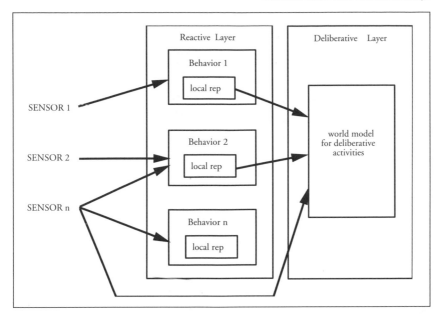

Figure 7. Sensing in the hybrid paradigm.

layer tightly couples acting and perceiving for a specific behavior or subtask.

Perception in a hybrid reactive-deliberative system takes different tracks, as shown in figure 7. The output from a sensor may be shared between the two layers: it may be directed to a motor behavior through a behavior-specific perceptual process, while at the same time cognitive functions may integrate the observations into a global model. The output of the behavior-specific representation can itself be integrated into a global model; in essence, the deliberative layer can eavesdrop on the reactive behaviors and expand on their structures to support reasoning, planning, and problem solving.

Architectural Variants Focusing on Sensing

The issue of how to organize sensing has recently been the subject of research efforts. Chen and Trivedi (1995) use a deliberative process to plan about sensing, especially how to take advantage of new information. Noreils and Chatila (1995) use a hybrid style of architecture that detects failures by monitoring the motor behavior from the deliberative layer. SFX (Murphy and Arkin 1992) attempts to keep monitoring and exception handling at the behavioral level, but will fail upwards. None of these three architectures seems to violate the basic association of local representations to behavior, and global models to deliberative layers. However, none sheds much insight into the process of constructing an adequate sensing hardware and software configuration at the behavioral level.

CSM Uses of Reactive Style

Both the 1994 and 1995 CSM teams used a reactive style architecture since the nature of the single navigation task did not require deliberation (e.g., path planning, map making, or reasoning). However, the entries differed in the use of internal perceptual representations for the behaviors. Although both entries used multiple sensors (i.e., vision, sonar, shaft encoders, inclinometers), the reactive paradigm effectively eliminated the issue of how to integrate such disparate modalities. The output of each sensor was directed to the user behavior, which handled integration locally, bypassing any global model.

The perception for the 1994 entry was composed of two reflexive behaviors. As you may recall, *follow-path* required only thresholding each image on the brightest pixels and taking the centroid in image coordinates. Each observation was independent of previous observations, and no internal representation, per se, was used. The advantage was that the behaviors were extremely fast. However, the overall system was brittle. The robot nearly veered out of bounds when a judge's shoe came into view, and then veered back in bounds following a patch of white dandelion thistles. Also, the path following and move-ahead behaviors were engineered solely for the competition; the software could not be used to guide the robot for any other path.

In contrast, both the *follow-path* and *avoid* behaviors for the 1995 entry used some type of explicit internal representation. The *follow-path* behavior used an internal model of a path. Following Dickmanns and Graefe (1988), the perceptual routine operated on six regions where the path boundaries were expected to appear in the image. The routine identified the best line in each region with a Hough transform and marked it as having either a negative slope (path turning to the left), positive slope (path turning to the right), or none (straight path). The resultant pattern was matched to a steering command via a table. Ambiguous patterns resulted in a "hold your course" action.

The *follow-path* representation was local; it was not used by the *avoid* or pan-camera behaviors. The *avoid* behavior accepted the preferred steering direction of the robot from *follow-path* in the form of a desired sector. It then used its sonar, following VFH (Borenstein and Koren 1991), to attempt to keep the robot in the free space nearest that sector. The *avoid* behavior maintained a local sector map. Similar to the occupancy grid used in VFH, *avoid* incremented or decremented belief in obstacles each sonar sensing cycle. The *pan-camera* behavior was responsible for turning the camera to the preferred steering direction (i.e., the center of the path).

Sensing Organization from Cognitive Psychology

The choice of motor control architecture can be viewed as providing a skeletal framework for the organization of sensing. However, as was seen in the previous section, the framework is very general and does not offer many insights into what types of sensors are appropriate for a task, if multiple sensors must be co-ordinated, or whether a task can be accomplished without perceptual models. This section summarizes insights from cognitive psychology about sensing and discusses how these insights can be applied to robotics. Cognitive psychology views sensing in terms of the inherent information that must be derived for a task. In particular, it offers a taxonomy of sensing information and some insight into when to use explicit perceptual representations. The performance of the 1995 CSM entry is used to illustrate the consequences of not considering the unique characteristics of each type of sensory information.

Taxonomy of Sensing Information

The choice of sensors and processing algorithms and how they are coordinated depends on the type of information that must be extracted. The traditional taxonomy of sensory information is a function of the mechanisms used for sensing; *proprioception* was derived from proprioceptors, which reported body movements relative to an internal frame of reference, while *exteroception* reflected how other receptors measured external information (Bruce and Green 1990).

Lee (1978) found this partitioning too restrictive for describing visual sensing activities and proposed an alternative taxonomy based on the content of the sensory information. In his taxonomy, *exteroception* supplies information about the layout of the environment and the position of relevant objects relative to the observer. Exteroception for the UGV competitions was used to determine the boundaries of a path visually or the remaining distance to an obstacle from sonar. *Proprioceptive* information concerns the movement of body parts relative to an internal frame of reference. Proprioception was used to determine where the robot has moved in the last few seconds. Finally, *exproprioception* reports on the position of the body, or parts of it, relative to the layout of the environment. Exproprioception was used in the 1995 entry to determine which way the camera mounted on the robot was pointing relative to the course boundaries.

This taxonomy can be helpful in integrating sensing and acting for two reasons. It directs the design process to focus on the information content of the sensors, rather than sensing modalities and algorithms. It also provides an opportunity for implicit assumptions to surface.

Figures 3 and 4 show the type of information associated with each behavior. Exteroception dominates because locomotion, especially road-following, is nominally concerned about where the road is. Certainly the *follow-path* in 1994, and the *follow-path* and *avoid* behaviors in 1995, relied on exteroceptive information. However the CSM entries also depended on proprioception and exproprioception. The experiences of the 1995 team highlight the dangers on concentrating solely on exteroception.

The need for proprioception in the UGV competitions arose in two ways. First, the entries for both years needed proprioception for dead reckoning about the robot's position. In 1994, the robot used the *move-ahead* behavior to continue straight ahead long enough to get past a visual distraction. In 1995, *avoid* relied on dead reckoning to update its local map of obstacles by estimating how far, and in what direction, the robot had traveled between readings. Second, proprioception was anticipated to be needed in the 1995 competition to sense inclines. The 1995 competition course included a wooden ramp which the robot could not go up at the maximum speed of five mph. The team created the *speed-control* behavior, which used a set of mercury switches as an inexpensive inclinometer. The *speed-control* behavior was not used in competition because the robot's maximum speed was left at 1.5 miles per hour (from 1994).

It is easy to underestimate the importance of proprioception. *Omnibot* and its successor *C2* had a very loose steering mechanism. The steer motor had shaft encoders, but because of the loose linkages, gearing, and grass conditions, the actual angle the robot turned might vary up to 15 degrees from the steer command. In the 1994 entry, this lack of accurate steering proprioception did not pose a problem. The vision processing for *follow-path* was simple and ran very fast. The robot could adjust its position relative to the course boundaries every 150 milliseconds. The high update frequency compensated for the lack of accurate proprioception about where the robot was actually steering.

However, in the 1995 entry, the algorithm was frequently unable to extract the boundaries because of lightly painted lines with low contrast to dead grass. In ambiguous cases, *follow-path* returned a "hold course" (no-op) command. Even though the more advanced vision code ran at the same update rate of 150 milliseconds, the poor visual conditions effectively dropped the update rate to closer to 500 milliseconds. If the robot had not turned sufficiently in the previous update cycle to stay on the path, it would continue to drift off course. This exacerbated the problems of detecting the course boundaries in the next vision update and accurately localizing the robot on the obstacle map.

The *pan-camera* behavior in the 1995 entry also relied on exproprioception, but was implemented as if it used exteroception. This led to an overall poor performance. For the 1995 competition, the CSM team used a variant of Dickmanns and Graefe (1988) which allowed the camera to pan. The use of pan mechanism was intended to permit the camera to follow the road while the vehicle turned to avoid obstacles. During implementation, the *pan-camera* behavior was given only exteroceptive information; it computed where to position the camera based on the camera's current relationship to the path. If the robot turned before the next image was collected, the camera position was incorrect because the robot body (and the camera) were now in a different position. Because of the substitution of exteroceptive information for the desired exproprioceptive information, the *pan-camera* behavior did not behave correctly on hairpin turns or slopes. The robot would turn in such as way as to cause the incorrectly positioned camera to interpret the right edge as the left boundary. This resulted in a steer command that drove the vehicle out of bounds.

Two Perceptual Systems

As noted earlier, many reactive systems make use of reflexive behaviors, relying on identifying a stimulus-response relationship between the robot's sensing capabilities and its task environment. Behaviors which can rely on stimulus-response like relations are generally faster than those which require intermediate processing. However, many behaviors make use of a local, internal representation. An important design issue for sensing is to discern when no model is needed. The need for explicit models is also a point of contention between traditional and ecological psychologists (Bruce and Green 1990).

The traditional—or indirect perception—camp maintains that some sort of inference or mediating process is required to extract the desired information from sensing observations. This traditional approach assumes that the mediating process will be operating over some model of the percept. The ecological, or direct perception, camp is based on the work of J. J. Gibson. Gibson argued that the necessary information can be obtained directly from the raw observations without constructing any intermediate representations or models. For instance, the robot does not have to ascertain whether an obstacle is a bush or a bale of hay in order to avoid it. In this situation, the time to contact, τ, with an object is a function of the optical flow field associated with the object (essentially, $1/$the rate that the observed object region is getting bigger). The object does not have to be identified as a bush or bale. τ is an *affordance* of the environment for detecting collisions that does not require the object to be modeled in any way. Gibson's approach is often referred to as the *ecological* approach because affordances are a function of the organism's ecological niche in its environment.

The two approaches to sensory processing are not necessarily mutually exclusive. Neisser (1989) cites physiological evidence that direct perception (i.e., the ecological model) describes the oldest form of perception, supporting stimulus-response types of behaviors. A second perceptual system evolved later to handle *recognition* types of activities, i.e., the traditional model-based view. The two perceptual systems dichotomy suggests that the robotic designer must determine whether there is an affordance in the environment that is detectable by the available sensors, or if a recognition style of perception is better suited for the task.

Unfortunately, the concept of two different perceptual systems does not resolve the question of what is direct perception versus a recognition-like model. Many animals have evolved specialized receptors; for example, frogs have been shown to respond visually to large moving objects (predators) and small moving objects (prey) (Cervantes-Perez 1995). In some regards, the use of subregions (i.e., selective perception) and directional filtering could be considered a software approximation of specialized retinal receptors. The issue of execution speed is not a good metric; our experiences suggest that recognition, or model-based, perception can be just as fast as direct perception methods. Both the 1994 and 1995 vision routines updated every 150 milliseconds. Our conclusion is that the real issue for a designer is to determine what information is in the environment and in what form it can be best exploited in a computationally efficient manner.

The 1994 and 1995 entries illustrate both sides of the dichotomy. In 1994, the *follow-path* behavior used a direct perception approach. The brightness of the white line served as the affordance for the boundary. The resulting perception was simple to program and executed rapidly. However, it was brittle. Because the robot was reacting to the centroid of the brightest pixels in the image, it did not exploit any knowledge about lines. The robot veered 30 degrees off course in one update cycle to move toward a judge's white shoes, even though the angular change in the course was much smoother.

In 1995, the *follow-path* behavior used a simple model of the road to attempt to construct a more robust algorithm. The vision processing component used what was known about the width of the course and the maximum rate of curvature to determine six subregions in the image where the boundaries should appear. It also used knowledge about the maximum rate of curvature to filter out edges which were not in the expected direction of the boundary. The best line for each subregion was identified by a Hough transform. The slope of each line in the subregions formed a mask, which served as an index function to a table of steering commands. By operating over subregions instead of the entire image and filtering out unlikely edge candidates, the model-based algorithm executed as quickly as the 1994 direct perception approach. The algorithm was demonstrated to be able to ignore distractions (such aswhite shoes or other white lines going perpendicular to the course) under test conditions. In the field, the algorithm did not perform adequately because of the errors in exproprioception compounded with the difficulty in extracting edges from faint white lines.

Conclusions: Guidelines

In this chapter, I have attempted to give some practical insight into the challenges and issues associated with sensing for mobility. The organization of sensing is left largely to the designer; motor control architectural styles provide a general framework but not much more. In order to aid the software designer, we offer a set of guidelines in keeping with the *action-oriented perception* philosophy.

• *Decompose the task(s) into functional desired activities.* This process will most likely have to be repeated several times as the designer attempts to get at the heart of the task and negotiates for sensing resources. The first iteration should result in the establishment of the style of architecture: hierarchical, reactive, or hybrid. Future iterations can then further partition the activities into behaviors or deliberative functions.

- *Establish the perceptual context.* The perceptual context of the mobile robot (the demands of the activity, the available sensors, and the inherent properties of the target environment) will influence how sensing needs can be satisfied and whether direct perception can be safely used. The 1994 entry used the competition to define a narrow ecological niche, while in 1995 the goal was to be able to follow different paths in both outdoor and indoor conditions.

- *Define the sensing needs for each activity in terms of proprioception, exteroception, and exproprioception.* This will influence the choice of sensors, requisite software processing and indicate the type of coordination necessary between sensors. The 1995 CSM entry typified the types of problems that can result from not adequately considering the task needs in terms of the information taxonomy.

- *Determine whether each sensing objective can be accomplished via direct or model-based methods.* The designer must establish whether there are any affordances that can be exploited by the sensing configuration. However, constraints on how the robot should act in response to unanticipated situations should not be overlooked. If the environment is well engineered and situations like judges wearing white shoes coming into view should not occur, then a direct perception approach such as that used by the 1994 CSM team may suffice. If a more portable behavior is desired, then a model-based approach may be more appropriate, as exemplified by the 1995 entry.

Even with these guidelines, the coordination and control of sensing is still as much of an art as is designing behaviors. Clearly the utility of any system depends on the functionality, simplicity, and reliability with which the components are arranged. I hope that as researchers pursue mechanisms for proving the correctness of configurations of behaviors, they will also find ways of constructing efficient systems which exploit the relationships between sensing and acting.

Acknowledgments

This work has been supported in part by NSF and ARPA under grant IRI-9320318 and the Colorado Space Grant Consortium. I would like to thank Dave Parish and Omnitech Robotics, Inc. for the donation of the *C2* base, the organizers of the AUVS UGV competitions, the many students who have been members of the CSM teams, and Dave Hershberger, who helped with the preparation of this chapter.

CHAPTER SEVEN

Vehicle Guidance Architecture for Combined Lane Tracking and Obstacle Avoidance

Bill Schiller, Yu-feng Du, Don Krantz, Craig Shankwitz, and Max Donath

The National Traffic Safety Board has indicated that in excess of 40 percent of heavy truck accidents are due to driver fatigue. Technologies that provide for collision avoidance and lane following can potentially "reduce urban and rural freeway accidents by a minimum of 30 and 35 percent, respectively. Accident reductions of this magnitude would eliminate approximately 71,000 accidents per year and $700 million in accidents costs" (Preston, Holstein, Otfeson, and Hoffman 1995).

Together with the Minnesota Department of Transportation, we are working on systems capable of taking over control of a semi tractor-trailer when drivers become incapacitated. Such systems must be able to provide for integrated speed and headway regulation, roadway following, obstacle (and other vehicle) detection, and collision avoidance. At the minimum, the control system should be able to drive the vehicle safely over to the shoulder (if and where it exists), slow down, and come to a complete stop.

In the first phase of the SAFETRUCK Program, we have been focusing on subsystems which prevent road departure accidents. The goal for these subsystems is to keep the vehicle in its lane. The tractor-trailer experimental testbed uses a new high accuracy, high bandwidth differential global positioning system (DGPS) capable of providing a real-time 5 Hz uninterpolated position of the tractor. This system is being integrated with an inertial measurement unit using a Kalman filter (Shankwitz, Donath, Morellas, and Johnson 1995; Bodor, Donath, Morellas, and Johnson 1996). We have experimentally shown that, after a period of continuous satellite lock, it is possible to track the motion of a truck using this DGPS and achieve dynamic accuracies with mean offset errors better than 4 centimeters (Bajikar, Gorjestani, Simpkins, and Donath 1997). Using the new steering system that we designed, we have further demonstrated that our system can take full steering control of a Navistar 9400 tractor trailer and keep it in its lane (Morellas, Morris, Alexander, and Donath 1997). This was accomplished using DGPS and a yaw rate gyro as the primary sensors. In subsequent phases, additional vehicle guidance systems will be investigated, including, for example, systems based on magnetic striping sensed by vehicle-mounted magnetometers. For safety reasons, it is important to test potentially high-risk vehicle sensing and control strategies on small vehicles before implementation on the semi tractor-trailer. The autonomous land experimental vehicle (ALX) was first designed to provide such a safe platform.

ALX was designed to solve a specific problem: navigating an a priori unknown outdoor road with paint-stripe lane boundaries, under varying sunlight conditions, while avoiding obstacles of unknown size, shape, number, and placement. The intent was to test out concepts for integrating lateral guidance and collision avoidance procedures. We do not expect that all the subsystems described in this chapter will be used on the truck testbed. However, the software and communication architecture described here represents an early prototype that allowed us to experiment with a variety of hardware configurations, software tools, system and sensor data integration issues and interprocessor communication procedures. We have developed two collision avoidance algorithms: one based on path tracking and the other on the virtual bumper. The differences between these algorithms is discussed here as well as our reasoning for selecting the virtual bumper for further development on the tractor-trailer. The vision-based guidance system described in this chapter is a precursor "placeholder" for introducing and evaluating lateral guidance within the overall system. Vision subsystems have limitations vis a vis all-weather operation and are not at present being considered for the truck. In fact, that is why we are currently using a DGPS system for the truck's lateral guidance. The ultrasonic range sensors have serious limitations as well, including bandwidth, signal to noise ratio, lateral spatial resolution, and wind effects. We expect that we will be using microwave and millimeter wave-based radar devices for obstacle detection and collision avoidance rather than ultrasonic range sensors.

We also developed a real-time simulated environment to aid in the design process. This simulated environment allowed us to debug the software and perform experiments indoors during the winter months. With the simulated environment, we were able to perform more efficient and controlled system testing as well as reduce our total system development time. The key was our emphasis on maintaining a high fidelity between the simulation and the final real-world implementation. Design could be performed on the controller using the simulation with confidence that the results of each iteration of test and redesign would apply directly to the final vehicle's performance outdoors.

During our design process, we studied many of the existing systems as reported in the literature (Du 1995; Shankwitz and Donath 1995). A survey of the literature showed that although there were many systems on robotic vehicles that were capable of detecting obstacles and avoiding collisions automatically, many of them were limited to indoor operation, relied on known environments, or suffered from inadequate lateral control (roadway following) functionality.

Figure 1. ALX.

System Design

ALX is based on an electric golf cart chassis and is equipped with control computers, actuators and feedback sensors, dead-reckoning sensors for position estimation, an array of up to sixteen ultrasonic sonar range sensors with overlapping fields for obstacle detection, and a vision system for roadway sensing.

System Device Overview

ALX (figure 1) was designed around a centralized processor system with several subsystems as shown in figure 2. Some of these subsystems are described briefly below.

Dead-Reckoning System

The dead-reckoning system consists of a set of dead-reckoning sensors, which include one two-axis fluxgate magnetometer, two clinometers, and one odometer (rear wheel encoder). The dead-reckoning system predicts the vehicle's position in Cartesian coordinate space based on position and velocity measurements from the suite of dead-reckoning sensors. Other entities sensed by ALX (roadway edges, obstacles, etc.) are then referenced using ALX's current computed position and orientation, i.e., the results of the dead-reckoning computation.

As with any other dead-reckoning systems, the certainty of ALX's coordinate accuracy decays as the traveled distance increases. This decay is due to slippage between the wheels and the road. The methods described here have demonstrated that successful operation is still possible despite the accumulated error of

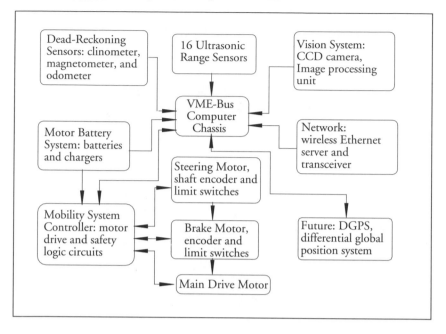

Figure 2. Hardware system layout of ALX.

such systems. A system for continuously correcting dead-reckoning results can improve the situation. DGPS is being tested for the truck and may be used later on ALX to correct position estimates.

Ultrasonic Range Sensing System

The ultrasonic range sensor system is used to detect obstacles and to allow ALX to compute and execute a trajectory around these obstacles. The information collected is accumulated and updated to construct a dynamic virtual map (see later) which provides information on the local environment to ALX. The range sensors are arranged on ALX to provide the ability to detect obstacles in front and to the side as shown in figure 3. The current design polls sensors at 10 Hz within each sensor group (1 to 16 sensors may be in each group). Only one sensor group is fired at a time. The firing sequence for the sensor groups is programmed to avoid crosstalk between sensors.

A VME-bus ultrasonic range sensor processing board was designed for ALX. The function of the sensor processing board is to coordinate the firing of the sensors and avoid potential crosstalk interference between them, measure the time-of-flight of the ranging echo pulse, and report range information to the main processor via a serial link which operates up to a maximum rate of 9600 baud.

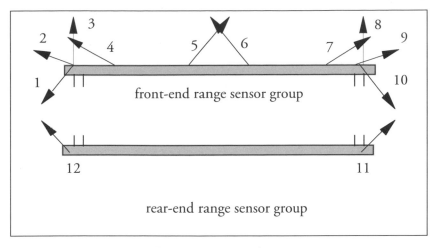

Figure 3. Range sensor layout.

Vision System

The vision system provides visual sensing of the roadway for ALX. It first determines the edges of the road from images taken by a CCD camera; then it passes this information to the microprocessor on ALX.

The image processing unit for the vision system is based on a DataCube MaxTD 200 image processor which incorporates a pipeline-processing capability (MaxVideo 200). The communication link between the image processor and the main control computer (a MVME 147SA) on ALX is established via ethernet (figure 4).

Mobility System Controller

The mobility system controller (MSC) contains the high-power control unit for the main drive motor, the steering motor, and the brake motor. The MSC uses pulse-width modulation (PWM) to control the speed of the main drive motor. The PWM frequency and duty cycle are supplied as inputs. The nominal PWM frequency is 10 KHz.

The MSC provides protection against illegal input commands (e.g., both "forward" and "reverse" commands simultaneously being active). It also provides a mechanical relay disconnect for the main drive motor when ALX is not in a safe state. The disconnect must be energized to supply power to the main drive motor. The MSC also detects the limit switch states of the brake and steering motors and cuts off drive power to the appropriate motor when a limit is reached.

Real-time Control Architecture

A real-time control architecture is used in our autonomous vehicle because of

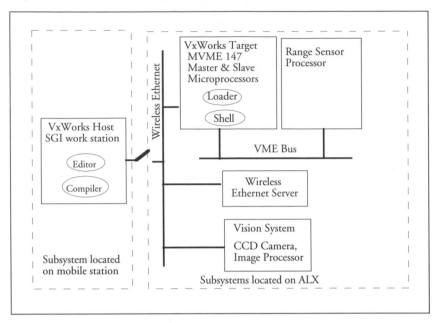

Figure 4. Cross development setup.

the ability to respond to events as they occur in the real world. For instance, consider the case when the vehicle is performing a specified task (i.e. road following) and an event occurs (i.e., obstacle is detected.) A real-time control approach allows for an immediate response to the event and for taking appropriate action (i.e. obstacle avoidance.) A traditional sequential controller on the other hand, will respond to the event based on a predefined order in which events are handled. Responding with actions in this predefined order usually will not satisfy time constraints for successful vehicle control.

By using Wind River's VxWorks real-time operating system to construct our computing architecture, we were able to develop an embedded real-time control system which differs from traditional control systems in that the sequence of actions is determined by real-time events occurring in the outside world.

Cross-Development Environment

The hardware for the ALX computer system includes one UNIX host system (an SGI workstation), two Motorola MVME 147SA microprocessors (the VxWorks target) and a DataCube image processor. The SGI workstation is used for software development and also contains an "image" of the VxWorks system, which is used to boot the MV 147SA targets. A Windata wireless Ethernet is used for intercomputer communications. The cross-development setup is illustrated in figure 4.

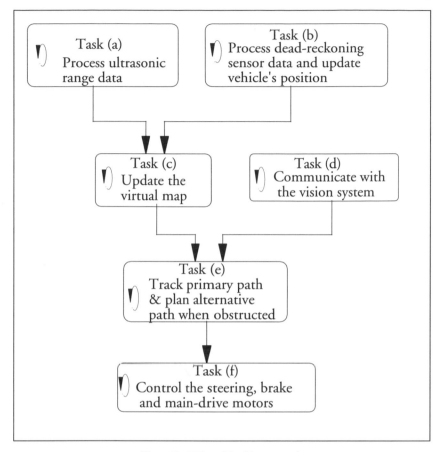

Figure 5. ALX multitasking structure.

Software development for ALX takes place on the UNIX host: an SGI worksta-tion which operates off an uninterruptable power supply (UPS) and can there-fore be taken outdoors. Program modules are written in C using the VxWorks library are compiled with a C cross-compiler and then downloaded to ALX. ALX then runs independently of the host workstation.

Multitasking Control Structure

The real-time computer control system for ALX is based on the complementary concepts of *multitasking* and intertask communications.

Multitasking provides the fundamental mechanism for control and reaction to multiple, discrete real-world events. The basic multitasking environment is provided by the VxWorks real-time kernel. Multitasking creates the appearance of many programs executing concurrently when, in fact, the kernel interleaves their execution on the basis of a scheduling algorithm. In the ALX control program, there are several tasks running "concurrently," as shown in figure 5.

The VxWorks multitasking kernel uses an interrupt-driven, priority-based task scheduler. With this preemptive priority-based scheduler, each task is assigned a priority, and the kernel ensures that the CPU will be allocated to the highest priority task that is ready to run.

The primary intertask communication mechanism used in the MVME 147SAs on ALX is message queues. Message queues allow a variable number of messages, each of variable length, to be queued in a first-in-first-out order. Any task can send and receive messages from different message queues, and multiple tasks can send and receive from the same message queue.

Visual Sensing of the Roadway

The goal of the vision system is to determine the location of the edges of the road in screen coordinates. To accomplish this goal, ALX uses a single CCD camera which is mounted six feet above the ground and is pointed forward and down. This camera provides an image that covers a field of view from five to thirty feet ahead of the cart; its average width (trapezoidal mapping) is twenty feet. The position of the lines in these images is determined using a blob analysis (or connectivity) algorithm.

Comparison of Blob Versus Edge Detection

Initially, two vision algorithms were evaluated: blob analysis and edge detection using a Laplace of Gaussian (LoG) operator. The evaluation of these approaches was based on three main criteria: (1) the ability to find the line in the image, (2) the ability to eliminate or ignore noise and reflections (large bright specular regions due to the sun), and (3) the ability to reject obstacles lying on the road that may be confused with the road edge. This evaluation was based on images consisting of white lines spray painted on green grass under varied lighting conditions. The algorithm which proved to be the most complete solution was selected.

Both blob analysis and edge detection find the edges of the road when the images are good. The advantages of blob analysis become apparent when the images have poor lighting and exhibit specular reflections due to the sun. Noise in the image is readily eliminated by discarding the blobs based on pixel count. All blobs with less than a minimum quantity of pixels are ignored. If a reflection creates a blob greater in pixel quantity than the minimum cutoff, the blob is most likely not shaped like a line. Therefore, this reflection can be eliminated based on measures of shape (i.e., perimeter^2/area). Conversely, edge detection does not handle reflections very well. Although the LoG operator provides smoothing to eliminate noise, it is still very susceptible to noise in the images. This is because reflections of the sun on the grass often exhibit sharper contrast than the edges of the road. When this occurs, the edges of the reflection are incorrectly considered to be lines.

Blob analysis is also superior to edge detection in rejecting the effects of obstacles on the road which appear in the image. The obstacles which ALX encounters are not shaped like a line. Therefore, blobs that are representative of obstacles are rejected as potential line data based on shape measures. Edge detection does not eliminate the obstacles as well as blob analysis. Edge detection finds the edges of the obstacles. If the obstacle is on or near the edge of the road, it is automatically considered part of the line and, as a result, skews the line data.

Due to the simplicity of the approach and the overall ability to eliminate noise and obstacles from the data, we decided to use blob analysis for the vision algorithm. Although many of the shortcomings of edge detection can be eliminated by adding further qualifying criteria for potential lines, we found that blob analysis provides adequate results without adding complexity to the algorithm.

However blob analysis has one major short coming. Blob analysis is only as good as the threshold selected for the image. However, it has been found experimentally that using a histogram-based thresholding method consistently reduced these images to the desired data (lines with some noise and obstacles).

Blob Analysis

Blob analysis is a relatively straightforward algorithm. It involves first thresholding the image (often first smoothed with a Gaussian filter). The resulting binary image is then evaluated for connectivity (connectivity analysis). In other words, neighboring pixels that are "on" or that have a value of one are grouped together. The resulting groups are considered blobs. The final step of blob analysis is gathering data about the blobs, for instance, their shape or size as well as their relationship to one another.

Although the blob analysis is straightforward, it is usually computationally expensive. Connectivity analysis alone has several algorithms designed to enhance computation time. Determining the relationship between blobs can also be costly.

The blob analysis algorithm discussed here addresses the problem of minimizing the computation time as our highest priority. Blobs relationships to one another are not calculated, as this is not a requirement of this system. Information about a blob being a parent or a daughter to another blob is not required for determining the edges of the road. Also the connectivity analysis algorithm has been created to allow for efficient determination of blobs. The details of the algorithms are discussed in the following subsections.

DataCube Image Processing System

The vision algorithm is executed on a MaxTD pipeline-based image processor. The MaxTD is a VMEbus-based computer that contains a Motorola MVME 167 (68040-based) processor and MaxVideo 200 pipeline hardware. This vision algorithm uses both the MV200 pipelines and the MVME 167 to perform the image processing (see figure 6 for flow chart). Similarly, the following subsections describe first the pipelines that are executed and then the processing performed by the Motorola processor.

The blob analysis requires four data pipelines. The first pipeline is used to capture the image. The results are passed to the second pipeline, which collects histogram data and also performs a thresholding operation. Next the third pipeline performs a three X three morphological filter. The third pipeline then uses the filtered image to create a run-length encoded image as well as a chain-coded image. The output of the morphological filter is displayed on the screen by a fourth pipeline with lines fit to appropriate blobs (the line fitting is discusses later). The input/output pipelines are not discussed as they are trivial implementation, but the two main processing pipelines will now be discussed.

Data Pipelines

A pipeline is a software-programmable hardware path on the MaxVideo 200 that performs a desired task (e.g., convolution) on the input data. The pixel values are sent through a pipeline as a stream of data, and the desired operation is performed on the image. All data pipelines are programmed using an application programming interface supplied by DataCube called ImageFlow.

The histogram and thresholding pipeline (Pipe2) is a multidestination pipeline. The destination surfaces are oApViewSurf and oMem4InSurf (figure 7). The DataCube system defines a surface as a block of memory which can be used by a pipeline. The oApViewSurf stores the data from the histogram operation, and the oMem4InSurf stores data from the thresholding operation. The important thing to remember about this pipeline is that having two destination surfaces saves time by performing two processes simultaneously. Of course the processes cannot have conflicting resources (both processes cannot use the same element). The oMem4InSurf stores the thresholded image and is the input for the next pipeline. Note that although the data for the histogram has been extracted by a pipeline, this data is evaluated on the MVME 167 for selecting an appropriate threshold value. In order to be time efficient, threshold selection is performed on the MVME 167 after completion of this pipeline while the next pipeline is executing. The threshold value selected by this method is then used on the following frame.

The other pipeline (Pipe3) is also a multidestination pipeline. The destination surfaces are oMem0InSurf, oMem1InSurf and oMem3InSurf and these

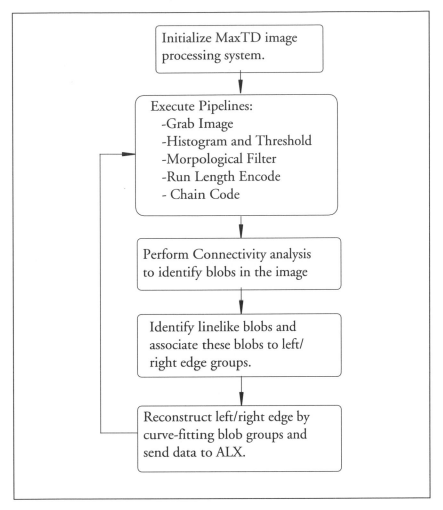

Figure 6. Simplified flow chart of blob analysis vision algorithm.

surfaces store data from the morphological filter, the chain-coding process and the run-length encoding process, respectively (figure 8).

The morphological filter is used to improve the quality of the thresholded image. This filter moves across the image looking at a three x three pattern of pixels and replaces the center pixel based on a look-up table (LUT) and the pixel patterns. This filter effectively eliminates isolated points and enhances the connectivity of blobs by filling in gaps in the connected regions. The output of the filter is passed on to the chain-coding and run-length encoding processes and is also stored in oMem0InSurf, which is used to display the results.

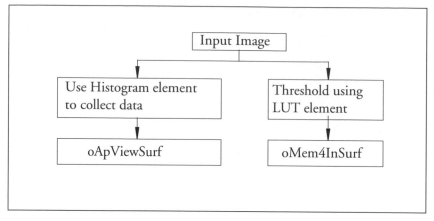

Figure 7. Threshold and histogram data pipeline.

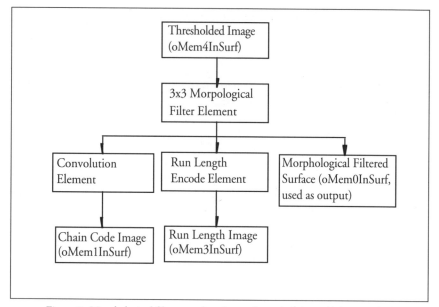

Figure 8. Morphological filter, run-length encode, and chain-code data pipeline.

The run-length encoded image contains information on the position of 0 to 1 and 1 to 0 transitions on each line of the binary image and is used in connectivity analysis (its use is discussed in the connectivity analysis subsection). The run-length encoding process takes as input the least significant bit (the bit representing on or off in the binary image) and provides an eight-bit output. For each pixel value of the output image, the seven least significant bits contain a

0	0	0	1	1	1	1	0
0	1	0	1	1	0	0	0
0	0	1	1	1	1	0	0

A. Binary Image

1	2	3	129	130	131	132	1
1	129	1	129	130	1	2	3
1	2	129	130	131	132	1	2

B. Run Length Encoded Image

Table 1. Example of a binary image(a)
and the corresponding run-length encoded image(b).

1	2	4
8	0	16
32	64	128

Table 2. 3 × 3 kernel.

count of the pixels since the last 0 to 1 or 1 to 0 transition in the binary image (counting from left to right). The most significant bit of each pixel value of the output image is the value of the binary image. Note that on the run-length encoded surface a count of 0 represents a distance of 128 times N (N being any positive integer) pixels from the last transition. Table 1 shows an example binary image and the corresponding run-length encoded image.

The chain-code image is the same as that used in Wensel and Seida (1993). Chain-code images usually contain information regarding the direction and length of a line segment of connected pixels. In this case, information about connected neighbors is only recorded. This is accomplished by convolving the image with the three x three kernel depicted in table 2.

Applying the above kernel to a binary image results in the chain-coded image having values from 0 to 255 depending on the values of the connected neighbors.

At this point the data pipelines used by this algorithm have been defined, but how are they executed? The input and output pipelines are initiated and execute continuously, but Pipe2 and Pipe3 cannot be continuous because of conflicts in resources. These pipes are programmed such that Pipe3 begins whenever Pipe2 is finished. Pipe2 begins when a dummy event is triggered. Therefore, a triggering of the dummy event causes both Pipe2 and Pipe 3 to execute in that order. To allow for efficient operation, the dummy event is triggered after the connectivity analysis has extracted the required data from the run-length encode and chain-coded images. Figure 9 shows the flow chart of the vision algorithm with the pipelines executing in this manner. This allows the pipes to execute while the MVME 167 is processing other data. Running the processes in parallel in this fashion accounts for approximately a twenty-five percent reduction in cycle time.

Connectivity Analysis

Once the run-length encoded and the chain-coded image have been generated by the Datacube MaxVideo 200, the next step is to perform the connectivity analysis. The connectivity analysis involves extracting desired information for each blob from the processed images. This process could have been implemented via Datacube pipelines; however, the programming process would have been tedious. Since the data to process has already been greatly reduced, a less involved programming task, which is also time efficient, can be implemented on the MVME 167 board. The connectivity analysis and the remainder of the program are executed on the MVME 167.

To extract the connectivity information, two data structures were created. The first is for a point in a blob, BlobPnt. The BlobPnt structure is a statically allocated array and contains information on the screen position of the blob point as well as the index (for the BlobPnt structure) of the next point in the blob. The second structure is for the segments of blobs, RawBlobs. RawBlobs is also a statically allocated structure and contains the indices of the beginning and last point of the blob in the BlobPnt structure. It also contains the pixel count for the blob.

The above structures do not store the blob number for each pixel. The blob number that each pixel is a part of is stored in that pixel's memory location in the run-length and chain-code images (the msb of the blob number is stored in the run-length image, and the lsb of the blob number is stored in the chain-code image, allowing for up to 65536 blobs). This approach quickly allows for checking as to which blob a pixel is a member of. The run-length and chain-code image are already being traversed using pointers. Checking a pixel's blob number involves incrementing the pointers and performing a logical OR. More importantly, this memory mechanism allows checking what blob a pixel belongs to without accessing the BlobPnt structure. This reduces the complexity of the connectivity analysis as well as the complexity of the BlobPnt data structure.

Data for the RawBlobs and BlobPnt structures are collected using the run-length encoded and chain-coded images (see figure 10 for the flow chart). The run-length encoded image is used to locate all the pixels that are set in the image,

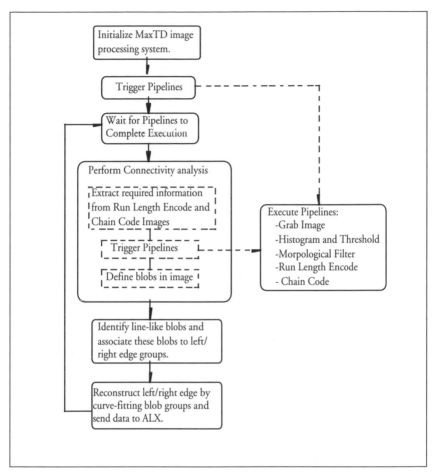

Figure 9. A modified flow chart for the vision algorithm.

and the chain-coded image is used to determine connectivity at these points. The image is traversed right-to-left and top-to-bottom by jumping only to set pixels using the information from the run-length encoding. The chain code is now used to determine If the neighbors above or to the right of the run of set pixels are also set (pixels below and to the left have not been visited yet). If there are no set neighbors, all of the points in the run are added to the BlobPnt structure and a new RawBlobs is added. The number of the new blob is now stored in the run-length and chain-coded image in the location of the set pixels for that blob. If there are set neighbors, the blob number of the RawBlobs is determined from the values at that pixel location of the run-length and chain-coded images. The run of set pixels is then added onto the appropriate RawBlobs structure and the blob

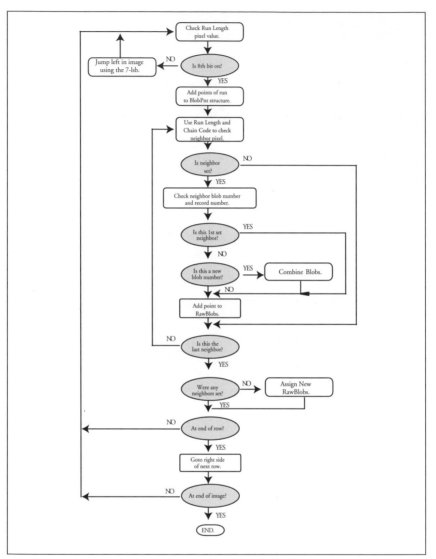

Figure 10. Connectivity analysis flow chart.

number is stored for each run point. When one run is connected to more than one RawBlob, all of the blobs are connected into one blob.

Blob Association and Curve Fitting

After the image has been completely traversed and the information is collected for the RawBlobs, the next step is to determine which blobs have acceptable line

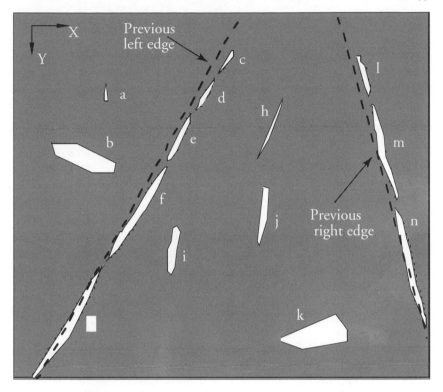

Figure 11. Binary image of the road with previous image lines.

shapes and to save these blobs. There are two criteria that are used for this evaluation: blob area and blob elongation (perimeter²/area).

Blobs that meet the minimum area and elongation requirements are saved in the GoodBlobs data structure. The data in GoodBlobs are considered as potential candidates for segments of the road lines. These blobs are associated with the left-side edge, the right-side edge, or are discarded; this process is called blob association.

To carry out this function correctly, a memory mechanism was used. The program keeps track of the road edges reconstructed in the previous image frame and then uses them as references for the current image's blob association. This mechanism is based on the assumption that the image-processing speed is reasonable in terms of ALX's operating speed so that the positions of the road edges in two consecutive images do not differ significantly. As shown in figure 11, with the previous edges (dashed lines) as references, some of the linelike blobs are associated together to represent either the left or right roadway edge; and some line-like blobs (for example, blob *"h," "j"* and *"i"*) are discarded because they cannot be associated with either the previous left edge or the previous right edge.

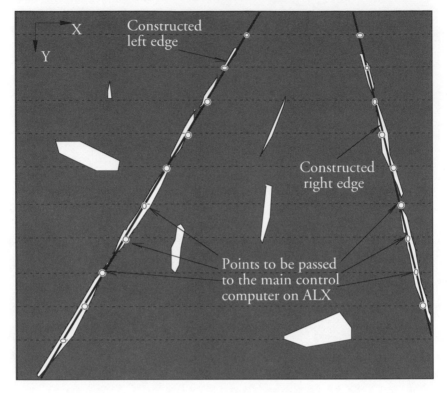

Figure 12. Reconstructed road edges.

After the blob association, a least-square curve fitting approach is used to construct a second-order polynomial curve which represents each of the two roadway edges. To represent the constructed road edges, ten evenly-spaced horizontal lines are scanned across the image, and the intersection points between the horizontal lines (dashed in figure 12) and the left (or right) edges are used to represent the left (or right) edge (figure 12). These intersection points are then transferred to the ALX computer for processing the road data. The results of the morphological filter and of the blob analysis and final road boundaries are displayed by the output pipeline on the MaxVideo 200.

Control Algorithms

We have developed and evaluated two separate control schemes for ALX: Path Tracking and the Virtual Bumper. Both approaches combine road following and obstacle avoidance for control of the vehicle and are discussed in this section.

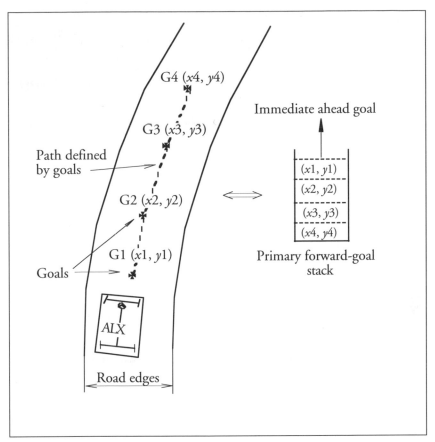

Figure 13. Illustration of the goal stack concept.

Path Tracking

The first approach we developed is Path Tracking. In this method we use the re-constructed road edges and a goal-generation scheme to form a path defined by goal points. At the same time a virtual map of the vehicle's environment is constructed using the range sensor data. When an obstacle is detected, the virtual map is used for planning an alternate collision-free path. The vehicle follows the prescribed path using a pure-pursuit algorithm.

For the path-tracking algorithm, the path, generated from either the visual processing unit or from an alternative path-planning algorithm used when the vehicle is obstructed, is represented by a finite number of goal points on the center-line of this path. The goals are defined in world coordinates and represent the positions which the vehicle is directed to reach. The coordinates of the goals are stored in a *goal stack*. Figure 13 shows an example of a path and its corresponding goal stack. The purpose of the goal stack is to allow ALX to retrace its steps if necessary to back up and go around an obstacle.

Once the immediate-ahead goal is determined, ALX uses a heading-control method which continuously (20 Hz) calculates the heading errors and issues steering commands accordingly.

Range Sensor Processing and Obstacle Avoidance

The on-board ultrasonic range sensors are used to detect obstacles and to map ALX's local environment.

Construction of the Virtual Map

The spatial information processing algorithm of ALX is based on the concept of a *virtual map*, a representation of the local area around ALX (see figures 13 and 14). This virtual map is constructed by a two-dimensional (2D) array and each unit of this array is called a *cell*. Since ALX is currently designed to operate only on a relatively flat surface, all the range sensor data is projected on this 2D Cartesian map, and sensor information is registered into the map cells. The virtual map is designed to be a square area about twice the length of the maximum sensing range along each edge and "scrolls" along under the robot as it moves. As ALX moves along, new "uncharted" areas appear on the leading edge of the map. Traversed areas "fall off" the trailing edge of the map, and all data associated with that part of the world are forgotten. The rationale for this is the short time frame for accurate position data provided by the onboard dead reckoning system. If ALX returns to an area previously visited, the position estimates will probably have accumulated enough error to make the saved data worthless.

The purpose behind constructing the virtual map is to determine the local traversibility; therefore, the map should have accurately and clearly delineated open space and obstacles. However, the use of ultrasonic range sensors can lead to a variety of systematic errors (Brown 1985; Beckerman and Oblow 1990). By systematic errors, we mean those errors that result from deterministic yet incorrect or biased interpretations of the raw data during processing.

Because of the relatively large beamwidth of the range sensor (about 15 degrees), we observed that there are several possible interpretations of the data from a given isolated scan. When combining data from different sensing positions or angles, erroneous initial interpretations will give rise to conflicts. To resolve conflict in the interpretation of the range sensor information, various stochastic methods have been used. In these methods, for each sensor scan, the profile of probability of the cells in the sensor cone has to be recalculated, and then every cell has to be updated. This is computationally expensive.

To identify and remove systematic errors arising from the processing of sparse sensor data, we have successfully adapted a nonstochastic method based on a multivalue labeling algorithm (Beckerman and Oblow 1990), which is briefly

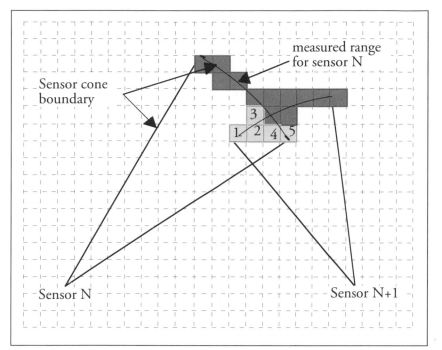

*Figure 14. Numbered cells receive conflict label
assignments from different sensor scans.*

described below. This method is much less computationally intensive compared to the stochastic methods, yet adequately handles systematic errors mainly caused by the range sensor's relatively wide beamwidth.

In order to label the cells, we process the portion of the virtual map within the boundaries of the sensor cone up to the measured range distance. Each cell inside this cone on the virtual map can be given a preliminary label as follows: if the sensor returns a "hit" and the distance from the origin of the cone to the center of the cell under consideration is greater than the sensed range, then the cell is given an assignment of "OCCUPIED." Otherwise, the cell is assigned to be "EMPTY." For example, in figure 14, for sensor $N+1$, both cell 1 and cell 2 are labeled as "OCCUPIED," while both cell 4 and cell 5 (well inside the boundary) are labeled as "EMPTY."

Besides a label, each cell is also assigned an attribute, which is the range of the sensor's actual return. This attribute is used in a relabeling algorithm to determine which sensor was closer to the detected obstacle. The closer the range sensor is to the object, the more confidence we have in the returned range value (provided that the returned range is greater than the sensor's minimum detectable range). Thus, when conflicting assignments arise, the cell label is as-

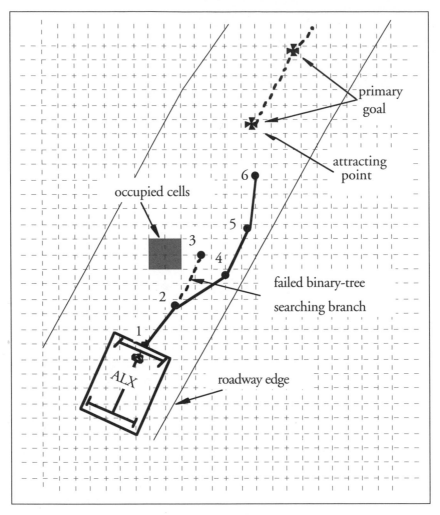

Figure 15. Searching for alternative path.

signed based on the sensor which is closest. For example, in figure 14, the cells receiving conflicting label assignments will be finally labeled in favor of sensor $N+1$.

Not all systematic errors can be treated in this way, however. Such a methodology is best suited to the case where the data are sparse, the patterns of conflict are simple, and the corrections are physically unambiguous.

In order to overcome these limitations, we have successfully developed a system that can generate topologically correct maps on line in real-time for ultrasonic range sensors. The methodology, based on self-organizing neural net-

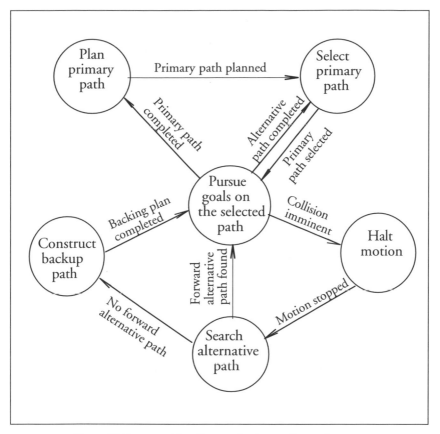

Figure 16. State transition diagram for the overall control strategy.

works, is described by Morrellas, Minners, and Donath. (1995) and Garlich-Miller and Donath (1996).

Alternative Path Generation

Alternative path generation is one of the key issues to achieve successful operations of ALX. The central issue for ALX's navigation is how quickly it can generate a safe alternative path when it detects obstacles in its original planned path. A graphic binary-tree search algorithm was developed for ALX's alternative path planning. This method uses the virtual map, which stores the occupancy of ALX's local environment, and an "attracting" location, which lies on the primary path of goal points. ALX tries to reach the attracting location while avoiding obstacles by searching for regions of "empty" cells. The algorithm tests each consecutive goal point by comparing the "footprint" of ALX with the occupancy of the virtual map under the footprint. If occupied, the algorithm tries a new goal point to the right and then to the left. If these are occupied, ALX backs up by one meter and iterates to find a new path around the occupied region (figure 15). This alternative path-planning method was successfully tested under a number of scenarios, ranging from a single obstacle near the lane boundary (requiring only slight trajectory corrections) to multiple obstacles that completely blocked the marked lane (requiring a reversal of direction to maneuver around the obstacles).

Overall Control Strategy

Figure 16 illustrates the overall control strategy of ALX's autonomous operation. ALX attempts to travel towards the top goal on the primary forward goal stack, which is constructed from the vision information, and then by using the virtual map, constructs a detouring goal stack when an obstacle is detected.

The Virtual Bumper

The second approach that we developed is based on the virtual bumper (Hennessey, Shankwitz, and Donath 1995). For the virtual bumper, we define a personal space around the vehicle (see figure 17). If an obstacle is sensed by the range sensors as having entered the personal space, a virtual force is computed and then applied to the vehicle through the actuators on board ALX. These forces (or torques) in effect "push" ALX away from the obstacle. The magnitude and direction of the virtual force is a function of the encroachment (as measured by the range sensors) into the personal space. This personal space can be characterized as a virtual bumper—a metaphor for its behavior. In effect, the deformation of the virtual bumper, or the rate of change of this deformation (based on the derivative of the range, or the closing rate) will result in an appropriately scaled force vector. The behavior of this virtual bumper can be programmed to mimic the behavior of a combination of linear and/or nonlinear springs and dampers (which can more generally be described as an impedance [Jossi and Donath 1995]). Although not described here, the shape of the virtual bumper can be modified to handle different scenarios (such as traveling through an intersection or traveling at different speeds.) The road, or more accurately the lane boundaries, also applies a virtual force to ALX that "push" it towards the center of the lane. This force can have the profile sketched in figure 17. The forces from the obstacles and the road are then summed together and transformed into speed and steering commands. The resulting control commands maneuver ALX to avoid obstacles while simultaneously attempting to keep ALX in the center of the lane.

Implementation of the virtual bumper requires three major components: generating road forces, generating obstacle forces, and transforming forces into control commands.

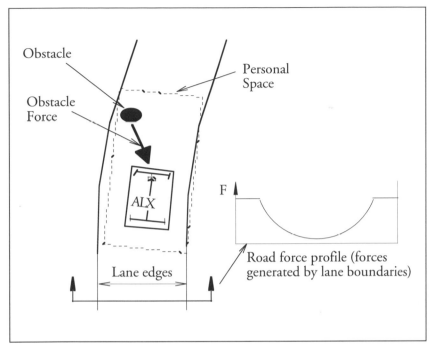

Figure 17. Virtual bumper—overview.

Road Force Generation

The virtual road force is generated as a function of the lateral offset from the center of the lane. The offset is calculated for a point ahead of the vehicle called PointAhead (the determination of this PointAhead is described below.) When there is no offset, there is no force. As the offset increases, so does the virtual force applied to the vehicle. The function used to calculate this road force is defined in equation 1. Figure 18 illustrates how this force is affected by some typical equation parameters.

$$RF = K_{rf} * \left(\frac{1}{\left(Offset_s + \frac{RW}{2} - |y| \right)^2} - \frac{1}{\left(Offset_s + \frac{RW}{2} \right)^2} \right) \tag{1}$$

where:

Krf	= Road force stiffness constant
y	= Lateral offset at PointAhead from center of road
RW	= Road width
$Offset_s$	= Sensitivity Offset, needed to prevent force from getting too large as y approaches $RW/2$

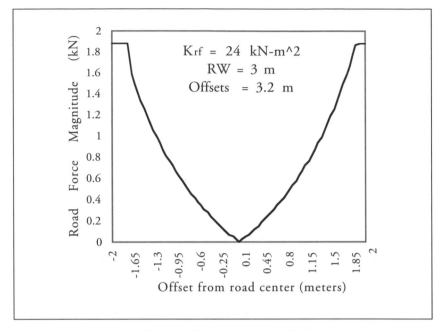

Figure 18. Virtual road force profile.

The calculated force is aligned normal to the vehicle's axis of travel and is positive if the offset is to the left of road center and negative if it is to the right of road center. Using a low flat valley at the center of the force profile (as in figure 4-5) results in the vehicle wandering from side to side about the lane center (not unlike human driving). For ALX, we intentionally implemented a discontinuity at the lane center to prevent this type of wandering.

The lateral offset could be measured from ALX's instantaneous position in the lane, but this would not take advantage of our knowledge regarding upcoming turns in the road. Instead, we define a point, called PointAhead, that is projected ahead of the vehicle by a specified distance (this distance is set by the user and is called the LookAheadDistance, equivalent to the preview typically associated with pursuit algorithms.) The lateral offset is then calculated for the position of PointAhead in the lane. This lateral offset is used for calculating the road force. Using this approach allows for improved lane tracking on curved road segments.

Obstacle Force Generation

The obstacle forces are generated by a similar method. First the range sensor readings are used to determine the location of any obstacles with respect to

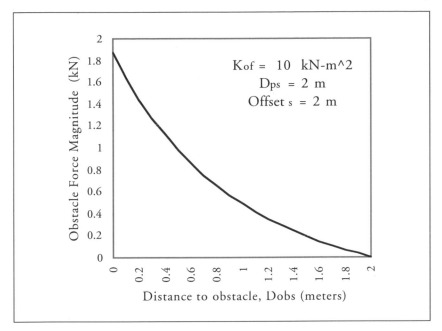

Figure 19. Virtual obstacle force profile.

ALX. If an obstacle is within ALX's personal space, the shortest distance from the obstacle to the vehicle is determined and the obstacle force is calculated from equation 2. Figure 19 shows a plot of the calculated forces for some typical equation parameters.

$$OF = K_{of} * \left(\frac{1}{\left(Offset_s + D_{obs}\right)^2} - \frac{1}{\left(Offset_s + D_{ps}\right)^2} \right) \qquad (2)$$

where:

Kof	= Obstacle force stiffness constant
Dobs	= Distance to obstacle
Dps	= Distance to edge of personal space or virtual bumper
Offset$_s$	= Sensitivity Offset, needed to prevent force from getting too large as D_{obs} approaches zero.

If the distance to the obstacle is greater than D_{ps}, the virtual force is set to zero. The obstacle force is also aligned normal to the vehicle's axis of travel and is positive if the obstacle is to the left of vehicle's center and negative if it is to the right of the vehicle's center.

Notice from the figures that the obstacle force and the road force functions have the same general form and magnitude. This is required for both types of forces to have the desired effect on the vehicle's control. For instance, if the magnitude for the obstacle force function is too low, the road force will drive the vehicle into an obstacle. Likewise, if the magnitude for the road force function is too low, an obstacle far from the vehicle can generate a force that will "push" ALX off the road. Therefore, it is important to select functions and function parameters that strike a balance between road following and obstacle avoidance behaviors.

Transforming Forces to Control Commands

Now that the virtual forces are calculated, they must be transformed into vehicle control commands. The virtual forces can have components in both the lateral and longitudinal direction. The lateral components are used for calculating lateral control commands (steering commands) and the longitudinal components are used for calculating velocity control commands. In this scenario, however, we will only calculate the lateral forces. Therefore, the virtual forces are only transformed into lateral control commands. The velocity control commands are determined using a heuristic approach based on the magnitude of the obstacle forces.

In order to better understand how we transform the lateral forces into lateral control commands, we will first discuss the lateral controller. The input to the lateral controller is the desired lateral offset, Y_{lat}. This desired lateral offset is a distance normal to the vehicle's direction of travel. The desired lateral offset and a distance which is set by the user (LookAheadDistance) are then combined to define a point, called SteerPoint, in vehicle coordinates. The angle of SteerPoint with respect to the vehicle's longitudinal axis is used to define a steering command (equation 3).

$$SC = \tan^{-1}\left(\frac{Y_{lat}}{LookAheadDistance}\right) \tag{3}$$

This steer command turns the front wheels to "aim" at the SteerPoint which is at a distance Y_{lat} to the side and a distance LookAheadDistance ahead of the vehicle.

The next step is to calculate the desired lateral offset from the virtual forces. This lateral offset is calculated using an impedance-based approach. A lateral impedance is first assigned to the vehicle. This impedance is assigned in software and can be representative of a mass, spring, and damper system. The road forces and the obstacle forces are then summed into a resultant. This resultant force is then applied to the system defined by the above specified impedance to determine the desired lateral offset (equation 4.)

$$Y_{lat} = \frac{F_{lat}}{Z_{lat}} \tag{4}$$

where

$Zlat$ = Specified lateral impedance

$Flat$ = Resultant lateral force

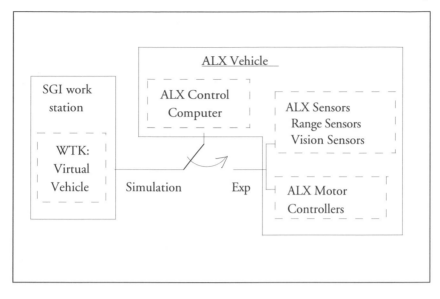

Figure 20. Real-time software is used to control the simulated vehicle as well as ALX.

The parameters of the impedance define how the lateral offset will respond to the input forces. These parameters are tuned to provide the desired system response.

The vehicle speed command is set based on the obstacle-generated virtual force. If there is no obstacle force, the speed command is SetSpeed. (SetSpeed is a parameter set by the user and must be set low enough to allow for obstacle detection by ultrasonic range sensors.) If there is a lateral obstacle force and the calculated steer command is within the physical limits of the vehicle, the speed command is set to half of the SetSpeed. The speed is reduced to allow for safer vehicle operation in the presence of obstacles.

One important scenario to note is what happens when the calculated steer command exceeds the steer limits of the vehicle. This occurs when ALX comes too close to an obstacle and would otherwise collide if it were to continue to move in the forward direction. In this case the vehicle is put into a reverse mode. While in this reverse mode, the steer command is set to be at ALX's physical steer limit in the direction opposite to that calculated in equation 3. This causes the vehicle to back up and rotate away from the obstacle. When the steer command calculated from equation 3 falls below the physical steer limits, ALX exits the reverse mode. ALX then starts forward again with a more desirable orientation with respect to the obstacle.

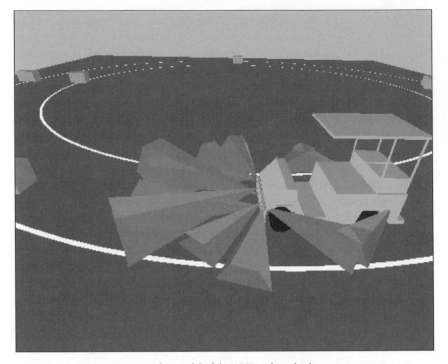

Figure 21. A graphic model of the ALX with multiple range sensors deployed. Each sensor's FOV is shown as a 3D cone.

Simulation Environment

For development of control algorithms for ALX and for our SAFETRUCK testbed, a simulation environment was developed. However, there are many drawbacks in developing control algorithms for a real-time system through simulation. For instance, it is difficult to determine how interprocess communication and the processing rate will affect the controller. Furthermore, once a control law has been determined, it must then be recoded for implementation on the real-time operating system. For these reasons, a nontraditional simulation environment was created.

For the simulation, only the vehicle, sensors, and the environment are simulated, while the vehicle control algorithms are executed in real-time on the ALX computer (figure 20). The vehicle, sensors, and environment are created in a 3D graphics package which runs on a workstation. In the 3D environment, the simulated vehicle can be moved and the simulated sensors (vision and range) calculate the appropriate measurements (see figure 21 for a 3D graphic model of ALX with range sensors). This data is passed to the ALX control computer through a network connection. The ALX computer processes this data as if it came from ALX's actual vision system and range sensors and determines the appropriate control action. The control action is then used by the ALX computer to calculate position and orientation based on a dynamic model of the vehicle. The new position and orientation is passed through another network connection back to the 3D simulation, and the vehicle is moved and the sensor data recalculated. This type of simulation approach allows for developing control laws while addressing real-time programming issues. Furthermore, the same software developed in simulation can be used on the actual vehicle.

It is important to note that the processing rate of the 3D simulation must be close to the sensor measurement output rate on the actual vehicle. This is because various control algorithms may be adversely affected by different sensor data rates. Therefore, the sensor data may have to be filtered to be used effectively. Keeping the simulation processing rate near the sensor output rate allows for developing appropriate filters for the sensor data through simulation.

Experimental Results

Both the path tracking and the virtual bumper algorithms were evaluated through a series of tests. We observed the ability of each algorithm to perform road following (no obstacles) as well as single- and multiple-obstacle environments. Emphasis was also placed on the ability of the algorithm to react to the vehicle's environment in real-time.

First the control approaches were evaluated based on road-following ability. When no obstacles are present, both algorithms guide the vehicle through similar paths and have similar computational requirements. Therefore, these experiments proved to be more a test of the vision system. The vision system guided ALX over a test track (figure 22) consisting of both straight sections and corners of varying curvatures under bright sunlight, overcast conditions, and low light intensity situations (i.e., dusk and dawn). The vision system proved to provide adequate information for both control algorithms.

Next the ability of the control algorithms to perform obstacle avoidance was tested. Through a series of tests it was determined that the path followed in a static obstacle environment is similar for both approaches. Figure 23 shows an example of ALX following a roadway which contains an obstacle near the middle of the road. The differences between these two algorithms will be described below in terms of the strengths and weaknesses that we observed through these experiments.

The path tracking algorithm has inherent strengths and weaknesses. One of its main weaknesses lies in the fact that it uses a recursive search to find an alternate path. The time to complete the search is significant and is a function of the virtual map cell size. Another weakness is that the virtual map approach does not work in a dynamic environment. Moving obstacles will corrupt the map.

Figure 22. ALX following a test "road."

On the other hand, this approach does have the ability to find a traversible path in a complicated environment. For instance, the alternate path search algorithm can find a path around a dead-end obstacle configuration. The weaknesses noted here led us to investigate the virtual bumper approach.

The virtual bumper algorithm also exhibits problems that need addressing. The primary weakness is the effect of a local minimum in the potential force field. This occurs in a cluttered environment when the forces of the obstacles balance with the forces of the road (i.e., dead end road.) This is an inherent pitfall for potential field approaches. Little work has been done here to alleviate this problem because we do not believe it will have a significant impact on our ultimate goal of vehicle control in a highway environment. For instance, if a control vehicle is on a highway with obstacle vehicles to the front and on both sides, it is in a local minimum. The effect of this local minimum is that the vehicle stays in this relative position until the traffic scenario changes and a path is available. This response is desirable, and is why we believe the mini-

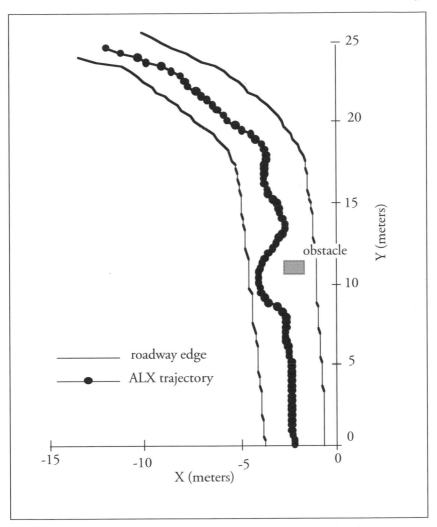

Figure 23. ALX following a roadway which contained an obstacle.

mum is not a significant issue in a structured highway driving environment.

There are also major benefits of the virtual bumper approach. First, this control approach responds quickly to obstacles in its environment without significant computational load and delays—a result of the approach in which the path is determined based on force calculations instead of a binary search. These force calculations require little computation and execution time is approximately constant regardless of obstacle configuration. Second, because of the reflexive nature of this approach, it can respond to stationary or moving obstacle environments.

These properties of the virtual bumper make it scalable to control a vehicle on a highway environment where it is absolutely necessary to handle dynamic environments in real-time.

Conclusion

ALX has proven to be a valuable tool for the preliminary investigation of vehicle sensing and control strategies at the system-integration level. To date, it has facilitated the evaluation of multitasking and intertask communication, real-time control protocols, vision-based lateral control, dead-reckoning based vehicle position estimation, watchdog safety subsystems (Krantz, Morris, Donath, and Johnson 1996) and ultrasonic sensor-based collision avoidance strategies. A simulation environment has been developed that has proven to be an effective tool for software and control algorithm development. Given the nature of ALX, vehicle dynamics are not an issue. The path tracking collision avoidance strategies used here might be appropriate for maneuvering in parking lots and in freight loading areas, but they probably have limitations that need to be addressed. They certainly would not apply to highway environments. However, the "virtual bumper" collision avoidance strategy discussed here provides a foundation for developing collision avoidance strategies for any vehicles, and in particular for large trucks, which may have to steer around obstacles rather than brake because of their high inertias. Higher risk strategies can be investigated on ALX without significant concern for human safety and vehicle damage. Other future technologies to be evaluated on ALX include millimeter wave radar (to replace the ultrasonic range sensors) for obstacle sensing and collision avoidance.

Acknowledgments

This project was partially supported by the Minnesota Department of Transportation; the Center for Advanced Manufacturing, Design, and Control (CAMDAC); the Center for Transportation Studies, and the ITS Institute at the University of Minnesota. We would like to acknowledge the assistance of our colleagues Micah Garlich-Miller and Jon Minners of the Robotics Laboratory.

PART THREE

Mobile Robot Architectures

In the context of this book, robot architectures refers to the arrangement of control software for the robot. Further we are concerned here with software architectures designed for use on physical robots from the outset, as opposed to well-known AI architectures which have been adapted to execute on robots as an experiment (e.g., GUARDIAN [Hayes-Roth 1995], and SOAR [Weismeyer 1989]). There has always been some skepticism in the community that there is any generality to be derived from using software architectures with robots, since the endeavor is usually more of an engineering art than a scientific discipline. Nonetheless, as discussed in the introduction to this book, in the past dozen years or so, some unifying principles have emerged among those research groups who are committed to seeing AI paradigms running usefully on mobile robots.

One such principle is that intelligent robots require both continuous and discrete event control capability executing in the same software framework. The control theory community has long known how to implement the former and has a large body of control laws for a variety of mechanisms (see for example, Dorf [1989]). Yet, there are few examples of control theory-based robots that can achieve high level goals such as find and fetch tasks (a notable exception is Saridis [1995]). This is due in large measure to the fact that there is a sharp rise in complexity as we move from from servo loops to interacting conjunctive goals, and for this, control theory has few solutions.

Researchers in AI robotics however, have discovered that continuous control and discrete event processing—that processing required to recognize goal-relevant state occurrences—need not co-exist in a homogeneous whole, but as two heterogeneous layers with some kind of syntactic differential between them. This is the essence of the "three layer" architecture for intelligent control of mobile robots, and Erann Gat's chapter gives a detailed account of the development of what could be considered a consensus architecture. The chapter by Firby and his colleagues describes a specific instance of using the first two layers of this architecture to integrate robot motion and vision control in one framework.

Several groups of researchers have been successful in integrating similar architectures which emphasize different aspects of discrete and continuous control due to past research roots or current endeavors. The chapter by Huosheng Hu and Michael Brady describes a layered control architecture whose development dates back to the beginnings of the AI robotics endeavors, and one which is motivated by a real-world production environment. Additionally, the control architecture realized is inherently distributed, making it particularly flexible to accommodate job shop changes. The roots of the Saphira architecture described by Kurt Konolige and Karen Myers date back to the Shakey and Flakey developments, but also makes use of the procedural reasoning system efforts of the late 1980s. This architecture includes a client-server communication system which makes it especially adaptable to different hardware platforms.

The entries to the AAAI Robot Competition have been of both the single and the multi-agent variety. Georgia Tech was one of the earliest groups to use multiple robots to accomplish competition tasks and the multi-agent robot system described by Ron Arkin and Tucker Balch was "commissioned" by ARPA for a real-world demonstration of their multi-agent control paradigm.

Finally, the chapter by Don Brutzman shows us that when moved from the laboratory to the field, robot software architectures must usually expand to encompass simulations and graphical interfaces. The underwater robot environments described in this paper represent some of the most difficult sensing and acting regimes in existence, and the paper gives us a detailed look at how flexible the architectures must be to deal with the real world.

R. Peter Bonasso

CHAPTER 8

Three-Layer Architectures

Erann Gat

In the mid-1980s Rodney Brooks touched off a firestorm of interest in autonomous robots with the introduction of the subsumption architecture[1] (Brooks 1986). At the time, the dominant view in the AI community was that a control system for an autonomous mobile robot should be decomposed into three functional elements: a sensing system, a planning system, and an execution system (Nilsson 1980). The job of the sensing system is to translate raw sensor input (usually sonar or vision data) into a world model. The job of the planner is to take the world model and a goal and generate a plan to achieve the goal. The job of the execution system is to take the plan and generate the actions it prescribes.

The sense-plan-act (SPA) approach has two significant architectural features. First, the flow of control among these components is unidirectional and linear. Information flows from sensors to world model to plan to effectors, never in the reverse direction. Second, the execution of an SPA plan is analogous to the execution of a computer program. Both are built of primitives composed using partial orderings, conditionals, and loops. *Executing* a plan or a program is easy (and therefore uninteresting) when compared with *generating* one. The information content is in the composition structure, not the primitives. The intelligence of the system (such as it is) lives in the planner or the programmer, not the execution mechanism. Research efforts through around 1985 focused almost exclusively on planning and world modeling.

By 1985 it was becoming clear that SPA had numerous shortcomings. Planning and world modeling turned out to be very hard problems, and open-loop plan execution was clearly inadequate in the face of environmental uncertainty and unpredictability. Several researchers in the mid 1980s suggested that a different execution mechanism was needed (Firby 1987, Agre 1987, Payton 1986). The SPA approach was so dominant at the time that this new work was labeled with the self-contradictory buzzword "reactive planning."

Subsumption is the best known departure from SPA. It is also popularly perceived as the most radical of its time. Ironically, in Brooks's seminal 1986 paper, Subsumption is presented as a compatible extension to SPA:

But what about each individual layer? Don't we need to decompose a single layer in the traditional manner? This is true to some extent, but the key difference is that we don't need to account for all desired perceptions and processing and generated behaviors in a single decomposition.

So in its original presentation, subsumption is, at least ostensibly, not a radical departure from SPA at all, but rather an attempt to make SPA more efficient by applying task-dependent constraints to the subsumption layers. This view is reinforced by the canonical diagram of subsumption, which shows all information flowing unidirectionally from sensors to actuators, just as in SPA.

Where subsumption departs radically from SPA is in its repudiation of plans (and indeed of symbolic representations in general [Brooks 1990]). From the details of Brooks's example it is clear that subsumption's layers are not decomposed "in the traditional manner" at all. Instead, they are simple networks of small finite state machines joined by "wires" which connect output ports to input ports. Subsumption provides only one mechanism for composing these basic building blocks to produce complex control mechanisms: the ability to override the contents of one wire with a value from another wire. This process is called suppression or inhibition, depending on whether it takes place at an input or an output port. Subsumption also advocates a development methodology consisting of layering progressively more complex task-specific control programs (called *behaviors*) on top of each other. However, subsumption provides no architectural mechanism to enforce (or even support) this methodology.

Subsumption achieved dramatic early success in the area of collision-free robot navigation. While SPA-based robots were pondering their plans, subsumption-based robots were zipping around the lab like R2D2. By the common metric that speed equals intelligence, subsumption appeared to be a major breakthrough.

Subsumption reached a pinnacle with a robot called Herbert, which was programmed to find and retrieve soda cans in an office environment (Connell 1989). (Brooks has recently launched an even more ambitious project called Cog, but as of this writing no results have been published.) While Herbert's capabilities were impressive even by today's standards, it also appeared to represent the limits of what could be achieved with subsumption. Herbert was very unreliable (there is no record of its ever having performed a complete can-retrieval task flawlessly), and no subsumption-based robot has ever matched its capabilities since.

One possible cause of subsumption's apparent "capability ceiling" is that the architecture lacks mechanisms for managing complexity. Quoting from (Hartley 1991)

> The most important problem we found with the subsumption architecture is that is it not sufficiently modular. The other problems described below are really side-effects of this one. Because upper layers interfere with the internal functions of lower-level behaviors, they cannot be designed independently and become increasingly complex. This also means that even small changes to low-level behaviors or to the vehicle itself cannot be made without redesigning the whole controller.

Figure 1. Tooth (left) and RockyIII (right).

Brooks proposes to solve this problem by reducing or even eliminating direct communications between modules. Instead behaviors would "communicate through the world." Except in a few cases ... we did not find this approach useful. The problem was that very similar states of the world could mean different things depending on the context...

Determining that one behavior is more high-level than another is sometimes completely artificial... Subsumption of low-level behaviors by high-level ones is not always appropriate. Sometimes the low level should override higher levels...

Hartley is taking issue with the most fundamental tenet of subsumption as a design methodology, saying in effect that the central (indeed the only) architectural mechanism that subsumption provides often doesn't work. (It should be noted that Hartley's critique only addresses subsumption as an engineering methodology, not as a model of human intelligence [Brooks 1991]. For such a critique, see Kirsh [1991].)

The years following the introduction of subsumption in 1986 saw a profusion of new robot control architectures, some developed more or less independently (e.g. Kaelbling 1988; Soldo 1990; Arkin 1990; Georgeff 1987; Simmons 1990) and others introduced as a direct response to subsumption's shortcomings (e.g. Rosenblatt 1989). One of the first robots to be built using one of these latter alternatives was Tooth (Gat 1994), which was completed in the summer of 1989. Tooth was a small robot (thirty centimeters by twenty centimeters) with simple sensors and limited computation (two eight-bit microcontrollers, each with about 2,000 bytes of memory), but it was a very capable robot nonetheless. Tooth was programmed to search for small objects (styrofoam coffee cups), pick them up in its gripper, and return them to a light-bulb beacon. A similar capability was demonstrated a year later on an outdoor robot, RockyIII (Miller 1991, Gat 1994) using the same control methodology. In contrast with Herbert,

Tooth and RockyIII were extremely reliable, running many dozens of trials without failing. (To be fair, Herbert was a much more ambitious robot, finding its soda cans using a structured-light vision system.)

The software that controlled Tooth and RockyIII (which I will refer to as T/R-III, not to be confused with the 3T architecture described later in this chapter) was a layered design like subsumption. However, unlike subsumption, T/R-III embraced abstraction rather than rejecting it. In subsumption, higher-level layers interface with lower level ones by *suppressing* the results of the lower-level computations and superseding their results. In T/R-III, higher-level layers interfaced with lower-level ones by *providing input or advice* to the lower-level layers (cf. Payton 1990; Agre 1990). In other words, layers in T/R-III provided layers of *computational abstraction* as well as layers of functionality.

Tooth and RockyIII were among the first autonomous robots capable of reliably performing a more complex task than simply moving from place to place, but they had one serious drawback: they were not *taskable*, that is, it was not possible to change the task they performed without rewriting their control program.

At least three different groups of researchers working more or less independently came up with very similar solutions to this problem at about the same time (Connell 1991, Gat 1991b, Bonasso 1991). All three solutions consisted of control architectures that comprised three main components: a reactive feedback control mechanism, a slow deliberative planner, and a sequencing mechanism that connected the first two components. Connell's sequencer was based on Subsumption; Bonasso used Kaelbling's REX/GAPPS system (Kaelbling 1989), and Gat's was based on Firby's reactive action packages (RAPs) system, as described in his 1989 dissertation (Firby 1989). Bonasso's group later adopted RAPs as their sequencing component, while Gat's sequencer was recently developed into a new language, ESL (Gat 1997).

Aside from the technical advances, there are two items of historical interest in Firby's dissertation. The first is that the title catch phrase was changed from "reactive planning" to "reactive execution," heralding a clean break from the SPA tradition. The second is that it contains the earliest description of the three-layer architecture that has now become the de facto standard (Firby 1989, figures 1.1 and 7.1). This original three-layer architecture was briefly implemented on JPL's Robbie robot (Wilcox 1987), but there is no record of the results. RAPs has since been used to control a number of real robots, including Uncle Bob (Elsaessar and Slack 1994), Homer (Gat and Dorais 1994), and CHIP (Firby 1996). The RAP-based three-layer architecture has come to be called 3T (Bonasso et al. 1996). Connell's subsumption-based architecture is called SSS. Gat's architecture is called ATLANTIS. It was first implemented on Robby in 1990 (Gat 1991b; 1992), and has since been implemented on a number of other robots (see the case study). The main differences between 3T and ATLANTIS are that first, that ATLANTIS used a different representation in its sequencing layer, one designed more for programming convenience than for use as a planner representation; and second, that the sequencer controlled the operation of the planner rather than vice versa. ATLANTIS also extended the then-existing RAPs action model to use continuous real-time processes rather than atomic operators, a feature which has since been incorporated back into the de facto standard.

The Role of Internal State

At this point the question naturally arises: why do so many independently designed architectures turn out to have such a similar structure? Are three components necessary and/or sufficient, or is three just an aesthetically pleasing number or a coincidence? I believe that there is a sound architectural rationale for having exactly three major components. It has to do with the role of internal state.

By way of motivation, consider the classic SPA architecture and two of its associated difficulties. First, because planning is time-consuming, the world may change during the planning process in a way that invalidates the resulting plan. (The same problem exists for world modeling.) Second, an unexpected outcome from the execution of a plan step can cause subsequent plan steps to be executed in an inappropriate context. (This problem often manifests itself as "running researcher syndrome," characterized by having to chase the robot to push the emergency stop button after it makes a wrong turn.)

To be fair, let us also consider a problem associated with Brooks-style reactive architectures. A reactive robot using ultrasonic sensors to control its motions sometimes can collide with obstacles when specular reflections produce readings that fail to indicate the obstacle's presence.

All three of these problems can be viewed as a result of the method used to manage stored internal state information (Gat 1993). Time-consuming computations like planning and world modeling generate internal state whose semantics reflect world states, whether they are past, present (in the case of world models) or future (in the case of plans). Plan execution also involves internal state, the program counter, which implicitly encodes the planner's expectations about the state of the world as execution proceeds. SPA gets into trouble when its internal state loses sync with the reality that it is intended to represent.

The reactive solution to this problem is to minimize the use of internal state as much as possible. If there is no state, then it cannot lose sync with the world, a sentiment often expressed by the slogan, "The world is its own best model." Unfortunately, extracting information from the world-as-its-own-model requires using sensors, which are unreliable and subject to occlusions. Sometimes a robot might do well to remember that there was a wall in front of it a little while ago and to conclude that the wall is probably still there despite the fact that it seems to have vanished according to the sonars. By eliminating internal state, the reactive approach avoids the problem associated with maintaining that state, but runs headlong into the problem of extracting reliable information about the world through sensors.

Three-layer architectures organize algorithms according to whether they contain no state, contain state reflecting memories about the past, or contain state reflecting predictions about the future. Stateless sensor-based algorithms inhabit the control component. Algorithms that contain memory about the past inhabit the sequencer. Algorithms that make predictions about the future inhabit the deliberator. Abstraction is used as a tool to isolate aspects of reality that can be tracked or predicted reliably and ignore aspects that cannot.

The Anatomy of the Three-layer Architecture

The three-layer architecture consists of three components: a reactive feedback control mechanism, a reactive plan-execution mechanism, and a mechanism for performing time-consuming deliberative computations. These components run as separate computational processes. This is most easily accomplished by using a multitasking or multithreaded operating system, but it can also be done by carefully coding the algorithms so they can be manually interleaved within a single computational process.

In 3T the components are called the *skill layer*, the *sequencing layer*, and the *planning layer*, respectively. In ATLANTIS these layers are called the *controller*, the *sequencer*, and the *deliberator*. The following discussion uses the ATLANTIS terminology, but as much as possible the description is generic to all incarnations of the three-layer architecture.

The Controller

The controller consists of one or more threads of computation that implement one or more feedback control loops, tightly coupling sensors to actuators. The transfer function(s) computed by the controller can be changed at run time. Usually the controller contains a library of hand-crafted transfer functions (called primitive behaviors or skills). Which ones are active at any given time is determined by an external input to the controller.

To distinguish between the code that implements a transfer function and the physical behavior produced by that transfer function when running on a robot in an environment, we shall capitalize the latter. Thus, a Behavior is a piece of code that produces a behavior when it is running. Primitive Behaviors are designed to produce simple primitive behaviors that can be composed to produce more complex task-achieving behavior (a job done, naturally, by the sequencer). Classic examples of primitive behaviors are wall-following, moving to a destination while avoiding collisions, and moving through doorways.

There are several important architectural constraints on the algorithms that go into the controller. First, computing one iteration of the transfer function should be of constant-bounded time and space complexity, and this constant should be small enough to provide enough bandwidth to afford stable closed-loop control for the desired behavior.

Second, the algorithms in the controller should *fail cognizantly*; that is, they should be designed to detect (as opposed to avoid) any failure to perform the function for which they were designed (cf. Noreils 1990). Rather than attempt to design algorithms that never fail (which is impossible on real robots), one can instead design algorithms that never fail to detect a failure. This allows other components of the system (the sequencer and deliberator) to take corrective action to recover from the failure.

Third, the use of internal state should be avoided whenever possible. An important exception to this rule is filtering algorithms, which rely on internal state, but can nevertheless be used in the controller. If internal state is used for other purposes, it should be *ephemeral*; that is, it should expire after some constant-bounded time. This way, if the semantics of the internal state do not reflect the true state of affairs in the environment, at least the time during which this error will manifest itself will be bounded.

Finally, internal state in the controller should not introduce discontinuities (in the mathematical sense) in a Behavior. In other words, a Behavior (which is a transfer function) should be a continuous function with respect to its internal state. It is the responsibility of the sequencer to manage transitions between regimes of continuous operation.

A number of special-purpose languages have been developed for programming the controller (e.g., Gat 1991a; Brooks 1989), but any language can be used as long as the architectural constraints are observed. Most of the special-purpose languages for programming the controller were developed at a time when robots could support only very small processors for which no other development tools were available. The current trend is to simply program the controller in C.

The Sequencer

The sequencer's job is to select which primitive Behavior (i.e., which transfer function) the controller should use at a given time, and to supply parameters for the Behavior. By changing primitive Behaviors at strategic moments, the robot can be coaxed into performing useful tasks. The problem, of course, is that the outcome of selecting a particular primitive in a particular situation might not be the intended one, and so a simple linear sequence of primitives is unreliable. The sequencer must be able to respond conditionally to the current situation, whatever it might be.

One approach to the problem is to enumerate all the possible states the robot can be in and precompute the correct primitive to use in each state for a particular task. Clever encoding can actually make this daunting task tractable for certain constrained domains (Schoppers 1987). However, this *universal plan* approach has two serious drawbacks. First, it is often not possible for a robot to know its current state, especially when unexpected contingencies arise. Second, this approach disregards the robot's execution history, which often contains useful information.

An alternative is to use an approach called *conditional sequencing*, which is a more complex model of plan execution motivated by human instruction following. Humans can achieve tasks based on very concise instructions in the face of a wide variety of contingencies (e.g., Agre 1990; Suchman 1987). Conditional sequencing provides a computational framework for encoding the sort of procedural knowledge contained in instructions. It differs from traditional plan execution in that the control constructs for composing primitives are not limited to the partial ordering, conditionals, and loops used to build SPA plans. Conditional sequencing systems include constructs for responding to contingencies, and managing multiple parallel interacting tasks.

It is possible to construct a conditional sequencing system in a traditional programming language like C, but because the control constructs are so much more complex than those provided by such languages, conditional sequencing is much more effectively done with a special-purpose language like RAPs (Firby 1989), PRS (Georgeff 1987), the Behavior Language (Brooks 1989), REX/GAPPS (Kaelbling 1987, Kaelbling 1989, Bonasso 1992), or ESL (Gat 1997).

There are two major approaches to the design of conditional sequencing languages. They can be complete languages in their own right with their own specialized execution semantics. RAPs and PRS take this approach. Or they can be layered on top of a syntactically extensible programming language like Lisp. This is the approach taken by the Behavior Language and ESL. Furthermore, the structure of the language can treat all possible outcomes of an action in a homogeneous fashion, or the language can be structured to recognize a privileged "nominal" result of an action and treat all other outcomes as "failures." Again, RAPs and PRS take the first approach; ESL takes the second.

Which approach one chooses depends on what one is trying to do. The RAPs/PRS approach results in a more circumscribed language that is suitable for use as a representation for an automated planner. The ESL approach, because it subsumes a traditional programming language, is more convenient to use and easier to extend, but more difficult to analyze.

The sequencer should not perform computations that take a long time relative to the rate of environmental change at the level of abstraction presented by the controller. Exactly how long a "long time" is depends on both the environment and the repertoire of Behaviors. Usually this constraint implies that the sequencer should not perform any search or temporal projection, but it might also constrain, for example, certain vision-processing algorithms from appearing in the sequencer, especially if computational resources are limited.

The Deliberator

The deliberator is the locus of time-consuming computations. Usually this means such things as planning and other exponential search-based algorithms, but as noted before, it could also include polynomial-time algorithms with large constants such as certain vision processing algorithms in the face of limited computational resources. The key architectural feature of the deliberator is that several Behavior transitions can occur between the time a deliberative algorithm is invoked and the time it produces a result. The deliberator runs as one or more separate threads of control. There are no architectural constraints on algorithms in the deliberator, which are invariably written using standard programming languages.

The deliberator can interface to the rest of the system in two different ways. It can produce plans for the sequencer to execute, or it can respond to specific queries from the sequencer. The RAPs-based 3T architecture takes the first approach (Bonasso et al. 1997). The ESL-based ATLANTIS architecture takes the second approach. This is a natural result of the fact that RAPs was designed specifically to serve as a plan representation for an automated planning system, and ESL was not. These two approaches are not mutually exclusive. RAPs does permit deliberative algorithms (called RAP-experts) to be invoked at run-time to answer specific queries, and the ATLANTIS sequencer can ask the deliberator to give it a complete plan, which it then executes. (This is being done in an application of ESL to autonomous spacecraft (Pell et al. 1996).)

Discussion

The architectural guidelines that govern the design of the three-layer architecture are not derived from fundamental theoretical considerations. Instead, they are derived from empirical observations of the properties of environments in which robots are expected to perform, and of the algorithms that have proven useful in controlling them. Robot algorithms tend to fall into three major equivalence classes: fast, mostly stateless reactive algorithms with hard real-time bounds on execution time, slow deliberative algorithms like planning, and intermediate algorithms which are fairly fast, but cannot provide hard real-time guarantees.

"Fast" and "slow" are measured with respect to the rate of change of the environment. In principle, if the rate of change of the environment is sufficiently slow (or, equivalently, if a planner were available that was sufficiently fast) the controller could contain a planner. (Note that this situation is essentially equivalent to the SPA architecture.) It is usually not possible to build planners that are fast enough to operate in this manner in realistic environments.

Case Study

To date at least half a dozen different robots have been programmed using some variation of the three-layer architecture (Gat 1992; Gat and Dorais 1994, Nourbakhsh et al.; Elsaessar and Slack 1994; Connell 1991; Firby 1996; Bonasso et al. 1997; Firby and Slack 1995. I will describe one of these here in some detail.

Alfred is a B12 robot built by Real World Interface (RWI). The B12 is a cylindrical robot, twelve inches in diameter, with a synchrodrive mobility mechanism. Encoders on the drive and steering motors provide fairly reliable odometry and dead reckoning, although the robot's heading tends to precess because of slight misalignments of its wheels. A development enclosure houses a Gespak 68000 computer and a radially symmetric ring of twelve Polaroid sonars (Biber 1980). The sonars are mounted on panels that are easily reconfigured. The sonar configuration was rotated fifteen degrees from the default factory configuration, resulting in one sonar pointing straight forward in the direction of motion and one sonar pointing directly to either side. (See figure 2.) This turned out empirically to make wall-following more reliable.

Alfred also used a Macintosh Powerbook Duo230 running Macintosh Common Lisp (MCL) mounted on top of the robot. The Duo was connect to the Gespak board through an RS-232 serial port running at 9600 baud. Alfred's controller ran on the Gespak board. The sequencer and deliberator were programmed in Lisp and ran on the Powerbook.

Alfred was programmed to compete in two events at the 1993 AAAI mobile robot contest (Nourbakhsh et al. 1993). The first event was called "escape from the office" and involved finding a route out of a room filled with furniture, and traversing across a large open area filled with cardboard boxes. The second event was called "deliver the coffee" and involved self-localization and path-planning in a maze.

Alfred placed second in the first event, and was the only robot to complete the second event. All the contest-specific code for the robot was written in three days by one person.

The following sections describe the control, sequencing, and deliberative layers on Alfred. These descriptions are faithful to the actual implementation used in the contest, and could no doubt be improved.

Control Layer

Alfred's control layer was implemented in a language for action (ALFA) (Gat 1991a), a programming language designed to enforce the control layer's architectural constraints. ALFA is a dataflow language with no looping constructs. It does, however, have state variables, making it Turing-complete. It is therefore possible to implement arbitrary algorithms in ALFA, and so ALFA's constraint en-

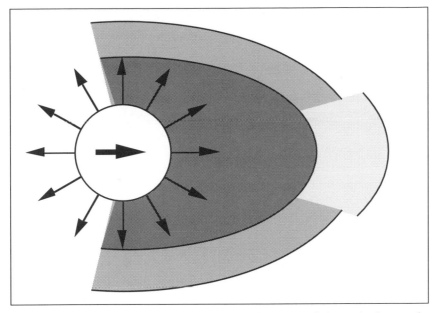

Figure 2. Schematic top-view of Alfred showing sonar directions (radial arrows) relative to the direction of motion (dark central arrow) and obstacle-detection regions.

forcement is far from perfect. The language does not make it impossible to violate the rules, just more difficult. Unfortunately, it turns out that ALFA's design also makes it more difficult to do things that should be allowed in the control layer. I no longer advocate the use of ALFA, preferring instead to use C or Lisp and a little self-discipline to enforce the architectural constraints.

Alfred's control layer had five interesting behaviors: obstacle avoidance, wall finding, wall alignment, wall following, and wandering. (It also had a number of uninteresting but nonetheless useful behaviors like turning in place.)

Obstacle avoidance was done as follows. First, the sonar data was preprocessed to indicate the presence or absence of an obstacle in each of five regions around the front of the robot. (The five rear-facing sonars were not used.) There was a near-field "hard obstacle" region close to the front of the robot (figure 2, dark shading), and three "soft obstacle" regions farther away. The hard obstacle region was divided into left and right regions that overlapped at the front sonar. The robot was able to detect collisions by monitoring its motor current. The obstacle regions were egg-shaped, extending farther from the robot toward the front than at the sides.

At the core of the controller code was the following safety algorithm that was always running:

IF there is a collision while moving forward

BACK UP slowly for a few seconds

ELSE IF there is a collision while moving backwards
STOP for a few seconds

ELSE IF there is an obstacle in one of the hard obstacle regions
STOP

ELSE IF there is an obstacle in one of the soft obstacle regions
set the current speed to SLOW

ELSE (there are no obstacles)
gradually increase forward speed up to a maximum value.

This code had the effect of slowing the robot down in the presence of obstacles and stopping the robot when it was in imminent danger of collision. By allowing any detected obstacle to immediately slow the robot down, but only a succession of clear readings to speed it back up again, the robot reliably slowed down in cluttered areas even if there was a lot of specular reflection.

The code uses internal state to remember collisions for a few seconds after they happen and to keep track of the current maximum speed. This use of internal state obeys the controller's architectural constraints in the first case because it is ephemeral, and in the second case because it is part of a filtering algorithm. The filtering algorithm might appear to violate the prohibition on state-dependent discontinuities, but this is not the case. The output of the controller is a continuous function of the state; it is the value of the state that changes discontinuously over time.

Ideally, the collision response routine would have been put in the sequencer, but because the robot detected collisions by monitoring motor current, by the time a collision was detected there was already quite a bit of mechanical stress built up in the robot's drive mechanism. Simply stopping the robot would have caused the robot's motor servo controller to attempt to maintain the motor's velocity at zero, which would have maintained this mechanical stress. Relieving the stress required backing up, and to accomplish this as quickly as possible, the response was implemented in the controller. This is a good example of how the lines between the components of the three-layer architecture can be blurred to accommodate reality.

Obstacle avoidance was done with the following algorithm:

IF there is an obstacle in the soft-left obstacle region and not in the soft-right region
    turn slowly to the right

ELSE IF there is an obstacle in the soft-right obstacle region but not in the soft-left obstacle region
    turn slowly to the left

ELSE
go straight, or turn toward a commanded heading.

This algorithm avoids obstacles only when the choice of turning direction is clearly dictated by the situation. When an obstacle is directly in front, the robot does not turn. This is because the control layer has no information on which to base the choice of a turning direction, and so this choice is deferred to the sequencer.

Wall finding was done by turning toward the sonar with the shortest range reading until the shortest reading was given by the forward sonar, and simultaneously moving forward until forced to stop by an obstacle in a hard obstacle region. This would reliably leave the robot facing the nearest object. When initiated near a wall, the robot would turn toward the wall.

Wall alignment was done by slowly turning the robot until a discontinuity caused by the onset of specular reflection was seen in the range reading returned by the forward sonar. When this procedure was begun while facing a smooth wall, the angle at which the discontinuity occurred was reproducible to better than one degree.

Wall following was done by serving the robot's heading to the reading on a side-facing sonar while moving forward. Although conceptually simple, the actual implementation is complicated by a number of factors.

The primary problem is that a straightforward negative-feedback servo loop off a side-facing sonar is unstable if the robot ever turns far enough toward the wall to cause a specular reflection on the side sonar. When this happens, it appears to the robot that the wall is suddenly very far away, and it will continue to turn toward the wall and eventually collide unless the safety module stops it. A similar effect happens when the robot passes an open door or an intersecting corridor.

There are two possible solutions to this problem. The first is to servo to the shortest reading on the side-facing sonar and its two adjacent sonars. The second is to use a model-based estimation algorithm such as a Kahlman filter to compute the distance to the wall. The solution used on Alfred was a model-based estimator (though not a Kahlman filter) that simply rejected any sonar reading that was much greater than the last known distance to the wall. The estimator also kept track of the robot's heading and odometer reading (i.e., the drive motor encoder reading) every time a valid sonar reading was taken. When an invalid sonar reading occurred, the robot turned toward the heading it was on during the last valid reading. If the robot traveled more than two meters without a valid reading, the robot stopped.

All of these primitive behaviors were implemented in less than 200 lines of ALFA code.

Sequencing Layer

Alfred's sequencing code was written in Macintosh Common Lisp version 2.0 (with one exception; see below), using a set of macros that later evolved into

ESL (Gat 1997). MCL 2.0 is a single-threaded Lisp, which made it impossible to implement multithreaded task management directly. MCL version 3 is multi-threaded, and all of the code and infrastructure described in this section have been much improved since Alfred's code was written.

The first contest event required the robot to search an office-like environment for a door, then traverse an obstacle-strewn area to a finish line. The door was opened between one and three minutes after the start of the event, and it could be in one of three different locations. The robot was told its initial orientation and the size of the room, but not its initial position nor the locations of obstacles.

Alfred determined its location by wandering randomly for one minute and keeping track of its maximum and minimum positions along the x and y axes. Wandering was done by augmenting the obstacle-avoidance code with an algorithm for choosing a turn direction when the choice was not clear from the current situation. This must be done with some care, or the robot can get stuck in an infinite loop. Alfred used the following algorithm: when an ambiguous obstacle avoidance situation was encountered, the robot would do an angular scan, turning first one way, then the other. The angle of the turn was gradually increased until the robot was able to move forward some threshold distance without triggering the scan. The scan angle was then reset to its initial value. Alfred's wander behavior was actually written in ALFA, although its use of stored internal state to produce discontinuous behavior indicates that it should be considered part of the sequencing layer.

Alfred then attempted to escape from the office by trying each of the three door locations in turn. It would move to the center of the office, point itself towards one of the doors, and turn on the follow-current-heading-with-obstacle-avoidance primitive. It would then wait until either it escaped the office (as indicated by its dead-reckoning position), in which case it headed toward the finish line, or a time limit was reached in which case it tried the next door. This task required no planning.

The second contest was much more interesting and challenging. The robot was put in a maze for which it had been given a complete and accurate map. However, the robot was given no information about its initial position or orientation. The robot's task was to search for a coffeepot hidden in the maze and deliver it to a given destination. The robot was given partial information about the location of the coffeepot. Of course, Alfred had no sensors capable of detecting a coffeepot, so it had to be told when the coffeepot was nearby, but otherwise Alfred completed the task with no cheating.

The key to Alfred's success was a combination of behaviors that allowed for reliable navigation of environments that were rich in walls, like mazes, and some creative representations. In addition to representing the a priori map of the maze in terms of open space, the robot was also given a description of the maze in terms of the wall assemblies it comprised. (With a little more time the robot could have been programmed to convert from one representation to the other automatically.)

The robot self-localized by first locating a wall. It did this by invoking the wall-finding primitive and then verifying that it had indeed found a wall rather than an obstacle by attempting to follow it for some distance (two meters). It then began to follow the wall, turning whenever the wall turned, and keeping track of the sequence of turns. Whenever it made a turn, it checked to see if the sequence of turns it had made created an unambiguous match with its a priori knowledge of the shapes of the wall assemblies in the maze. (This was done by the deliberator.) As soon as it had a match, the robot knew where it was. It then began a systematic search of the possible locations of the coffeepot, followed by a traversal to the delivery location.

Note that the algorithms in the sequencer make extensive use of internal state (keeping track of which door location is being tried, maintaining records of the robot's position, etc.) but no search or temporal projection.

Deliberative Layer

The deliberative layer did the matching of Alfred's self-localization sequence to the a priori map and also planned paths for traveling between locations. Both algorithms were simple exhaustive searches made tractable by the fact that the search space was bounded by the size of the maze.

By the standards of AI, the deliberative layer was trivial and uninteresting, which is precisely what makes the three-layer architecture nontrivial and very interesting. The use of a sequencing layer makes it possible (in fact, easy) to use trivial and uninteresting algorithms to control real robots performing complex tasks.

Conclusions

The three-layer architecture arises from the empirical observation that effective algorithms for controlling mobile robots tend to fall into three distinct categories: (1) reactive control algorithms which map sensors directly onto actuators with little or no internal state; (2) algorithms for governing routine sequences of activity which rely extensively on internal state but perform no search; and (3) time-consuming (relative to the rate of change of the environment) search-based algorithms such as planners. The three-layer architecture is based on the premise that algorithms of the first (second) type can provide effective computational abstractions for constructing interfaces to algorithms of the second (third) type. This conclusion has apparently been reached independently by at least three different groups of researchers.

Algorithms of the first and third type can be programmed in conventional programming languages. Algorithms of the second type appear to benefit significantly from specialized languages with sophisticated control constructs. Attempts to construct languages to enforce the constraints imposed on algorithms of the first type have been largely unsuccessful.

In retrospect, in the story of the three-layer architecture there may be more to be learned about research methodology than about robot control architectures. For many years, the field was bogged down in the assumption that planning was sufficient for generating intelligent behavior in situated agents. That it is not sufficient clearly does not justify the conclusion that planning is therefore unnecessary. A lot of effort has been spent defending both of these extreme positions. Some of this passion may be the result of a hidden conviction on the part of AI researchers that at the root of intelligence lies a single, simple, elegant mechanism. But if, as seems likely, there is no One True Architecture, and intelligence relies on a hodgepodge of techniques, then the three-layer architecture offers itself as a way to help organize the mess.

The three-layer architecture is by no means the last word in either architectures or organizational tools. It largely ignores, for example, issues like sensor processing, learning, and world modeling. Such algorithms may turn out to fit nicely within the existing structure, or it may prove necessary to extend the architecture to incorporate them. This promises to be fertile ground for future research.

Acknowledgments

Pete Bonasso and Robin Murphy provided extensive and thoughtful comments on an early draft of this chapter. David Miller and Marc Slack provided useful comments on an early draft of section 1. This work was conducted at the Jet Propulsion Lab, California Institute of Technology, under a contract with the National Aeronautics and Space Administration.

Note

1. There is no consensus on the definition of the word "architecture" in the context of software systems. In this chapter, I will use the word to mean a set of constraints on the structure of a software system.

CHAPTER 9

The Saphira Architecture for Autonomous Mobile Robots

Kurt Konolige and Karen Myers

M obile robots, if they are to perform useful tasks and become accepted in open environments, must be *autonomous*: capable of acquiring information and performing tasks without programmatic intervention. Autonomy has many different aspects; here we concentrate on three central ones: the ability to attend to another agent, to take advice about the environment, and to carry out assigned tasks. All three involve complex sensing and planning operations on the part of the robot, including the use of visual tracking of humans, coordination of motor controls, and planning. We show how these capabilities are integrated in the Saphira architecture, using the concepts of coordination of behavior, coherence of modeling, and communication with other agents.

What are the minimal capabilities for an autonomous mobile agent? Posed in this way, the question is obviously too broad; we would like to know more about the task and the environment: What is the agent supposed to do—will it just have a limited repertory of simple routines, or will it have to figure out how to perform complex assignments? Will there be special engineering present in the environment, or will the agent have to deal with an unmodified space? How will its performance be judged? Will it have to interact with people, and in what manner?

As has become clear from the mobile robot competitions at the last three AAAI national conferences (Simmons 1995), the more restricted the environment and task (the less open-ended), the better mobile agents can perform. Designers are adept at noticing regularities and taking advantage of them in architectural shortcuts. As a consequence, contest creators have become more subtle in how they define the rules, striving to reward mobile agents that exhibit more autonomy. To do so, they have had to grapple with refinements of the questions just posed. Although there may be no definitive answers, we can try to address these questions, like the contest creators, by articulating a scenario in which the autonomous agent must perform. To push our research, we have tried to make the environment and task as natural and open-ended as possible, given current limitations on the robot's abilities.

Fortunately, in designing a scenario, we had outside help. In March 1994 we were approached by the producers of the television science program "Scientific American Frontiers," who were interested in showcasing the future of robotics. After some discussion, we decided on a scenario in which our robot, Flakey, would be introduced to the office environment as a new employee and then asked to perform a delivery task. To realize the scenario, Flakey would need at least the following capabilities:

Attending and following: A supervisor would introduce Flakey to the office by leading it around and pointing out who inhabited each office. Flakey would have to locate and follow a human being. It would also have to know if a human was present by speech, e.g., going to an office door and inquiring if anyone was present.

Taking advice: Advice from the teacher would include map-making information such as office assignments and information about potential hazards ("There's a possible water leak in this corridor"). It would also include information about how to find people ("John usually knows where Karen is").

Tasking: Flakey would have to perform delivery tasks using its learned knowledge. The task was chosen to illustrate the different types of knowledge Flakey had: maps, information about office assignments, and general knowledge of how to locate people. There was to be no engineering of the environment to help the robot; it would have to deal with offices, corridors, and the humans that inhabited them, without any special beacons, reflective tags, or markers. Any machine-human communication would use normal human-human modalities: speech and gestures.

The scenario was made more difficult by three factors: there were only six weeks to prepare; the supervisor (Alan Alda) would have no knowledge of robotics; and the scenario was to be completed in one day, so the robot hardware and software had to be very robust. We converged on this scenario because it was the most open-ended one we could think of that could be done with current equipment and algorithms and because it would hint at what future mobile agents would be like.

We believe that any mobile agent able to perform well in an open-ended scenario such as this one must incorporate some basic features in its architecture. Abstractly, we have labeled these the three "Cs": coordination, coherence, and communication.

Coordination

A mobile agent must coordinate its activity. At the lowest level there are effector commands for moving wheels, camera heads, and so on. At the highest level there are goals to achieve—getting to a destination, and keeping track of location. There is a complex mapping between these two goals, which changes depending on the local environment. How is the mapping to be specified? We have found, as have others, (Connell 1992; Gat 1992; Firby 1987; Arkin 1990) that a layered abstraction approach makes the complexity manageable.

Coherence

A mobile agent must have a conception of its environment that is appropriate for its tasks. Our experience has been that the more open-ended the environment and the more complex the tasks, the more the agent will have to understand and represent its surroundings. In contrast to the behaviorist theory that "the environment is the model" (Connell 1990), we have found that appropriate, strong internal representations make the coordination problem easier and are indispensable for natural communication. Our internal model, the local perceptual space (LPS), uses connected layers of interpretation to support reactivity and deliberation.

Communication

A mobile agent will be of greater use if it has the ability to interact effectively with other agents. This includes the ability to understand task commands as well as integrate advice about the environment or its behavior. Communication at this level is possible only if the agent and its respondent internalize similar concepts, for example, about the spatial directions "left" and "right." We have taken only a small step here by starting to integrate natural language input and perceptual information.

In the remainder of this chapter, we describe our approach to autonomous systems. Most of the discussion is centered on a system architecture called Saphira that incorporates the results of over a decade of research in autonomous mobile robots. Our emphasis is on the integration of a variety of representations and reasoning techniques to achieve a complete mobile robotic system—one that can follow a person around, listen and respond to humans, learn a map of the environment, and navigate with dexterity and robustness.

The Robot Server

The Saphira architecture is designed to operate with a robot server, that is, a mobile robot platform that provides a set of robotic services in a standard format. The client/server paradigm abstracts Saphira from the particulars of any one robot and enables us to port it readily to different robots, as long as they adhere to the server protocol.

The robot server is responsible for controlling the low-level operation of the motors based on commands from a client, and for operating the sensors and

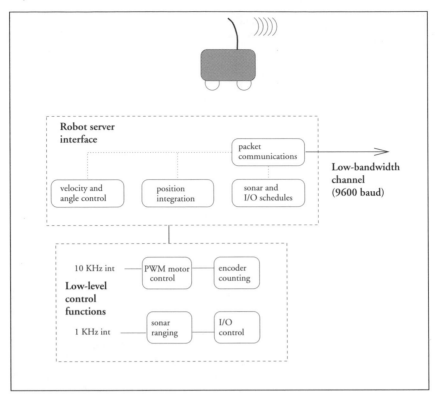

Figure 1. Server operating system.
Basic services include motor control, position integration, and sensor control.
These services are derived from motor actuators and sensors on the robot.

packaging the results to send back to the client. Figure 1 shows a typical server operating system. On a fast interrupt cycle, the server controls power to the motors and checks encoder readings. On a slower cycle, it manages the sonars and any other sensors or communications devices. On top of the low-level controls, the server implements a set of basic services.

Movement control: forward and reverse velocity, angular heading. The server has setpoints for velocity and heading and controls the motors on a fast servo cycle (10–50 milliseconds) so that the robot maintains the setpoint values. The client sends commands to change the setpoints, thus controlling robot motion at a slower cycle (100 milliseconds).

Position integration: The server updates the robot's internal dead-reckoned position using information from the encoders.

Sonar and other sensors: The server manages the sensors, controlling the timing of the sonar and any other devices such as a camera pan/tilt head. The client can send commands to change the sensor schedules.

Figure 2. Saphira servers.
Top left (a): Flakey has a camera with stereo splitter on top, and a radio ethernet link. A
Sparc station multiprocessor is shown in the open compartment.
Stereo sonars ar the small discs around the bottom. Top right (b): Khepera is a tiny robot with
a differential drive, IR sensors, and an optional gripper.
Bottom left (c) Erratic. Bottom right (d): Pioneer.
Erratic and Pioneer are two smaller versions of Flakey with the same
motion and sonar capabilities, but no vision system.

Communication: The server sends an information packet to the client every
100 milliseconds, containing information on the position, velocity, and sensor
readings. It receives commands from the client to update its setpoint variables
and sensor schedules.

By using setpoint control, the server can communicate with a client over a low-bandwidth channel with some latency because the high-speed servo control of motors and sensors is done locally. For example, we have successfully controlled a robot by running Saphira on a remote host machine with a telephone connection to the site of the robot server.

With vision sensors, the amount of information processing required means that either all visual processing must be done on board, or the bandwidth of the communication must be increased. We have used the former method, producing stereo range information for obstacle avoidance and people tracking, and packaging the results into a small number of bytes for use by the Saphira client (see the tracking people subsection).

Most current mobile robot platforms can support the kind of server operations specified in the protocol. To date, Saphira has controlled four different robotics platforms.

Flakey (SRI International). This is a custom mobile robot platform first built in 1984 (figure 2a). Its shape is an octagonal cylinder, approximately .5 meters in diameter and one meter high. Two driven wheels 7 inches in diameter are located on the sides, and passive casters balance it front-to-back. Flakey's sensors include a ring of 12 sonar sensors on the bottom, and a stereo camera pair mounted on a pan/tilt head. Flakey also has a speaker-independent continuous speech recognition system called CORONA, developed at SRI, and a standard text-to-speech program for speech output. The speech interface is integrated as part of the Saphira client, rather than the robot server.

Erratic and Pioneer (SRI International and Real World Interface, Inc.). Erratic is a smaller version of Flakey with the same differential drive and sonar sensors, but without the vision capabilities (figure 2c).[1] Pioneer (figure 2d) is a commercial version of Erratic made by Real World Interface, Inc.

Khepera (Swiss Federal Institute of Technology). Khepera is a tiny robot only 2 inches wide, with differential drive wheels and IR proximity sensors (figure 2 b). It also has add-on modules for vision and gripping.

B14/B21 (Real World Interface, Inc.). These are commercially-made research mobile robots with a full range of sensing capabilities, including sonars, IR proximity, and vision systems. Instead of differential drive, they have a synchro-drive system in which three driven wheels turn in unison (Jones and Flynn 1993).

The Saphira client, which controls the high-level operation of the robot, can exist either on the robot itself, or off board on a host computer. The smaller robots typically have room only for the server, and the Saphira client runs on an off-board–host computer. Pioneer is an interesting intermediate case: Saphira can run on a laptop on top of the robot, or on an off-board host connected by a radio modem.

On Flakey and the B14/B21 robots, all systems run on board. Flakey has a two-processor Sparc station configuration, with one processor dedicated to the server and the vision system, the other to Saphira and a speech understanding system.[2]

Both Flakey and Erratic performed well in past AAAI robot competitions in 1992–1994 (Congdon 1993; Konolige 1994, 1995).

Stereo Vision System

While sonars and IR proximity sensors are useful for obstacle avoidance and low-resolution surface extraction, passive vision produces much more data and is potentially the best sensing modality for mobile robots. On the downside, visual images must be processed to produce useful information such as range or recognized objects, and such processing is expensive and unreliable. As processing costs go down, we expect many more mobile robots will use visual sensing as their primary modality.

The vision system on Flakey consists of two cameras synchronized to capture stereo images. These images are input to a stereo algorithm using the census method (Zabih and Woodfill 1994), which results in full-frame dense stereo maps at a rate of about 2.5 Hz. Figure 3 shows a stereo pair and the results of the stereo algorithm on the pair. The stereo results are coded so that closer objects are whiter.

The stereo results can be interpreted directly as range information, and we use them in several ways, such as to identify surfaces that could be possible obstacles by matching their height against the ground plane, or to find and track personlike objects.

A short description of the tracking algorithm is given in the methodology and use subsection.

The Saphira Architecture

The Saphira architecture (Saffiotti, Ruspini, and Konolige 1993; Saffiotti, Ruspini, and Konolige 1995; Congdon 1993) is an integrated sensing and control system for robotics applications. At the center is the LPS (see figure 4), a geometric representation of space around the robot. Because different tasks demand different representations, the LPS is designed to accommodate various levels of interpretation of sensor information, as well as a priori information from sources such as maps. Currently, the major representational technologies are a grid-based representation similar to Moravec and Elfes's (1985) occupancy grids, built from the fusion of sensor readings; more analytic representations of surface features such as linear surfaces, which interpret sensor data relative to models of the environment; and semantic descriptions of the world, using structures such as corridors or doorways (artifacts). Artifacts are the product of bottom-up in-

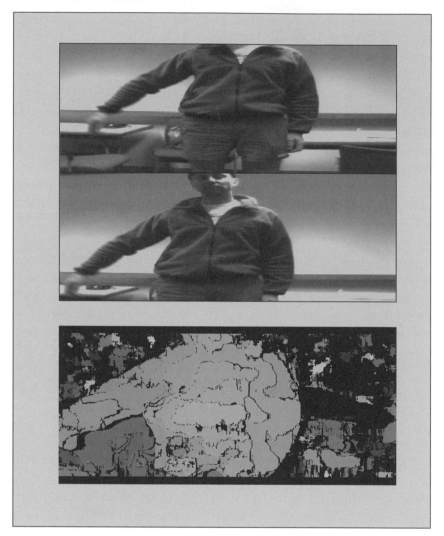

Figure 3: The top picture is a stereo pair from Flakey's cameras. The images are 640 x 240 pixels. The bottom pair shows the results of the census stereo algorithm: closer areas are coded white, farther areas black. Census algorithms are from John Woodfill of Interval Research Corporation.

terpretation of sensor readings, or top-down refinement of map information.

The LPS gives the robot an awareness of its immediate environment and is critical in the tasks of fusing sensor information, planning local movement, and integrating map information. The perceptual and control architecture make constant reference to the local perceptual space. The LPS gives the Saphira architecture its representational coherence. As we will subsequently show, the interplay of sensor readings and interpretations that takes place here lets Saphira constantly coordinate its internal notions of the world with its sensory impressions. One can think of the internal artifacts as Saphira's beliefs about the world, and most actions are planned and executed with respect to these beliefs.

In Brooks's terms (Brooks 1986), the organization is partly vertical and partly horizontal. The vertical organization occurs in both perception (left side) and action (right side). Various perceptual routines are responsible for both adding sensor information to the LPS and processing it to produce surface information that can be used by object recognition and navigation routines. On the action side, the lowest level behaviors look mostly at occupancy information to do obstacle avoidance. The basic building blocks of behaviors are fuzzy rules, which give the robot the ability to react gracefully to the environment by grading the strength of the reaction (e.g., turn left) according to the strength of the stimulus (e.g., distance of an obstacle on the right).

More complex behaviors that perform goal-directed actions are used to guide the reactive behaviors and to utilize surface information and artifacts; they may also add artifacts to the LPS as control points for motion. At this level, fuzzy rules blend possibly conflicting aims into one smooth action sequence. Finally, at the task level, complex behaviors are sequenced and their progress is monitored through events in the LPS. The horizontal organization comes about because behaviors can choose appropriate information from the LPS. Behaviors that are time-critical, such as obstacle avoidance, rely more on very simple processing of the sensors because it is available quickly. However, these routines may also make use of other information when it is available, such as prior information from the map about expected obstacles.

Behaviors

At the control level, the Saphira architecture is behavior-based: the control problem is decomposed into small units of control called basic behaviors, like obstacle avoidance or corridor following. One of the distinctive features of Saphira is that behaviors are written and combined using techniques based on fuzzy logic (see Saffiotti, Ruspini, and Konolige (1993) and Saffiotti (1996) for a more detailed presentation). Figure 5 shows the main components of behavior processing in Saphira.

Each behavior consists of an update function and a set of fuzzy rules. The purpose of the update function is to extract information from the LPS and turn it into a set of fuzzy variables appropriate for the behavior. For example, an obstacle-avoidance behavior might have the following variables, indicating where the robot's path is blocked:

front-left-blocked

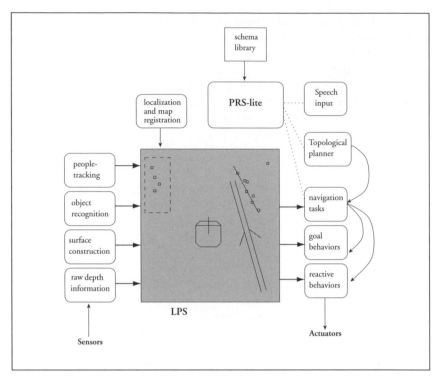

Figure 4: Saphira system architecture. Perceptual routines are on the left, action routines on the right. The vertical dimension gives an indication of the cognitive level of processing, with high-level behaviors and perceptual routines at the top. Control is coordinated by PRS-Lite, which instantiates routines for navigation, planning, execution monitoring, and perceptual coordination.

front-right-blocked
side-left-blocked
side-right-blocked

Each fuzzy variable takes a value from the interval [0,1], indicating the degree to which its condition holds. Fuzzy variables are computed using a transfer function from the state of the LPS to the variable. Suppose we consider the left front of the robot to be completely blocked if there is an obstacle 10 centimeters away, and unblocked if there is nothing within 100 centimeters. In between we would like the value of front-left-blocked to be intermediate between 0 and 1. Its transfer function looks like figure 6.

The fuzzy variables are the inputs to a set of fuzzy control rules of the form

$A \rightarrow C$,

where A is a fuzzy formula composed of fuzzy predicates and the fuzzy connectives AND, OR, and NOT, and C is a control action. For example, the rules for ob-

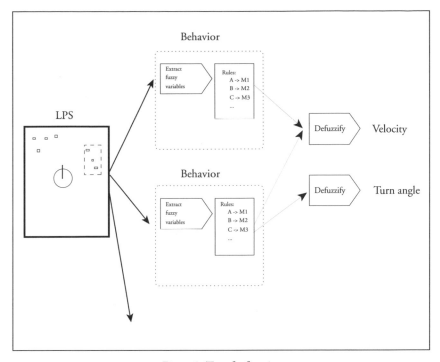

Figure 5. Transfer function.

stacle avoidance could be written as:

> front-left-blocked AND (NOT front-right-blocked AND (NOT side-right-blocked)
>   → turn right
> front-right-blocked AND (NOT front-left-blocked) AND (NOT side-left-blocked)
>   → turn left
> front-right-blocked OR front-left-blocked → slow down

Note that these rules refer to both the heading and velocity of the robot. In general, the robot may have many control channels, each with the ability to perform some motion function. Flakey and all robot servers for Saphira have at least the ability to turn to a heading and maintain a velocity; other functions include grippers or manipulators, pan or tilt heads for a camera, and so on. A behavior can affect as many of these control channels as it needs to, while leaving the others alone.

The results of a rule application is a desirability function, which states how much the behavior would like to see a particular control value. For each control channel, the results of all the behavior rules for that channel are averaged to give the final control value. The averaging includes a weighting function based on two properties: priority of a behavior and its activation context. Behaviors that

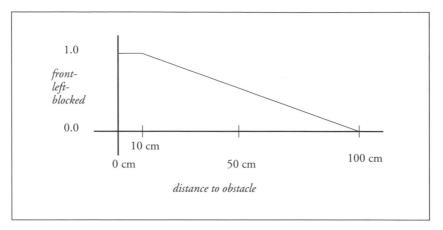

Figure 6. Fuzzy behaviors. Each behavior contains a function for calculating appropriate fuzzy variables from the LPS and a set of rules that give the desirability of possible actions. The outputs of the behaviors are combined and a control value is chosen for each control channel.

are more important are given higher priorities; for example, avoiding obstacles has a higher priority than wall-following because we don't want the robot to bump into anything. However, allowing the collision-avoidance behavior complete control over the robot, even when there are no obstacles, is not reasonable because in this context wall-following should take precedence. So, while priorities are fixed, the context of activation changes and the controls of the behaviors are blended according to the priority of the behavior and how active it is. We call this weighting context-dependent blending, since it takes into account how much a behavior should respond in a particular context.[3] Figure 7 shows an example of context-dependent blending in operation as the robot follows a wall and avoids an obstacle.

Context-dependent blending has proven to be an effective technique for coordinating reactive and goal-oriented behaviors. Behaviors are not just switched on and off; rather, their preferences are combined into a tradeoff desirability. An important consequence is that the preferences of the goal-seeking behaviors are still considered during reactive maneuvers, thus biasing the control choices toward the achievement of the goals. In the example above, suppose that the obstacle is right in front of the robot (for example, the robot ended up facing the wall) and can thus be avoided by turning either right or left; then the combined behavior prefers the side that better promotes corridor following.

It is interesting to compare context-dependent blending with the artificial potential field technique, first introduced by Khatib (1986) and now extensively used in the robotic domain (Latombe 1991; Arkin 1990). In the potential field

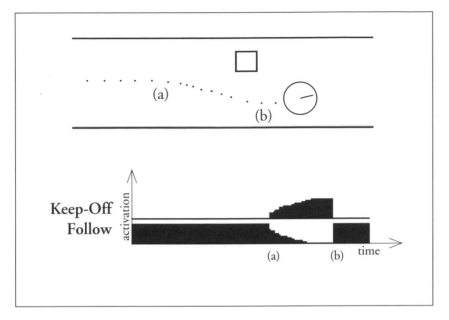

Figure 7. Context-dependent blending of following and avoiding behaviors. After point (a), the keep-off behavior starts to become active, and its higher priority dominates the follow behavior. At point (b), the obstacle is passed, and follow resumes.

approach, a goal is represented by a potential measuring the desirability of each state from that goal's viewpoint. For example, the goal of avoiding obstacles is represented by a potential field having maximum value around the obstacles; and the goal of reaching a given location is represented by a field having minimum value at that location. At each point, the robot responds to a pseudoforce proportional to the vector gradient of the field. Although there are some technical differences, in general the fuzzy rule approach can also be seen as generating a desirability gradient showing the best direction for the robot to move at each point in the field. The primary difference, however, is in how the complex control problem is decomposed. The fuzzy control approach allows us to partition control actions according to desired behaviors of the robot and then to combine the behaviors through context-dependent blending. By contrast, the potential-field method forces us to think about how to change a global potential field to achieve a particular result, conceptually a much harder task. Interestingly, the motor schema approach (Arkin 1990) brings a behavior orientation to potential fields by decomposing the global field into a set of subfields, each designed to accomplish a particular goal.

Coherence

Reactive behaviors such as obstacle avoidance often take their input directly from sensor readings, perhaps with some transformation and filtering. More goal-directed behaviors often benefit from using artifacts, internal representations of objects or object configurations. This is especially true when sensors give only sporadic and uncertain information about the environment. For example, in following a corridor, a robot will be unable to sense the corridor with its side sonars while traversing open doorways or junctions. It would be foolish to suspend the behavior at this point, since, over a small distance, the robot's dead-reckoning is good enough to follow a "virtual corridor" until the opening is passed.

In other situations, an artifact may represent an artificial geometric entity that guides the behavior. Such situations occur frequently in human navigation. For example, when crossing a street we tend to stay within a lane defined by the sidewalks on either side, even when there is no painted crosswalk. Similarly, in the follow-corridor behavior, the robot is guided by a lane artifact that is positioned a foot or so in from the corridor walls.

In accordance with these behavioral strategies, artifacts in Saphira come from three sources.

- A priori information. Typically, the robot will start with a map of the corridors and offices in its environment.

- Perceptual features. When a perceptual process recognizes a new object, it may add that object to the list of artifacts.

- Indirectly, from other artifacts or goal information. For example, if the user gives the command "move 3 feet forward," a goal artifact is created at a position three feet in front of the robot.

Artifacts always have a class (WALL, CORRIDOR, POSITION, etc.), geometric information about their position and extent, and a unique identity, so that no two artifacts in the same class are the same. They may also have information about geometrical dependencies with other artifacts.

Normally, artifacts in the LPS are updated based on the robot's dead-reckoning mechanism, which is reliable only over short distances. Coherence is the property of updating artifact positions in the LPS based on perception, so that the robot's model of the environment stays registered with the robot's position as it moves. To understand how this works, we refer to the following diagram:

feature <==> object hypothesis <==> artifact

Features are constructs based on sensor information, usually representing surface information. A typical feature would be a linear surface, represented by a straight segment in the LPS.

An object hypothesis is a set of features that could correspond to a real-world object. For example, two breaks in a linear surface could be a doorway, and these two features might be grouped together to form a doorway hypothesis. Object hypotheses do not have any particular identity—a doorway hypothesis does not have information that it is the doorway to a particular office.

All three types of representations—features, object hypotheses, and artifacts—coexist in the LPS. As the diagram implies, there is no strict relationship in how one is created or manipulated by another. Depending on the task, it is possible to go in several different directions. In map-building, for example, features are grouped into object hypotheses, which are then recognized as artifacts. Although this process is mostly bottom-up, there is also an important top-down component, in which previously-recognized artifacts are matched against current hypotheses, and only those hypotheses which refer to possible new objects are given the status of artifacts.

In practice, we have found that the introduction of artifacts greatly simplifies the design of behaviors, by allowing us to decouple the problem of control from the problems of interpreting noisy sensor data. Our behavior-writing methodology has been to first write small rule sets for elementary types of movements based on simple artifacts, like follow a line or reach a location; and then focus on the strategies to keep these artifacts anchored to the right features in the environment. The resulting behaviors often proved to be more robust than purely reactive controllers.

In this chapter, we cannot describe all of the ways in which the feature-to-artifact connection is made. We will concentrate on two areas: feature extraction from perceptual information, and the process of anchoring, in which current artifacts are kept coherent with the environment by matching against features or object hypotheses.

Extracting Features

To navigate through extended regions, Saphira uses a global map that contains imprecise spatial knowledge of objects in the domain, especially walls, doorways, and junctions of corridors. Using a map depends on reliable extraction of object information from perceptual clues, and we (as well as others) have spent many frustrating years trying to produce object interpretations from highly uncertain sonar and stereo signatures (see, for example, Drumheller 1985; Leonard, Durrant-Whyte, and Cox 1990; Moravec and Elfes 1985). The best method we have found is to use extended aperture sonar readings, perhaps augmented with depth information from the stereo system. As Flakey moves along, readings from the side sonars are accumulated as a series of points representing possible surfaces on the side of the robot. This gives some of the resolution of a sensor with a large aperture along the direction of motion. By running a robust linear feature algorithm over the data, we can find wall segments and doorways with some degree of confidence.

The utility of this technique is that it yields reliable linear features with almost no false positives. False positives are difficult to deal with, because using them for localization puts the robot at the wrong position in its internal map, and subsequent matches against features will fail. In general it's better to miss a few features and err on the conservative side in accepting features, since dead-reckoning works reliably for short periods.

Extracting wall and doorway features makes it easy to build a global map automatically by having Flakey explore an area. The map is imprecise because there is error in the dead-reckoning system and because the models for spatial objects are linear; e.g., corridors are represented as two parallel straight lines. As features are constructed, they can be combined into object hypotheses, matched against current artifacts, and promoted to new artifacts when they are not matched. In practice, we have been able to construct a reliable map of the corridors in SRI International's Artificial Intelligence Center, along with most of the doorways and junctions. Some hand editing of the map is necessary to add in doorways that were not found (because they were closed, or the robot was turning and missed them) and to delete some doorway artifacts that were recognized because of odd combinations of obstacles.

Anchoring

Artifacts exist as internal representations of the environment. When the physical object that an artifact refers to is perceived by the sensors, we can use this information to update the position of the artifact with respect to the robot. This is necessary to guarantee that behavior using the artifact operates with respect to the actual object, rather than with respect to an a priori assumption. We call anchoring the process of first matching a feature or object hypothesis to an artifact, and then updating the artifact using this perceptual information (see Saffiotti 1994 for more on anchoring).

In Saphira, the structure of decision making for the anchoring problem takes the following form (see figure 8): As features are perceived, Saphira attempts to convert them to object hypotheses, since these are more reliably matched than individual features. These hypotheses are matched against artifacts existing in the LPS. If they match against an artifact, the match produces information for updating (anchoring) the artifact's position. If not, they are candidates for inclusion as new artifacts in the map.

If an artifact that is in view of the perceptual apparatus cannot be matched against an object hypothesis, then Saphira tries to match it against individual perceptual features. This is useful, for example, when the robot is going down a hallway and trying to turn into a doorway. Only one end of the doorway is initially found because the other end is not in view of the side sonars. This information is enough to anchor the doorway artifact and allow the robot to proceed with the door-traversing behavior.

Artifacts that have no perceptual support when they should (i.e., when they

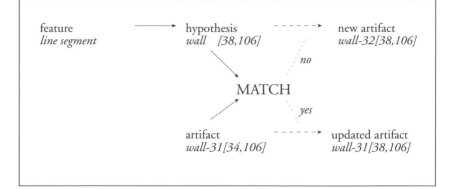

Figure 8. Structure of decision making for the anchoring problem.

are in the range of the cameras or sonars), are candidates for reaping from the LPS. In general, the reaping process must take into account the environment of the robot. For example, walls and corridors are fixed structures that are always present, while doors can be closed (and therefore do not show up as features). The most obvious candidates for reaping are transient objects such as obstacles. At present we do not have any general theory of how to represent the dynamic aspect of objects and its relation to artifact recognition, but rely on special-purpose algorithms for each type of object.

Figure 9 shows an example of anchoring in Saphira. The picture shows the LPS in two consecutive moments during corridor following. The corridor-following behavior acts with respect to a corridor artifact, represented by the two double lines. This artifact is initially placed by the planning and executive levels based on map information (a). Note that the position of the artifact does not correspond to that of the actual wall, visible from the clusters of sonar readings (small dots); this may be because the map is incorrect or, more commonly, because of the inaccuracy of self-localization. As enough sonar readings are gathered, Saphira's perceptual routines infer the existence of two parallel walls (marked by "W") and hence form a corridor hypothesis ("C"). The artifact is then anchored to this hypothesis (b), and the movement now proceeds with respect to the actual corridor. If one wall is obscured by obstacles or a doorway, then the other will be used to anchor the corridor. Anchoring provides a closed-loop response whenever the relevant sensor data are available. When data are not available, e.g., if the walls become obscured, artifacts act as assumptions for movement.

Currently, anchoring is successfully used by individual behaviors or activity schemas that control behavior. For example, it is used by the doorway-traversing behavior to track the location of the doorway as it moves into or out of a room.

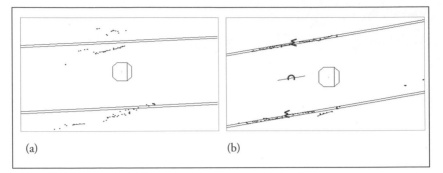

Figure 9. Anchoring a corridor artifact to sensor readings for corridor following.

It is also used to keep the robot globally registered with respect to a map. The registration process is sufficiently robust that the original map the robot makes does not have to be very precise (and it can't be, if dead-reckoning is poor). The anchoring process will keep the robot's position updated with respect to the relevant objects in the environment, assuming, of course, that the robot can find and match objects of the right sort. For instance, going down a long corridor with no features, the robot will stay correctly registered in the center of the hallway, but the error in its longitudinal position will grow. So it's important to find doorways or breaks in the corridor at reasonable intervals. Using the anchoring strategy on corridors, doorways, and junctions, we have been able to keep the robot localized for arbitrarily long periods (i.e., until the batteries run low) as it navigates the corridors of the Artificial Intelligence Center.

Anchoring thus helps to correct uncertain prior information by using perception and keep the robot localized on a map as it navigates. But there are still several problems we have not addressed with this scheme. One is that sonar percepts are, in general, not adequate to keep the robot localized in complex environments. For example, in crowded rooms, the robot quickly becomes confused because it cannot find a sufficient set of long linear segments to match. To solve this problem, we are considering correlation-based algorithms using the stereo vision system. By keeping track of a number of small surface patches that are sufficiently distinctive as features, we hope to be able to use the same registration algorithms to localize the robot reliably in complex indoor and outdoor environments.

A second problem is that of place recognition: localization when the robot has no knowledge of its current position. Alessandro Saffiotti, who worked with the authors on Flakey's fuzzy behaviors, has ideas for solving this task based on the use of fuzzy sets to represent locational uncertainty (Saffiotti and Wesley 1996; Saffiotti 1996).

Tracking People

Saphira incorporates a simple people-tracker based on stereo information. The tracking algorithm does not perform correlations on successive temporal frames to keep track of the object. Instead, it looks for personlike objects in each successive frame without reference to previous ones, formulates a hypothesis, and then passes it to the LPS registration routines. "Personlike objects" are detected by a matching process running on the stereo data. Three bands of range information at torso height are examined for a shape profile the width of an adult. If two of the three bands agree, then a person is detected at the center of the shape. Because we are using only a portion of the stereo information, we can run the person-tracker at a 10-Hz rate.

The registration algorithm makes a decision about whether the hypothesized person is the same as one represented by an artifact and either updates the artifact position or creates a new one. We keep a simple velocity model of person artifacts, which helps the registration process to make better matching decisions. The velocity model is also used by a centering process which can keep the camera center locked on the person being tracked. If a person artifact does not receive support for a period of time, it is removed from the LPS.

Interestingly, the registration process makes it possible to follow people around corners and through doorways, where they may be temporarily lost from sight. The artifact represents their most likely position, and the vision routines keep searching this area until the person is reacquired or cannot be found.

One limitation of the current system is its inability to distinguish different people. The range resolution of the system is coarse enough that distinguishing people by shape is not possible, even without the complication of motion, arm position, and so on.

Controlling Executive: PRS-Lite

Behaviors provide low-level situated control for the physical actions affected by the system. Above that level, there is a need to relate behaviors to specific goals and objectives that the robot should undertake. This management process involves determining when to activate or deactivate behaviors as part of the execution of a task, as well as coordinating them with other activities in the system. PRS-Lite (Myers 1996), a reactive controller based loosely on the Procedural Reasoning System (PRS) (Georgeff and Ingrand 1989; Myers 1993) fills this role within Saphira.

Many of the core capabilities provided by PRS-Lite are shared by most current-generation task controllers. These include the smooth integration of goal-driven and event-driven activity, timely response to unexpected changes in the world, and the hierarchical decomposition of tasks. Several additional capabilities, however, distinguish PRS-Lite from other reactive control systems (including the original PRS). These include the management of continuously interacting processes, a rich set of declarative control mechanisms, and a generalized goal semantics that replaces concepts of success or failure with levels of goal satisfaction.

Overview

The representational basis of PRS-Lite is the activity schema, a parameterized specification of procedural knowledge for attaining a declared objective. This procedural knowledge is represented as an ordered list of goal-sets, whose successive satisfaction will yield the overall objective of the schema. A goal-set is composed of one or more goal statements (or goals), each consisting of a goal operator applied to a list of arguments. A goal-set can be optionally identified by a label unique to its schema. Intuitively, a goal-set corresponds to an ordered sequence of goals that are to be achieved as an atomic unit. A compiler transforms the schema specifications into parameterized finite-state machines (performing optimizations where appropriate), whose arcs are labeled with individual goal-sets to be achieved. Activity schemas are launched by instantiating their parameters and intending them into the system. Such instantiated schemas are referred to as intentions. Multiple intentions can be active simultaneously, providing a multitasking capability.

Different modalities of goals are supported, as summarized in figure 10. Broadly speaking, goal types can be categorized as action or sequencing. Action goals ground out in either executable functions (called primitive actions), tests on the state of the environment (as represented in the internal world model), or the activation or deactivation of intentions and behaviors. This last ability enables the hierarchical decomposition of goals. Sequencing goals provide conditional goal execution and sophisticated goal ordering beyond the default of linear processing, as well as various forms of parallelism.

Overall, PRS-Lite can be used to generate and manage a forest of directed graphs whose nodes each represent a goal-set from some activity schema. The root node of each graph represents a top-level goal, with its successors generated by hierarchical goal refinement. We refer to the set of active graphs at a given point in time as the current intention structures for the system. The leaf nodes of the intention structures are called the current nodes, and their associated goal-sets the current goal-sets. Note that an intention structure can have multiple current nodes because of the inclusion of parallel sequencing goals in the schema definition language.

An executor manages intentions at runtime. It repeatedly operates a short processing cycle in which it considers the current goal-sets in each intention structure, performs any actions required to achieve their constituent goals, and updates the set of current nodes (as appropriate). The decision to limit processing to a single goal-set for each leaf node in an intention structure ensures over-

Action Goals:

Test	check a condition
Execute	execute a primitive action
=	assignment of local variables
Wait-for	wait for a condition
Intend	dispatch intentions (block / nonblock)
Unintend	terminate intentions

Sequencing Goals:

If	conditional goals
And	parallel goals (with join)
Split	parallel goals (without join)
Goto	branching to labeled goals

Figure 10. PRS-Lite goal modalities.

all responsiveness to new events. Given the granularity of processing, responsiveness is dependent on the number of active intentions, the degree of parallelism in those intentions, the size of goal-sets, and the underlying primitive actions that are executed. The design has proven adequate for the tasks considered to date (as discussed later).

Goal Modalities

Action goals supply the most basic operations in the system. *Test* goals provide the ability to test beliefs about the current state of the external world. Within Saphira, beliefs are characterized by a combination of the Local Perceptual Space and a set of environment variables. *Execute* goals provide for the execution of primitive actions, which may perform internal bookkeeping, the setting of environment variables, or the triggering of specific external actions by the system. External actions for Flakey include the generation of an utterance by the speech synthesis module and the invocation of a route planner. = goals enable the binding of local variables within an intention.

Intend goals lead to the activation of both intentions and behaviors. As such, they enable the hierarchical expansion of intentions through repeated goal refinement. *Unintend* goals provide the complementary ability to explicitly terminate active intentions before they run their full course. This ability is critical when operating in dynamic, unpredictable domains, where rapid switching among activities is essential. Intentions can be assigned priorities that determine the order in which they are processed by the executor. Intentions can also be named when activated, allowing them to be referenced by other intentions (in particular, *Unintend* intentions).

A critical feature of *Intend* is that it supports the invocation of intentions in either nonblocking or blocking mode. In nonblocking mode, the intention is activated and control proceeds to the next goal. In essence, the nonblocking intention is spawned as an independent process within the context of the parent intention; the nonblocking intention will persist either until it completes or until its parent intention terminates. In contrast, blocking mode disables updating of the current goal within the parent intention until the child completes. Any intentions activated earlier by the parent intention will continue to be processed. Degrees of blocking are also supported: an intention can be blocked until a designated success criteria is satisfied. This capability is valuable for controlling behaviors implemented as fuzzy rules, which provide a natural metric for defining degrees of success (namely, the fuzzy predicates that model the world state). As a simple illustration, Flakey has a *:face-direction* behavior that orients the robot toward a designated heading. This behavior is invoked with different thresholds of blocking in different contexts, depending on how critical it is to be precisely oriented to that heading.

Wait-for goals enable limited suspension of an intention until a certain condition or event occurs. The *Wait-for* goal modality is critical in the framework in that it enables synchronization among concurrent intentions through the use of shared variables. An illustration is provided in the next section.

The sequencing goals enable more sophisticated goal-ordering and selection mechanisms than does the default of linear processing of goal-sets. Sequencing goals can be nested to arbitrary depths, yielding a rich framework for specifying control strategies. *If* goals support conditional activation of a goal. *Goto* goals support nonlinear flow of control within an activity schema by allowing a current goal-set to be mapped to any other labeled goal-set in the schema. Iteration can be specified through appropriate combinations of *If* and *Goto* goals. Two forms of parallelism are provided by the *Split* and *And* goal modalities. *Split* parallelism spawns sets of independent concurrent goals, with control in the parent intention proceeding to the successor goal-set. Each thread of activity for the spawned goals continues until it completes or the parent intention terminates (similar in spirit to the nonblocking mode of intending). In contrast, *And* parallelism treats the parallel goals as a unit; processing of the parent intention suspends until each of the threads occasioned by the *And* subgoals terminates.

Methodology and Use

Goal-directed behavior is produced by intending schemas for satisfying individual tasks. Reactive, event-directed behavior is produced by launching intentions

```
(defintention :plan-and-execute
    :params (dest)
    :goals
    '((:plan
        (AND
          (EXECUTE (say "Planning path to ~a" dest))
          (EXECUTE (setq *failed-execution* nil))
          (= plan (find-path *cur-region* dest))) )
        (IF (null plan) (GOTO :finale))
        (INTEND :monitor-planex () :blocking nil)
        (INTEND :follow-path ((path . plan))
        :blocking t :name follow-it)
        (IF *failed-execution* (GOTO :plan))
        (:finale
          (IF (null plan)
            (EXECUTE (say "No passable routes")))) ) ) )

(defintention :monitor-planex
    :params ()
    :goals
    '((:monitor (WAIT-FOR *failed-execution*))
      (:cleanup (UNINTEND 'follow-it)) ))
```

Figure 11. Activity schemas for directed navigation.

that employ *Wait-for* goals that suspend activity until some condition or event transpires.

A common idiom for the design of activity schemas is to define an umbrella intention for a specific objective, which in turn invokes both a lower-level intention for achieving the objective and one or more "monitor" intentions (thus combining goal- and event-driven activities). Monitors use *Wait-for* goals to detect changes in the world that could influence the actions required to achieve the overall objective of the top-level schema. Certain monitors identify failure conditions that would invalidate the approach being taken for the current task. Others provide reactivity to unexpected events that require immediate attention. Monitors can also check for serendipitous effects that eliminate the need for certain goals in active intentions, and modify the intention structures accordingly.

To illustrate the use of the various goal modalities and idioms, figure 11 presents simplified versions of activity schemas used by Flakey to perform basic navigation tasks. The schema *:plan-and-execute* encodes a procedure for generating and robustly executing a plan to navigate to a designated destination. The destination is specified as a parameter to the schema and is represented as an artifact in the LPS, thus linking abstract notions of place to the robot's beliefs about its environment.

The initial goal-set in the schema (with the label *:plan*) employs an *And* goal applied to three subgoals to perform certain initializations. The first *Execute* subgoal invokes a function "say" that performs a speech generation command. The second *Execute* goal initializes the environment variable **failed-execution**, which is used to encode information about the status of plan execution. This variable is an example of state information within PRS-Lite that provides coordination among intentions (as described further below). The final subgoal invokes a function "find-path" that produces a topological plan for navigating from the current locale to the destination. Navigation within Saphira is at the level of regions (doors, junctions, hallways); the route planner produces a sequence of such regions that should be traversed to reach the target destination.

After performing the necessary initializations, the schema intends a non-blocking monitor intention *:monitor-planex*, followed by a blocking intention *:follow-path*, in the spirit of the umbrella idiom described above. This latter intention (not shown here) cycles through the computed path, launching various lower level intentions as required to navigate between successive regions in the generated path. The lower-level intentions may encounter difficulties, which they signal by setting the environment variable **failed-execution**. The *Wait-for* goal in the *:monitor-planex* intention would detect such an event and then process the goal (*Unintend follow-it*). Satisfying this goal would deactivate the *:follow-path* intention, with the monitor intention then terminating. If no lower-level intention signals a failure, the blocking intention *:follow-path* will eventually complete, enabling processing of the remainder of the *:plan-and-execute* intention. The *:monitor-planex* intention is terminated automatically when its parent intention *:plan-and-execute* terminates.

Figure 12 displays a snapshot of the intention structures at a point during a run in which Flakey uses the above schemas to execute a delivery task.[4] Each line in the display consists of an initial marker, indicating whether the intention is blocking (*) or nonblocking (o), the name of the activity schema (e.g., *Deliver-Object*), a unique identifier for the particular instantiation of the schema (e.g., a label such as *Follow-It* if one was specified in the *Intend* goal, else an assigned name such as I3674), and either the next state of execution (for an intention) or *B* (for a behavior). At the instant captured by this display, PRS-Lite has two intentions active at the highest level (corresponding to two distinct user-specified objectives): *Deliver-Object* and *Avoid*. The *Avoid* intention has only one active thread at this point, namely the behavior for avoiding collisions (*Avoid-Collision*). Note though that in the past or future, this intention may trigger many other activities. Of more interest is the state of execution for the *Deliver-Object* intention. At its topmost level, this parent intention has the single child intention *Plan-and-Execute,* which in turn is executing the *:follow-path* schema while simultaneously monitoring for execution failures (via *Monitor-Planex*). As

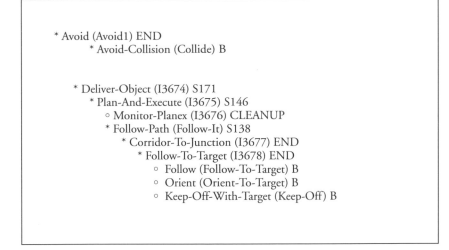

```
      * Avoid (Avoid1) END
            * Avoid-Collision (Collide) B


      * Deliver-Object (I3674) S171
            * Plan-And-Execute (I3675) S146
                  ○ Monitor-Planex (I3676) CLEANUP
            * Follow-Path (Follow-It) S138
                  * Corridor-To-Junction (I3677) END
                  * Follow-To-Target (I3678) END
                        ○ Follow (Follow-To-Target) B
                        ○ Orient (Orient-To-Target) B
                        ○ Keep-Off-With-Target (Keep-Off) B
```

Figure 12. Snapshot of the intention structures during execution of a delivery task.

part of the path-following schema, the robot is currently moving from a corridor to a junction, which in turn has activated an intention to move toward a specific target. At the lowest level, three behaviors are activated simultaneously, namely *Follow*, *Orient*, and *Keep-Off-With-Target*.

Discussion

PRS˚-Lite provides a powerful and natural framework in which to specify and manage the purposeful activities of a robot. The system itself is compact (less than 500 lines of Lisp code, including executor, compiler, and display manager), especially in comparison to the original PRS. It has proven to be sufficiently fast over a broad range of tasks, with the intention execution loop easily fitting into Saphira's overall cycle time of 100 milliseconds. Precise figures for the cycle time of the PRS-Lite executor are not available, but the combination of behavior and task control lies somewhere in the range of 5 to 30 milliseconds (on a Sparc-2 processor). This is very fast, considering that on average there are 10 to 15 intentions in operation, monitoring various conditions and coordinating behaviors.

One novel capability of PRS-Lite within Saphira is its ability to manage behaviors implemented as fuzzy rules. A key feature of such behaviors is the smoothness of activity that results from rule blending. However, sequencing languages (including activity schemas) model task-level events as discrete actions connected by explicit transitions, even when the tasks themselves ground out in continuous processes. This separation of task and behavior levels leads to discontinuities in the resultant activities of the system. As an illustration, consider the task of navigating to an office in a given corridor and then entering it. Flakey has activity schemas defined for the navigation and doorway-crossing, each of which employs an appropriate set of behaviors. A straightforward approach to the overall task would be to execute a navigation intention to reach the office and then a doorway-crossing intention to enter the office. But the termination of the corridor navigation intention prior to the activation of the doorway-crossing intention leads to jerky, unnatural motion by the robot. For smoother operation, the doorway-crossing behaviors must be activated before the robot reaches the office (i.e., while the corridor navigation behaviors are still active). The corridor navigation behaviors should terminate once the robot is sufficiently far down the corridor to enable successful completion of the doorway-crossing intention. Such intention-level blending can be specified in the PRS-Lite goal language, using a combination of monitors and thresholded blocking of intentions.

Communication

At this point, our ideas about communicating have been strongly influenced by the Natural Language Understanding community, especially the plan-based theory of speech acts (Allen 1983). Eventually, we would like to have a complete understanding system that would perform intention recognition on the speaker's utterance and form appropriate plans. For the scenario, we concentrated on the area of referent identification, matching the speaker's terms to objects in the immediate environment of the robot. In this section we describe the speech input system and the schemas that carry out advice-taking and tasking commands.

Speech Input

We were fortunate to have an excellent speech-recognition system, developed at SRI, called CORONA. CORONA has speaker-independent recognition models that need no training, although it will have better accuracy with individually-tuned models. CORONA accepts a BNF grammar of phrases and produces strings of the words spoken. On a Sparc 10-51, it operates at about twice real-time on the simple grammar we used, i.e., a five-second sentence would take about ten seconds to recognize.

One of the hardest problems in voice communication is letting the supervisor know when Flakey has heard an utterance and what the state of its understanding is. We employed several techniques:

Keying. There can be a lot of extraneous chatter during interactions. The grammar was created with a keyword initiation, so that only phrases beginning with the word "Flakey" were recognized. This worked extremely well; it was natural to address commands and statements to the robot in this fashion. A nice additional feature would be to use directional interpretation of sound sources for getting Flakey's attention; we currently do not have this capability.

Process status. CORONA employs an "endpointer," a period of low speech energy, to signal the end of a speaker phrase. From this point there is a delay until the speech is processed; the speaker can be confused about whether his input was received, and whether it was recognized. We implemented a simple end-of-speech flag: Flakey says "um" when the endpoint is reached. Thus the speaker can tell that his input was received and is being processed.

Results. It is important to give feedback to the speaker about the interpretation of his input. For example, if the speaker says "turn left," and it is interpreted as "go forward" (a not altogether unknown occurrence), the speaker will be mystified by the robot's behavior. So Flakey acknowledges each spoken command, either by paraphrasing it or by nodding its cameras in recognition. If the phrase was not recognized, Flakey said "duh?" or "what?" Crude, but effective.

Gestures

We were ambitious enough to want gesture recognition as part of the attention process. The idea was to use a mixture of speech and gesture for reference, e.g., "This office (point to the right or left) is Karen's." We did manage to extract enough information from the stereo system to recognize left or right-pointing arms but did not have enough time to integrate it correctly with the speech input, even for simple reference. This would be a good project for future work, with a more elaborate natural-language understanding system.

We implemented a simple but surprisingly sufficient set of activity schemas to perform the scenario. They fall into several categories: direct motion commands ("turn around"), sensor-based movement ("follow me," "follow the corridor"), tasks ("get the file from Karen"), and information ("this is John's office").

Direct Motion

These are direct commands to move forward or turn, or to look (move the cameras) in certain directions, e.g., "look behind you." Direct motion commands are implemented as simple sequential behaviors with well-defined ending conditions and short timeouts. For example, if Flakey is told to move forward while facing a wall, it will turn away from the wall and move forward about one meter, since collision avoidance is active at all times. It would be smarter, of course, to recognize that it is not possible to move forward and state this fact. But in our current implementation Flakey does not check for possibility of carrying out commands; it only tries to do the best it can.

Attending and Following

These commands involve coordination of sensing and acting, mediated by artifacts in the LPS. Even very simple activity schemas, when coordinated with sensing, can give the appearance of a well-trained robot with humanlike capabilities.

The Attending schema finds the closest personlike object and brings Flakey to face the person at a distance of about 1 meter. The command "look at me" or "find me" triggers this schema. Flakey performs a scan from the current camera position to the extreme left and right position of the pan–tilt head, giving a full 360-degree field of view. The first personlike object detected by the stereo tracking algorithm (see the tracking people subsection) is placed in the LPS, and an activity schema positions the robot to face the object and keep the cameras centered on it. Success of the Attending schema is indicated by saying "here I am;" failure, after a full scan, by "I can't find you!"

The Following schema uses the same kind of movement and sensor control to track a person. If there is no person currently in view, the Attending schema is invoked. Once found, the person is kept centered in the cameras, using the spatial information returned from the tracking algorithm. The activity schema keeps Flakey about 1–1.5 meters from the person as much as possible (top speed of 300 millimeters per second) while avoiding obstacles. If the person is lost, Flakey looks in the most likely area for a while but does not attempt to reattend, since if there are other people around, it may acquire the wrong one. Flakey's vision system cannot distinguish individuals.

Both these behaviors worked well in practice. Mr. Alda was able to lead Flakey through several corridors and doorways at SRI, with only minor problems in reacquisition.

Information

This is one of the most interesting areas for robot/human interaction. The hard problem is relating robot-centered representations of the world to human-centered ones. For example, when the supervisor says, "…this office…," the robot must understand that there is an object in the current focus of dialogue that is being referred to. The point of contact, for the robot, is in the artifacts of the LPS. Flakey has enough background knowledge to infer that doors can lead to offices, even though it cannot recognize an office per se. So the phrase "this office" is linked to the nearest doorway in the robot's perceptual space.

In general the problem of reference resolution can be phrased in terms of abductive inference: find an object that, if assumed as the referent, would make the speaker's phrase carry reasonable information (Hobbs, Stickel, Appelt, and Martin 1993). For the scenario demonstration, we did not use a general inference method to determine reference, since we decided beforehand that we would only refer only to offices, people, and certain other objects. But in general the problem of reference for robots will require some of the same tools that have been used in computational linguistics. However, robots do enjoy one advantage: since they also perceive the world, they can draw on a repertoire of perceived objects as referents (in philosophical terms, they are situated in the word). Instead, the problem becomes one of matching the artifacts of the robot's representation with the linguistic expressions of the speaker. We have formulated a theoretical foundation for this interchange (Myers and Konolige 1992), but it was not applied in the scenario. Other more complex theories of knowledge and action have been developed in a logical framework (Moore 1980; Lespérance and Levesque 1995); we expect to see more application of these theories as robots become more sophisticated in their interactions.

Another type of information used by the robot is knowledge of how to locate people, since delivery tasks often involve finding someone. In general this is a planning problem, with reasoning about where someone is or who might have information about where that person is. For the scenario, we implemented a simple routine that would first check the person's office (using speech output and waiting for a reply) and then start looking for people who might know where the person is. More sophisticated routines might check a personal calendar, or compile a list of likely places, or perform inference about knowledge prerequisites for action, and so on. Here again the problem of reference emerges. Phrases such as "Karen is around the corner" would be hard to interpret, so we settled on a set of place-names that could be used: offices, corridors, and open areas such as the library. These were all places that Flakey could learn from the supervisor, since there were artifacts (doors, corridors, junctions) that could be identified with the area.

One lesson we learned from attempting to give Flakey advice of this sort is that the closer a match between the robot's perceptual categories and the human's, the easier and more foolproof the exchange of information. For example, if Flakey had no concept of a corridor, it would be almost impossible to tell it the name of the corridor (e.g., "J-wing") and expect it to be internalized in an effective way. Suppose Flakey were to store its current position in association with the corridor name. Then the command "Go to J-wing" would cause Flakey to go back to the same location, even if another location in the corridor were much closer. Commands such as "follow the corridor" wouldn't make any sense at all.

Tasking

A robot is supposed to perform useful tasks. For the scenario, Flakey was a delivery robot, whose main task was to deliver messages and manuscripts. While performing these tasks, Flakey maintained the goals of obstacle avoidance and localization. These required no overt planning and the requisite behaviors were invoked automatically. In more complicated situations, for example where the robot must explore to find a new route, there might be explicit planning for localization.

Navigation plans were computed by graph search on the learned topological map and then executed by PRS-Lite. More complicated procedures were constructed as conditional navigation plans: find person X, ask him/her where person Y is, and then go to that location. These plans were simple enough that we just created PRS-Lite schemata for them. A major failure in the plan (e.g., person X not found) caused the robot to instantiate an alternative schema. The most complicated plan Flakey executed was going to Karen's office and finding out she wasn't there; then going to John's office, asking him where Karen was, finding and getting a report from her, and returning to deliver it.

Discussion

There are two basic areas where our work on Saphira has differed in design and emphasis from others. The first is in the area of coherence: by mediating interacts between perception and action through the LPS, we have been able to abstract away some of the difficulties found in interpreting goal-directed behavior relative to the perceptual state of the robot. This is especially true of tasks that cannot rely on current perceptions to formulate correct action sequences. Typical here is the task of following a person around a corner. As the person turns the corner, the perceptual system can no longer track him: there is nothing in the perceptual space on which to base a "follow" behavior. By providing an artifact that represents the best estimate of the person's position, Saphira can still perform the follow behavior on the expectation of reacquiring perceptual information after a short while.

The second distinctive aspect of our work is in the area of coordination, both the coordination of basic behaviors and the scheduling of behaviors to perform high-level tasks. Context-dependent blending is a general methodology to form complex controllers by composing basic behaviors. Basic behaviors are simple functions on a local state written to satisfy a single goal over a small range of environments (the context). As such, they are relatively easy to write and to debug—they should also be easier to learn in the future. Complex behaviors to achieve multiple goals or operate over wider environmental conditions are composed out of simpler ones by using fuzzy context rules. This is in general an easy operation if the preconditions of the basic behaviors have been clearly stated. Interestingly, this compositional methodology can be formally analyzed using the tools of multivalued logics. In a related work (Saffiotti, Konolige, and Ruspini 1995), we have shown several properties that link behavior composition to goal decomposition: for example, we can prove, under certain assumptions, that if two behaviors individually promote two goals, then their conjunctive blending promotes the conjoint goal in the conjoint context. Formal groundedness is an important feature of our compositional methodology to form complex behaviors.

Obviously, our approach also has its problems. Fuzzy behaviors implement a local "greedy" method, gradient descent, that is highly reactive and simple to compute. Like any local technique, however, fuzzy behaviors can be trapped in local minima. It is the responsibility of higher level intentions to instantiate only behaviors for which gradient descent is appropriate based on some global analysis or to monitor execution to detect local minima and failures. In practice, it is not always easy to find the right contextual condition for a behavior.

A related problem in our experience has been that tuning the parameters of the fuzzy rules may be difficult. Although the decomposition of complex behaviors into simpler ones makes them simpler to write, some behaviors required many days of experimental debugging. We are currently exploring the possibility to automatically synthesizing basic behaviors from specifications and using learning techniques to improve a behavior's performance.

Numerous task-level controllers for managing the activities of mobile robots have been built in recent years (Firby 1994b; Gat 1992; Nilsson 1994; Payton, Rosenblatt, and Keirsey 1990; Simmons 1994), many of which provide services similar to those in Saphira. However, two aspects of the PRS-Lite controller within Saphira set it apart from other systems. One is that PRS-Lite builds many key control constructs into the schema language itself, rather than leaving them implicit in the procedural workings of the controller. The second is its thresholded goal semantics, which enables task-level blending of fuzzy behaviors.

In our experiences of writing over fifty schemas for a variety of different tasks, the expressiveness of PRS-Lite has proven to be mostly adequate. However, certain extensions would simplify the task-control effort. One would be to add a database to provide explicit, declarative representations of beliefs about the world, thus enabling more general reasoning capabilities. Currently, this state information is stored in a combination of the Local Perceptual Space and a set of environment variables. A more significant change would be to add some limited deliberation to enable selection among multiple candidate schemas rather than direct dispatch of a single designated schema. The database and deliberation capabilities were explicitly excluded from the original system for fear that their computational overhead might eclipse the limited processing time available for each perceive-act cycle. Given that there is available cycle time, it would be interesting to modify the system to be more declarative in this manner.

Acknowledgments

We have worked closely with Enrique Ruspini and Alessandro Saffiotti, who are primarily responsible for the ideas and code behind the fuzzy control behaviors of Saphira. They are also responsible for many of the most interesting features of

Saphira, and we are grateful for their participation in this project. We would also like to thank John Woodfill of Interval Corporation for allowing us to use his stereo vision programs on Flakey.

Notes

1. As vision systems become smaller and use less power, there is a possibility of equipping small robots like Pioneer with interesting vision capabilities. Newton Labs of Washington has developed a small color vision sensor that extracts colored blobs from images in real-time, and we have used this system on Pioneer to find and approach soda cans. SRI is developing a small real-time stereo vision system for Pioneer, similar to the one on Flakey.

2. At the time of the demonstration, Flakey had a single on-board processor, which ran the vision algorithms and basic motor control. The rest of the work was done by an off-board Sparcstation connected through a radio Ethernet.

3. For averaging to make sense, the rules in a behavior should not suggest dramatically opposite actions in the same state. Our coding heuristic has been to make sure that rules with conflicting consequents have disjoint antecedents. Other authors have preferred to use more involved choice functions.

4. To improve the understandability of the robot's actions, PRS-Lite maintains an intention display that summarizes the intention structures at the end of each execution cycle. The intention display provides a concise overview of the motivation for the actions being undertaken by the system at any point in time, thus conveying to an observer why the robot is behaving in a certain manner.

CHAPTER TEN

The Animate Agent Architecture

R. James Firby, Peter N. Prokopowicz, and Michael J. Swain

The goal of the Animate Agent Project is to design software systems for intelligent robotic agents working in the world alongside human beings. Such agents need to be able to pursue a wide variety of goals and interact naturally with people when deciding which goals to achieve and how to achieve them. As a starting point, the Animate Agent Project must deal with the following four issues:

Interaction with the real world. The agent must deal with natural, dynamic environments that include other agents and processes. It must be able to adapt its actions to the details of a changing environment and cope with unexpected changes, problems, and opportunities.

Using context to simplify perception. The agent must take advantage of task and environmental constraints to specialize and focus visual processing resources to make effective use of visual sensors.

Software reuse for multiple goals. The plans, algorithms, and knowledge representations the agent uses should be modular and parameterizable so they can be reused in a variety of situations to help achieve a variety of goals.

Object representation. The agent must be able to coordinate its activities with people in a natural way. In particular, human communication presumes the ability to refer to individual objects in the world, so the agent must be able to find, identify, and act on objects as well.

The animate agent architecture addresses these issues using a two level model for encoding robot behavior: a lower level consisting of continuous processes that control the robot's sensors and effectors, and a higher level consisting of a reactive plan executor that selects sequences of actions and programs the lower level at run-time. This two level approach is designed to cope with the following issues:

The details of the world. There are a huge number of details that affect precisely what actions an agent should take to achieve its goals. Many are unimportant from a planning point of view but become critical during the actual execution of the plan. Going through a door is a reasonable plan step even if an agent doesn't know whether the door has a knob, a handle, or a latch that will each require somewhat different actions to actuate. The architecture does run-time action selection so that details like these can be dealt with when the actual latch type becomes apparent.

Dynamic situations. In real situations other agents and processes change things unpredictably, and an agent's actions do not always have their intended effects. The details of the agent's situation can change unexpectedly and might be unpredictable in advance. The architecture includes ways for confirming that actions and plans are actually having their intended effects and for changing plans when situations change.

Contingencies, problems, and opportunities. In many situations there are a large number of routine things that can go wrong while executing a plan. An agent might drop something it is carrying, it might lose track of a target it is following, or it might stumble across the hammer it is going to the workshop to fetch. The architecture incorporates methods for handling routine problems and opportunities as a standard part of the agent's capabilities.

The control of continuous processes. An agent's actual movements are usually controlled by continuous processes. The architecture supports the description and use of continuous processes as well as discrete plan steps.

The integration of purposive vision. Current research in vision processing strongly suggests that perceptual routines aimed at a specific task are more effective than routines aimed at general "scene understanding." The architecture is designed to support purposive visual processing by specializing visual tasks in context and tightly linking them to other control processes.

CHIP is the Animate Agent Laboratory robot at the University of Chicago. As shown in figure 1, CHIP is built on a Real World Interface Inc. three-wheeled synchro-drive mobile base. This base is surrounded by an octagonal bumper and supports a body roughly three feet high. Around the middle of the body are eight sonar sensors and on top is a pair of color cameras mounted on a computer-controlled pan-tilt platform. At the front of CHIP's body, where it can reach the floor, is a Heathkit Hero robot arm augmented with force and contact sensors to get tactile feedback from the gripper. Onboard, CHIP carries a 68000 computer to manage the sensors and control the arm and a 68030 computer to run the skill control processes. Video from CHIP's cameras is broadcast offboard to a DataCube image processing system attached to a Sparc-20 workstation, where all vision processing is done.

The software controlling CHIP consists of a variety of connected systems, as shown in figure 2. The low-level motor and sensor processing software is written in "C" and runs onboard. The concurrent, perceptual-motor skills that make up CHIP's modular control system are written in Chicago Robot Language (CRL) (Firby 1994b), with some running onboard the robot and others running offboard on a Macintosh computer. The onboard and offboard components are linked via a radio-ethernet. The reactive action plan (RAP) system (Firby 1995; Firby 1994a; Firby 1989) for task-level sequencing of the modular skills is written in Lisp and runs offboard on the Macintosh, where it interfaces to the CRL

Figure 1. The robot CHIP.

skill system. Vision processing is done offboard on the Sparc-20 and communicates with other skills and the RAP system via ethernet (Kahn and Swain 1995).

The next section of this chapter describes the software architecture used to program CHIP. The subsequent section describes the knowledge representations (*i.e.*, the skills and RAP plans) used in the competition. The vision rou-

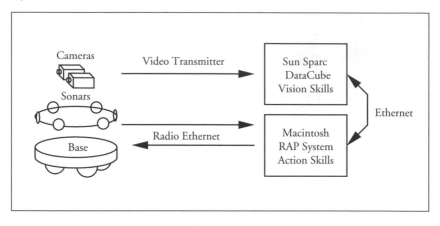

Figure 2. Software systems for CHIP.

tines section discusses the vision skills used during the competition, and finally, the conclusion of this chapter includes some thoughts on future work.

The Software Architecture

The Animate Agent Architecture organizing CHIP's plans and algorithms is shown schematically in figure 3. It consists of a reactive task execution system, using a hierarchical library of discrete plans and plan steps, and a continuous control system using composable modules called skills. At run-time, the execution system assembles the skills into sequences of control programs to satisfy CHIP's goals.

A two-level architecture is used to allow the encoding of two quite different, but complementary, types of robot behavior. The skill level supports the description of continuous control processes, while the task execution level supports the description of multistep plans. The skill level is implemented on CHIP using CRL, while task execution is implemented using the RAP system.

The Skill Level

Many low-level robot activities are most easily described, and most effectively implemented, as continuous, feedback control loops. For example, tracking an object visually, moving up to an object, or grasping an object are all processes that require fast transformation of sensor data (image data, sonar data, or dead reckoning position) into target coordinates and moving an actuator (the camera, the robot, or the gripper) toward those coordinates.

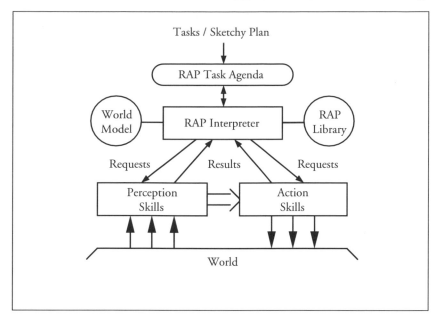

Figure 3. The animate agent architecture.

A central theme in the Animate Agent Project is the study of ways to modularize behaviors and then mix and match in various ways to achieve different tasks. Thus, low-level feedback loops in the animate agent architecture are implemented using modular CRL skills. A modular system allows the actual feedback loops controlling CHIP to be changed dynamically at execution time as CHIP's goals change. The CRL system is designed with four characteristics:

- *It controls sensors and actuators in real-time.* All of CHIP's sensor processing and actuator control is done through skills.

- *It is modular.* Skills are designed to be building blocks for control loops with many skills running together to control the robot.

- *It is reconfigurable.* The RAP system can put skills together in different combinations to carry out different actions in the world at different times.

- *It signals when specific states become true.* In addition to controlling the robot, skills signal when states are attained or change in the world. The RAP system interprets these signals to determine the end points of the activities it has programmed into the skill system.

CRL defines three building blocks for modular control systems: skills, signals, and channels. Skills are separate control routines that can be enabled and disabled independently and asynchronously. Skills communicate with one another and with the robot sensors and actuators through channels. In addition, active

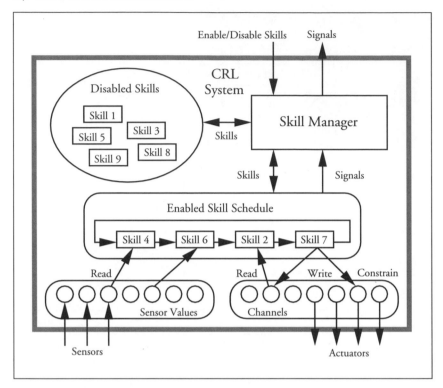

Figure 4. The CRL system.

skills can generate signals to the RAP system in response to things they find interesting in the world.

A schematic view of the CRL system is shown in figure 4. When skills are enabled, they are moved to a schedule of active skills, and as they are disabled, they are removed from the schedule. The CRL system is continually cycling through the active schedule and running each skill in turn. A skill can examine the current state of all sensors and channels and decide whether and how to alter the value of a channel. Sensor values come directly from sensors (or sensor drivers), and some channels are connected to actuators (or actuator drivers). A single skill can include a tight feedback loop from sensors to actuators, or a feedback loop can be built using multiple skills that communicate through channels. As skills are enabled and disabled, they move to and from the active schedule, altering the active feedback loops and hence altering the robot's behavior.

Skills communicate back to the RAP system by sending asynchronous signals. Signals can be generated for any reason that the skill writer deems important. For example, a tracking skill might send a signal when it has locked on to a target and another signal if it loses track of the target. A skill to move the robot might signal when it gets stuck and can't move, and so on. Each signal consists of the skill generating the signal, the signal name, and any additional information the skill wants to add. The RAPs that enable a skill can use or ignore the signals from that skill as they see fit since the same signals might mean different things in different plans. An action process for approaching a given target might be used to move up to a fixed location in the world, or it might be coupled with a visual tracking skill to follow a moving target. A signal saying that the target has been reached might mean the task is complete when approaching, or it might mean the object is too close when following.

As an example, some of the skills from the office cleanup domain are shown schematically in figure 5. The track-small-object skill takes in color images from CHIP's cameras, computes the target coordinates of the object, and writes those coordinates out to the target coordinate channel. The move-and-avoid skill reads from the target coordinate channel and CHIP's sonars to compute speed and steering commands for CHIP's motors. Together, these skills move CHIP toward a small moving object. It is also possible to enable the pan-to-target skill to keep the camera pointing at the target when CHIP turns to avoid obstacles (as shown). Alternatively, the track-small-object skill could be disabled and the dead-reckon-target skill enabled in its place to move CHIP toward a particular location based on dead reckoning rather than visual tracking.

The Task Execution Level

In a complex dynamic world, the best a planner can do is create a plan that needs to be refined further at run-time when actual states of the world can be determined directly. Such a sketchy plan will consist of steps at various levels of abstraction, from quite vague to quite detailed, depending on the information the planner has available and the amount of change expected from other agents and processes in the world.

The RAP system is designed to carry out complex, multistep sketchy plans in dynamic, natural environments. It takes task goals (either as a plan from a planner or, in the case of the International Joint Conference on Artificial Intelligence (IJCAI) Competition, as top-level goals) and breaks them down into steps that can be accomplished by activating a set of skills (Firby 1989; Firby 1994b). To do this refinement effectively, the RAP system must choose the method for carrying out a task at run time, confirm that the method executed for a task has the intended effect, synchronize task execution with the real world, and react quickly to routine dangers and opportunities. These tasks are outlined further in the following sentences:

- *Choose the method for carrying out a task at run-time.* When it is time to execute a plan task, the RAP system must check the world and choose the most appropriate way to carry out the task in the actual situation that exists.

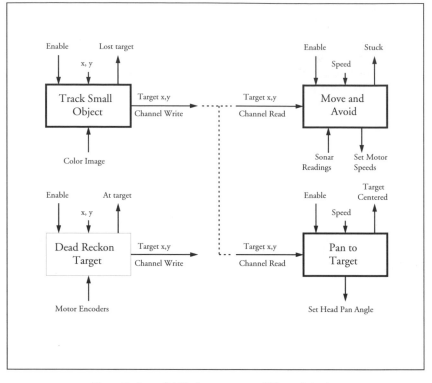

Figure 5. A set of skills that can create different behaviors.

- *Confirm that the method executed for a task has the intended effect.* In a dynamic world, the method chosen for a task may fail to work as expected. The RAP system must be able to detect such situations and try a different method.
- *Synchronize task execution with the real world.* Although plans consist of discrete steps, actual action takes the form of enabling sets of skills and waiting for them to achieve changes in the world over time. The RAP system must ensure that plan expansions and method execution stay synchronized with the continuous changes they are causing in the world.
- *React quickly to routine dangers and opportunities.* A robot will seldom be completely focused on a single task. It will need to deal with routine dangers and opportunities like running low on fuel or noticing money on the floor. The RAP system must allow concurrent tasks to watch for these situations and switch control to them quickly should such a situation arise.

The RAP system is shown schematically in figure 6. The tasks from the sketchy plan form the initial contents of the task agenda; the system's under-

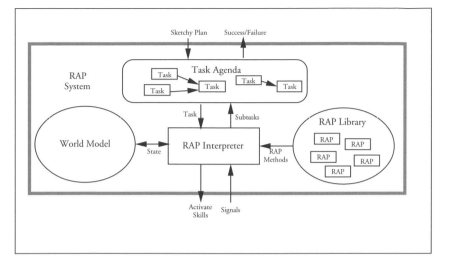

Figure 6. The RAP system.

standing of the current world state is maintained in the world model; and the
hierarchical methods that define task refinements reside in the RAP library.

The RAP interpreter pursues tasks on the agenda according to the following
algorithm: (1) Select the next task to run from the agenda. (2) If the task is satisfied, as defined in the RAP succeed clause, go on to the next task. (3) If the task
is a primitive, execute it and go on to the next task. (4) If the task is not satisfied
and nonprimitive, select a refinement method that matches the current situation, as defined in the RAP method context clauses. (5) Instantiate the method
by creating a subtask for every step and placing them on the agenda with appropriate ordering constraints. (6) Place the current task back on the agenda to run
after all of its subtasks have completed. (7) Loop back to select the next task.

This looping continues as long as there is a task on the agenda that is eligible
to run. Tasks may become ineligible to run temporarily because they are
blocked waiting for signals from the skill system or because they are constrained
to follow tasks that have not yet run. However, during this time, concurrent
paths of execution are still pursued by the RAP system if any are available on the
task agenda.

The RAP system is designed to achieve goals in a dynamic environment. Doing method selection at run-time enables RAP tasks to select the best method
even when the world is changing or contains details that cannot be predicted in
advance. RAP methods also include other RAP tasks as subgoals, and the resulting
hierarchy helps the system to cope with complexity by specializing actions

through many different levels of detail. To further increase robustness, a RAP task includes a success test to confirm that a method has succeeded in achieving its goal. If the success test is false after a method has completed, the RAP task continues to run, selecting alternative methods until the success test is satisfied or there are no methods to try. This tenacious execution allows a task to recover when the information it uses to select a method is incorrect, when actions don't have their intended effects, or when the situation changes while a method is executing.

Along with the ability to describe task plans and switch easily between tasks as the situation requires, the RAP system also maintains a record of what it knows about the current world state. Ideally, all of the succeed and context checks done by the system would refer directly to the state of the world so that they would always make use of the most up-to-date information possible. However, real sensors have finite ranges, fields of view, and processing power, so there is no way for the system to sense everything in its environment at the same time. The world model keeps information available using rules that alter memory in response to the success and failure of tasks and the contents of signals from the skill level.

The Knowledge Representation

The animate agent architecture defines the framework in which CHIP is programmed. However, it is the skills and RAPs that encode CHIP's knowledge about how to carry out tasks in the world.

Our goal while creating skills and RAPs for CHIP has been to encode behaviors that can be used to achieve a wide variety of goals. The first step has been to assemble a broad set of skills and low-level RAPs to manage CHIP's effectors. This set forms the building blocks for all higher-level RAP tasks.

The next step has been the adoption of an object centered view of the world. CHIP's skills and RAPs are structured to separate the designation of objects in the world (i.e., tracking) from the skills and plans that act on those objects. This separation allows actions to be extended to new object types by adding new tracking routines for designating those types. The object centered view also encourages a general "designate," "go-to," "orient," and "act" structure for basic activities on objects. This structure can be seen in all of CHIP's high-level RAPs.

To illustrate these ideas, this section of the paper describes in detail the skills and RAPs used by CHIP at the IJCAI-95 Robot Competition. CHIP went into the "office cleanup task" with a relatively general-purpose strategy for cleaning up a room. Broadly, the strategy was to scan an entire area systematically, and as collectible trash objects were identified, pick them up and deposit them in the nearest appropriate trash receptacle. The RAPs encoding this strategy are built up from a collection of more general purpose operations designed to be the building blocks for CHIP's future behavior.

The knowledge representation for the cleanup domain consists of thirty skills and sixty-three RAPs. All of the skills and most of the RAPs are reusable for similar tasks. Only a few of the mapping and highest level RAPs are specific to the trash task.

Skills

The skills used on CHIP break down into several categories: basic effector motions, gathering information, tracking targets, acting on targets, and monitoring for problems.

Basic Effector Skills

CHIP has basic skills for moving its arm, gripper, head, and body. These skills correspond to generic actions and can be used to accomplish a wide variety of tasks. However, these skills incorporate very little feedback from the external environment, so they can only be employed effectively when the situation around the robot is well known.

CHIP's arm extends straight out in front of its body and has shoulder, elbow, and wrist joints. To position the arm, there is a skill to move the arm so that the wrist is a given distance away from the body and above the floor, and another skill to move the wrist to a given pitch and roll. There is also a skill to open or close the gripper to a given position as well as a separate skill to open the gripper until its sensors report that the gripper is empty. This latter skill is used to drop things and is much more robust than trying to drop something by opening the gripper to a fixed width. All of these skills generate a signal when the arm, wrist, or gripper has reached the desired position. All three skills also monitor relevant touch sensors on the arm and gripper and will stop moving the arm and signal that it cannot move if something is bumped. These basic arm skills are:

(position-arm out up)
(position-wrist pitch roll)
(position-gripper width)
(open-gripper)

CHIP's cameras are mounted on a pan/tilt head. There are two skills to position that head:

(pan-to angle)
(tilt-to angle)

Each skill generates a signal when the head reaches the appropriate angle.

There are three simple skills to move CHIP forward and backward and turn CHIP a given angle:

(roll-forward distance speed)

(roll-backward distance speed)
(turn-relative angle speed)

Each of these skills generates a signal when the correct distance or angle has been covered. All three skills monitor touch sensors and signal that the robot is stuck if something is bumped.

Gathering Information

There are four simple state sensing skills:

(report-arm-data)
(report-gripper-data)
(report-head-data)
(report-position-data)

These skills are really an artifact of the implementation of the animate agent architecture used to control CHIP at the robot competition. The values of all CHIP's basic sensors, like joint angles, speeds, heading, etc., are available directly to all skills within the CRL system. However, because of the distributed nature of CRL, this information cannot be directly queried by the RAP system. Hence, the RAP system must maintain its own model of the state of the robot and update that model when necessary by enabling skills that generate the relevant data in the form of signals. These skills generate signals specifying the configuration of CHIP's effectors.

CHIP also has skills for reporting the values of its range sensors:

(report-sonar-values)
(report-freespace-values divisions)

The first of these reports the values of the eight sonar sensors, and the other processes camera images to generate free space distances in front of the robot. The free space skill is based on an algorithm used by Horswill that looks for the edges where obstacles meet the floor (Horswill 1993). When enabled, these skills generate signals that include the appropriate sensory data. Note that the visual freespace algorithm requires use of the camera and only makes sense when the camera is pointed in an appropriate direction.

During the trash collection task, the signals from these skills are not directed to the RAP system, but to the occupancy grid-mapping system. The RAP system controls when the skills are enabled, but their effect is to update CHIP's maps.

CHIP has two crucial visual skills for finding objects in the world:

(find-small-objects)
(find-hausdorff model)

The first of these visual skills looks for all of the small objects in the current camera field of view and classifies each according to type. The second looks for places in the current field of view that match a given model using a Hausdorff distance metric for judging similarity. The algorithms used by the small object finder and the Hausdorff matcher are described in more detail in the vision routines section. Each of these skills generates two types of signal: the first is generated for each object found, and gives its type and location; the second is generated when the skill has finished processing an image.

During the trash-collecting task, the signals generated by these skills when an object is found are also sent directly to the object-mapping system and not to the RAP system. However, the RAP system receives the "processing complete" signals so it will know when the skill is done.

Acting on Specific Objects and Locations

CHIP has three skills that can be used to specify target locations:

(track-*x-y* *x y*)
(track-small-object *x y* failures)
(track-hausdorff model failures)

The first skill simply designates a fixed point in the world using dead-reckoning. The second skill tracks a small object in the world and continually updates its position relative to CHIP. The third skill tracks an object using the Hausdorff matcher. All three skills write the tracked object's location to the target location channel.

The two visual tracking skills incorporate a number of assumptions about the world to make them function more effectively. The small object tracker locks onto and tracks any small object; it does not attempt to classify the object while it is tracking. As a result, the tracker must be given the initial location of the object to be tracked. The Hausdorff tracker assumes there is only a single object in the field of view that matches the model and will get confused if there are more. Each visual tracker also has a parameter specifying the maximum number of frames in a row that the target can be lost before a lost target signal is generated. If the target never moves out of the field of view, these skills do not generate any signal.

Once a target location is being tracked, there are a number of actions that CHIP can take to act on that location. The first of these is to keep the camera head pointed at the location:

(pan-to-target)

When CHIP is tracking an object and moving at the same time, the camera head must continually be adjusted to remain pointed at the object.

The second activity that CHIP needs to be able to do is to move toward the current target location. This activity is encoded as two skills: one for converting the target location into a target heading and range, and one for moving in the direction of the target while avoiding obstacles.

(head-to-target at-radius near-radius)
(move-and-avoid speed buffer horizon)

The first of these skills generates a signal when the robot gets near the target and when it reaches the target. The second skill uses a very simple potential field-based algorithm (Arkin 1987) for avoiding obstacles using CHIP's current sonar readings parameterized by a minimum distance allowed to obstacles and a horizon beyond which obstacles are ignored. This skill generates a signal if CHIP is not making progress toward the target heading.

CHIP can turn toward the current target location without moving toward it using the skill

(turn-to-target speed buffer near-angle)

This skill signals when the robot is facing near the target. It also backs the robot up slowly if possible to keep the arm from hitting anything.

CHIP also needs to pick up targeted objects. This activity is broken down into two skills: one to line the robot up precisely with the target, and one to move forward and grasp the object at the target location:

(orient-to-target standoff range-error angle-error)
(roll-forward-and-grasp speed max-distance)

The first of these skills is required because CHIP cannot move its arm from side to side and therefore must line its body up precisely with an object before it can reach out to grasp it. During the trash cleanup competition, CHIP needed to be aligned to a piece of trash within one degree before it could pick it up.

Once CHIP is precisely aligned with an object the second skill moves CHIP forward to grasp the object. This skill moves CHIP until the gripper sensors say that something is within its grasp and then closes the gripper to fixed pressure. Conceptually, this action should probably be encoded as a skill to move the robot forward until the sensors say to stop, and a separate skill to close the gripper. However, they were encoded as a single skill to increase robustness by decreasing the time between detecting the object to be grasped and closing the gripper. This skill signals when it has successfully completed a grasp, when it has moved a specified distance without finding anything to grasp, and when it has closed the gripper but nothing seems to be in it. The first signal indicates success, while the other two arise when the robot is misaligned, the object moves, or when closing the gripper accidentally squeezes the object out of its grasp.

Monitoring States of the World

Finally, CHIP uses a small set of skills for monitoring various states in the world and signaling problems. The first of these skills monitors the gripper sensors and signals if they change state:

(monitor-gripper)

This skill is typically used to detect an object that is dropped while it is being carried from one place to another.

There are also three skills that monitor the sonars and signal when something gets too close to CHIP's front, back, or arm:

(forward-safe radius)
(backward-safe radius)
(turn-safe radius)

These skills are used concurrently with other skills to signal when problems are arising. For example, when CHIP is rolling forward to pick up a piece of trash, the direction in front of the robot is monitored to make sure it stays safe. However, when the robot is rolling forward to drop a piece of trash in a trash bin, the monitor skill is disabled so it will not detect the trash bin as an obstacle as the arm moves over the top of it.

The last skill used in the trash cleanup competition monitors the emergency stop button and signals an emergency when that button is pressed. This skill is always enabled:

(emergency-stop)

Primitive RAPs

The interface between the RAP system and the skill system is in the form of RAP methods that enable and disable skills. To allow the most flexible use of CHIP's skills in RAP methods, access to each skill is encoded into a "primitive" RAP. When executed, such a RAP enables the appropriate skill and waits for it to generate a signal that means success or a signal that means failure.

For example, to move the pan/tilt head the following RAP is used:

```
(define-rap  (primitive-pan-to ?angle)
   (succeed (and (head-pan angle ?b)
                 (within (- ?angle ?b) 0.02)))
   (method
     (primitive
       (enable (pan-to ?angle))
       (wait-for (:pan-at ?a) :SUCCEED (head-pan-angle ?a))
       (wait-for (:pan-stuck ?a) :FAIL (head-pan-angle ?a))
       (disable :above))))
```

This RAP describes a task for placing the camera head at a given pan angle. If the current head-pan-angle is specified in the RAP world model to be within 0.02 radians (about one degree) of the desired angle, the task is complete and the RAP succeeds. If not, the single method defines a primitive plan to enable the pan-to skill and then waits for it to generate a :pan-at signal. The method also waits for the skill to generate a :pan-stuck signal just in case the head cannot move. In either case, when a signal arrives, the method finishes by disabling the skills it enabled.

The final argument to the wait-for clause specifies a change to make in the world model if the corresponding signal arrives. A complete task encoding within the RAP system includes defining rules to change the RAP world model according to the results of executing each task. A general syntax for these rules is described in Firby (1995) but for many RAPs, the wait-for result can be treated as a direct assertion into the RAP world model. In the example above, the wait-for clauses are such that when a primitive-pan-to task completes, the RAP world model will hold the pan angle that the head actually reached.

There are similar primitive RAPs that correspond to each of the robot effector and information-gathering skills discussed previously:

```
(primitive-arm-move ?x ?y)
(primitive-wrist-move ?tilt ?twist)
(primitive-gripper-move ?position)
(primitive-gripper-open)
(primitive-pan-to ?angle)
(primitive-tilt-to ?angle)
(primitive-roll-forward ?dist ?speed)
(primitive-roll-backward ?dist ?speed)
(primitive-turn-relative ?angle ?rs)
(primitive-find-small-objects ?type)
(primitive-find-hausdorff ?type ?range ?failures)
(primitive-report-arm-data)
(primitive-report-gripper-data)
(primitive-report-head-data)
(primitive-report-location-data)
(primitive-report-sonar-values)
(primitive-report-freespace-values ?divisions)
```

At this level of abstraction, the directed information gathering skills are packaged via primitive RAPs that are exactly like any other primitive. For example

```
(define-rap (primitive-find-small-objects ?type)
    (method
      (primitive
        (enable (find-small-objects ?type))
        (wait-for  (:small-objects-found ?num)
                   :SUCCEED (found-small-objects ?num))
        (disable :above))))
```

A key idea in our architecture is that agent activity is created by assembling networks of skills that close feedback loops through both sensing and action. When viewed as building blocks for these networks, sensing and acting skills are conceptually the same type of entity. For example, the target designation skills are packaged as primitive RAPs in the same way and become

```
(primitive-track-x-y ?x ?y)
(primitive-track-small-object ?x ?y ?error)
(primitive-track-hausdorff ?type ?range)
```

The primary difference between these tracking RAPs and the information gathering RAPs is that tracking RAPs complete only when an error is signaled:

```
(define-rap (primitive-track-small-object ?x ?y ?error)
    (method
      (primitive
```

```
(enable (track-small-object ?x ?y 3 ?error))
(wait-for (:lost-target) :FAIL)
(disable :above))))
```

In normal circumstances, target tracking primitives are used in conjunction with action primitives that complete when the desired task is complete. Also notice in this example that the failure count (the number of times the tracker is allowed to lose and reacquire the target) passed to the skill being activated is built in as the constant 3. A more general formulation of the RAP library would use different failure counts according to the expected difficulty of tracking the object in the current situation.

Similarly, targeted action skills are represented as primitive RAPs:

```
(primitive-pan-to-goal)
(primitive-move-to-goal ?ts ?rs ?drange)
(primitive-turn-to-goal ?rs ?drange)
(primitive-orient-to-goal ?standoff ?drange ?dangle ?ts ?rs)
(primitive-approach-and-grasp ?speed ?maxdist ?press)
```

However, many of these primitives actually enable a set of skills, either to monitor additional safety conditions or because the skills only make sense as a group. For example

```
(define-rap (primitive-move-to-goal ?ts ?rs ?drange)
    (futility-threshold 1)
    (method
      (primitive
        (enable  (forward-safe 20)
                 (head-to-goal ?drange ?drange)
                 (move-and-avoid ?ts ?rs 2.0 100 170))
        (disable :above)
        (wait-for (:at-goal ?x1 ?y1 ?h1) :SUCCEED (at ?x1 ?y1 ?h1))
        (wait-for (:near-goal ?x1 ?y1 ?h1) :SUCCEED (at ?x1 ?y1 ?h1))
        (wait-for (:stuck ?x1 ?y1 ?h1) :FAIL (at ?x1 ?y1 ?h1))
        (wait-for (:front-danger) :FAIL))))
```

A more general formulation might separate these skills to give more flexibility in describing plans, but that wasn't necessary for the trash cleanup task.

However, a special case requiring a different combination of motion skills did arise in the trash domain. The primitive-move-to-goal described above causes CHIP to stop between segments of a larger motion plan. If two move-to-goal tasks are executed in a sequence, the move-and-avoid skill that controls CHIP's motors is disabled in between. To avoid that stop, two other primitive RAPs were defined that signal when approaching their goal but do not disable the skills they have started:

```
(primitive-move-to-goal-smooth ?ts ?rs ?drange)
(primitive-turn-to-goal-smooth ?rs ?dangle)
```

Thus, while the RAP system moves on and invokes the next task in the sequence, CHIP's skills are still moving toward the last task's goal, and a smooth transition occurs between tasks.

Moving smoothly from one skill set to the next is a general problem, and this simple solution for multistep motion tasks may point toward a more general solution.

There are two more primitive motion RAPs implemented on CHIP for the trash cleanup task

(primitive-move-to-x-y ?x ?y ?ts ?rs ?radius1 ?radius2)
(primitive-turn-to-x-y ?x ?y ?rs ?dangle)

These RAPs simply group together a target designation skill (*i.e.*, track-x-y) and the corresponding action skills. Again, this is a representational shortcut that isn't required; the same behavior can be generated by a RAP method that executes primitive-track-x-y and primitive-move-to-goal concurrently. The details of the primitive-move-to-x-y RAP are

```
(define-rap (primitive-move-to-x-y ?x ?y ?ts ?rs ?radius1 ?radius2)
   (method
    (primitive
     (enable  (forward-safe 15.0)
             (track-x-y ?x ?y)
             (head-to-goal ?radius1 ?radius2)
             (move-and-avoid ?ts ?rs 5.0 80.0 120.0))
     (disable :above)
     (wait-for (:at-goal ?x1 ?y1 ?h1) :SUCCEED (at ?x1 ?y1 ?h1))
     (wait-for (:stuck ?x1 ?y1 ?h1) :FAIL (at ?x1 ?y1 ?h1))
     (wait-for (:front-danger) :FAIL))))
```

Finally, the last primitive RAP is

(primitive-monitor-gripper)

This RAP is used to notice if the robot drops something it is carrying. That skill was separated out because it needs to overlap a variety of other primitive tasks as CHIP carries objects around. The other safety skills are incorporated into motion primitives and do not have separate RAPs.

The RAP Hierarchy

A hierarchy of more abstract RAPs is built on top of the primitives. The hierarchy is currently defined by the subgoals that we believe will be generally useful for other tasks in the future. Only at the very top of the hierarchy does information specific to trash cleanup come into play.

Moving the Robot

The first set of composite RAPs used on CHIP encodes simple methods for moving CHIP to a designated location. Four RAPs are used for this task:

(turn-to-location ?x ?y ?rs ?dangle)

```
(go-to-location ?x ?y ?ts ?rs ?drange)
(go-to-goal ?ts ?rs ?drange)
(travel-to-goal ?ts ?rs ?drange)
```

The first of these RAPs enables the primitive actions needed to turn CHIP to face a particular location. Actually moving CHIP to a location is handled by travel-to-goal, which enables primitives in sequence to turn toward the currently tracked goal location and then move up to it. The go-to-goal and go-to-location RAPs give two different interfaces to travel-to-goal. Go-to-goal is used when some other task is already tracking the goal (a visual tracker in the trash cleanup task), and go-to-location is used to start up a dead-reckoning location tracker when no other tracking task is running in parallel. Both go-to-goal and go-to-location also have methods for making sure that the robot's current location is up-to-date.

One method for go-to-location and the method used by travel-to-goal are shown below (?ts and rs are translation and rotation speeds, and ?drange is the desired minimum distance from the goal):

```
(define-rap (go-to-location ?x ?y ?ts ?rs ?drange)
    (succeed (and   (my-location ?x1 ?y1 ?h1)
                    (within (delta (- ?x1 ?x) (- ?y1 ?y)) ?drange)))
    ...
    (method
      (context (my-location ?x1 ?y1 ?h1))
      (task-net
        (parallel
          (t2 (primitive-track-x-y ?x ?y) (until-end t3))
          (t3 (travel-to-goal ?ts ?rs ?drange))))))

(define-rap (travel-to-goal ?ts ?rs ?drange)
    (method
      (task-net
        (sequence
          (t1 (primitive-turn-to-goal-smooth ?rs 0.4))
          (t2 (primitive-move-to-goal ?ts ?rs ?drange))))))
```

There are also composite RAPs for moving CHIP's arm around:

```
(position-arm ?place)
(position-wrist ?place)
(arm-fold)
```

The first two allow symbolic names to be used to specify standard arm and wrist configurations. In particular, for the trash cleanup task, CHIP's arm needs to be positioned down near the floor for grasping, up high for dropping trash in the waste basket, and tucked in for carrying things from place to place. CHIP's wrist also has to be positioned up (level with the ground) for grasping and carrying, and down out of the way when CHIP is searching for objects visually. The arm-fold RAP is used to tuck CHIP's arm away when it is not in use.

As an example, the position-wrist RAP is

```
(define-rap (position-wrist ?place)
    (succeed (wrist-position ?place))
    (method
      (context (= ?place UP))
      (task-net
        (t1 (primitive-wrist-move 0.0 0.0))))
    (method
      (context (= ?place DOWN))
      (task-net
        (t1 (primitive-wrist-move -1.57 0.0)))))
```

These abstract RAPs are somewhat specialized for the trash cleanup task since they specifically encode appropriate arm and wrist configurations for the actions required for that task. However, the idea of canonical actuator configurations for particular tasks seems reasonable, and these specialized examples stand in for a more developed model of such behavior.

Acting on an Object

The basic modularity concept encoded into the primitive RAPs and skills is the separation of tasks for tracking objects and locations in the world from the tasks for acting on those objects and locations. This same separation appears in the higher level RAPs as a focus of attention. All of CHIP's high level RAPs are designed to act on the current focus of attention, so before CHIP can act on an object or location it must select that object or location as the focus of attention. The introduction of a focus of attention means that action plans are encoded in an indexical-functional way.

CHIP's action plans also break naturally into three broad categories: plans for approaching the focus, plans for orienting to the focus in preparation for taking an action, and plans for acting on the focus in various ways. For the trash cleanup task, it was only necessary to flesh out some of the different types of approach and orientation behaviors that a robot like CHIP might require.

The most elaborate hierarchy of focus based plans are the RAPs for approaching the current focus of attention. Five RAPs were required to encode all of the combinations of actions needed to turn CHIP to face the focus, move within visual tracking range of the focus, start tracking the focus and move toward it, and when close enough, ensure that the focus is roughly in front of CHIP. Those RAPs are

```
(go-to-focus ?mapping ?ts ?rs ?standoff ?drange ?dangle)
    (go-to-focus-basic ?ts ?rs ?standoff ?drange ?dangle)
      (go-to-focus-aux ?ts ?rs ?standoff ?drange ?dangle)
        (approach-focus-visually ?ts ?rs ?drange ?dangle)
          (track-visually ?type ?x ?y)
```

The go-to-focus RAP enables whatever mapping primitives are desired to run in parallel with moving the robot toward the focus (such as sonar or vision based occupancy grid building). The go-to-focus-basic RAP ensures that CHIP's current location with respect to the focus is known, and go-to-focus-aux contains different methods for the various cases in which CHIP is too far or too close to track the focus visually, CHIP doesn't know how to track the focus visually (i.e., the target is an object without a good tracking method), or CHIP is too close to the focus and must back away. The track-visually RAP selects and enables an appropriate primitive tracker for the object type (if one is known) and is used by approach-focus-visually, which appears in the go-to-focus-aux methods that require visual tracking. All of these RAPs eventually generate go-to-location or go-to-goal subtasks.

Orienting to the focus so that it can be manipulated is a critical task for CHIP in the trash cleanup domain. CHIP's body must be precisely aligned to enable the gripper to reach around or over an object simply by moving the body back and forth. This orientation is accomplished with two RAPs:

```
(orient-to-focus ?purpose)
(orient-to-focus-aux ?offset ?drange ?dangle ?ts ?rs)
```

The first RAP selects appropriate parameters for the second RAP according to the purpose of the orientation. Preparing for a grasp requires much more precise, and hence slower, orientation than preparing to drop something in the waste basket.

An example method from the orient-to-focus-aux RAP is shown below:

```
(define-rap (orient-to-focus-aux ?offset ?dr ?da ?ts ?rs)
    ...
    (method
      (context (and   (focus-object ?class ?type)
                      (focus-location ?x ?y)))
      (task-net
        (sequence
          (t0 (primitive-pan-to 0.0))
          (parallel
            (t1 (track-focus-visually ?type ?x ?y))
            (t2 (primitive-orient-to-goal ?offset ?dr ?da ?ts ?rs)))
          (t3 (primitive-report-location-data))))))
```

In this method, the camera is fixed straight forward, and the object is tracked visually while CHIP lines up with it.

Once CHIP is properly oriented to an object, it can perform one of two actions in the cleanup domain: it can pick the object up, or it can drop something into the object. The RAPs for these tasks are

```
(pickup-focus)
    (pickup-focus-aux ?ts ?max-dist)
    (pickup-focus-cleanup)
(drop-into-focus ?ts)
```

The pickup-focus RAP is interesting because it must cope with CHIP failing to get hold of the object it is trying to pick up. On the whole, CHIP performs very reliably in the trash cleanup domain, and what little special error handling is required has been removed from the RAPs shown for clarity. However, picking trash up off the floor is relatively unreliable, and failing to get hold of the desired piece of trash can leave CHIP's arm and gripper in unexpected states. For example, CHIP may actually have the object wedged in its gripper but be unable to sense that it is there. In that case, it must open its gripper wide to make sure it is empty before folding its arm away. To ensure that this cleanup operation happens, the pickup-focus method encodes a two step method. The first step actually tries to pick up the focus object, and if it succeeds then the method finishes up immediately. However, if it fails, the method proceeds to the second step, which puts the gripper and arm in known, safe states.

```
(define-rap (pickup-focus)
    (succeed (arm-holding ?class ?type))
    (method
      (context (pickup-params ?type ?ts ?max-dist))
      (task-net
        (sequence
          (t0 (pickup-focus-aux ?ts ?max-dist)
              (wait-for :succeed :terminate)
              (wait-for :fail :proceed))
          (t1 (pickup-focus-cleanup))))))
```

This simple technique for putting the robot in a safe state after failure can be used in a wide variety of situations.

The drop-into-focus RAP is a good example of a multistep plan:

```
(define-rap (drop-into-focus ?ts)
    ...
    (method
      (context (and (focus-location ?x ?y)
                    (my-location ?x1 ?y1 ?h1)))
      (task-net
        (sequence
          (t0 (calculate-range-to-x-y ?x1 ?y1 ?x ?y => ?range))
          (t2 (position-arm up))
          (t3 (primitive-roll-forward (- ?range 55) ?ts))
          (t4 (primitive-gripper-open))
          (t5 (primitive-roll-backward (- ?range 20) ?ts))
          (parallel
            (t6 (arm-fold))
            (t7 (primitive-gripper-move 1)))))))
```

This action is also prone to error in the trash cleanup task. If the orient-to-focus task that precedes it does not actually achieve the precision that it believes it has, then moving forward may cause a collision or the gripper may not end up over the focus and the object dropped will fail to go in. Unfortunately, CHIP did not have any good way of sensing either of these situations during the IJCAI-95 competition and there was no good way to detect or correct such failures. Hence, the RAP for the drop-into-focus task does not encode any failure correction strategies (fortunately, crossing our fingers seemed to be effective during the actual competition). Notice also that the calculation of the actual distance to move forward (and backward) uses constants that effectively hard code the reach of the arm when it positioned up.

The drop-into-focus RAP also includes an example of a function call encoded as a RAP task. The calculate-range-to-x-y step in the method looks like a RAP task but it ends up as a simple function call. Two RAPs like this were used in various methods for the trash cleanup task:

```
(calculate-range-to-x-y ?x1 ?y1 ?x ?y => ?range)
(calculate-angle-to-x-y ?x1 ?y1 ?h1 ?x ?y => ?angle)
```

Finally, carrying is encoded as a separate task that monitors the gripper in parallel with moving: RAPs used for carrying are

```
(carry-to-focus ?mapping ?ts ?rs ?standoff ?drange ?dangle)
    (monitor-gripper-holding ?class ?type)
```

The need to specify a separate carrying task complicates the reuse of subtasks because all methods must make a distinction between moving to a location and carrying something to a location. This example of problems in creating a truly modular task hierarchy is discussed in more detail in Firby (1996).

The carry-to-focus RAP executes a go-to-focus task in parallel with a monitor-gripper-holding task:

```
(define-rap (carry-to-focus ?mapping ?ts ?rs ?standoff ?dr ?da)
    (method
      (context (and (focus-object ?class ?type)
                    (arm-holding ?class1 ?type1)))
      (task-net
        (parallel
          (t0 (speak :carry ?type1 ?type))
          (t1 1 (monitor-gripper-holding ?class1 ?type1)
              (until-end t2))
          (t2 (go-to-focus ?mapping ?ts ?rs ?radius ?dr ?da))))))
```

Unlike many of the previous RAP examples, this method has not been cleaned up, and it includes a special step in which CHIP says what it is doing. This step was encoded into the method for the IJCAI-95 competition so that CHIP would give a running commentary on its progress to the audience. Adding such steps might seem simple, but they complicate the task hierarchy considerably. In this instance, an additional task, monitor-gripper-holding, is also required. The primitive-monitor-gripper task would work, but it does not say anything (*i.e.*, speak) if the object gets dropped. Monitor-gripper-holding executes primitive-monitor-gripper and watches for that task to fail, indicating that the object has been dropped, and then executes a speak task to say what has dropped. To know what to say, monitor-gripper-holding has to be passed the class and type of object being carried. Of course, in general, the actions required for CHIP to talk about what it is doing should not be hard coded into the plans used to act in the world.

Mapping the World

In addition to acting in the world, CHIP needs to map the location of objects and obstacles. A map of objects is needed so that CHIP can remember the location of trash and trash cans, and a map of obstacles is needed so that CHIP can select good observation points and tell when all pieces of trash have been collected. For the trash cleanup task, CHIP maintains four maps: a map of object locations, a map of where it has looked for trash, a map of where it has looked for trash cans, and a map of occupied space.

CHIP records the locations of objects like trash and trash cans in a simple database which is updated automatically whenever the find-small-objects or find-hausdorff skills are used. To keep track of where CHIP has looked, a binary grid in global coordinates is also maintained for each of these skills. Whenever CHIP uses one of these skills, the wedge of floor space imaged by the skill is recorded in the appropriate grid by setting the points covered by the image. The grid showing where CHIP looked for small objects during the final event of the IJCAI-95 competition is shown in figure 7.

To map occupied space, CHIP uses a simple occupancy grid technique (Borenstein and Koren 1991; Elfes 1989). The occupancy map is updated whenever the report-sonar-values or report-freespace-values skills are enabled. During the competition, the sonar skill was enabled by the go-to-focus task whenever CHIP moved. The occupancy grid generated during the final event of the competition is shown in figure 8.

Connecting the object database directly to sensing skills is a shortcut that works for CHIP because both the small object finder and the Hausdorff matcher actually identify an object's type. Manipulation of the object database at a higher level of RAP plan is all that will be needed to make use of less specific sensor data like an object's color or shape. However, the binary grids that CHIP uses to keep track of where it has looked for trash and trash cans is a very specialized trick. A different approach will be needed to generalize CHIP's plans for searching to allow any type of object. CHIP cannot be expected to maintain a separate grid for every type of object it knows about.

Data are fed into all these maps from low-level skills, but CHIP's RAP-level plans make use of the maps via two functions accessed as RAP steps:

(query-object-set ?relation ?x ?y ?class => ?x1 ?y1 ?type)
(find-unobserved-spot ?type ?x ?y ?heading ?minx ?maxx => ?x1 ?y1)

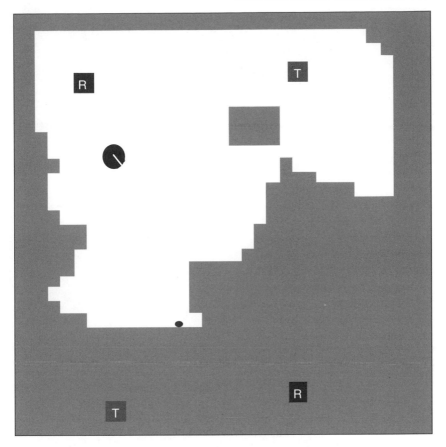

Figure 7. Areas searched for trash during the competition. Trash cans and recycling bins are marked as squares. A piece of trash is shown as a dot.

The query-object-set function is used to query the object database to find an object with the specified relationship to a location in the world. Current defined relations let CHIP ask which object of the specified class is closest to or farthest from the given location. In the trash cleanup domain, the defined classes were trash and trash bin. The function returns the location of the selected object and its type. In the trash domain, types were cup, can, trash can, and recycling bin.

The find-unobserved-spot function is used to select a good place on the floor to look at when searching for an object. It takes the object type, CHIP's current position, and the minimum and maximum ranges of CHIP's cameras as arguments. Simple heuristics are used to prefer to explore areas that can be seen by turning the pan/tilt head, then those that can be explored by turning the robot, and finally those that require moving to a new vantage point. In addition to ex-

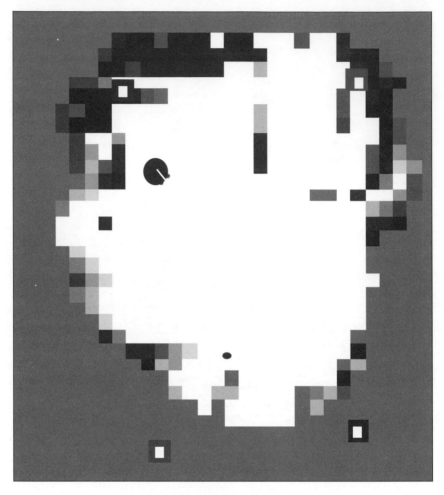

Figure 8. Occupancy map generated during the competition.

amining the appropriate binary observation grid, this function uses the occupancy grid to ensure that all observation targets are actually accessible. Furthermore, because the office environment at the competition was sealed by walls and closed doorways, once CHIP had checked every accessible area for trash, it knew that no more trash existed in the office and the task was complete.

Searching for an Object

The final major subtask needed in the trash cleanup domain is using the map as a basis for searching for trash and trash cans.

The RAP plans for selecting a piece of trash implement a loop to check for a known piece of trash in the object map, if none is known to select a previously unobserved location and move to bring it into view, then to observe the location with the small object finder (which will place any trash objects seen into the object map), and repeat. Those RAPs are:

```
(search-for-object ?class ?mapping ?ts ?rs)
    (select-closest-object ?class)
        (comb-the-world ?class ?mapping ?ts ?rs)
        (comb-the-near-world ?class ?mapping ?ts ?rs)
        (select-unobserved-spot ?class => ?x ?y)
        (observe-spot ?x ?y ?standoff ?mapping ?ts ?rs)
            (look-for-class ?routine ?class)
```

The search-for-object RAP implements the searching loop and invokes select-closest-object, which queries the map structures using query-object-set. If no object of the correct type is known, then comb-the-world is invoked, which selects a location to observe, moves there and looks, and repeats until an object of the correct type is actually found. Comb-the-world will fail when there are no areas left unobserved, meaning that the trash cleanup task is done. The levels in the hierarchy implement the heuristics of looking nearby before actually moving.

CHIP uses the same RAPs to find trash cans and recycling bins. However, search-for-object was specialized during the competition to implement additional heuristics if the class being looked for was trash can or recycle bin. In particular, unlike pieces of trash, trash cans can be seen all the way across the office, and there were exactly two trash cans and two recycling bins. This information led to the heuristic that CHIP use a known trash can if it was facing toward one or look around first if it was facing away from a known can and the other trash can had not yet been found. The result of this heuristic was for CHIP to find all four receptacles early and then always move to the closest can of the appropriate type.

The result of successfully executing a search-for-object task is to set the focus of attention to the selected object.

Putting It all Together

Finally, putting it all together, the top-level algorithm for the cleanup task is:
1. Select a piece of trash. If one is known in the database, use it, else search.
2. Go to the trash.
3. Pick it up.
4. Select an appropriate trash can. If a good one is known, use it, else search.
5. Go to the trash can.
6. Drop off the trash.
7. Repeat.

This algorithm is implemented using two RAPs:

(clean-up-trash)
   (put-object-away ?class)

The clean-up-trash task is the top level goal given to CHIP and it loops over put-object-away with class trash until no more trash can be found. Put-object-away directly implements the basic algorithm as:

```
(define-rap (put-object-away ?oclass)
    ...
    (method
     (task-net
      (sequence
        (t0 (arm-fold))
        (t1 (search-for-object ?oclass :sonar 30 0.4)
            ((focus-object ?oclass ?otype) for t1b))
        (t2 (go-to-focus :sonar 30 0.4 80 10 0.1))
        (t3 (orient-to-focus :pickup))
        (t4 (pickup-focus)
            ((and  (arm-holding ?oclass ?type)
                   (can-for ?type ?cclass)) for t5))
        (t5 (search-for-object ?cclass :sonar 20 0.4))
        (t6 (carry-to-focus :sonar 30 0.4 100 10 0.1))
        (t7 (orient-to-focus :drop-off))
        (t8 (drop-into-focus 10))))))
```

The can-for annotation on step t4 looks in memory for the appropriate kind of trash bin for the type of trash found and picked up.

This basic plan may encounter a number of problems: there may be no pieces of trash to be found, a piece of trash may be unreachable, pickup might fail, the trash might be dropped while moving, or there may be no accessible trash can. The first problem is caught by this plan as a failure of step t1, and it means the cleanup task is complete. The second problem results in a failure of step t2 and is dealt with by the memory update rules associated with go-to-focus. When a go-to-focus task fails, the focus object is removed from the object map, resulting in its causing no more problems. If the pickup step fails, or the piece of trash is dropped, this plan fails but clean-up-trash keeps looping and tries again. If no trash cans can be found, then this plan fails and so does clean-up-trash.

Vision Routines

One of the primary goals in developing the animate agent architecture has been to integrate purposive vision with other aspects of intelligent agent control. Within our architecture, all vision processing is done in the context of a specific task, and that task can be used to focus vision-processing skills on specific aspects of the environment. In addition, complex vision-processing tasks that require executing a series of "perceptual primitives" are easily encoded as multistep RAP methods.

In programming CHIP for the office cleanup task, the most difficult problem was getting useful information about the world out of visual images. Most of the skills and RAPs were relatively straightforward once reliable visual routines were produced. Therefore, this section of the paper describes the two primary visual routines in detail: the Hausdorff, template-matching routine used to find trash cans, and the small object finder used for finding and classifying pieces of trash.

Finding Objects Using Template Matching

One way to find objects in a visual image is to search the image for an area that matches a known template of the object. For example, one might try to match a template of the edges of a known object against the edges in a scene. On CHIP we have implemented a template matcher that uses binary edge features and a search algorithm based on the Hausdorff distance metric. The software we use was produced by Cornell's Robotics and Vision laboratory (Huttenlocher and Rucklidge 1992) and is publicly available.

The basic idea of our template matcher is to look for edges in a scene that "line up" with the features in a template. However, the actual arrangement of the target's features in an image depends on how the object is viewed, so the matcher must search over a wide range of possible attitudes and scales.

For the objects in the office cleanup task, we can restrict the expected viewpoints a priori because we know that objects are in a known orientation, (e.g., the trash cans were right-side up, not on their sides or upside down). Thus, we only need to worry about viewing the object from different locations on the plane of the floor. Furthermore, the trash cans were round, so they look the same when viewed from different directions. Also, the possible distance to an object can always be bounded, because of limited camera resolution at large distances and limited field of view up close. Thus, the template matcher only has to search for our object as seen from a single direction at a restricted number of scales.

However, an object template must still consist of a set of models because, as a robot approaches a round trash can, the top rim of the can becomes more circular, whereas from a distance it appears as a line or thin ellipse. This deformation is not well approximated as a simple resizing, so we use six models for a trash can (figure 9) taken from different distances. The search takes no longer than with a single model, because each model is searched for over one-sixth the range of possible distances that would be covered by a single model.

Having restricted the attitudes and scales over which the matcher must search, it is still necessary to compare template matches at all possible locations in the image. The Hausdorff distance is a particularly good metric for judging the fit between a template and image. The Hausdorff metric gives a single num-

Figure 9. Edge models of the IJCAI trash can taken from distances of seventy-five cm to three meters.

ber that describes the "visual distance" between two sets of points and is described thoroughly in papers from the Cornell lab (Huttenlocher 1992). The Hausdorff distance is the maximum distance from any point in one set to its nearest neighbor in the other set. If each point in one set (e.g., the template) is coincident with some point in the other set (e.g., the image), the Hausdorff distance is zero. If there is even one point in the template that is two pixels away from its nearest neighbor in the image, while all other points are coincident, the Hausdorff distance between the sets is two. The distance can also be computed in the other direction—normally, the two distances are not equal.

Careful a priori restrictions of the viewpoint space are generally not enough to make Hausdorff-distance template matching practical. For example, it takes about ten to twenty seconds to search a 512 x 484 image with typical edge density, using a Sparc 20 processor. A more serious problem than search time is that the number of false positive matches (i.e., mirages) increases linearly with the area actually searched. It is hard to find matching thresholds that reliably find the target, if it is present, without the number of false positives actually exceeding the number of correct matches. If you look hard enough, a simple shape such as that of the trash can will almost always appear somewhere in a cluttered scene.

Therefore, we reduce the search space further by looking only in parts of the image that contain colors which indicate the possible presence of a target object. In typical scenes, this color-based region of interest greatly restricts the possible location of the object in the scene and hence reduces the template viewpoint search space (figure 10). The space can be further reduced if it is known a priori how high off the ground plane the target will be when found. Often, it is known that the object will be on the floor, for example. In this case, the ROI

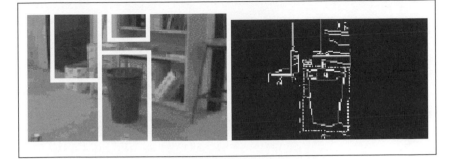

Figure 10. An original image with the color
ROIs outlined and the edges matched and model found.

can be projected onto the ground plane (or any plane) to find the minimum and maximum distances that the object can be at and still fall within the ROI. We use these distances to choose the templates that are consistent and to restrict the range of scales to be applied to those templates.

Once a target has been found in the image, we verify that the apparent size of the object agrees with the distance to the object, as determined by triangulation. If the object is known to be on the floor, then its height in the image determines its distance from the camera. If this distance is not within 10 percent of the distance determined from the scale factor and the known distance of the original template model, the match is ignored.

Finding and Recognizing Small Isolated Objects

We have found that feature-template matching is useful for a broad range of objects in cluttered scenes, but it is still somewhat expensive to compute. In some situations, more specialized algorithms can find and classify objects much more quickly and at least as reliably. In cases where the object can be expected to be against a uniform background (such as a floor), we use a binary feature-vector classification algorithm. The algorithm has four steps.

First, an edge operator is run over the visual scene to create a binary edge image, which is then segmented into connected regions (figure 11). Very small and very large regions are filtered out.

Second, the size, aspect ratio, average color, edge density, fraction of white, and contour regularity (combined standard deviation of the boundary points from horizontal and vertical lines) are computed for the points in each region.

Third, the resulting feature vector for each region is classified against a set of fuzzy exemplars by choosing the nearest neighbor within a maximal allowable distance. We create the fuzzy exemplars by presenting a group of objects of the same class (such as soda cans, styrofoam cups, and wads of paper) and comput-

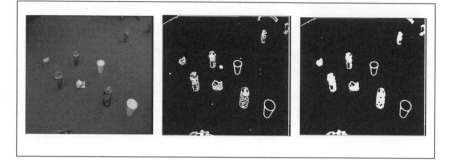

Figure 11. Image processing to identify small isolated objects. The raw edge image is in the middle with the isolated connected regions on the right.

ing the average features and their deviations. Distances to the exemplars are computed relative to the deviation of each exemplar's features.

Finally, the relative location of each object with respect to the robot is computed by triangulation from the height of the camera and the angle of the line of sight to the bottom of the object, with the assumption that the object lies on the floor.

This operation can find and identify small objects at the rate of one object per second on a Sparc 20 processor.

Once an object is found, it can also be tracked as the robot approaches it. The image trajectory is computed by estimating the velocity and acceleration of the object through the image. With the estimated velocity and acceleration, we can predict an object's location in the next image and restrict processing to a small region based on the previous size of the object in the image and centered at its predicted location. By reducing the processing area and also reducing the image resolution, we can track the object reliably at three to five cycles per second.

Conclusions

This chapter describes the animate agent architecture and the way it integrates modular control, real-time vision processing, and reactive plan execution. The chapter also describes the skills and RAPs built within the architecture to control our robot CHIP at the IJCAI-95 robot competition. That task required implementing skills and plans; finding, identifying, and tracking objects; and manipulating those objects in simple ways. It also required integrating these pieces into coherent plans to systematically pick up all the trash in the office and to deal with contingencies like missing a grasp, dropping something being carried, or seeing ghost trash or trash cans because of sensing errors. The resulting implementation used thirty skills and sixty-three RAPs. Of these, only the two top-level RAPs were specific to just the cleanup task—most of the RAPs and skills are reusable for other tasks because they encode relatively generic actions like finding an object, picking an object up, and moving to a new location, while coping with changes and failures in a real-world environment.

Our experience at the robot competition has proven the architecture to be very successful. It was possible to encode all of the plans needed for the competition using the system as designed, without having to code around shortcomings. In addition, the system worked very efficiently and controlled the robot well in real time. The architecture also proved excellent for the integration of vision-based skills with all other aspects of robot control. Finally, the use of two representation levels, skills and RAPs, works very well and leads to a natural encoding of both control processes and sequential task methods.

We also learned some lessons about the representation of task knowledge while encoding the trash cleanup task. First, it is relatively easy to define low-level skills and tasks that can be reused in many higher-level plans (i.e., arm and robot motion tasks or visual skills). Second, an object centered view of the world works well and leads to task definitions that separate object strategies from the actions that manipulate the objects. Third, we learned that this modularity is somewhat more difficult to maintain at the higher levels of the task hierarchy. In particular, the need for separate carry and go-to tasks in the trash cleanup domain means that all higher-level plans must distinguish between carrying an object and just moving from place to place.

Overall, we are very happy with the performance and versatility of the system. The robot performs well and is easy to program. In particular, the way that the top-level put-object-away plan corresponds to the natural description of the task is very important. We are currently continuing to flesh out CHIP's RAPs to deal with more actions, more types of objects, and more object orientations.

CHAPTER ELEVEN

Cooperative Multiagent Robotic Systems

Ronald C. Arkin and Tucker Balch

Teams of robotic systems at first glance might appear to be more trouble than they are worth. Why not simply build one robot that is capable of doing everything we need? There are several reasons why two or more robots can be better than one:

- *Distributed action:* Many robots can be in many places at the same time.
- *Inherent parallelism:* Many robots can do many, perhaps different things at the same time.
- *Divide and conquer:* Certain problems are well suited for decomposition and allocation among many robots.
- *Simpler is better:* Often each agent in a team of robots can be simpler than a more comprehensive single robot solution.

No doubt there are other reasons as well. Unfortunately there are also drawbacks, in particular regarding coordination and elimination of interference. The degree of difficulty imposed depends heavily upon the task and the communication and control strategies chosen.

In this chapter, we present our approach to multiagent robotics in the context of two major real world systems.

The first system is part of the Defense Advanced Research Projects Agency's (DARPA) unmanned ground vehicle (UGV) Demo II program. In this program, we have studied the ways in which reactive control can be introduced to the coordination of teams of HMMWVs (Jeeplike vehicles) working together in dynamic, unstructured, and hazardous environments. We will discuss elements of this system, specifically the design of formation behaviors; means for specifying missions for robotic teams using the MissionLab system; and team teleautonomy, where an operator can influence the behavior of a collection of robots, not just one at a time, in subsequent sections within this chapter..

The second system we present is the three-robot team that won the AAAI Clean-up-the-Office competition in 1994.

Related Work and Background

We will first briefly review a sampling of relevant research in multiagent robotics and then present some background in schema-based reactive control.

Multiagent Robotic Systems

Fukuda was among the first to consider teams of robots working together (Fukuda et al. 1989). His cellular robot system (CEBOT) is a collection of heterogeneous robotic agents which are capable of assembling and disassembling themselves. Imagine, for example, a self-assembling ship in bottle. This ability to allow complex structures to be constructed on-site and the additional capability of reconfiguring the combined units is of potentially great value for a wide range of applications in space-constrained environments.

Mataric, in her dissertation research at the Massachusetts Institute of Technology, has studied adaptive cooperative behavior in a collection of homogeneous robotic agents, the so-called Nerd Herd. Using a behavior-based subsumption-style architecture (Mataric 1992), she demonstrated, in hardware, group behaviors such as flocking and foraging in a team of 10-20 robots. Of interest is the phenomenon of interference that occurs because the robots, at times, get in each other's way. In our team of robots used for the AAAI competition, (described in a later section), kin recognition is used as a means for distributing the agents more uniformly through the environment, keeping them apart and thus reducing interference.

Parker, now at the Oak Ridge National Laboratories, developed the Alliance architecture as a means for expressing and controlling heterogeneous teams of robotic systems (Parker 1993). Researchers at the University of Michigan have used distributed artificial intelligence techniques to control small groups of robots (Lee et al. 1994). There is also extensive research being conducted in Japan on multirobot teams (1992).

Canadian researchers have developed a useful taxonomy for characterizing the various research approaches being developed (Dudek et al. 1993). They are subdivided along the following lines:
- Team size: one, two, size-limited, and size-infinite
- Communication range: none, near, infinite
- Communication topology: broadcast, addressed, tree, graph
- Communication bandwidth: high, motion-related, low, zero
- Team reconfigurability: static, coordinated, dynamic
- Team unit processing ability: nonlinear summation, finite state automata, push-down automata, turing machine equivalent
- Team composition: homogeneous, heterogeneous

Another starting point for further understanding of the general issues and research efforts ongoing in robotic teams appears in Cao's review article (Cao et al. 1995).

Reactive Schema-Based Behavioral Control

Reactive behavioral control (Arkin 1995) is now a well-established technique for providing rapid real-time response for a robot by closely tying perception to action. Behaviors, in various forms, are the primary building blocks for these systems, which typically operate without conventional planning or the use of global world models.

Schema-based systems (Arkin 1989) are a form of reactive behavioral control that are further characterized by their neuroscientific and psychological plausibility, the absence of arbitration between behaviors (schemas), the fusion of behavioral outputs through the use of vector summation in a manner analogous to the potential fields method (Khatib 1985), inherent flexibility due to the dynamic instantiation and deinstantiation of behaviors on an as-needed basis, and easy reconfigurability through the use of high-level planners or adaptive learning systems.

Motor schemas are the basic building blocks of a schema-based system. These motor behaviors have an associated perceptual schema which provides only the necessary sensory information for that behavior to react to its environment, and ideally nothing more. Perceptual schemas are an embodiment of action oriented perception, where perception is tailored to the needs of the agent and its surrounding environment. Each motor schema produces a single vector that provides the direction and strength of the motor response for a given stimuli. All of the active behaviors' vectors are summed together, normalized, and sent to the actuators for execution.

Another coordination operator, temporal sequencing, ties together separate collections of behaviors (assemblages) and provides a means for transitioning between them (Arkin and MacKenzie 1994). Typically, perceptual triggers are defined which monitor for specific events within the environment. If a relevant event is detected, a state transition occurs resulting in the instantiation of a new behavioral assemblage. Finite state acceptor (FSA) diagrams are typically used to represent these relationships. Examples of these diagrams appear in the Mission Specification and the Team of Trash-Collecting Robots Sections.

Formation Control

This section, and the two subsequent ones, will focus on multiagent research in support of DARPA's UGV Demo II program. The goal of this project is to field a team of robotic scout vehicles for the U.S. Army. At present, scout platoons

Figure 1. One of Lockheed-Martin's HMMWVs.
Photograph courtesy Lockheed Martin.

are composed of four to six manned vehicles equipped with an array of observation and communication equipment. The scouts typically move in advance of
the main force, to report on enemy positions and capabilities. It is hoped that
robotic scout teams will do as well as humans for this task, while removing sol-
diers from harm's way. Lockheed-Martin has built four prototype robot scout
vehicles, based on the HMMWV (figure 1). This section outlines the design of an
important behavior for scout teams: formation maintenance. The next two sections look at related issues: a way for humans to express military missions for
robot team execution and a way to provide variable levels of human intervention during an ongoing mission.

Scout teams use specific formations for a particular task. In moving quickly
down roadways for instance, it is often best to follow one after the other. When
sweeping across desert terrain, line-abreast may be better. Furthermore, when
scouts maintain their positions, they are able to distribute their sensor assets to
reduce overlap. Army manuals (U.S. Army 1986) list four important formations
for scout vehicles: diamond, wedge, line, and column. Four simulated robots
moving in these formations are pictured in figure 2.

Motor Schemas for Formation

The formation behavior must work in concert with other navigational behaviors. The robots should concurrently strive to keep their relative formation positions, avoid obstacles, and move to a goal location. Formation behaviors for
two, three, and four robots have been developed and initially tested in simula-

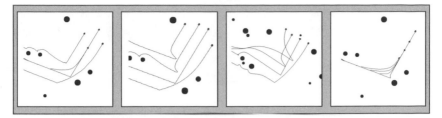

Figure 2. Four robots in leader-referenced diamond, wedge, line, and column formations executing a 90-degree turn in an obstacle field.

tion. They have been further tested on two-robot teams of Denning robots and Lockheed-Martin UGVs. The formation behaviors were developed using the motor schema paradigm within Georgia Tech's MissionLab environment. Each motor schema, or primitive behavior, generates a vector representing a desired direction and magnitude of travel. This approach provides an easy way to integrate behaviors. First, each vector is multiplied by a gain value; then all the vectors are summed, and the result is normalized. The gain values express the relative strength of each schema. A high-level representation of this behavioral integration is illustrated as pseudocode in figure 3.

The formation behavior itself comprises two main components: a perceptual schema detect-formation-position, and a motor schema maintain-formation. The perceptual schema determines where the robot should be located based on the formation type in use, the robot's relative position in the overall formation, and the locations of the other robots. Maintain-formation generates a vector towards the correct position, with the magnitude based on how far out of position the robot finds itself.

Three different approaches for determining a robot's position in formation are described in Balch and Arkin (1995). Here we will present the unit-center approach, where the position depends on the locations of the other robots, the overall unit heading, and the formation type. A unit-center is computed by averaging the positions of all the robots involved in the formation; then each robot determines its own formation position relative to that center.

A vector generated by maintain-formation always directs the robot from its current position toward the formation position. It varies from zero magnitude to a maximum value depending on how far out of position the robot is (figure 5):

- Ballistic zone: The robot is far out of position, so the output vector's magnitude is set at its maximum, which equates to the schema's gain value, with its directional component pointing towards the center of the computed dead zone.

- Controlled zone: The robot is somewhat out of position, and the output vector's magnitude decreases linearly from a maximum at the farthest edge of the zone to zero at the inner edge. The directional component is toward the dead zone's center.

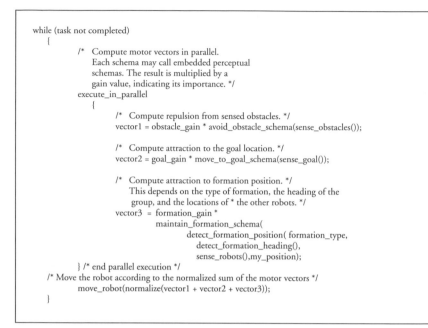

```
while (task not completed)
    {
            /*  Compute motor vectors in parallel.
                Each schema may call embedded perceptual
                schemas. The result is multiplied by a
                gain value, indicating its importance. */
        execute_in_parallel
            {
                    /*  Compute repulsion from sensed obstacles. */
                    vector1 = obstacle_gain * avoid_obstacle_schema(sense_obstacles());

                    /*  Compute attraction to the goal location. */
                    vector2 = goal_gain * move_to_goal_schema(sense_goal());

                    /*  Compute attraction to formation position. */
                        This depends on the type of formation, the heading of the
                        group, and the locations of * the other robots. */
                    vector3  = formation_gain *
                            maintain_formation_schema(
                                detect_formation_position( formation_type,
                                    detect_formation_heading(),
                                    sense_robots(),my_position);
            } /* end parallel execution */
    /* Move the robot according to the normalized sum of the motor vectors */
            move_robot(normalize(vector1 + vector2 + vector3));
    }
```

*Figure 3. Pseudo-code showing the behavioral assemblage for a robot to
move to a goal, avoid obstacles, and maintain a formation position.*

- Dead zone: The robot is within acceptable positional tolerance. Within the dead zone, the vector magnitude is always zero.

Pseudocode for this computation and for determining the robot's formation position are given in figure 4. These behaviors were ported to Lockheed-Martin's UGVs and successfully demonstrated at Demo C on two UGVs in Denver, Colorado, in the summer of 1995.

Mission Specification for Multirobot Systems

Another pressing problem for the UGV Demo II program in particular and for robotics in general is how to provide an easy-to-use mechanism for programming teams of robots, making these systems more accessible to the end-user. Toward that end, the MissionLab mission specification system has been developed (MacKenzie, Cameron, and Arkin 1995). An agent-oriented philosophy is used as the underlying methodology, permitting the recursive formulation of societies of robots.

A society is viewed as an agent consisting of a collection of either homogeneous or heterogeneous robots. Each individual robotic agent consists of assem-

```
detect_formation_position(formation_type, formation_heading, robot_positions)
        /*  The unit-center is the average of the robot locations. */
        unit_center = average(robot_positions());

        /* Now compute where the robot should be if in perfect position.
           A lookup table stores the proper positions for each robot for
           each type of formation. The value must be rotated and added
           to the unit-center to shift from local to global coordinates. */

        local_position = lookup_table[formation_type, my_position_number];
        correct_position = rotate(local_position(), formation_heading()) + unit_center;
        return(global_position);

maintain_formation_schema(correct_position, current_position)

        /*  Compute the vector from the present position of the
            robot to the correct position for formation. */
        initial_vector = correct_position - current_position;

        /*  Adjust the magnitude of the vector according to the
            equations in the text, based on dead-zone-radius and
            controlled-zone-radius. */
        vector = adjust(initial_vector, dead_zone_radius, controlled_zone_radius);
        return(vector);
```

*Figure 4. Pseudocode for the detect-formation-position perceptual
schema and the maintain-formation-position motor schema.*

blages of behaviors, coordinated in various ways. Temporal sequencing (Arkin
and MacKenzie 1994) affords transitions between various behavioral states which
are naturally represented as a finite state acceptor. Coordination of parallel behaviors can be accomplished via fusion (vector summation), action-selection, priority (e.g., subsumption) or other means as necessary. These individual behavioral
assemblages consist of groups of primitive perceptual and motor behaviors which
ultimately are grounded to the physical sensors and actuators of a robot.

An important feature of MissionLab is the ability to delay binding to a particular behavioral architecture (e.g., schema-based, SAUSAGES, subsumption) until
after the desired mission behavior has been specified. Binding to a particular
physical robot occurs after specification as well, permitting the design to be both
architecture- and robot-independent.

MissionLab's architecture appears on the left of figure 6. Separate software libraries exist for the abstract behaviors and for the specific architectures and
robots. The user interacts through a design interface tool (the configuration edi-
tor) which permits the visualization of a specification as it is created. The right
side of figure 6 illustrates an example MissionLab configuration that embodies

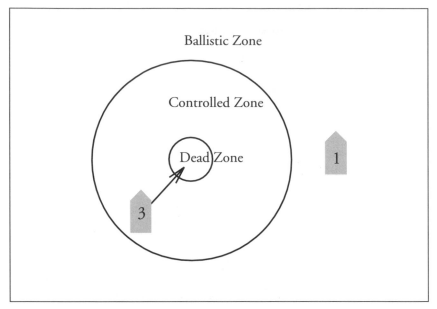

Figure 5. Zones for the computation of maintain-formation magnitude.

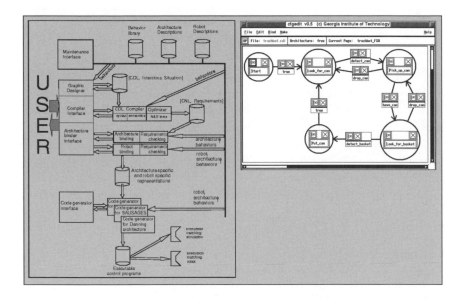

Figure 6. MissionLab. The system architecture appears on the left. A finite state configuration corresponding to the AAAI Robots appears on the right. This FSA differs slightly from the version implemented in figure 12.

the behavioral control system for one of the robots used in the AAAI robot competition. The individual icons correspond to behavior specifications which can be created as needed or preferably reused from an existing repertoire available in the behavioral library. Multiple levels of abstraction are available, that can be targeted to the abilities of the designer, ranging from whole robot configurations down to the configuration description language for a particular behavior.

After the behavioral configuration is specified, the architecture and robot types are selected and compilation occurs, generating the robot executables. These can be run within the simulation environment provided by MissionLab (figure 7 top), or through a software switch, they can be downloaded to the actual robots for execution (figure 7 bottom).

MissionLab was demonstrated at UGV Demo C in the summer of 1995 to military personnel. MissionLab is available via the world wide web at: www.cc.gatech.edu/aimosaic/robot-lab/research/MissionLab.html.

Team Teleautonomy

Another important control aspect is concerned with the real-time introduction of a commander's intentions to the ongoing operation of an autonomous robotic team. We have developed software in the context of the UGV Demo II program to provide this capability in two different ways:

- The commander as a behavior. In this approach a separate behavior is created that permits the commander to introduce a heading for the robot team using an on-screen joystick (figure 8 left). This biases the ongoing autonomous control for all of the robots in a particular direction. Indeed, all other behaviors are still active, typically including obstacle avoidance and formation maintenance. The output of this behavior is a vector which represents the commander's directional intentions and strength of command. All of the robotic team members have the same behavioral response to the operator's goals and the team members act in concert without any knowledge of each other's behavioral state.

- The commander as a supervisor. With this method, the operator is permitted to conduct behavioral modifications on-the-fly. This can occur at two levels: For the knowledgeable operator, the low-level gains and parameters of the active behavioral set can be adjusted directly if desired, varying the relative strengths and behavioral composition as the mission progresses. For the normal operator, behavioral traits ("personality characteristics") are abstracted and presented to the operator for adjustment. These include such things as aggressiveness (inversely adjusting the relative strength of goal attraction and obstacle avoidance) and wanderlust (inversely varying the strength of noise

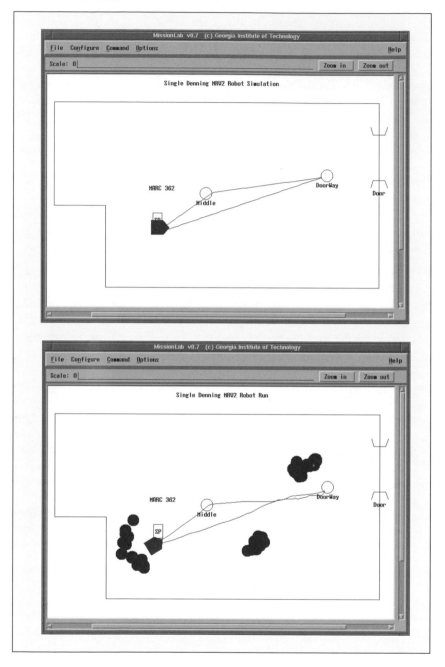

Figure 7. Execution of robot behaviors in MissionLab. Top: Simulated run on Denning robot. Bottom: Same code executed on actual Denning robot.

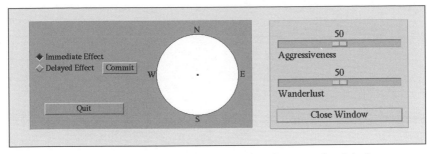

Figure 8. Left: On-screen Directional Control Right: Personality slider bars.

relative to goal attraction and/or formation maintenance) (figure 8 right). These abstract qualities are more natural for the operator unskilled in behavioral programming and permit the concurrent behavioral modification of all of the robots in a team according to the commander's wishes in light of incoming intelligence reports.

An example illustrating the utility of the directional control approach is in the extrication of teams from potential traps. Figure 9 shows a run using two of our Denning mobile robots. The active behaviors include avoid-static-obstacle, move-to-goal, and column-formation. The robots wander into the box canyon and become stuck trying to make their way to the goal point specified behind the box-canyon (top left photograph). The operator intervenes, using the joystick to direct the robots to the right. While moving, they continue to avoid obstacles and maintain formation. Once clear of the trap (top right photograph), the operator stops directing the robots, and they proceed autonomously to their goal. The overall execution trace is depicted at the bottom of figure 9.

The directional control team teleautonomy software has been successfully integrated by Lockheed-Martin into the UGV Demo II software architecture and was demonstrated in simulation to military observers during UGV Demo C. Both directional and personality control have been integrated into the Mission-Lab system described above and are available in the MissionLab release via the world wide web. Additional information on team teleautonomy can be found in Arkin and Ali (1994).

A Team of Trash-Collecting Robots

This section describes a team of robots designed for trash-collecting. Specifically, the task for these robots is to gather items of trash, primarily red soda cans, and deposit them near blue wastebaskets. They must operate in an office environment that includes obstacles like tables and chairs. The design we present builds

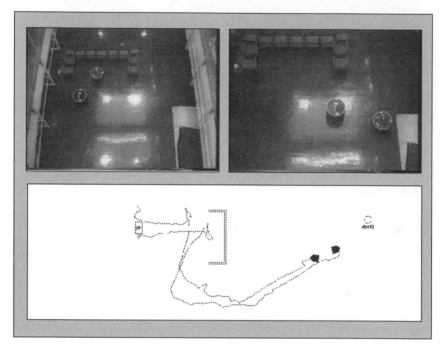

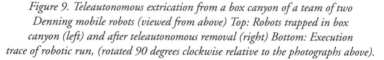

*Figure 9. Teleautonomous extrication from a box canyon of a team of two
Denning mobile robots (viewed from above) Top: Robots trapped in box
canyon (left) and after teleautonomous removal (right) Bottom: Execution
trace of robotic run, (rotated 90 degrees clockwise relative to the photographs above).*

on motor schema research presented in earlier sections of the chapter. These
robots show how simple individual primitive behaviors may be combined, sequenced and instantiated on several robots to yield a successful cooperating
team. A detailed account of this effort is available in Balch et al. (1995).

Io, Ganymede, and Callisto (figure 10) were built primarily with off-the-shelf,
commercially available components. The base was purchased as a radio-con-
trolled tank with two separately motorized treads. Motor and perceptual schemas
run on a PC-compatible motherboard, while control and sensing tasks are implemented on a separate microcontroller board. Each robot is equipped with a forward-looking color camera and a gripper for grasping trash (figure 11).

The robots use color vision to find trash items (attractors), other robots (kin),
and wastebaskets. To facilitate the vision task, the robots were painted bright
green, trash items are presumed to be red (cola cans) and wastebaskets are blue
recycling containers. A set of sequenced behavioral assemblages, presented next,
leads the robots through the states necessary to complete the task.

Figure 10. Ganymede, Io, and Callisto.

Behaviors for Trashcollecting

This task lends itself to a sequential state-based solution: search for trash objects; if one is found, move towards it; if close enough, grasp it; now look for a wastebasket; and so on. The sequence of states is naturally represented as an FSA. The sequence developed for our robots is depicted in figure 12. Partial pseudocode for the FSA is shown in figure 13.

We first examine the behavioral design starting at the highest level of abstraction, then successively narrow our focus to lower levels of the sensor software. Each state, or behavioral assemblage, in the FSA represents a group of activated perceptual and motor schemas. Outputs of the active motor schemas are combined as described earlier and output for motor control. Pseudocode for one of the assemblages, wander-for-trash is listed in Figure 14.

Image Processing for Kin Recognition

We now focus on the perceptual component of the wander-for-trash behavior concerned with kin recognition. The perceptual schema sense-robots uses a combination of vision and short-term memory to track other robots. When another robot is detected visually, its position is noted and added to a list of robots recently seen (a check is made to ensure there are no duplicate entries). Entries are removed after sixty seconds, when they get stale. Short-term memory is important since nearby agents are often lost from view as the

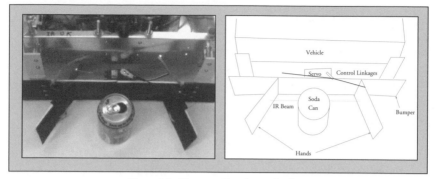

Figure 11. Close-up of trash manipulator.

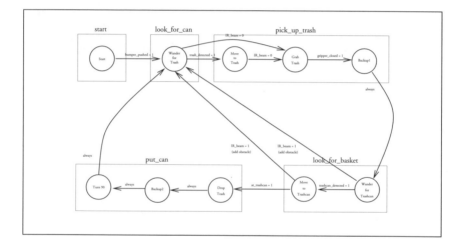

Figure 12. Implemented robot behavioral state diagram for the trash-collecting task. The blocks correspond to the more abstract states depicted in figure 7. Some additional transitions were added for fault-tolerance.

robot moves or turns. Pseudo-code for sense-robots appears in figure 15.

Robots are detected visually in the find-robots-in-image routine (figure 16). We were limited to simple image processing since complex schemes would limit the robot's real-time performance, or might not have fit in the limited RAM. Overall, the approach is to isolate colored blobs in the robot camera's view, then use simple trigonometry to estimate the locations of objects associated with the blobs in the environment. Processing for green blobs finds the positions of other visible robots (kin).

The first step is to extract separate red, green and blue components from the image. One might begin the search for green objects by simply inspecting the

```
state = START;
do forever
        /*
         * Execute behavioral assemblages according to which state the
         * agent is in.
         *
         * bumper_pushed == 1    means one of the contact sensors is pushed
         * ir_beam == 1          means the IR beam in the gripper is intact. *
         *                       It is 0 if the beam is broken, in the case of
         *                       a potential trash object.
         */
        switch(state)
            case START:
                do forever
                        start();
                        if (bumper_pushed == 1)
                            state = WANDER_FOR_TRASH;
                            break; /* out of do forever */
                break; /* out of this state */
            case WANDER_FOR_TRASH:
                do forever
                        wander_for_trash();
                        if (bumpers == 0 and ir_beam == 0)
                            state = GRAB_TRASH;
                            break; /* out of do forever */
                        else if (trash_detected == 1)
                            state = MOVE_TO_TRASH,
                            break; /* out of do forever */
                break; /* out of this state */
            case MOVE_TO_TRASH:
                do forever
                        move_to_trash();
                        if (trash_detected == 0)
                            state = WANDER_FOR_TRASH;
                            break; /* out of do forever */
                        else if (bumpers == 0 and ir_beam == 0)
                            state = GRAB_TRASH;
                            break; /* out of do forever */
                break; /* out of this state */
        /* OTHER STATES DELETED FOR BREVITY */
```

Figure 13. Partial pseudocode implementing three states of the FSA for a sequenced trash-collecting behavior. This is the highest level control code for each robot.

green image component, but a problem with using just one of the color components occurs because many bright objects (e.g., specular reflections) have strong red and blue components in addition to green. In other words, one cannot infer that an object is green just because it has a large green component alone. To get around the problem, a supercomponent for each primary color was computed

```
wander_for_trash()

        /* Compute motor vectors in parallel.
        Each schema may call embedded perceptual
        schemas. The result is multiplied by a
        gain value, indicating its relative strength. */
    execute_in_parallel

            /* Compute repulsion from sensed obstacles. */
            vector1 = obstacle_gain * avoid_obstacle_schema( sense_obstacles());

            /* Compute noise vector */
            vector2 = noise_gain * compute_noise();

            / Compute repulsion from sensed robots. */
            vector3 = robot_gain * avoid_robot(sense_robots()); }

        /* Move the robot according to the normalized sum of the * motor vectors
    */move_robot(normalize(vector1 + vector2 + vector3));
```

Figure 14. Pseudocode for the wander-for-trash state.
In this state, the robot is repulsed by other robots.

first. Supercomponents for one color are computed by subtracting each of the other color components from it. Supergreen, for example, is computed as green - (red + blue). So a white blob (as in a specular reflection) will have low supergreen component, while a green blob will have a bright supergreen component. This approach significantly improves performance when searching for specifically colored objects. A sample luminance and supergreen image are shown in figure 17. Notice how well the green robot stands out.

After the green supercomponent is computed, the resultant image is thresholded so that pixels below a certain value are set to 0; those above are set to 255. Although the system is not extremely sensitive, the best performance results when the threshold value is tuned for ambient lighting conditions. Groups of adjoining bright pixels (255) are classified as a blob if there are more than a certain number of them in the group. The minimum blob size is typically set to 100 pixels. The angular offset (azimuth) to the object is computed from the field of view of the camera (pixels per degree). We are able to compute range to an object by finding the lowest pixel of the corresponding blob. Since all perceptual objects (trash, robots and wastebaskets) rest on the floor and the camera sits at a fixed height above the ground, all objects the same distance away will lie equally low on the image plane. Range is estimated using the trigonometric relation:

$r = h / \tan^{-1}\theta$

```
sense_robots()

        /*  Remove stale memories of other robot locations. */
        robot_list = age(robot_list);

        /*  Get a list of visually acquired robots. */
        visual_robots = find_robots_in_image();

        /*  Add new visually-acquired robots to the list, and
            refresh the memory of ones that we've seen again. */
        for (each robot in visual_robots)
            if (robot not in robot_list)
                add_to_list(robot_list, robot);
            else
                refresh(robot_list, robot);
        return(robot_list);
```

Figure 15. Pseudocode for the sense-robots perceptual schema.

where r is range, h is the camera height, and θ is the apparent angle to the bottom of the object from the center of the image. θ is computed by counting pixels from the center of the image to the bottom of the blob, based on the number of degrees covered by one pixel. In a final step, the range and azimuth data are converted to Cartesian coordinates within the robot's reference frame. The entire process takes about one second.

Performance of the Trash-Collecting Team

The robots competed in three preliminary trials and in the final competition, winning the clean-up task at the AAAI-94 Mobile Robot Contest (Simmons 1995). In our laboratory, the robots have sometimes gathered as many as twenty soda cans in ten minutes. But in the best run at the contest, the robots collected only 15 cans. One reason for not equaling the earlier performance is that the contest required the use of black wastebaskets, rather than the blue ones the robots had been designed for.

The competition team revised the image processing software to seek dark objects, as opposed to blue ones in the move-to-trashcan phase. Unfortunately, this led to robots occasionally "hiding" soda cans under tables or other shadowy areas, as they confused them with wastebaskets. Finally, we took advantage of another perceptual clue for wastebaskets: the fact that from a robot's point of view all wastebaskets must cut through the horizon. In other words, part of the

```
find_robots_in_image()
    detected_robot_list = empty;

    /* grab the image */
    image = digitize_image();

    /* enhance and threshold green component */
    for (each pixel x and y )
        supergreen[x,y] = image.green[x,y] - (image.red[x,y] + image.blue[x,y]);
        thresholded[x,y] = threshold(threshold_value, supergreen[x,y]);

    /* extract blobs of pixels above the threshold from the green image */
    blobs = find_blobs(thresholded, min_blob_size);

    for (each blob in blobs)

    /* compute range and azimuth to the blob based on camera parameters */
        blob.range = camera_height * arctan(blob.bottom_pixel * degrees_per_pixel);
        blob.azimuth = blob.center_pixel * degrees_per_pixel;

    /* estimate the other robot's relative position, +x is forward */

        local_robot = convert_from_polar(blob.range, blob.azimuth);

    /* convert into global coordinates and add to list */
        global_robot = rotate(local_robot, -current_heading) + current_position;

        add_to_list(detected_robot_list, detected_robot);

    return(detected_robot_list);
```

Figure 16. Pseudo-code for find-robots-in-image, which processes a color image to find the green blobs corresponding to other robots. For these computations, the center of the camera image is assumed to be [0,0] and negative azimuth is to the left. The robot's egocentric coordinates have +y straight ahead and +x to the right. The robot tracks its position and the position of other robots.

wastebasket is below camera level and part of it is above camera level. This ruled out most nonwastebasket blobs.

Except for the complications regarding black wastebaskets, the system performs very well. The robots easily find red soda cans and move quickly towards them. The robot-robot repulsion is usually obvious to the observer and clearly helps the team spread out in the search phase.

Figure 17. A robot's-eye view of a laboratory scene including another green robot, two red soda cans and a blue wastebasket. The image on the right shows the image after processing to highlight green pixels. Notice how well the robot stands out.

Summary and Open Questions

In this chapter we have presented several of the many aspects of multiagent control. These include the coordination of motion to maximize effort as seen in formation maintenance; methods by which programming of multiagent systems can be made easier through the use of visual programming using tools such as MissionLab; and methods by which a human operator can effectively interact with teams of mobile agents without becoming overwhelmed by the sheer numbers of robots. Two very different problem domains have motivated our research: military scouts and janitorial robots. Successful implementations of many of these ideas have been completed in these domains.

Other important questions still confront multiagent robotics researchers. A few include

- How can we introduce adaptation and learning to make these systems more flexible within a changing environment?

- How can we ensure robust interrobot communication that is both task and environment sensitive?

- How well will these ideas scale to large swarms of robots on the order of perhaps ten thousand or more?

- How can biological systems inform us to ensure we are providing a sound ecological fit of the robot to its environment, producing long-term survivable systems?

Our laboratory and others continue to pursue answers to these and other important questions regarding cooperative multiagent robotic systems.

Acknowledgments

Funding to support this research has been provided by the National Science Foundation under Grant IRI-9100149 and DARPA/ONR under Grant N00014-94-1-0215. Doug MacKenzie and Khaled Ali provided the figures for MissionLab and team teleautonomy respectively and are primarily responsible for their development. Matt Morgenthaler and Betty Glass at Lockheed-Martin were primarily responsible for the porting of software developed in Georgia Tech laboratories to the UGV Demo II vehicles. Development of the trash-collecting robots was funded by the CIMS/ATT Intelligent Mechatronics Laboratory at Georgia Tech. The AAAI provided a generous grant for travel to the AAAI-94 competition in Seattle.

CHAPTER TWELVE

Toward Advanced Mobile Robots for Manufacturing

Huosheng Hu and Michael Brady

The mobile robots, sometimes called autonomous guided vehicles (AGVs), currently deployed in flexible manufacturing are used primarily for transporting material or for cleaning. The vast majority are wire-guided, typically following a signal-carrying wire or tracking a visible line on the floor (Hollier 1987; Premi and Besant 1983; Tsumura 1986). These vehicles have enjoyed considerable success mainly because of the end-point accuracy that they can achieve. However, they can only follow predetermined paths issued by a central control station. Such AGVs need, and have, very limited sensing capabilities and in the presence of obstacles can only stop. Installation of wire guides can be costly and disruptive; but, more significantly, modifications are comparably expensive. If anything goes wrong with the central control station, it may cause the whole team of autonomous mobile robots to stop.

Considerable progress has been made recently in the design and implementation of experimental mobile robots that can cope with an unknown or dynamically changing environment (Borenstein and Koren 1989; Brooks 1986; Giralt, Chatila, and Vaisset 1984; Harmon 1987; Jarvis and Byrne 1988). They are characterized by rapid, real-time response to unexpected obstacles based on sensor-based control. It is essential for a mobile robot to work safely in industry. However, real-time implementation of path planning and environment learning are equally important for a mobile robot to do something useful, such as acquiring pallets, transporting materials, and cleaning warehouses. But most path planning and environment learning algorithms today are intrinsically inefficient and unsuited to real-time operation. As a result, most mobile robots built to date are far from having the fully autonomous competence needed for reliable and useful industrial applications, which in turn poses a tough challenge:

- *Robots are fast, multi-degree of freedom devices* for which the plant kinematics changes as fast as the device moves. This is particularly challenging for robot arm control, but is nontrivial for vehicle control too.

- *It is necessary to sense the environment in order to determine how to act.* The key advantage of mobile robots is that they can potentially operate in an environment that is variable and uncertain, hence sensing is vital. As it is rarely the case that any single sensor suffices for all situations, sensor data-fusion is necessary (Brady et al. 1990). Since sensor data is intrinsically noisy, the control system must be able to deal with uncertain information. Sensors with high bandwidths have inevitable processing latency, reducing the stability margin of the system.

- *Practically useful mobile robots must operate in real time.* It is useful to distinguish a number of control layers, which in turn poses the challenge of a multirate, multilevel system. Typically, an obstacle avoiding control loop operates at about 25 Hz. A global path planner needs to be able to deliver set points to the low-level control layers and be able to replan paths in case obstacles are encountered, which might operate at 1–5 Hz. In fact, the ability to repair a plan is much more useful than an optimal path planner for operation in a real world.

- *Systems that are fielded in practice must be fail-safe, hence have redundant sensing, processing and actuation.* By processing, we mean reasoning, planning, recognizing, and modeling. To be fail-safe, the processing should be distributed.

- *Real systems are judged by performance, not by papers.* Much mobile robotics research focuses on theory and simulated environments. The solutions being given in many papers are often computationally expensive and may not be feasible for practical applications.

Over the past eight years, we have built a series of mobile robots for practical application, in close collaboration with industry. Our work has always been aimed at addressing generic research issues. Some of the principles that have guided our work are described in this paper. We begin with motivations for working on mobile robots in the next section. The Representation and Planning section presents our work on planning for mobile robots to operate in a dynamic manufacturing environment autonomously and efficiently. The Dynamic Localization section addresses how to cope with uncertainty in a real world during localization. In the Structure and Coordination section, architecture issues that are key to the design and construction of real robots are addressed. We then describe the modularity and scalability to build complex mobile robots, and conclude this chapter with a brief summary.

Motivations

Clearly, there are many motivations for working on mobile robots. First, as in our case, one might approach a problem from the standpoint of engineering science. In that case, one starts with a range of specifications of actual practical problems, for example cleaning a baggage handling area at an airport, acquiring palletized objects in the loading bay of a factory, etc., and sets about defining a system that can meet the specifications. Primarily, success is judged by whether or not one's system meets the specifications and, assuming that it does, to what extent it can cope with likely problems, is easily fixed, is costed attractively, and can be adapted to similar problems.

A second motivation may be to shed some light on human cognition. Such work may be considered good if it provides an explanation of certain observed cognitive behavior, for example dealing with conflicts in reasoning or goals, and more importantly if it leads to testable predictions whose results are not known in advance but which turn out to be as predicted. Other motivations we have encountered include the desire to study control systems and the desire to study artificial intelligence.

We are sure that there is very good work, entirely sited within the study of human intelligence and based on mobile robots, or components of such systems. For example, there has been some superb research on the control of attention and eye movements by motor physiologists, and some excellent work on motion perception by psychophysicists. Our difficulty is certainly not with such work, but with systems that claim or advocate a close relationship between engineering and studies of humans. The limiting factor in the design of real robot systems turns out to be humble components such as motors, transmission elements, gear boxes, and sensors such as TV cameras.

The human eye controller, for example, has many degrees of freedom actuated by a mass of muscles that transmit power through tendons bathed in sinovial fluid. Unfortunately, no motor currently available, or likely to be available for many years to come, even remotely matches the performance of muscles, and sinovial fluid is almost frictionless. From an engineering standpoint, it is folly to build systems with more than a minimal number of degrees of freedom, in order to maximize stiffness, minimize friction loss, and maximize the parameters (e.g. acceleration, torque) that determine the usefulness of the system.

This fundamental difference is inevitably reflected in higher level functions such as trajectory planners, path planners, and mission planners. Examples abound. Exactly similar comments apply to sensors: the TV camera is nowhere near the performance of the human eye, nor will it be for many years. In turn, the peculiar characteristics of TV cameras, for example poor dynamic range, low speed, anisotropy, uniformity, yet linearity, predetermine strategies for motion computation, intensity change detection, and ultimately stereo and recognition.

Representation and Planning

Planning embraces a broad range of abilities, and for manufacturing purposes, it is useful to distinguish four: *Mission planning* or *task planning* is the process of determining the requirements and constraints for the global tasks and obtaining an optimal schedule for multiple goals. *Global path planning* aims to find a collision-free path (a set of intermediate points) for a mobile robot to follow from the start position to the goal position. In contrast, *local path planning* or *obstacle avoidance* generates relatively local detours around sensed obstacles while following a globally planned path. Finally, *trajectory planning* generates a nominal motion plan consisting of a geometrical path and a velocity profile along it in terms of the kinematics of the individual robot.

Global path planning has traditionally been treated as a purely predictive process where complete knowledge is assumed a priori about the environment either in the form of a qualitative or a quantitative model. For instance, in the graph-searching approach, a graph is created that shows the free spaces and forbidden spaces in the robot's environment. A path is then generated by piecing together the free spaces or by tracing around the forbidden area (Brooks 1983; Kambhampati and Davis 1986; Takahashi and Schiling 1989). In contrast, the potential field approach uses a scalar function to describe both objects and free space. The negative gradient of the potential field precisely gives the direction to move to avoid obstacles (Barraquand and Latombe 1991; Hwang and Ahuja 1992; Warren 1989). The main feature of these approaches is that a complete sequence of steps that solve a problem or reach a goal is determined before taking any action. Recovering from error and dealing with unexpected events is usually left as a subsequent execution stage. As a result, such planning systems are inherently open-loop (or off-line) and are unable to handle unmodeled disturbances in the real world.

Recent work in planning has aimed to overcome this limitation. A variety of proposals have been made to develop the idea of a situated agent (Agre and Rosenschein 1995), a software object that is intended to be in continuous interaction with the world. Sadly, the vast majority of situated agents inhabit only a simulated world in which the problems of noise, uncertainty, and clutter are absent (but see Rosenschein and Kaelbling [1986] for a notable exception).

Our work has concentrated on path planning for a mobile robot to operate in a dynamic manufacturing environment autonomously and efficiently. Figure 1 shows a situation in which there are three robots operating in the same environment. They try to reach their goal positions along predefined paths. Robot 1 transfers tools from the *Tool Store* to *Workstation 4* along a preplanned path, but encounters an unexpected obstacle (a pallet in this case). Since the path has been completely blocked, the robot has to backtrack to take an alternative path. A question that naturally arises is which decision should be made next time when the same task is commanded: try this path again or not? If tried, the pallet may still be there; if not, the pallet may already be moved away. Similarly, robot 2 meets an unexpected object (a box in this case) when it transfers finished parts to the *Warehouse*. It may sidestep the obstacle incurring extra path traversal cost, but should it take this into account the next time it plans the same path? In

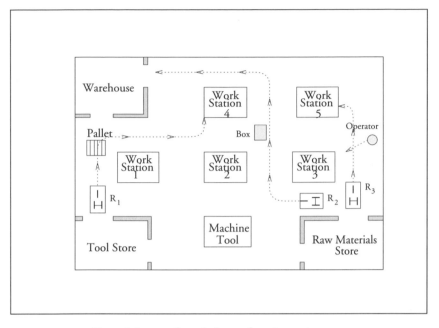

Figure 1. Layout of a typical manufacturing environment.

contrast, robot 3 detects a moving object (a person in this case) when it deliveries raw materials to Workstation 5. Should the robot wait or should it try another path? How should it learn something new from this experience?

The important issue being addressed is how to model such a dynamic, uncertain environment to provide a solution for an optimal path constrained by the real world. Since a centralized and complicated model for a dynamic environment needs more time to compute, thereby reducing the system's response speed, we employ several simple models, each tuned to a different range and resolution of situations for different tasks, shown in figure 2. In other words, this multimodel control architecture takes the real-time capability and the expected task-achieving behaviors into account. Data sampled by different physical sensors are used to maintain different model dynamically.

A system that plans under uncertainty must maintain multiple possibilities for the state of the world, and associate with each some degree of belief. Some alternative world states will be more likely than others; for example, the system must allow for the possibility that the sensor data are incorrect. New sensor data about the world must be used to update these possibilities and beliefs; some alternatives may be ruled out and new alternatives generated, while others may become more or less likely. Therefore, we have proposed a probabilistic approach to the path planning problem for our mobile robots (Hu 1992). Two

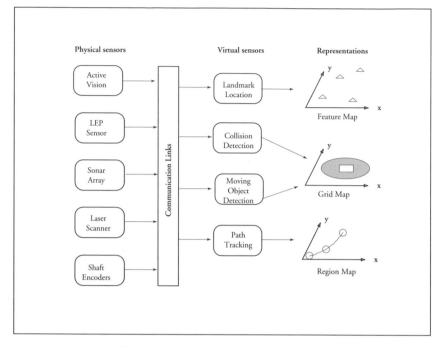

Figure 2. Multiple sensors and multiple models.

types of world knowledge have been used in our approach to achieve real-time performance. One is a priori information about the robot's environment, which is considered relatively static. The other is updated information acquired by the sensors as the robot moves around, which is normally unpredictable and changes dynamically.

We have used a topological graph G to represent the free space of the robot's environment, weighted by a scalar cost function $C(\mathbf{x}(k))$ in which $\mathbf{x}(k)$ is the robot's state or the node in graph G. The cost function represents the effort for a mobile robot to move from the state $\mathbf{x}(k-1)$ to the next state $\mathbf{x}(k)$. This consists of two parts: a deterministic cost $T(\mathbf{x}(k))$ and an uncertainty cost $U(\mathbf{x}(k))$ as follows:

$$C(\mathbf{x}(k)) = T(\mathbf{x}(k)) + U(\mathbf{x}(k)) \qquad (1)$$

The deterministic cost depends on path parameters such as length, width, and straightness, which are easy to model. To quantify uncertainty, we have built statistical models to form uncertainty costs for unexpected events (Hu and Brady 1992). These uncertainty costs are updated by available sensor data when the robot moves around. Given an initial state $\mathbf{x}_s$ and the goal state $\mathbf{x}_g$, an optimal path is found by choosing a sequence of admissible decisions

$$\pi = \{\mathbf{a}(0), \mathbf{a}(1), ..., \mathbf{a}(N-1)\} \tag{2}$$

in such a way as to minimize the accumulated cost (expectation) expressed by the sum

$$J = E\{C[\mathbf{x}(N)] + \sum_{k=0}^{N-1} C[\mathbf{x}(k), \mathbf{a}(k), \mathbf{d}(k)]\} \tag{3}$$

subject to the system constraints

$$\mathbf{x}(0) = \mathbf{x}_s \qquad \mathbf{x}(N) = \mathbf{x}_g \qquad \mathbf{a}(k) \in \mathbf{A} \qquad \mathbf{x}(k) \in \mathbf{X} \tag{4}$$

where $E\{\cdot\}$ denotes the expectation operation, $C[\mathbf{x}(N)]$ is the terminal cost, $\mathbf{A}$ is defined to be the admissible decision space, $\mathbf{X}$ is the state space (or nodes in a search graph), and $\mathbf{d}(k)$ is a random disturbance.

In our design, the global planner described above generates alternative subgoals dynamically when the robot is traveling along a preplanned optimal path. In other words, it is always assumed that the next node of the preplanned path may be blocked by unexpected obstacles. If this turns out to be true, the local planner can backtrack along these subgoals without delay. However, if nothing happens when the robot is approaching the next node, the alternative subgoals provided by the global planner will be ignored. Both global path planning for optimal paths and local path planning for obstacle avoidance are implemented in real time. Figure 3 shows a flow chart of such an implementation. Dynamic replanning is performed as necessary, based on the decisions that are rooted in sensory information (Hu and Brady 1994).

Figure 4 shows a situation in which there are two unexpected obstacles along the way. Based on prior information and previous traversals, the robot computes the optimal path, a straight line, and moves towards the goal. When the sensors report an obstacle on the way, the robot has to backtrack along an alternative path planned dynamically by the global path planner. The robot travels along the new path until it encounters another obstacle. Once again, the robot backtracks and eventually reaches the goal along the alternative path. It should be noted that the obstacle information obtained during this traversal is used to update the cost function, C_{ij}, of the two corresponding portions of the path in the topologic graph G for subsequent traversals.

Figure 5 shows that an optimal path is planned based on information gathered from the last traversal. In this way, the robot is able to adapt to changes in its environment, rather than repeatedly trying the original planned path. Note that the weighted search graph G is updated dynamically whenever information is available. The uncertainty costs will decrease exponentially during subsequent traversals even though those arcs are not chosen and no new sensor data are available. The robot will be able to try the previous path again. This is the problem of modeling persistence and change discussed above (Hu 1992).

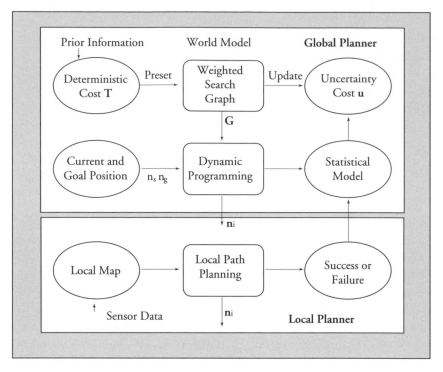

Figure 3. Global planner and local planner.

Dynamic Localization

A fundamental problem for a mobile robot is locating itself in its environment. Estimation of position and orientation based on conventional dead-reckoning (shaft encoders) for a mobile robot leads to cumulative errors, and the robot soon gets lost. Therefore, position correction must be made sufficiently often. To reach its destination with reasonable accuracy, the robot requires external sensors and sensor fusion algorithms to relate knowledge about its environment to information obtained from its sensors.

In our work, we have built on an industrial system that used a feature-based approach to localization based on artificial beacons, shown in figure 6. A laser scanner using a HeNe laser diode (class 3) is located on the physical center of our mobile robot. It is scanned in azimuth at a constant speed of 3 Hz and provides beacon information (x_i, y_i, ϕ_i) whenever it sees a passive retroreflecting target i. Note that in figure 6, XOY is the world frame, $X_r O_r Y_r$ is the robot frame, and $X_s O_s Y_s$ is the scanner frame. The target positions (x_i, y_i) are known accurately by surveying the environment in advance. The position of the robot is deter-

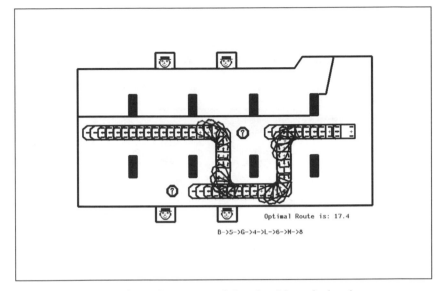

Figure 4. Avoiding unexpected obstacles with two backtracks.

mined by integrating beacon information (x_i, y_i, ϕ_i) and odometry $\mathbf{u}(k) = [d(k), \alpha(k)]$ where $d(k)$ is wheel rotation distance and $\alpha(k)$ is the steering angle.

Assume that the system model describes how the robot state $\mathbf{x}(k)$ (referenced to the physical center of the robot) changes over time in response to a control input $\mathbf{u}(k)$:

$$\mathbf{x}(k + 1) = \mathbf{F}(\mathbf{x}(k), \mathbf{u}(k)) + \mathbf{w}(k) \tag{5}$$

where $\mathbf{w}(k)$ is the state noise with a zero-mean Gaussian distribution $\mathbf{N}((\mathbf{0}, \mathbf{Q}(k))$, and $\mathbf{F}(\mathbf{x}(k), \mathbf{u}(k))$ is the nonlinear function:

$$F = \begin{bmatrix} x(k) + d(k)\cos\alpha(k)\cos(\theta(k)) \\ y(k) + d(k)\cos\alpha(k)\sin(\theta(k)) \\ \theta(k) + d(k)\sin\alpha(k) / (D + C) \end{bmatrix} \tag{6}$$

where $(D + C)$ is the distance from the steer point to the center of the rear axle, as shown in figure 6.

The measurement model is an angle observation ϕ_i in terms of the system state $\mathbf{x}(k)$ and the position of the beacon being detected, $B_i = [x_i, y_i]$, under the assumption of zero-mean Gaussian noise, i.e. $\mathbf{v}(k) \sim \mathbf{N}(\mathbf{0}, \mathbf{R}(k))$:

$$\mathbf{z}(k) = \mathbf{h}(B_i, \mathbf{x}(k)) + \mathbf{v}(k) \tag{7}$$

where the measurement function $\mathbf{h}(B_i, \mathbf{x}(k))$ is also nonlinear, and is given by

$$\mathbf{h}(B_i, \mathbf{x}(\text{k})) = \arctan (y_i - y(k) / x_i - x(k)) - \theta(k) \tag{8}$$

Since both models are nonlinear, the extended Kalman filter (EKF) algorithm

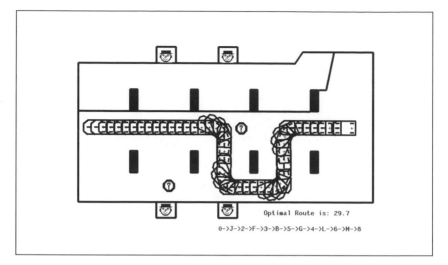

Figure 5. The robot learns something new from previous traversals.

is used. It operates in a "prediction-observation- matching-correction" cycle to provide an estimate of the robot location.

Prediction:

The predicted state $\hat{\mathbf{x}}(k + 1|k)$ and its covariance $\mathbf{P}(k + 1|k)$ are

$$\hat{\mathbf{x}}(k + 1|k) = \mathbf{F}(\mathbf{x}(k|k), \mathbf{u}(k)) \qquad (9)$$

$$\mathbf{P}(k + 1|k) = \nabla\mathbf{F}\mathbf{P}(k|k)\,\nabla\mathbf{F}^{\mathrm{T}} + \mathbf{Q}(k) \qquad (10)$$

where $\mathbf{Q}(k)$ is the system noise, assumed to be zero-mean Gaussian noise. $\nabla\mathbf{F}$ is the Jacobian of the transition function (Brady et al. 1990), obtained by linearization $\partial\mathbf{F}/\partial\mathbf{x}$.

Observation:

We have the current observation provided by the laser scanner

$$\mathbf{z}(k + 1) = \mathbf{h}(B_p, \hat{\mathbf{x}}(k + 1|k + 1)) + \mathbf{V}(k) \qquad (11)$$

and the predicted observation calculated by

$$\hat{\mathbf{z}}(k + 1) = \mathbf{h}(B_p, \hat{\mathbf{x}}(k + 1|k)) \qquad (12)$$

Matching:

The innovation or measurement residual $V(k + 1)$ is obtained using

$$V(k + 1) = \mathbf{z}(k + 1) - \hat{\mathbf{z}}(k + 1) \qquad (13)$$

and the innovation covariance $S(k + 1)$ is given by

$$S(k + 1) = \nabla\mathbf{h}\mathbf{P}(k + 1|k)\,\nabla\mathbf{h}^{\mathrm{T}} + \mathbf{R}(k + 1) \qquad (14)$$

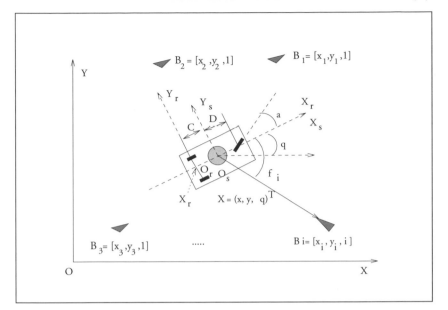

Figure 6. The localization system based on angle observations.

where the Jacobian $\nabla\mathbf{h}$ is found by linearization $\partial h\,/\,\partial x$.

For each measurement, we use a validation gate to decide whether it is a match or not:

$$\varepsilon\,(k+1) = V(k+1)\mathbf{S}^{-1}(k+1)\,V^{\mathrm{T}}(k+1) \le GT \tag{15}$$

where GT is the validation gate, see (Bar-Shalom and Fortmann 1988) for more details on how to choose. If a measurement falls into such a gate, we get a successful match. Otherwise, we simply ignore it and look for the next target measurement.

Correction:

Finally, the updated filter gain $\mathbf{W}(k+1)$, the state $\mathbf{x}(k+1|k+1)$, and the covariance matrix $\mathbf{P}(k+1|k+1)$ are

$$\mathbf{W}(k+1) = \mathbf{P}(k+1|k)\,\nabla\mathbf{h}^{\mathrm{T}}\mathbf{S}^{-1}(k+1) \tag{16}$$

$$\mathbf{x}(k+1|k+1) = \hat{\mathbf{x}}(k+1|k) + \mathbf{W}(k+1)\,V(k+1) \tag{17}$$

$$\mathbf{P}(k+1|k+1) = \mathbf{P}(k+1|k) - \mathbf{W}(k+1)\mathbf{S}(k+1)\,\mathbf{W}^{\mathrm{T}}(k+1) \tag{18}$$

To initialize the robot position and orientation, we modified a dynamic triangulation (DT) algorithm proposed in McGillem and Rappaport (1988) to calculate the scanner position recursively as long as three targets have been detected. As shown in figure 7, initial position, $\mathbf{x}_0$, of the robot is calculated by DT process and sent to Kalman filtering (KF) process. Two processes, DT and KF,

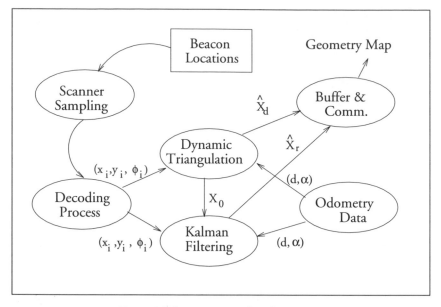

Figure 7. Software structure of our laser scanner.

operate in parallel and send their results to the communication process, which is in charge of distributing them to other processes.

In this way, the robot's position and orientation are predicted by dead reckoning and corrected by sensed information provided by a laser scanner. Figure 8 presents a comparison of data by triangulation (thin curve) and Kalman filter (thick line). This is implemented recursively to reduce the discrepancy between the planned and actual states of a robot, which increase, as does the state uncertainty, when no sensor measurements are made. The Kalman filter has the property that, under certain reasonable assumptions, it is the optimal state estimator. Note that it is not without problems in practice. Among the more severe of these are (1) the difficulty of computing a good *initial* state estimate; (2) the difficulty of determining appropriate gain matrices; and (3) the difficulty of identifying and approximating real plants in the simple form shown. The Kalman filter has been much used at Oxford (Borthwick and Durrant-White 1994; Leonard and Durrant-White 1992; Rao, Durrant-White, and Sheen 1993) and elsewhere to guide robot vehicles, track moving shapes, and compute egomotion.

Structure and Coordination

As we described in earlier sections, any robot system or autonomous mobile

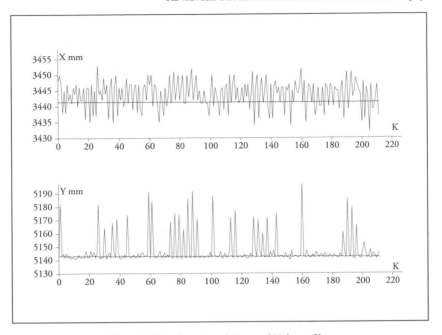

Figure 8. Data by triangulation and Kalman filter.

robot needs constantly to process large amounts of sensory data in order to build a representation of its environment and to determine meaningful actions. The extent to which a control architecture can support this enormous processing task in a timely manner is affected significantly by the organization of information pathways within the architecture. The flow of information from sensing to action should be maximized to provide minimal delay in responding to the dynamically changing environment. A distributed processing architecture offers a number of advantages for coping with the significant design and implementation complexity inherent in sophisticated robot systems. First, it is often cheaper and more resilient than alternative uniprocessor designs. More significantly, multiple, possibly redundant, processors offer the opportunity to take advantage of parallelism for improved throughput and for fault tolerance. Note that we distinguish the design of a processing structure (architecture) from its realization in hardware and/or software.

Over the past two decades, a good deal of thought and effort has been dedicated to the design of architectures to tame complexity and achieve new heights of performance. Two principal designs have been adopted: *functional* and *behavioral* decomposition. Functional decomposition follows the classical top-down approach to building systems. The entire control task of a mobile robot is divided into subtasks which are then implemented by separate modules. These functional modules form a chain through which information flows from the robot's environment, via the sensors, through the robot, and back to the environment via actuators, closing the feedback loop. Most previous mobile robots have been based on this approach, including, for example, hierarchical (Daily et al. 1988) and blackboard (Harmon 1987) architectures; but both of these have inherent limitations, including poor use of sensory information, reduced bandwidth causing bottlenecks, and difficulty in dealing with uncertainty.

In contrast, behavioral decomposition is a bottom-up approach to building a system. A behavior encapsulates the perception, exploration, planning, and task execution capabilities necessary to achieve one specific aspect of robot control. That is, each behavior is capable of producing meaningful action, and several such can be combined to form increasing levels of competence (Brooks 1986). This design method has enjoyed popularity recently. In the subsumption architecture, for example, control is distributed among those task-achieving behaviors that operate asynchronously. Higher layers can subsume the operation of the lower ones when necessary, only one layer actually controlling the robot at any one time. Since each layer achieves a limited task, it requires only that information which is useful for its operation. But the implementation of higher layers of competence still poses a problem. More careful initial design in specifying the communications and modularity is required. Moreover, the higher levels often rely on the internal structure of lower levels, thus sacrificing modularity.

Neither of these approaches suffices, since the control of a mobile robot is so complex that one cannot strictly adhere to one decomposition scheme while completely ignoring the other. Each has benefits and drawbacks. We have developed and implemented an architecture that is, we contend, a blend of the best features of each. It consists of a distributed community of sensing, action, and reasoning nodes. Each of them has sufficient expertise to achieve a specific subtask, following a hierarchical decomposition scheme. Few of them are composed of a single task-achieving behavior as in a behavioral decomposition scheme. The key point is that the control task of the mobile robot is distributed among a set of behavior experts that tightly couple sensing and action, but which are also loosely coupled to each other, as shown in figure 9. In this way, sensor data can be used directly in a corresponding layered control task to form a task-achieving behavior. This differs from the functional decomposition in which the combination of subtasks is a single processing chain. To function effectively, each layer requires a significant amount of self-knowledge to allow it to decide what information it can supply to others, how best to recover from local errors, as well as what to do if no information is sent from other layers.

Basically, there are two subsystems in our design: a layered perception system and a layered control system. The layered perception system is used for active sensor control and distributed sensor fusion to support a layered control strategy. The layers process raw sensor data from internal sensors (tachometer, encoder, resolver) and external sensors (sonar, vision, laser scanner, lateral effect

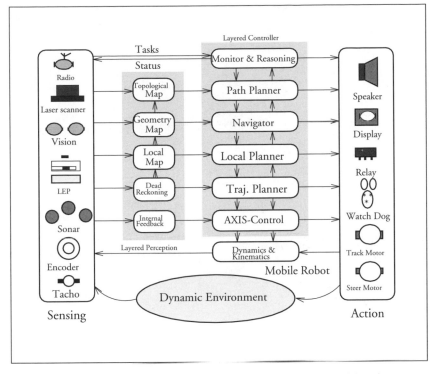

Figure 9. A distributed real-time control architecture for Oxford Mobile Robots.

photodiode LEP range sensor [Pears and Probert 1993]) to build up models in a bottom-up manner. All the sensing layers operate independently and are loosely coupled. Communication between them is used to realize sensor data fusion and coordination of different sensors and actuators.

The design of the layered controller is based on the observation that different tasks require different response times. The lower levels perform simple, general tasks such as *smooth path guidance* and *obstacle avoidance* for fast reactivity. The higher levels perform more complex, situation-specific tasks such as *path planning* and *monitoring*. All layers operate in parallel (Hu, Brady, and Probert 1993). Such a design has been adopted in several different mobile robots in our group, three of which are shown in figure 10, to implement real-time sensing, planning, and control. It should be noted that each layer of our distributed real-time architecture consists of a control node and a sensing node. Each sensing node delivers a representation, which, in the context of a given task, causes a corresponding control node to generate commands.

We have recently built a new mobile robot with four rugged wheels for outdoor applications. Such a robot has a carlike kinematics: one DC motor with a differential gearbox for driving two back wheels, and another DC motor with

Figure 10. Three Oxford AGVs.

leading screw for steering front two wheels. It is fully modular from sensors to actuators based on the modular architecture which we present in the next section.

Modularity and Scalability

There are several issues that concern the realization in hardware or software of distributed architectures such as those described above. For example, one key issue is granularity: a fine-grained architecture is generally considered to comprise many thousands of individual processing elements, while a coarse-grained architecture comprises just a few tens or hundreds. In every case, there is a trade-off between computation and communication. Granularity greatly influences software design. We have adopted a coarse granularity based upon a well-developed theory of interprocess communication and commercially available processors to implement it.

LICA Concept

To implement the system proposed above, we have developed a processing mod-

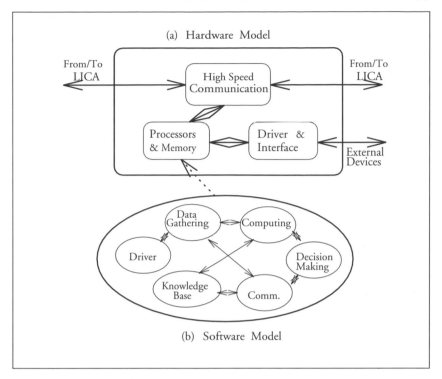

Figure 11. Diagram of LICA concept. (a) Hardware model. (b) Software model.

ule that we call a *Locally Intelligent Control Agent* (LICA). It is based on the concept shown in figure 11. Note that figure 11(a) briefly presents its typical hardware configuration, and figure 11(b) shows its typical software configuration. The LICA design is a standard approach to the design and construction of a complex system and to maximizing modularity. It is independent of any particular processor. Central to such a design is the concept of communication sequential processes (CSP), which was developed by Hoare (1985). Although we originally implemented the LICA concept using *transputer* technology (Hoare 1985), we have also built LICA implementations using other processors such as SIEMENS 80C166 and PowerPC.

The transputer was designed to execute CSP efficiently and specifically for dedicated applications in embedded real-time systems. Its high-speed serial links (up to 20 MBit/s) provide a convenient way to build a parallel processing computer architecture. It has outstanding capability for input and output, and an efficient response to the interrupts. These features are supported by a timesharing (multiprogramming) operating system, which is built into the chip. An application program can therefore be structured naturally as a collection of loosely coupled parallel processes, modeling the parallel structure of the environment in which they are embedded. In essence, we exploit the channel communication architecture provided by transputers, but use more powerful processors for computation.

Dozens of LICAs have been built for a variety of purposes, including high level planning, low-level vehicle control, and sensor data interpretation and fusion. Figure 11(a) shows the logical functions of a typical LICA, which includes a driver and interface to external sensors and motors, computing power and memory, as well as high speed serial links. A pair of RS-422A drivers and receivers are included in a LICA for the point-to-point link signals to be carried at a speed of 20 MBit/s for a distance of up to 30 meters. A range of different computing TRAMs (TRAnsputer Modules), sensing TRAMs (sonar TRAMs, vision TRAMs, etc.), and interface TRAMs (A/D, D/A, digital I/O, RS232, etc.) can be used on LICAs to implement different tasks demanded by applications (Hu, Brady and Probert 1993).

The software of each LICA contains its own localized function and its own localized knowledge source, as shown in figure 11(b). The LICAs run independently, monitoring their input lines and sending messages on their output lines. There is no shared memory. Once a LICA has input data to work on, the data are processed and the results are held for a certain predefined time for other LICAs to read. If no valid data are available, the LICA gives up its input process and continues with other processing.

A Modular Architecture

The LICA encourages a modular approach to building complex control systems for intelligent mobile robots to perform navigation, planning, and control tasks in real time. The LICA-based modularity offers flexibility in changing the system configuration between the different applications by exploiting point-to-point communications. It provides a degree of robustness and reliability, as well as a cost-effective solution to problems of designing complex robot systems.

Figure 12 shows that the proposed control system is built from twenty-three LICA boards. Since control of the vision head and visual tracking require high computing power, nine LICAs are used at the beginning. Currently, the number of LICA boards is reduced to five, since one PowerPC LICA has been used (see figure 16). Other sensors, such as sonars, an LEP, and a laser scanner require much less computing power, and only three or four LICAs are used. It should be noted, however, that the number of LICAs for each task-achieving behavior, such as path planning and obstacle avoidance, is flexible and can be easily changed. This depends upon the system time constraints in a particular application. The topology of the network can be reconfigured flexibly by twisted link cables according to different experiments or applications.

Figure 13 shows the corresponding software structure. It is implemented by

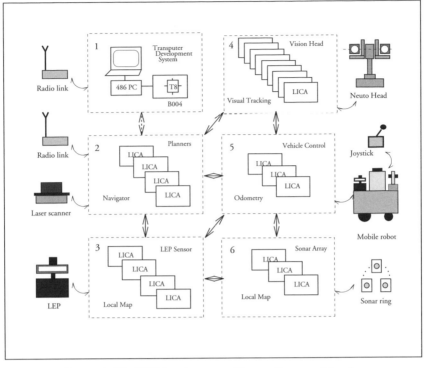

Figure 12. The LICA-based system architecture for our mobile robot.

INMOS C, which is a special configuration language able to distribute processes over a network of transputers and to create a multiprocessor system very quickly. There are six main processes, each of which in turn consists of many subprocesses which exploit the support of parallelism in transputers. All the processes are correspondingly mapped into the LICA-based transputer network shown in figure 12 and operate in parallel. A typical mapping for the active stereo vision head onto the LICA architecture is sketched in the next section to show scalability of the system. The mapping for other sensors and the layered controller can be found in (Hu, Brady, and Probert 1993).

The Scalability of the System

The LICA design not only provides modularity for building a complex robot system, but also provides scalability to the system to enable it to be used for different applications. Figure 14 shows that the LICA architecture can be scaled in three ways. The top diagram shows an ASIC version of LICA, used to increase its

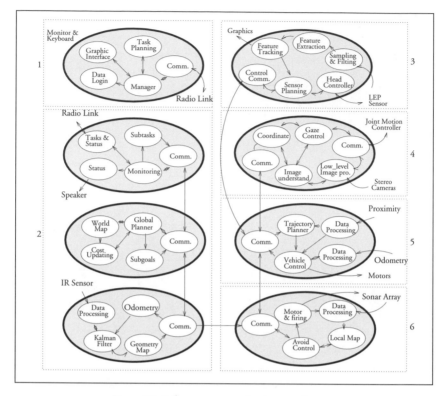

Figure 13. Software structure for the control system.

capability of interfacing to different sensors and actuators. The microprocessor 80C166 is currently used, but this can be easily changed to other processors. The middle diagram shows the normal version of LICAs, which combine the power for computing and the power for interfacing external devices. Finally, the bottom diagram shows LICAs with high computing power gained by adding Texas C40, IBM PowerPC, or DEC Alpha into LICA architecture. Such LICAs are particularly required by high bandwidth systems such as real-time vision systems.

A LICA-based active vision system (Du and Brady 1994) is one such example that demonstrates the system's scalability. The vision system enhances the visual navigation capabilities of the system when it is confronted with a dynamic environment. Based on a four degree-of-freedom stereo robot head, the vision system is able to actively change its geometry to adapt to the task requirements and is able to plan and execute accurate camera motions (Hu et al. 1995). Figure 15 shows that the system has several functional blocks, namely

- *The stereo head* and its *motion controller* are responsible for carrying out the desired joint motions. The stereo head has four degrees of freedom, and is

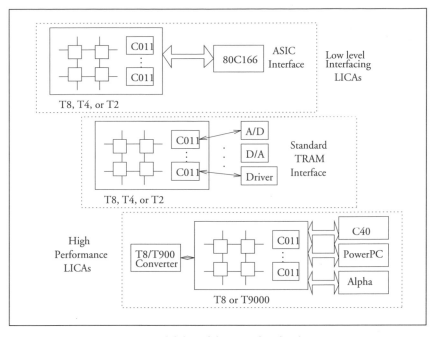

Figure 14. Scalability of the LICA-based architecture.

driven by four high-performance DC motors. Real-time joint motion is controlled by PID controllers working at 2.93 kHz.

- *The gaze controller* is responsible for generating and controlling a set of useful behaviors which are important for visual information processing.
- *The low level image processing* is generally task independent. It provides on demand a set of low level visual features and an estimate of visual motion, and transmits them to high level image processing and the gaze controller.
- T*he high level image processing* is used to interpret the information according to the task requirements. Head-vehicle coordination controls the overall behavior of the active vision system and information exchange between vision and the vehicle controller. It must initialize appropriate behaviors and image processing algorithms to achieve its current purpose.

The computing/control platform of the active vision system is first implemented using a network of thirty-two T800 transputers on nine LICA boards. To maintain compactness, two transputer-based frame grabbers are used to capture the images. The network topology can be changed both locally and globally to implement specific tasks. For low-level image processing (monocular image processing for the left and right cameras) short length pipelines and intensive parallelism are used to provide high sample rate and short latency. These are key

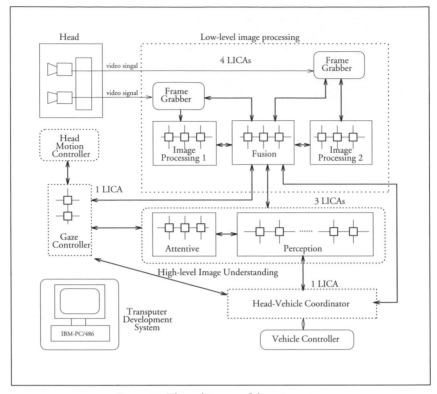

Figure 15. The architecture of the vision system.

to achieving the real-time control of actions (head motions). The data fusion represents middle-level image processing, and the perception corresponds to the high level reasoning and image understanding. This architecture enables us to integrate various strategies and algorithms into the system. Figure 16 shows that a PowerPC LICA has been used to replace five T800 transputer LICAs.

Figure 17 shows that the vision head performs saccade motion for tracking initialization by moving both cameras. Then it keeps tracking the target to implement pursuit motion. Note that the image positions of the target at both cameras are kept in the centre of the image frames.

Figure 18 presents a image sequence of visual tracking. A torch held by a person is moving at a speed of about 10 centimeters per second. The vision head tracks its light and locates its position and angle relative to itself. Then such information is used to calculate the moving speed and the steering required for the robot to pursue it. The robot will follow the spotlight within a certain safe distance (1.5 meters) and will backtrack if the torch is too close (i.e., distance between the robot and the torch is less than 1.5 meters).

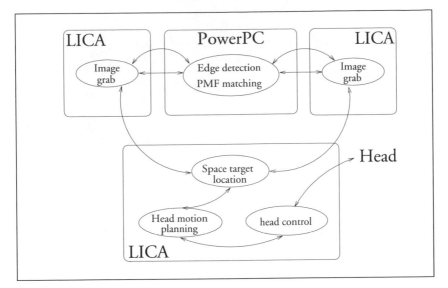

Figure 16. A new version of the LICAs.

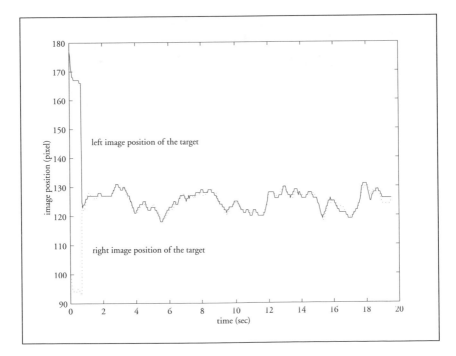

Figure 17. Tracking target motion after initialization.

Figure 18. The spotlight tracking by the vision head on the AGV.

Conclusions

The use of mobile robotics for parts handling and delivery is increasingly common in the manufacturing industry. There are hundreds of fielded systems in the world (Hollier 1987). Nearly all of them are tracked or line following, because currently such systems are far more accurate than free ranging systems that locate their position using retroreflecting beacons (Premi and Besant 1983). Since an industrial environment is complex and dynamic, it is impossible for a designer to foresee all of the circumstances that might be faced by a mobile robot in continuous, long-term interaction with such an environment. Any fully autonomous mobile robot must possess a considerable degree of autonomy, such as robust navigation, obstacle avoidance, dynamic planning, and environment learning. In other words, it should be able to adapt its behavior flexibly to unexpected situations and dynamic changes in the environment without explicitly being told what to do at each moment. It is essential to build a decentralized control system in industrial applications to obtain high reliability and flexibility.

Major application opportunities are currently opening up in outdoor mobile robotics: (1) stockyard parts acquisition and delivery, (2) subsea, (3) dockside automation, (4) inshore navigation, (5) civil construction, and (5) parts delivery inside nuclear power stations. All of these are characterized by imperfect information generated by application-specific sensors from which decisions must be made in real time. In each case, a fixed environmental model suffices, with occasional updates. Cases (1), (2), and (3) predominantly require advances in sensing and sensor-based obstacle avoidance; case (4) requires primarily sensor data-fusion; and case (5) requires high accuracy (typically 1 centimeter over a range of 100 meters). Applications that are often talked about but which seem to have very limited likelihood of being fielded over the next decade include object delivery in hospitals and offices; robot "guide dogs," and sentries, e.g. in prisons. It is fun to imagine far-out applications; measurable progress will come from work on real problems.

Acknowledgments

We wish to thank Penny Probert and Hugh Durrant-Whyte for many insightful conversations, Professor Alan Pugh for his encouragement, and the staff at GCS for their continuing support. Thanks to Fenglei Du (Now at Amherst Systems Inc.), Fuxing Li, and many people within the Oxford Robotics Research Group for contributing toward the project. Thanks also to the EPSRC DIP for their financial support under grant GR/K39844.

CHAPTER THIRTEEN

The *Phoenix* Autonomous Underwater Vehicle

Don Brutzman, Tony Healey, Dave Marco, and Bob McGhee

The *Phoenix* autonomous underwater vehicle (AUV) is a robot for student research in shallow-water sensing and control (figure 1). *Phoenix* is neutrally buoyant at 387 pounds (176 kilograms) with a hull length of 7.2 feet (2.2 meters). Multiple propellers, thrusters, plane surfaces, and sonars make this robot highly controllable. The underwater environment provides numerous difficulties for robot builders: submerged hydrodynamics characteristics are complex and coupled in six spatial degrees of freedom, sonar is problematic, visual ranges are short, and power endurance is limited. Numerous *Phoenix* contributions include artificial intelligence (AI) implementations for multisensor underwater navigation and a working three-layer software architecture for control. Specifically we have implemented the execution, tactical, and strategic levels of the rational behavior model (RBM) robot architecture. These three layers correspond to hard-real-time reactive control, soft-real-time sensor-based interaction, and long-term planning, respectively. Operational software functionality is patterned after jobs performed by crew members on naval ships. Results from simple missions are now available.

In general, a critical bottleneck exists in AUV design and development. It is extremely difficult to observe, communicate with and test underwater robots because they operate in a remote and hazardous environment where physical dynamics and sensing modalities are counterintuitive. Simulation-based design using an underwater virtual world has been a crucial advantage permitting rapid development of disparate software and hardware modules. A second architecture for an underwater virtual world is also presented which can comprehensively model all necessary functional characteristics of the real world in real time. This virtual world is designed from the perspective of the robot, enabling realistic AUV evaluation and testing in the laboratory. Three-dimensional real-time graphics are our window into the virtual world, enabling multiple observers to visualize complex interactions.

Networking considerations are crucial inside and outside the robot. A networked architecture enables multiple robot processes and multiple world components to operate collectively in real time. Networking also permits worldwide observation and collaboration with other scientists interested in either robot or

Figure 1. Phoenix AUV testing in Moss Landing Harbor, California.

virtual world. Repeated validation of simulation extensions through real-world testing remains essential. Details are provided on process coordination, reactive behaviors, navigation, real-time sonar classification, path replanning around detected obstacles, networking, sonar and hydrodynamics modeling, and distributable computer graphics rendering. Finally in-water experimental results are presented and evaluated.

This chapter describes software architectures for an autonomous underwater robot and for a corresponding underwater virtual world, emphasizing the importance of 3D real-time visualization in all aspects of the design process. Recent work using the *Phoenix* AUV is notable for the successful implementation and integration of numerous software modules within multiple software layers. The three-layer software architecture used is the RBM, consisting of reactive real-time control (execution level), near-real-time sensor analysis and operation (tactical level), and long-term mission planning and mission control (strategic

Figure 2. Phoenix AUV shown in test tank (Torsiello 1994).

level) (Byrnes et al. 1996; Marco, Healey, and McGhee 1996). In effect, a higher robot software layer also exists: an off-line mission assistant that uses rule-based constraints and means-ends analysis to help human supervisors specify mission details, followed by automatic generation of strategic level source code. Results for simultaneous operation of the three onboard robot software layers (running an autogenerated mission) have been verified by virtual world rehearsal and in-water testing (Davis 1996; Davis, Brutzman, Leonhardt, and McGhee 1998).

Theoretical development stresses a scalable distributed network approach, interoperability between models, physics-based reproduction of real-world response, and compatibility with open systems standards. Multiple component models are networked to provide interactive real-time response for robot and human users. Logical network connectivity of physical interactions is provided using standard sockets and the IEEE standard distributed interactive simulation (DIS) protocol (IEEE 1995). Implementation of the underwater virtual world and autonomous robot are tested using the actual *Phoenix* AUV (figure 2).

In order to support repeatability of our results, documentation and source code are available electronically (Brutzman 1996a, 1996b). Current work includes model validation as well as adaptation of hydrodynamics and controls coefficients for other submersibles. Ongoing work also includes making 3D graphics and networking compatible with the Virtual Reality Modeling Language

(VRML 97) to permit Internet-portable rendering and interaction with any computer connected to the World Wide Web.

In this chapter, we will discuss motivations for AI approaches in underwater robotics, describe robot hardware for *Phoenix*, examine the RBM software architecture, detailing the execution, tactical, and strategic levels, and describe robot networking. We will also discuss virtual worlds, visualizing control algorithms, and AUV-virtual world communications which permit real-time physics-based response in the laboratory. We then discuss interactive 3D computer graphics and sonar visualization, evaluate experimental results, and point out areas for future work. The chapter closes with conclusions, references, and pointers to a repository for software and documentation.

Motivation

Untethered underwater robots are normally called autonomous underwater vehicles (AUVs), not because they are intended to carry people but rather because they are designed to intelligently and independently convey sensors and payloads. AUVs must accomplish complex tasks and diverse missions, all while maintaining stable physical control with six spatial degrees of freedom (i.e., posture, meaning 3D position plus 3D orientation).

The underwater environment is highly challenging. Hydrodynamics forces are surprisingly cross-coupled between various axes because of asymmetric vehicle geometry and the nonlinear drag "added mass" of water fluid carried along with moving vehicles. Active sonar returns provide precise range but poor bearing accuracy and can be subject to frequent dropouts. Sonar range maxima are highly frequency-dependent. At moderate ranges (beyond several hundred meters) sonar paths can bend significantly because of continuous refraction from sound speed variation, which is caused by changes in water temperature, salinity, and pressure (i.e., depth). Vision is only possible for short ranges (tens of meters at best) and is often obscured if water is turbid. Underwater vision also requires powerful lighting, which is an unacceptable power drain because of already-severe power and propulsion endurance constraints. Laser sensors are usable to an approximately 100 meter range and provide good range and bearing data but remain expensive, hard to tune, and subject to turbidity interference. Typically little or no communication with distant human supervisors is possible. When compared to indoor, ground, airborne, or space environments, the underwater domain typically imposes the most restrictive physical control and sensor limitations upon a robot. Underwater robot considerations remain pertinent as worst-case examples relative to other environments (figure 3).

A large gap exists between the projections of theory and the actual practice of underwater robot design. Despite numerous remotely operated vehicles (ROVs)

Complex Hydrodynamics

- coupled in six spatial degrees of freedom
- accompanying "added mass" of water
- instability can be severe or fatal

Sonar

- accurate ranges but poor bearings
- numerous nonlinear factors affecting reverberation and attenuation
- sonar path bending at long ranges because of sound speed profile (SSP) effects

Vision and Laser

- refraction and turbidity range limits
- lighting requires excessive power

Endurance Typically a Few Hours

- limited power available
- places constraints on all other equipment

Navigation

- ocean currents vary with time, location
- acoustic navigation requires calibrated prepositioned transponder field
- GPS and inertial methods are possible

Communications

- tether is an unacceptable encumbrance
- acoustics are limited in bandwidth, range
- optics have extremely limited range

Figure 3. Environmental constraints for underwater robots are severe.

and a rich field of autonomous robot research results, few complete AUVs exist and their capabilities are limited. Cost, inaccessibility, and scope of AUV design restrict the number and reach of players involved. Interactions and interdependencies between hardware and software problems are poorly understood. Equipment reliability and underwater electrical connections are constantly challenging. Testing is difficult, tedious, infrequent and potentially hazardous. Meaningful evaluation of results is hampered by overall problem complexity, sensor inadequacies, and human inability to directly observe the robot in situ. Potential loss of an autonomous underwater robot is considered intolerable because of tremendous investments in time and resources, the likelihood that any failure will become catastrophic, and difficulty of underwater recovery.

Underwater robot progress is slow and painstaking for other reasons as well. By necessity most research is performed incrementally and in piecemeal fashion. For example, a narrow problem might be identified as suitable for solution by a particular AI paradigm and then examined in great detail. Conjectures and theories are used to create an implementation, which is tested by building a model or simulation specifically suited to the problem in question. Test success or failure is used to interpret validity of conclusions. Unfortunately, integration of the design process or even final results into a working robot is often difficult or impossible. Lack of integrated testing prevents complete verification of conclusions.

AUV design must provide autonomy, stability, and reliability with little tolerance for error. Control systems require particular attention since closed-form solutions for many hydrodynamics control problems are unknown. AI methodologies are thus essential for numerous critical robot software components. Historically, the interaction complexity and emergent behavior of multiple interacting AI processes has been poorly understood, incompletely tested, and difficult to formally specify (Shank 1991). We are happy to report that these problems can be overcome. Our three-layer robot software architecture, in combination with a physically and temporally realistic virtual world, has enabled effective research, design, and implementation of an autonomous underwater robot.

The charter of the Naval Postgraduate School (NPS) Center for AUV Research group is to support graduate student thesis research. Certainly there is no shortage of problems that underwater robotics researchers might work on. We believe that having a clear and compelling objective is fundamentally important. *Mission drives design.* A well-defined goal provides priorities that can be understood by a large research group, clear criteria for making difficult design trade-offs, and a finish line: success metrics are defined. We have chosen shallow-water minefield mapping as our driving application. At the 1995 Symposium on Autonomous Vehicles for Mine Countermeasures (MCM) (Bottoms 1995), consensus was reached that all technical components exist which are needed to build effective MCM AUVs. Our motivating goal is to demonstrate such a vehicle. We intend to demonstrate that there are no fundamental technical impediments to mapping shallow-water minefields using affordable underwater robots. We are integrating component technologies necessary for underwater autonomy in a working system and are making good progress toward reaching that goal.

Related Efforts

Over a dozen other research groups are active in underwater robotics. The Massachusetts Institute of Technology (MIT) Sea Grant Laboratory has deployed several *Odyssey*-class AUVs notable for open-ocean and under-ice oceanographic exploration, leading to the possibility of autonomous oceanographic sampling networks (AOSNs) (Curtin et al. 1993). The Florida Atlantic University (FAU) ocean engineering department has built a series of vehicles which include fuzzy logic controllers and special sensing techniques (Smith and Dunn 1994). The Woods Hole Oceanographic Institute (WHOI) Deep Submergence Lab (DSL) has specialized in long-term bottom monitoring, acoustic communications, and remotely teleoperated task-level supervision of manipulators (Sayers, Yoerger, Paul, and Lisiewicz 1996). An excellent introductory text on underwater robot design and control is Yuh (1995). Annual AUV technical symposia are sponsored in alternate years by the IEEE Oceanic Engineering Society (OES) and the Autonomous Undersea Systems Institute (AUSI).

Important Problem Domain for AI

Despite many handicaps, the numerous challenges of operating in the underwater environment force designers to build robots that are truly robust, autonomous, mobile, and stable. This fits well with a motivating philosophy of Hans Moravec:

> ... solving the day to day problems of developing a mobile organism steers one in the direction of general intelligence.... Mobile robotics may or may not be the fastest way to arrive at general human competence in machines, but I believe it is one of the surest roads. (Moravec 1983).

Hardware

Detailed knowledge regarding robot capabilities and requirements is a necessary prerequisite for designing and implementing robot software. Overview descriptions of the *Phoenix* AUV and related research appear in Brutzman and Compton (1991). Both an external view and internal vehicle component arrangements are shown in figures 4 and 5.

Designed for research, the *Phoenix* AUV has four paired plane surfaces (eight fins total) and bidirectional twin propellers. The hull is made of pressed and welded aluminum. The vehicle is ballasted to be neutrally buoyant at 387 pounds (176 kilograms) with a hull length of 7.2 feet (2.2 meters). Design depth is very shallow at 20 feet (6.1 meters). Two pairs of sealed lead-acid gel batteries provide vehicle endurance of 90-120 minutes. Since battery electrical

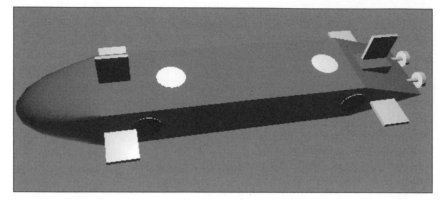

Figure 4. Exterior view of NPS Phoenix AUV.

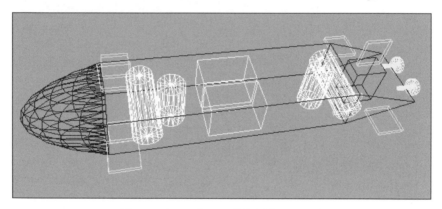

Figure 5. Internal view of NPS Phoenix AUV.

discharge produces hydrogen gas, hydrogen absorber pellets reduce the potential hazard of explosion. Twin propellers provide five pounds of force (lbf) (22.5 N), with resulting speeds up to two knots (approximately one meter per second). A free-flooding (vented to water) fiberglass sonar dome supports two forward-looking sonar transducers, a downward-looking sonar altimeter, a water speed flow meter, and a depth pressure cell. Five rotational gyros mounted internally are used to measure angles and rates for roll, pitch, and yaw respectively. Small cross-body thruster tunnels were locally designed and built for the *Phoenix* AUV. An in-line bidirectional propeller inside each thruster can provide up to two lbf (8.9 N). Detailed schematics and specifications of all *Phoenix* AUV hardware components are presented in Torsiello (1994).

The primary computer for low-level hardware control is a GesPac 68030 running the OS-9 operating system. A significant recent hardware improvement was the addition of a Sun Sparc5 Voyager laptop workstation, with the display monitor removed to save space. Also connected is a paddlewheel speed sensor, depth sensor, DiveTracker acoustic navigation system (Flagg 1994), global positioning system (GPS), differential GPS (DGPS), and inertial navigation system (INS) equipment (Bachmann, et al. 1996), as well as Ethernet local-area network (LAN) connections between onboard computers and (optionally) to external networks. Twin sonars have 1 centimeter resolution out to 30 m maximum range, with the ST725 (725 KHz) having a 1 degree wide by 24 degree vertical beam, and the ST1000 (1 MHz) a 1 degree conical beam. Each sonar is steered mechanically in the horizontal plane in 0.9 degree increments.

Software Overview

The *Phoenix* AUV is primarily designed for research on autonomous dynamic control, sensing, and AI. Software control of the vehicle is provided at a low level, corresponding to maneuvering control of plane surfaces and propellers, as well as at a high level, corresponding to strategic planning and tactical coordination. Sensors are also controlled via execution level microprocessor-hardware interfaces, although some sensor functions may be optionally commanded by the intermediate tactical level, such as steering individual sonar transducer heading motors during classification.

Because of the large variety of critical tasks an autonomous underwater robot must perform, a robust multilevel software architecture is essential. Underwater robot software architectures are a particular challenge because they include many of the hardest problems in robotics, control, and AI over short, medium, and long time scales.

Rational Behavior Model (RBM)

The software architecture used by the *Phoenix* AUV is the rational behavior model (RBM) (Byrnes 1993; Byrnes, et al. 1996). The RBM is a trilevel multiparadigm software architecture for the control of autonomous vehicles. Execution, tactical, and strategic levels correspond roughly to direct interaction with vehicle hardware and environment, intermediate computational processing of symbolic goals, and high-level planning, respectively. The three levels of RBM correspond to levels of software abstraction which best match the functionality of associated tasks. Temporal requirements range from hard-real-time requirements at the execution level, where precise control of vehicle sensors and propulsion is necessary to prevent mission failure or vehicle damage, to soft-real-time long-term planning at the strategic level.

RBM provides an overall structure for the large variety of *Phoenix* AUV soft-

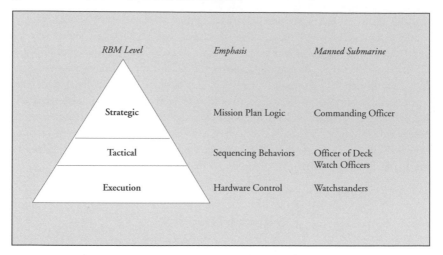

Figure 6. Rational behavior model (RBM) software architecture (Holden 1995).

ware components. A particular advantage of RBM is that the three levels of RBM can be informally compared to the watchstanding organization of a submarine crew (i.e., a manned AUV). Watchstanders operating vehicle sensors, the propulsion plant, and diving station controls correspond to the execution level. Precise real-time control is needed at this level. The officer of the deck (OOD) is represented in the tactical level, carrying out the commanding officer's (CO's) orders by sending individual commands capable of being carried out by watchstanders at the execution level. Because of the diversity of tactical tasks and the complexity of some orders from the CO, the OOD has assistants at the tactical level to assist in their decomposition. These departments (navigation, sonar, path replanner) permit the OOD to concentrate on sequencing and coordinating overall vehicle operation rather than exhaustively directing every detail. Finally the CO is responsible for mission generation and successful completion. CO tasks include mission-related planning and decision making, all performed at the strategic level. This architectural relationship is illustrated in figure 6 (Holden 1995).

Human analogies are particularly useful for naval officers working on this project who already know how to drive ships, submarines, and aircraft, since they provide a well-understood partitioning of duties and a clearly defined task lexicon. The naval analogies used here merely express common and essential robotics requirements using terminology familiar to the many officer students who have worked on *Phoenix*. This approach permits them to apply at-sea experience and domain knowledge intuitively. The RBM paradigm continues to serve well as a formal robot architecture which scalably composes numerous critical processes having dissimilar temporal and functional specifications.

RBM Three Levels Summarized

Execution level software integration includes physical device control, sense-decide-act, reactive behaviors, connectivity, a mission script language, and stand-alone robustness in case of loss of higher levels. Tactical level software includes OOD coordination of parallel tactical processes, telemetry vector state variable updates as a form of shared memory, sonar control, sonar analysis and classification, path planning, DiveTracker acoustic navigation, DiveTracker acoustic communications, DGPS/GPS/INS navigation, and fail-safe mission abort if strategic level commands are lost. Strategic level software integration includes cross-language message passing, linking of dissimilar binary executables, and several functionally equivalent strategic level variations: missions prescribed by Prolog rules, static mission scripts or an off-line mission generation expert system. There are numerous three-level robot architectures and many are similar to RBM.

Operating Systems and Compilers

Interestingly enough, operating system and compiler considerations have been most notable for their incompatibilities rather than their power. Aside from multitasking and interprocess communications, we have not yet found it necessary (or desirable) to take advantage of real-time operating system constructs. The execution level resides on a GesPac 68030 under OS-9 written in Kernighan and Richie (K&R) C, a precursor to ANSI-C. The tactical and strategic levels currently reside on the Voyager Sparc5 laptop under Solaris UNIX, written in ANSI-C and Prolog, respectively. Additionally, tactical and execution software can identically compile under SGI Irix 5.3 UNIX in ANSI-C. Compilation of single version source files across a variety of operating system architectures and language variants is achieved through use of #ifdef and *Makefile* constructs (Brutzman 1996s). This prevents "versionitis" or multiple file versions, which inevitably leads to programmer confusion, incompatible source code interoperability and wasted effort. We are continuing this interoperability trend by porting to the well-supported public domain compiler *g++* (GNU-ANSI-C/C++).

Hierarchical Versus Reactive

Only a few years ago, robot architecture designers seemed preoccupied with bipolar arguments between hierarchical and reactive approaches. Hierarchical stereotypes included phrases like deliberative, symbolic, structured, top down, goal-driven, explicit focus of attention, backward inferencing, world models, planning, search techniques, strictly defined goals, rigid, unresponsive in unpredicted situations, computation-intensive, and highly sophisticated performance. Reactive stereotypes included phrases like subsumptive, bottom up, sensor-driven, layered, forward inferencing, robust subsuming behaviors, avoidance of both dynamic planning and world models, somewhat random behavior, success without massive computations using well-considered behaviors, difficulty scaling up, elusive stability and nondeterministic performance. RBM is a hybrid architecture that is hierarchical at the top layer, reactive at the bottom layer, and a mixture in between. Real-time responsiveness varies correspondingly at each level. From our experience with *Phoenix,* it appears clear that a three-layer hybrid architecture is essential for a robot that must meet a broad range of timing requirements. Similar three-layer hybrid architectures now appear to be the norm for many mobile robots.

World Models

Numerous *Phoenix* AUV theses and source code implementations have been handicapped by inadequate end-to-end hardware and software functionality within the vehicle. Such constraints are common for AUVs. Availability of networked hydrodynamics and sonar models for integrated simulation during robot development have been invaluable for development of robot control algorithms. This approach has permitted realistic development of software in all three software levels, independently and in concert, first in the virtual world and then in the real world.

Declaring that combined models create a virtual world rather than a simulation is not an overstatement. From the robot's perspective, the virtual world can effectively duplicate the real world if robot hardware and software response is identical in each domain. In effect, this is a type of Turing test from the robot's perspective. Such a concept is controversial, perhaps especially among reactive behavior-based approaches which assume world models are unavoidably overcomplicated and use "the world is its own best model" (Brooks 1986). In our case, the challenges of the underwater environment eliminate relying on world availability throughout robot development. Development of a virtual world architecture that can realistically support the robot architecture has produced a new paradigm for robot software development (Brutzman 1992a, 1993, 1994).

Execution Level

In 1994 the execution level was the only software that effectively existed inside the *Phoenix* AUV. A second networked version of execution level was adapted to run in conjunction with developmental tactical routines and the underwater virtual world. A disastrous hydrogen explosion that required over a year to repair occurred in 1994. During this reconstruction period, many changes and enhancements were made to the AUV software. Unfortunately, the two versions of execution level software grew far apart as they progressed, with the in-water version emphasizing new hardware interfaces (Healey and Marco 1995) and the virtual world version emphasizing increased functionality (Brutzman 1994).

Two Versions into One

The top priority for 1995 efforts was to merge the two different versions of the execution level. The in-water code was painstakingly reintegrated with the virtual world version, one function at a time. This approach permitted frequent testing in the virtual world as well as continuous execution level accessibility to other tactical level work which proceeded in parallel. Laboratory bench tests were also conducted to ensure that software functions controlled the proper hardware and that direction of rotation of moving components was correct. A single version of the combined execution level source code had to run on different computer architectures, using different compilers, and with different physical and logical interfaces. The new source code also had to run identically in the real world and the virtual world, all without error. This effort was successful (Burns 1996; Brutzman 1996b).

Telemetry State Vector

The execution level runs in a tight sense-decide-act loop and provides real-time control of vehicle sensors and effectors. Sensor data and effector orders are recorded in a telemetry state vector. This state vector is updated at the closed loop repetition rate, typically 6-10 Hz. The state vector is used for recording mission data, sharing critical parameters among all tactical processes, and providing a data-passing communications mechanism which permits identical operation in the real world and the virtual world (described later). State vector parameters, message-passing semantics, and relation to flow of control are described in detail in Brutzman (1994).

Vehicle Control

As current AUV research indicates, a great variety of control modes are possible for controlling vehicle posture and movement. A primary goal for the execution level is to provide robust open-loop and closed-loop control using propellers, cross-body thrusters, and fin surfaces. Direct open-loop control of all these effectors is available, singly or in combination. Closed-loop control is available for course, depth, and position, either in waypoint-follow mode or hover mode. Waypoint-follow mode relies on propellers and plane surfaces, which works well while transiting but poorly when stationary. Hover mode relies on propellers for short-range longitudinal motion and thrusters for lateral, vertical, and rotational motion. Hover mode allows precise station keeping in position, heading, and depth, at least while dead-reckoned position and ocean current set and drift estimates are accurate.

HELP		*Provide keywords list*
WAIT	#	*Wait/run for # seconds*
WAITUNTIL	#	*Wait/run until clock time*
QUIT		*Do not execute any more*
RPM	# [##]	*Prop ordered rpm values*
COURSE	#	*Set new ordered course*
TURN	#	*Change ordered course #*
RUDDER	#	*Force rudder to # degrees*
DEPTH	#	*Set new ordered depth*
PLANES	#	*Force planes to #*
THRUSTERS-ON		*Enable vertical and*
		lateral thruster control
NOTHRUSTER		*Disable thruster control*
ROTATE	#	*Open loop rotation control*
NOROTATE		*Disable open loop rotate*
LATERAL	#	*Open loop lateral control*
GPS-FIX		*Proceed to shallow depth,take GPS fix*
GPS-FIX-COMPLETE		*Surface GPS fix complete*
GYRO-ERROR	#	*Degrees of gyro error*
		[GYRO + ERROR = TRUE]
LOCATION-LAB		*Vehicle is operating in lab using virtual world.*
LOCATION-WATER		*Vehicle is operating in water w/o virtual world.*
POSITION	#	*## [###] Reset dead reckon,*
		i.e. navigation fix.
ORIENTATION	# ## ###	*(phi, theta, psi)*
POSTURE	#a #b #c #d #e #f	
		(x, y, z, phi, theta, psi)
OCEANCURRENT		*#x #y [#z]*
TRACE		*Verbose print statements*
STANDOFF	#	*Change standoff distance*
		for WAYPOINT-FOLLOW, HOVER
WAYPOINT		*# X #Y [#Z]*
HOVER		*[#X #Y] [#Z] [#orientation]*
		[#standoff-distance]

Figure 7. Mission script language.

Mission Script Language

In keeping with our goal to make vehicle control understandable, we have implemented execution level functionality using a series of script commands. Each command consists of a keyword followed by a variable number of parameters. The mission script language controls operating modes and state flags in the execution level. A subset of the mission script language appears in figure 7.

Commands can originate from tactical level processes, a prepared mission script file, or a human operator. Each command is designed to be unambiguous and readable either by the robot or by people. Prescripted missions and tactical communications are intelligible because they sound similar to OOD orders and ship control party communications aboard ship. We believe this approach has general applicability for most AUVs. Another feature is text-to-speech conversion in the virtual world, simplifying human monitoring of mission progress. Overall execution level functionality also includes plotting telemetry results, replaying recorded mission telemetry data, and acting as network interface to sensor and hydrodynamics models when operating in the virtual world.

Tactical Level

Of the three levels of the RBM architecture, the tactical level was the last developed onboard *Phoenix*. Creation of an OOD module is crucial. The OOD controls the flow of information between other levels and within the tactical level, yet cannot become overburdened by unnecessary details. By forking parallel processes, the OOD creates several departments which are available to assist in processing commands and sensor data. Reuse of execution level functions and data structures reduces the amount of unique code needed by the tactical level. A modular interface design permitted the departments and OOD to be developed simultaneously. Figure 8 shows interprocess communications (IPC) from OOD to strategic level, execution level, and other tactical level processes (Leonhardt 1996).

Properly implementing IPC is crucial. Forked UNIX processes have duplicate variable stores but do not share memory. Consequently, state variable changes in the parent (OOD) and children processes (navigation, sonar, replanner) must be performed individually for each process. We use standard UNIX pipes for this communication because the tactical level is always within a single processor (Stevens 1992). BSD-compliant sockets are used for communications to the execution level because that operates on a different processor (or even on a different network). Separate communication channels are used for updating state vectors and exchanging orders and acknowledgments.

Navigation

The navigation module is a parallel forked process of the tactical level. It uses an asynchronous discrete Kalman filter to filter GPS satellite navigation data received from a Motorola 8-channel GPS–DGPS unit and ranges received from a commercial short baseline sonar range system (DiveTracker).

The *Phoenix* is designed for precision navigation requiring position accuracy

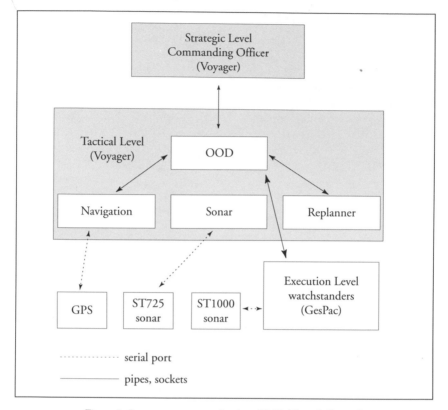

Figure 8. Interprocess communications (IPC) (Campbell 1996).

of 1 meter. The standard deviation of the position available from GPS is approximately 60 meters, with DGPS being accurate within 2 meters. The Dive-Tracker short baseline acoustic ranges have a geometry-dependent standard deviation within 20 centimeters (with an occasional range out to 33 centimeters), which can cause a transiting position uncertainty of 1-3 meters. Using raw positions results in fix-to-fix position uncertainty, control chattering, and hydrodynamic stability problems for *Phoenix*. Kalman filtering corrects these difficulties.

Kalman filtering is a method for recursively updating an estimate of the state of a system by processing a succession of measurements. The *Phoenix* implementation uses a model-based movement estimator for state, combined with measurements, to produce the most probable estimate of the vehicle's position. A discrete Kalman filter is used to process measurements, and the use of acoustic range data requires an extended Kalman filter mode of operation because of the nonlinearity of range measurements (Bachmann 1996).

Accurate and efficient navigation from point to point also requires knowledge of the local ocean currents to prevent undershooting or overshooting the intercept course toward the desired location. If a vehicle fix determines that the vehicle is not where the motion model predicts, then the likely causes are either ocean current or AUV speed and heading errors. Using a nonzero mean movement model (where input vehicle speed is assumed truth) results in the filter solving for both an updated position data and estimates of ocean current. Estimated ocean currents are actually the combined sum of actual ocean current, errors in reported speed, and heading errors. The ocean current values produced can thus change with the vehicle heading, but the root mean squared value of the currents will converge to a steady state number. This number can be resolved to x-y or set-drift (polar) components for dead reckoning use. As with most processes at the tactical level, the algorithmic basis for this approach is similar to techniques used by human navigators.

By monitoring the difference between a motion model and measurements, the Kalman filter can determine if it has possibly lost track or received a bad measurement. If the difference is briefly too high, then the measurement is ignored. If the difference is too high for longer than fifteen seconds, then it is assumed that the filter has lost track. Upon loss of track, the tactical level is informed and the OOD requests surfacing to gain a GPS fix and reset the filter state and parameters. This GPS-FIX procedure is designed to work equally well in hover and waypoint control. Full navigator details are in McClarin (1996) and Bachmann, McGhee, Whalen, Steven, Walker, Clynch, Healey, and Yun (1996).

Real-Time Sonar Classification

Real-time sonar classification and run-time collision avoidance are essential for AUV autonomy and survivability. An off-line sonar classification expert system was originally written using the CLIPS expert system shell (Brutzman, Compton, and Kanayama 1992; Brutzman 1992b). Successful development of rules was originally dependent on the support of the expert system rule-matching engine. Once the expert system was developed, translation to C was practical, and the optimized sonar classifier is now capable of running in real-time to meet robot sensing requirements (Campbell 1996).

The sonar module initializes sonar transducer parameters for maximum range scale, orientation change step size, and transmitter power settings. Three sonar search control modes are available: transit search, sonar search, and rotate search. The transit search consists of a 60 degree sonar scan in front of the AUV. This search is primarily conducted for collision avoidance. The other two modes are conducted in a search area to detect, localize, and classify any unknown objects. Sonar search and rotate search are 360 degree searches. Sonar search is performed by mechanical rotation of the sonar head, whereas rotate search is accomplished with the sonar head fixed while the full *Phoenix* body performs a 360 degree rotation.

Sonar processing begins with filtering, thresholding, and smoothing of the raw sonar data to produce a return bearing and range. The returns are then fitted to line segments using parametric regression. Line segments are started when a sliding window locates four returns that form an acceptable line. Points are subsequently added based on distance from the line segment and the acceptability of the new resultant line segment. Completed line segments are then combined based on proximity and orientation.

To remove the directionality effects of sonar scan rotation, comparison of line segments is performed by first using the segment that is more clockwise relative to the AUV. Once objects and line segments are formed, heuristic rules are applied to classify the objects. The last part of the classification process is to relay object information in a manner suitable for path planning purposes. A circle representation is used with the center at the centroid of the object. Particularly long line segments (i.e., walls) are converted to a set of small adjacent circles. This methodology works. Additional experimental results are needed to ensure that system coefficients are properly tuned for current *Phoenix* sonars.

Imminent collision avoidance is achieved with a simple relative bearing and range check for all valid returns that contribute to any line segment. If a return does not contribute to a line segment, it is not evaluated and is treated as a spurious return. We have developed more robust imminent collision avoidance algorithms independent of near-real-time sonar classification using the second steerable sonar. Using multiple noninterfering sonars permits the use of search techniques that are otherwise mutually exclusive when sharing a single sonar transducer head. The collision avoidance sonar (usually the ST725) is directly controlled by the execution level for reliability and rapid response.

Path Planning and Replanning

Path planning is a tactical function. The strategic level contains the CO and controls the overall mission plan. The CO decides (in general terms) where the ship will operate. Meanwhile, achieving the ordered track is the responsibility of the tactical level OOD. To determine a safe route to the location the CO has requested, the OOD tells the tactical-level replanning department the desired location and the ship's present position. The sonar department (by means of the OOD) provides the replanning department with the current physical environment—where all the "circled" obstacles are. The replanning department takes this data and provides the OOD with the best path to the CO's ordered location after adding a safety distance around any obstacles. If a new obstacle is found by sonar while the ship is transiting, the OOD will call upon the replanning department to check the path. Replanning does not constantly process data but rather is called when the OOD needs it.

As a final step, smooth motion planning algorithms are applied to the output of the circle world path replanner in order to provide precise control of *Phoenix* and allow for rapid travel around obstacles without slowing into hover mode (Brutz-

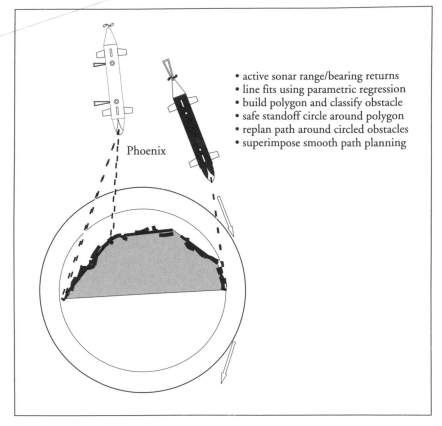

- active sonar range/bearing returns
- line fits using parametric regression
- build polygon and classify obstacle
- safe standoff circle around polygon
- replan path around circled obstacles
- superimpose smooth path planning

Phoenix

Figure 9. Obstacle detection, classification, localization, and avoidance.

man 1992b; Kanayama 1995; Leonhardt 1996; Davis 1996). Hover mode is inefficient when transiting waypoints because it requires *Phoenix* to stop and maintain posture at a given location. Given the turning radius of a vehicle, smooth motion planning allows the vehicle to go from one point to another along a path that does not require the vehicle to perform instantaneous changes in direction. Thus the vehicle does not need to rotate in place when negotiating around obstacles. Replanner details are in Leonhardt (1996). Figure 9 illustrates the end-to-end process of detecting, classifying, localizing, and avoiding a sonar obstacle.

Strategic Level

The RBM strategic level is typically written in Prolog, a language for predicate logic. The strategic level implements a planning capability by sequencing mis-

- Symbolic computation only, contains mission-independent doctrine predicates and current mission guidance predicates
- No storage of internal vehicle or external world state variables
- Rule-based implementation, incorporating rule set, inference engine and working memory (if required)
- Noninterruptible, not event driven
- Directs tactical level via asynchronous message passing
- Messages may be either commands or queries requiring Boolean responses
- Operates in discrete (Boolean) domain independently of clock time
- Building blocks: goals
- Abstraction mechanism: goal decomposition (backwards chaining) and rule partitioning (forward chaining); both are based on goal-driven reasoning

Figure 10. RBM characteristics for strategic level (Byrnes 1996).

sion phases and backtracking when necessary to provide appropriate guidance to the tactical level as portions of the mission succeed or fail. Strategic level design criteria appear in figure 10.

Manually produced early versions of the strategic level worked properly but became large and complex. Strategic level code was streamlined by separating mission-independent doctrine from mission-specific guidance. With practice, the strategic level Prolog code is relatively simple to read, produce, and run. An example strategic level mission follows in figure 11, where TASK might be a combination of GPS fix, drop marker, radio report, and return home.

The strategic level can also take the form of a deterministic finite automata (DFA). A mission controller initiates the phase associated with the current DFA node upon arrival, transitioning to a new node when the current node's phase completes successfully (or aborts because of a time out). A representative mission phase template appears in figure 12. Individual tactic predecessors and successors can be composed using this template to create missions of arbitrary complexity (Davis 1996a; Davis Brutzman, Leonhardt, and McGhee 1996b).

Advantages of the strategic level DFA structure are twofold. First, an arbitrary mission can be modeled simply as a set of phases that are executed in an order

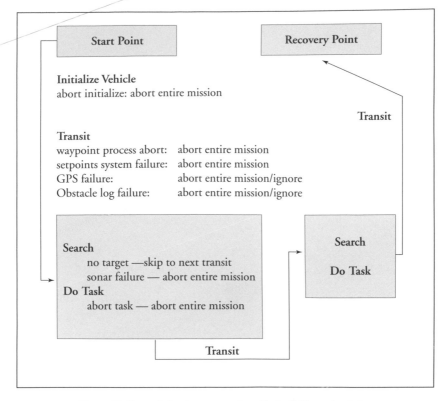

Figure 11. Strategic level representation of minefield search mission.

defined by the transitions of the DFA. Second, mission control using the Prolog search engine is powerful enough that complex behavior can be implemented without needing computationally intensive mathematical calculations. Arithmetic is confined to the tactical level; conceptual mission planning is confined to the strategic level.

Since a prime motivation for *Phoenix* is shallow water countermine operations, the mission generation process must be substantially simpler than writing Prolog programs if typical human operators are to deploy the AUV. One solution to this problem combines a graphical user interface for mission planning and specification together with a goal-driven expert system for strategic level code generation.

There are three aspects to the AUV mission generation expert system. The first is a mission planning tool, which specifies vehicle launch and recovery positions and indicates what the mission is supposed to accomplish. Means-ends analysis then computes a sequence of phases which can accomplish the desired mission. Failure of any single phase will cause a mission to either abort or follow an alter-

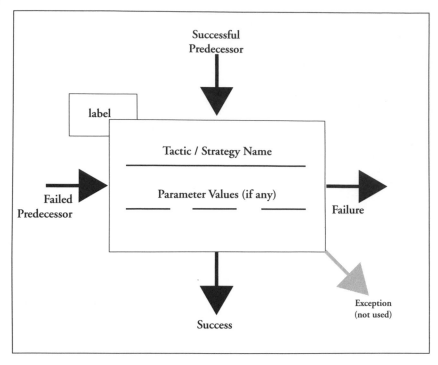

Figure 12. Template for tactic and strategy composition.

nate failure-recovery phase (Byrnes 1996). Because there might be multiple phase sequence solutions for a mission, each solution generated by the system is the next solution found as opposed to an optimal solution. In addition, missions generated through means-ends analysis are linear and proceed phase-by-phase to the end. In any case, users are allowed to choose among the candidate solutions generated (Davis 1996a; Davis Brutzman, Leonhardt, and McGhee 1996).

More complicated missions can take full advantage of this strategic level DFA structure. They are specified phase-by-phase using the second piece of the mission generation expert system, the mission specification tool. This tool allows an experienced user who understands the DFA structure of the strategic level to define missions one phase at a time. Regardless of whether the mission planning tool or the mission specification tool is used, the system automatically checks input for correctness and logic and will not allow specification of an invalid mission (Leonhardt 1996; Holden 1995; Davis 1996; Davis, Brutzman, Leonhardt, and McGhee 1996).

The final aspect of this system is the code generation facility. By using specified phases, either the mission planning or mission specification tool, and templates for valid phase types (such as hover or search) the system can generate executable code in either Prolog or C++. Earlier theses demonstrated that the strategic level can be equivalently instantiated using either the Prolog backwards chaining engine or the CLIPS forward chaining engine. Alternate languages are possible because there are multiple ways to plan. Backwards chaining can be unambiguously implemented using forward chaining, forward chaining can be unambiguously implemented using backwards chaining, and both can be implemented using fully enumerated decision graphs. Use of C++ has become possible because improved understanding and tighter constraints on mission primitives have eliminated the need for the full functionality of the Prolog search engine. Nevertheless, such simplifications were only possible following extended experimentation using Prolog code.

Extensive testing of autogenerated Prolog and C++ code has been conducted in the virtual world, and successful in-water testing has been conducted at the *Phoenix* AUV test tank, Moss Landing Harbor, and the NPS swimming pool. Further in-water tests are planned. Accomplishment of our goal of simplifying mission generation is indicated by a significant reduction in the time required for mission coding (minutes when using the expert system as opposed to hours without it). Finally, syntactic programming errors have been completely eliminated by the source code autogeneration system, and logical programming errors have been substantially reduced.

Robot Networking

Perhaps surprisingly for a small robot, networking is a major consideration. Within the Phoenix AUV is an Internet-connectable local-area network (LAN) This feature enables network communications between and within the three software levels, external connectivity in laboratory via tether cable, and, optionally, external connectivity during harbor testing. Remote connection of the LAN to the campus Internet backbone is achieved using multiple wireless bridge boxes. Multicast backbone (MBone) connectivity permits local or worldwide transmission of audio, video, and DIS streams (Macedonia and Brutzman 1994). World Wide Web links to online software documentation, multiple research group accounts, and properly networked LANs with group access around campus further strengthened this software development collaboration. Ease of use and remote access translate into significant productivity gains and regular discovery of new capabilities. We expect to someday extend this approach underwater by developing Internet protocol over sea water (IP/SW) connectivity (Brutzman and Reimers 1995). We discuss other network considerations in the virtual world connectivity section that follows.

Figure 13. Underwater virtual world for an AUV (Brutzman 1994).

Virtual World

The harsh environment in which an AUV must operate calls for extra precautions in its design to prevent damage to or loss of the vehicle. We have developed a medium-scale virtual environment which enables meaningful end-to-end testing of robot software and hardware in the laboratory (figure 13). As noted in earlier work on the virtual world:

> It is tremendously difficult to observe, communicate with and test underwater robots, because they operate in a remote and hazardous environment where physical dynamics and sensing modalities are counterintuitive. An underwater virtual world can comprehensively model all necessary functional characteristics of the real world in real-time. This virtual world is designed from the perspective of the robot, enabling realistic AUV evaluation and testing in the laboratory. 3D real-time graphics are our window into the virtual world, enabling multiple observers to visualize complex interactions. A networked architecture enables multiple world components to operate collectively in real-time, and also permits world-wide observation and collaboration with other scientists interested in the robot and virtual world. (Brutzman 1994)

The objective of the underwater virtual world is to reproduce real-world robot behavior with complete fidelity in the laboratory. Many questions pertain. What is the software architecture required to build an underwater virtual world for an autonomous underwater vehicle? How can an underwater robot be connected to a virtual world so seamlessly that operation in the real world or a virtual world is transparent to the robot? How can 3D real-time interactive computer graphics support wide-scale general access to virtual worlds? Specifically, how can computer graphics be used to build windows into an underwater virtual world that are responsive, accurate, and distributable and represent objects in openly standardized formats and provide portability to multiple computer architectures? Overview answers to these questions are provided here. Detailed analyses and example solutions are presented in Brutzman (1994). In effect, the virtual world requires a separate software architecture for networked world models that complements the robot software architecture.

The real world is a big place. Virtual worlds must similarly be comprehensive and diverse if they are to permit credible reproductions of real-world behavior. A variety of software components have been shown to be necessary. In every case, 3D real-time visualization has been a crucial tool in developing AUV software. Ways to scale up and arbitrarily extend the underwater virtual world to include very large numbers of users, models, and information resources are also incorporated in this work.

Virtual world capabilities were utilized for testing and verification throughout the software development process. Use of this tool allows a number of programmers to work independently and in concert. Virtual world capabilities have been incrementally improved to match increased vehicle software capabilities, such as

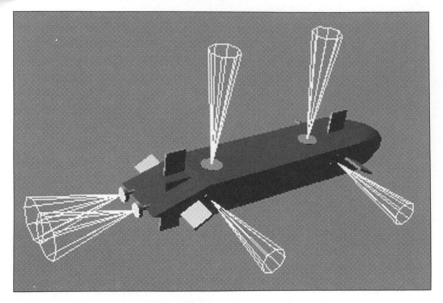

Figure 14. Detailed hydrodynamics and control visualization is essential.

hydrodynamics and controller response rendering (figure 14). Scientific visualization techniques have provided further significant benefits (Brutzman 1995).

Visualizing Control Algorithms

Designing an AUV is a complex task. Many capabilities are required for an underwater mobile robot to act capably and independently. Stable physical control, motion control, sensing, path planning, mission planning, replanning, and failure recovery are example software components that must be solved individually for tractability. The diversity and dissimilarity of these many component subproblems preclude use of a single monolithic solution paradigm.

Vehicle control algorithms are implemented using either thrusters (hovering modes), planes, rudders, or propellers (cruise modes), or all effectors in combination. Control algorithms for the following behaviors are included: depth control, heading control, open-loop rotation, open-loop lateral motion, waypoint following, and hovering. Control algorithms are permitted to operate both thrusters and planes, rudders, and propellers simultaneously when such operation does not provoke mutual interference. Most *Phoenix* control code has been developed and tested in conjunction with the construction of a real-time six degree-of-freedom hydrodynamics model. Design, tuning, and optimization of control algorithms in isolation and in concert is the subject of active research

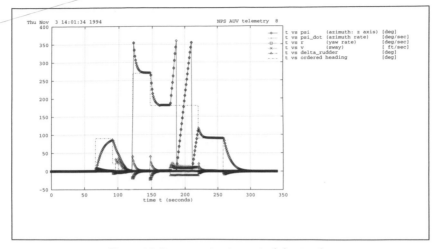

Figure 15. Representative time-series behavior plot.

(Healey and Lienard 1993; Healy, Marco, and McGhee 1996; Fossen 1994; Marco and Healey 1996) and remains an important area for future work. Control algorithm robustness is a particularly important topic since potentially fatal nonlinear instabilities are possible and vehicle reliability is paramount.

Typical efforts at hydrodynamic development are based on mental interpretation of multiple time-series such as figure 15. Dozens of 2D time-series plots are necessary for quantitative performance analysis, but this approach remains notoriously difficult to use when attempting to mentally integrate and visualize all aspects of vehicle behavior. The successes of individual control algorithms created as part of this effort were highly dependent on 2D and 3D visualization techniques. Complete derivations of the full hydrodynamics model and corresponding control equations are in Brutzman (1994, 1996).

A challenging example scenario for an AUV is evaluating vehicle control stability when transitioning from stable submerged control to intentional surface broaching in figures 16 and 17. This scenario exercises the real-time buoyancy model developed in Bacon (1995). Real-time 3D observation of such scenes is an essential tool when developing and testing algorithmic models.

AUV-Virtual World Communications

RBM is a multilevel architecture; consequently, communications between levels must be formally defined. Communications between robot and virtual world must also be clearly specified. Defining communications includes establishing a physical path for data transfer as well as defining the syntax and protocol of ex-

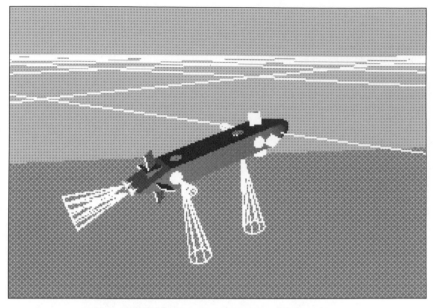

Figure 16. Evaluating control response while broaching.

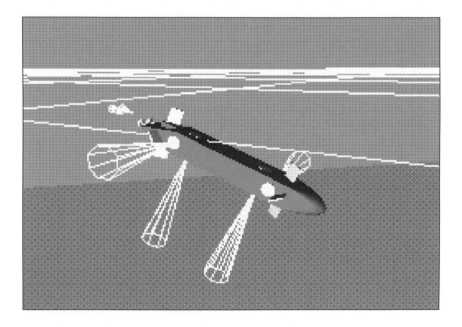

Figure 17. Evaluating control response after broaching.

changed messages. Our design objectives include reliability and clarity so that messages are easily created and easily understood, either by software processes or by people. Details follow that illustrate the precise relationships between robot, virtual world, and graphics-based user viewing windows.

Two kinds of messages are defined for use between robot and virtual world. The first is the telemetry vector, which is a list of all vehicle state variables pertinent to hydrodynamic and sensor control. Telemetry vectors are passed as a string type. The second kind of message allowed is a free-format commands. Free-format command messages are also string types, starting with a predefined keyword and followed by entries which may optionally have significance depending on the initial keyword. Messages with unrecognized keywords are treated as comments. These two kinds of messages (telemetry and commands) can be used for any communication necessary among robot-related entities. Employment of string types facilitates data transfer between different architectures, data transfer via network sockets, and file storage. String types also ensure that all communications are readable by both robot and human, a trait that is particularly useful during debugging. An open format for command messages permits any user or new application to communicate with little difficulty.

Within the AUV, the basic communications flow between execution level and tactical level is straightforward. All telemetry vectors are sent from the execution level to the tactical level, providing a steady stream of time-sensitive, rapidly updated information. The tactical level may send commands to the execution level as desired, and the execution level may return informational messages between telemetry vectors as appropriate. Nonadaptive tactical level functionality can also be provided by carrying out prescripted mission command files. Telemetry vector records and command messages are logged in separate mission output files for postmission analysis and replay.

The telemetry vector serves several essential purposes. In addition to providing a steady stream of information from the execution level to the tactical level, the telemetry vector also serves as the data transfer mechanism between execution level and virtual world. Efficient communications between robot and virtual world are essential if rapid real-time 10 Hz robot response is to be maintained. The telemetry record is a concise and complete way to support all of these data communications requirements. Figure 18 shows in detail how the flow of control proceeds and the telemetry vector is modified during each sense-decide-act cycle. Robot execution software is designed to operate both in the virtual world and in the real world. While sensing in the virtual world, distributed hydrodynamics and sonar models fill in pertinent telemetry vector slots. While sensing in the real world, actual sensors and their corresponding interfaces fill in pertinent telemetry vector slots. In either case, the remainder of the robot execution program that deals with tactical communications, command parsing, dynamic control, and interpretation is unaffected. While operating in the virtual world, robot propulsion and sensor commands are communi-

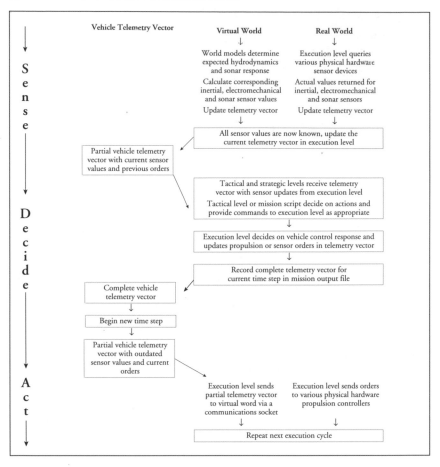

Figure 18. Data flow via the telemetry vector during each sense-decide-act cycle.

cated via the same telemetry vector. While operating in the real world, robot propulsion and sensor commands are sent directly to hardware interfaces for propellers, thrusters, planes, rudders, sonar steering motors, etc. Again, almost all parts of the robot execution program are completely unaffected by this difference. This networked architecture is essentially transparent to the robot, permitting identical AUV operation in the real world or virtual world.

The telemetry vector is therefore a key data transfer mechanism. Telemetry vector updates also define the communication protocol between execution level and virtual world. As might be expected, this works well because the execution level program follows the common robotics cyclic paradigm of sense-decide-act. Figure 19 provides an overview of the telemetry vector update sequence as an alternate means of portraying the validity of this approach. Given the perhaps-

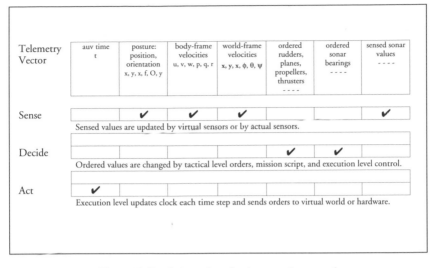

Telemetry Vector	auv time t	posture: position, orientation x, y, x, f, O, y	body-frame velocities u, v, w, p, q, r	world-frame velocities x, y, x, φ, θ, ψ	ordered rudders, planes, propellers, thrusters ----	ordered sonar bearings ----	sensed sonar values ----
Sense		✔	✔	✔			✔

Sensed values are updated by virtual sensors or by actual sensors.

Decide					✔	✔	

Ordered values are changed by tactical level orders, mission script, and execution level control.

Act	✔						

Execution level updates clock each time step and sends orders to virtual world or hardware.

Figure 19. Local viewpoint of active sonar in test tank.

worst-case computational complexity of underwater world models, this networked virtual world software architecture for real-time performance in the laboratory also appears applicable to other robot domains.

Interactive 3D Graphics

Several important requirements are needed for the creation of object-oriented graphics viewers for visualizing a large-scale virtual world. Open standards, portability, and versatility are emphasized over platform-specific performance considerations in order to support scaling up to very large numbers of users, platform types, and information sources. The OpenInventor graphics tool kit and scene description language has all the functionality needed. The potential integration of network connections to logically extend graphics programs is also examined.

A good graphics tool kit for building a virtual world viewer must meet many requirements (Foley and van Dam 1990). Rendered scenes must be realistic, rapidly rendered, permissive of interaction, and capable of running on both low-end and high-end workstations. Graphics programmers require a wide range of tools to permit interactive experimentation and scientific visualization of real-world datasets (Thalmann 1990). The ability to read multiple data formats is also important for a programmer using scientific and oceanographic datasets. Scientific data format compatibility can be provided by a number of data function libraries which are open, portable, reasonably well standardized and usually independent of graphics tools (Fortner 1992). Viewer programs need to be capable of examining high-bandwidth information streams and large archived scientific databases. Thus the ability to preprocess massive datasets into useful, storable, retrievable graphics objects will be particularly important as we attempt to scale up to meet the sophistication and detail of the real world. Adequate standardization of computer graphics and portability across other platforms is also desirable but has been historically elusive.

OpenInventor is an object-oriented 3D graphics tool kit for graphics applications design (Strauss and Carey 1992). Based on the Open GL graphics library, OpenInventor provides high-level extensions to the C++ (or C) programming language and a scene description language. It is designed to permit graphics programmers to focus on what to draw rather than how to draw it, creating scene objects that are collected in a scene database for viewpoint-independent rendering.

The ability to store graphics objects as readable, editable files is especially appealing for the creation of large-scale virtual worlds. Since the performance of computer graphics is highly dependent on the computational complexity of scenes to be rendered, it is inevitable that truly large-scale world scene databases will eventually overload viewing graphics workstations. Such overload will occur regardless of the efficiency of viewpoint culling algorithms and graphics pipeline optimizations, unless partitionable and networked scene databases are used. Furthermore, since populating a virtual world is a task that needs to be open and accessible to large numbers of people, an open graphics data standard is needed for virtual world construction. The ability to selectively load graphics objects and scenes from files is an important distribution mechanism that can take advantage of World Wide Web connectivity.

Ubiquitous portability for analytic, hypermedia, network, multicast, and graphics tools is therefore an essential feature for virtual world model builders. A superior alternative is now available using the VRML specification (Carey, Marrin, and Bell 1997). VRML is the World Wide Web standard for interactive 3D representation. VRML scene description files are the best approach for object definitions in a large-scale virtual world (Brutzman 1997).

Sonar Visualization

Sensor differences distinguish underwater robots from ground, air, and space-based robots. Oceans are generally opaque to visible light at moderate-to-long ranges; consequently vision-based video systems are ordinarily of use only at short distances and are unreliable in turbid water. Vision systems also usually re-

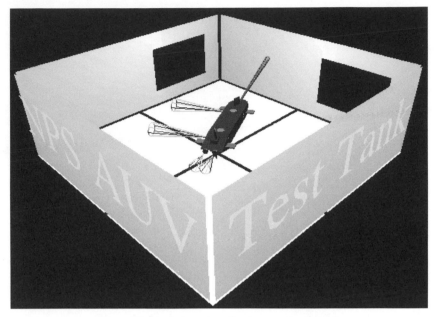

Figure 20. Local viewpoint of active sonar in test tank.

quire intense light sources which deplete precious energy reserves. In comparison to underwater computer vision, active and passive sonar (acoustic detection) has long been a preferred sensing method because of the long propagation ranges of sound waves underwater.

However, sound waves can be bent by variations in depth, temperature, and salinity. A variety of problems including ambient noise, multipath arrival, fading, shadow layers, masking, and other effects can make sonar use difficult. Since active sonar typically provides good range values with approximate bearing values, algorithms for sonar recognition are much different from vision algorithms. In the short sonar ranges used by *Phoenix,* simple error probabilities and linear geometric sonar relationships are adequate. Figure 20 shows the perspective gained by observing AUV sonar from an "over the shoulder" perspective, one of several vantage points needed when developing sonar classification algorithms.

Sonar is the most effective detection sensor used by underwater vehicles. Thus, sonar visualization is particularly important when designing and evaluating robot software. Sonar parameters pertinent to visualization and rendering include sound speed profile (SSP), highly variable sound wave path propagation, and sound pressure level (SPL) attenuation. Several questions are prominent. How can a general sonar model be networked to provide real-time response despite high computational complexity? How can scientific visualization techniques be applied to outputs of the sonar model to render numerous interacting

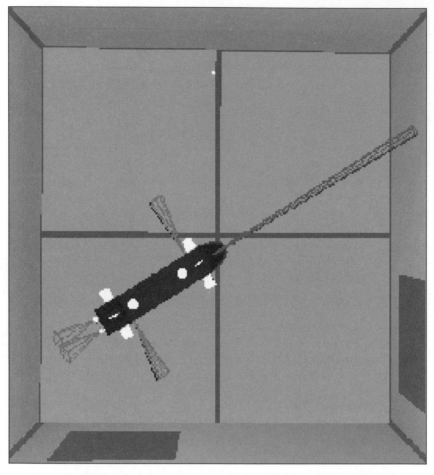

Figure 21. Hand-crafted geometric sonar model for AUV test tank (Brutzman 1994).

physical effects varying in three spatial dimensions and time? Initial investigations indicate that this area may yield significant results. The high dimensionality of sonar data is best served by scientific visualization techniques.

Sonar sensing is crucially important (Stewart 1992). Previously only a single geometric sonar model was available for *Phoenix*, derived by hand to model the AUV test tank (figure 21). Although effective in a small regular volume, this approach was too limited and did not permit easy addition of artificial targets or obstacles. We adapted the computational geometry routines included in the OpenInventor interactive 3D graphics library to shoot rays into the scene database to produce a general geometric sonar model. Now the same scene

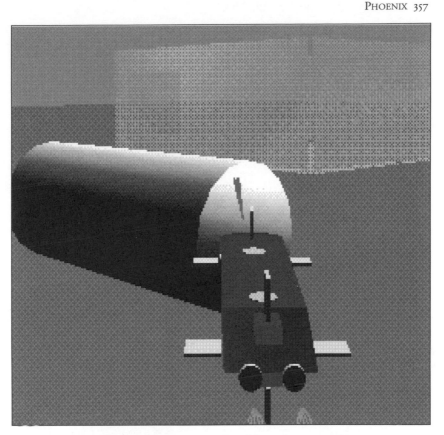

Figure 22. A general geometric sonal model uses the same graphics scene database to produce highly detailed sonar ranges and bearings in real time. Note sonar return from interior of recovery tube.

database (made up of OpenInventor and VRML files) can be used for both virtual world visualization and arbitrary real-time 3D sonar ray intersection calculations (figure 22) (Davis 1996a; Brutzman et al. 1996).

Experimental Test Results

Once *Phoenix* functionality was correct in the virtual world, test tank experiments were conducted to fine tune hardware and properly move the AUV through the water. Diving, forward, backward, lateral, and rotational movement checks were all performed during these test tank experiments. However, the cali-

*Figure 23. Phoenix AUV maneuvering to enter a docking tube
using onboard sonar (Davis 1996a, 1996b).*

bration of speeds during these movements could not be tested because of the relatively small size of the test tank (6 meters x 6 meters x 2 meters deep).

The next vehicle tests were performed in the relatively calm sea water harbor in Moss Landing California. A variety of logistical problems were overcome, but a seemingly endless series of minor hardware failures then thwarted each attempt to run a complete minefield search. Although a complete mission was never accomplished beginning to end, all components of the mission were individually exercised. We now believe that the functionality and logic of the AUV software is correct (Brutzman et al. 1996). Remaining tests include repeated mission testing, verification of aggregate software behavior under a variety of scenarios, tuning of control constants, and validation of both hydrodynamics and sonar models in the virtual world. Recent results include precise vehicle maneuvering and rendezvous with a docking tube (Davis 1996, Davis et al. 1996) (Figure 23). Much more experimental testing awaits.

Future Work

An underwater vehicle which can transit through waypoints and hover in the presence of currents enables a variety of capabilities which are not possible for vehicles that must maintain forward way to remain hydrodynamically stable. We intend to examine whether the *Phoenix* hull form can stably approach and neutralize a moored mine-like object. Figure 24 is a notional diagram that shows how sonar can be used to carefully approach a target broadside, keep station against the ocean current, take confirming video, and attach a beacon or neutralizing device using a simple one- or two-degree-of-freedom effector. For low sea states, we see few limiting factors in this approach.

Phoenix is only directly controllable in five degrees of freedom since roll is unconstrained. Pitch stabilization is straightforward using vertical thrusters. Testing will determine whether roll stabilization is also necessary, perhaps by using an additional thruster. We are further interested in development of automatic diagnostics that reconfigure control algorithms to handle equipment faults. We also intend to explore local measurement of cross-body ocean current flow using acoustic Doppler current profilers (ADCPs) in order to permit precise maneuvering in the midst of highly varying flow fields and high sea states. Finally, future work on underwater virtual world networked graphics includes compatibility with common Web browsers using the VRML (Brutzman 1996).

Conclusions

The underwater environment is extremely challenging for robots. Counterintuitive hydrodynamics response, poor visual capabilities, complex sonar interactions, communications inaccessibility, and power endurance are significant design constraints. Robot builders must provide stable control and reliable operation at all times because of the unacceptably high cost of failure. A variety of AI processes must be used for planning, sensing, and other complex tasks.

Systems integration is significant because of the many sensors and effectors required for nontrivial operation. The *Phoenix* AUV demonstrates that a three-layer robot architecture can be effective at combined system control over time scales ranging from hard-real-time sense-decide-act response to temporally unconstrained mission planning.

Using an underwater virtual world for interactive 3D graphics rendering is an essential capability for effective AUV development. The networked software architecture and various results described here demonstrate that a real-time physically based underwater virtual world is feasible. It enables repeated testing of all aspects of underwater vehicle control, stability, sensing, autonomy and reliability. Graphics viewer requirements include scientific visualization and portability

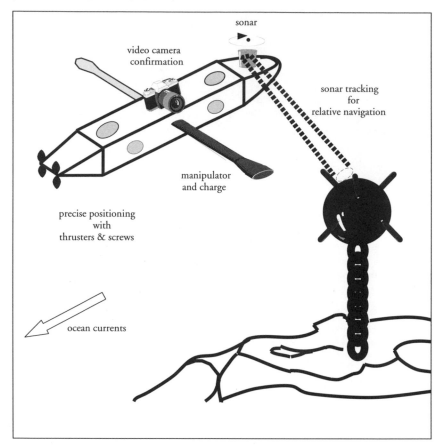

Figure 24. A mobile stable AUV might precisely place an explosive charge on an underwater mine.

across multiple platforms. The use of multicast DIS messages, Web access, and VRML scene descriptions that include dynamic behaviors promise the possibility of scaling to very large numbers of participants. Network connectivity allows us to use the global Internet as a direct extension of our desktop computers, permitting global collaboration on a routine basis.

After years of effort, the RBM architecture is fully instantiated onboard the *Phoenix* AUV and is being successfully tested and refined by in-water testing. A networked underwater virtual world has been crucial to this development project. Experimental results indicate we are close to demonstrating that affordable underwater robots can operate autonomously in challenging environments.

Bibliography

Agre, Phillip E., and Chapman, David. 1990 What are Plans For? *Robotics and Autonomous Systems* 6:17-34.

Agre, Phillip E., and Chapman, David. 1987. Pengi: An Implementation of a Theory of Activity. In *Proceedings of the Tenth International Joint Conference on Artificial Intelligence*. San Francisco: Morgan Kaufmann Publishers.

Agre, Phillip E., and Rosenschein, S. J. 1995. *Special Issue of Artificial Intelligence*. Amsterdam: Elsevier Science Publishers.

Albus, J. S. 1990. Hierarchical Interaction Between Sensory Processing and World Modeling in Intelligent Systems, In *Proceedings of the Fifth IEEE International Symposium on Intelligent Control*, 866-875. Los Alamitos, Calif.: IEEE Computer Society Press.

Allen, J. F. 1983. Recognizing Intentions From Natural Language Utterances. In *Computational Models of Discourse*, ed. M. Brady and R. Berwick, 107–166. Cambridge, Mass.: The MIT Press.

Aloimonos, John. 1990. Purposive and Qualitative Active Vision. In *DARPA Image Understanding Workshop*. San Francisco: Morgan Kaufmann Publishers.

Ambros-Ingerson, J., and Steel, S. 1988. Integrating Planning, Execution and Monitoring. In *Proceedings of the Seventh National Conference on Artificial Intelligence*, 83-88. Menlo Park, Calif.: AAAI Press.

Andersen, Claus S.; Madsen, Claus B.; Sorensen, Jan J.; Kikeby, Neils O. S.; Jones, Judson P.; and Christensen, Henrik I. 1992. Navigation Using Range Images on a Mobile Robot. *Robotics and Autonomous Systems* 1(1): 147-160.

Anderson, T. L., and Donath, M. 1990. Animal Behavior as a Paradigm for Developing Robot Autonomy. *Robotics and Autonomous Systems* 6(1990): 145-186.

Andreson, Fred P.; Davis, Larry S.; Eastman, Roger D.; and Kambhampati, Subbarao. 1985. Visual Algorithms for Autonomous Navigation. In *Proceedings of the IEEE International Conference on Robotics and Automation*, 856-861. Los Alamitos, Calif.: IEEE Computer Society Press.

Arbib, M. 1981. Perceptual Structures and Distributed Motor Control. In *Handbook of Physiology—The Nervous System II*, ed. V. B. Brooks, 1449-1465. Bethesda, Maryland: American Physiological Society.

Arkin, Ronald. C. 1995. Reactive Robotic Systems. In *Handbook of Brain Theory and Neural Networks*, ed. M. Arbib, 793-796. Cambridge, Mass.: The MIT Press.

Arkin, Ronald. C. 1990. Integrating Behavioral, Perceptual and World Knowledge in Reactive Navigation. *Robotics and Autonomous Systems* 6 (1990): 105–122.

Arkin, Ronald. C. 1989. Motor Schema Based Mobile Robot Navigation, *International Journal of Robotics Research* 8(4): 92-112.

Arkin, Ronald. C. 1987a. Motor Schema Based Navigation for a Mobile Robot: An Approach to Programming by Behavior. In *Proceedings of the IEEE International Conference on Robotics and Automation*, 264-271. Los Alamitos, Calif.: IEEE Computer Society Press.

Arkin, Ronald. C. 1987b. Towards Cosmopolitan Robots: Intelligent Navigation in Extended Man-Made Environments. Technical Report, COINS 87-80, University of Massachusetts at Amherst.

Arkin, Ronald. C., and Ali, K. 1994. Integration of Reactive and Telerobotic Control in Multi-Agent Robotic Systems. Paper presented at the Third International Conference on Simulation of Adaptive Behavior, Brighton, England, Aug.

Arkin, Ronald C., and MacKenzie, D. 1994. Temporal Coordination of Perceptual Algorithms for Mobile Robot Navigation. In *IEEE Transactions on Robotics and Automation*, 10(3): 276-286.

Arkin, Ronald. C., and Murphy, R. R. 1990. Autonomous Navigation in a Manufacturing Environment. *IEEE Transactions on Robotics and Automation* 6(4): 445-444.

Arkin, Ronald. C.; Riseman, E.; and Hanson, A. 1987. Visual Strategies for Mobile Robot Navigation. In *Proceedings of the Workshop on Computer Vision*, 176-181. Los Alamitos, Calif.: IEEE Computer Society Press.

Bachmann, E. R.; McGhee, R. B.; Whalen, R. H.; Steven, R.; Walker, R. G.; Clynch, J. R.; Healey, A. J.; and Yun, X. P. Evaluation of an Integrated GPS/INS System for Shallow-Water AUV Navigation (SANS). Paper presented at the IEEE Oceanic Engineering Society Conference AUV 96, Monterey, California, 3-6 June.

Bacon, Daniel Keith Jr. 1995. Integration of a Submarine into NPSNET. Master's thesis, Naval Postgraduate School, Monterey, Calif. (www.-npsnet.cs.nps.navy.mil/npsnet.)

Bajikar, S.; Gorjestani, A.; Simpkins, P.; and Donath, M. 1997. Evaluation of In-Vehicle GPS-Based Lane Position Sensing for Preventing Road Departure. Paper presented at the IEEE Conference on Intelligent Transportation Systems, Boston, 9-12 November.

Balch, T., and Arkin, R. C. 1995. Motor Schema-Based Formation Control for Multiagent Robot Teams. In *Proceedings of the First International Conference on Multiagent Systems*, San Francisco, California, ed. Victor Lesser, 10-16. Menlo Park, Calif.: AAAI Press.

Balch, T.; Boone, G.; Collins, T.; Forbes, H.; MacKenzie, D.; and Santamara, J. 1995. Io, Ganymede and Callisto—A Multiagent Robot Trash-Collecting Team. *AI Magazine* 16(2): 39-51.

Ballard, Dana H. 1991. Animate Vision. *Artificial Intelligence* 49(1): 57-86.

Ballard, Dana H., and Brown C. M. 1982. *Computer Vision*. Englewood Cliffs, N.J.: Prentice-Hall.

Bar-Shalom, Y., and Fortmann, T. E. 1988. *Tracking and Data Association*. Boston: Academic Press.

Barraquand, J., and Latombe, J. C. 1991. Robot Motion Planning: A Distributed Representation Approach. *International Journal of Robotics Research* 10(6): 628-649.

Beckerman, M., and Oblow, E. 1990. Treatment of Systematic Errors in the Processing of Wide-Angle Sonar Sensor Data for Robotic Navigation. *IEEE Transactions on Robotics and Automation* 6(2): 136-145.

Bellman, R. 1957. *Dynamic Programming.* Princeton, N. J.: Princeton University Press.

Bellutta, P.; Collini, G.; Verri, A.; and Torre, V. 1989. Navigation by Tracking Vanishing Points. Paper presented at the AAAI Spring Symposium on Robot Navigation, March, Stanford, Calif.

Betke, M., and Gurvits, L. Mobile Robot Localization Using Landmarks. Technical Report, SCR-94-TR-474, Siemens Corporate Research, Princeton, N. J.

Biber, C. 1980. The Polaroid Ultrasonic Ranging System. In *Proceedings of the Sixty-Seventh Conference of the Audio Engineering Society.* New York: Audio Engineering Society.

Bodor, R.; Donath, M.; Morellas, V.; and Johnson, D. 1996. In-Vehicle GPS-Based Lane Sensing to Prevent Road Departure. Paper presented at the Third Annual World Congress on Intelligent Transport Systems, Orlando, Florida, October 14-18.

Bonasso, R. Peter 1992. Using Parallel Program Specifications For Reactive Control of Underwater Vehicles. *Journal of Applied Intelligence* 2(2): 201-223.

Bonasso, R. Peter 1991. Integrating Reaction Plans and Layered Competences Through Synchronous Control. In *Proceedings of the Twelfth International Joint Conference on Artificial Intelligence*, 1225-1231. San Francisco: Morgan Kaufmann Publishers.

Bonasso, R. Peter, and Dean, T. L. 1996. Robots With AI: A Retrospective on the AAAI Robot Competitions and Exhibitions. In *Proceedings of the Thirteenth National Conference on Artificial Intelligence,* 1321. Menlo Park, Calif.: AAAI Press.

Bonasso, R. Peter; Firby, R. J.; Gat, E.; Kortenkamp, David; Miller, D.; and Slack, M. 1997. Experiences with an Architecture for Intelligent, Reactive Agents. *Journal of Experimental and Theoretical Artificial Intelligence* 9(2): 237-256.

Borenstein, Johann, and Koren, Yoram 1992. Noise Rejection for Ultrasonic Sensors in Mobile Robot Applications. In *Proceedings of the IEEE International Conference on Robotics and Automation*, 1727-1732. Los Alamitos, Calif.: IEEE Computer Society Press.

Borenstein, Johann, and Koren, Yoram 1991a. Histogramic In-Motion Mapping for Mobile Robot Obstacle Avoidance. *IEEE Transactions on Robotics and Automation* 7(4): 535-539.

Borenstein, Johann, and Koren, Yoram 1991b. The Vector Field Histogram—Fast Obstacle Avoidance for Mobile Robots, *IEEE Transactions on Robotics and Automation*, 7(3): 278-288.

Borenstein, Johann, and Koren, Yoram 1989. Real-Time Obstacle Avoidance for Fast Mobile Robots. *IEEE Transactions on Systems Man and Cybernetics* 19(5): 1179-1186.

Borenstein, Johann,; Everett, B.; and Feng, L. 1996. *Navigating Mobile Robots: Systems and Techniques.* Wellesley, Mass.: A. K. Peters, Ltd.

Borthwick, S., and Durrant-Whyte, H. F. 1994. Dynamic Localization of Autonomous Guided Vehicles. In *Proceedings of the 1994 IEEE International Conference on Multisensor Fusion and Integration for Intelligent Systems*, 92-97. New York: IEEE.

Bottoms, A., ed., 1995. Symposium on Autonomous Vehicles for Mine Countermeasures, Naval Postgraduate School, Monterey, California, April.

Brady, J. M.; Durrant-White, H. F.; Hu, H.; Leonard, J. J.; Probert, P. J.; and Rao, B. S. Y. 1990. Sensor-Based Control of AGVs. *IEE Journal of Computing and Control Engineering* 1(2): 64-70.

Brooks, Rodney A. 1991. Intelligence Without Representation. *Artificial Intelligence* 47 (1-3): 139-160.

Brooks, Rodney A. 1990. Elephants Don't Play Chess. *Robotics and Autonomous Systems* 6: 3-15.

Brooks, Rodney A. 1989a. The Behavior Language User's Guide. Artificial Intelligence Laboratory Memo 1227, Massachusetts Institute of Technology, Cambridge, Mass.

Brooks, Rodney A. 1989b. A Robot That Walks; Emergent Behaviors From a Carefully Evolved Network. *Neural Computation* 1(2): 253.

Brooks, Rodney A. 1986. A Robust Layered Control System for a Mobile Robot. *IEEE Transactions on Robotics and Automation.* 2(1):14-23.

Brooks, Rodney A. 1985. Visual Map Making for a Mobile Robot. In *Proceedings of the IEEE International Conference on Robotics and Automation,* 824-829. Los Alamitos, Calif.: IEEE Computer Society Press.

Brooks, Rodney A. 1983. Solving the Find-Path Problem by Good Representation of Free Space. *IEEE Transactions on Systems, Man and Cybernetics* 13: 190-197. HU

Brown, M. K. 1995 Feature Extraction Techniques for Recognizing Solid Objects with an Ultrasonic Range Sensor. *IEEE Transactions on Robotics and Automation,* 1(4): 191-205.

Bruce, V., and Green, P. R. 1990. *Visual Perception: Physiology, Psychology and Ecology .* Hillsdale, N. J.: Lawrence Erlbaum Associates.

Brutzman, Donald P. 1997 Graphics Internetworking: Bottlenecks and Breakthroughs. In *Digital Illusion,* ed., Clark Dodsworth. Reading, Mass.: Addison-Wesley.

Brutzman, Donald P. 1996a. NPS Phoenix AUV Software Reference, November 1996. Naval Postgraduate School, Monterey, Calif. (www.stl.nps.navy.mil/~auv/software_reference.html)

Brutzman, Donald P. 1996b. Tutorial: Virtual World for an Autonomous Underwater Vehicle (AUV). Paper presented at the IEEE Oceanic Engineering Society Conference OCEANS 96, Fort Lauderdale, Florida, September 23-26. (www.stl.nps.navy.mil/~auv/uvw_tutorial.html)

Brutzman, Donald P. 1995. Virtual World Visualization for an Autonomous Underwater Vehicle, Paper presented at the IEEE Oceanic Engineering Society Conference OCEANS 95, San Diego, California, October 12-15. (ftp://taurus.cs.nps.navy.mil/pub/auv/oceans95. ps. Z)

Brutzman, Donald P. 1994. A Virtual World for an Autonomous Underwater Vehicle, Ph.D. diss., Naval Postgraduate School, Monterey, Calif. (www.stl.nps.navy.mil/~brutzman/dissertation)

Brutzman, Donald P. 1993. Beyond Intelligent Vacuum Cleaners. In Instantiating Real-World Agents: Papers from the 1993 Fall Symposium. AAAI Technical Report FS-93-03, 23. Menlo Park, Calif.

Brutzman, Donald P. 1992a. From Virtual World to Reality: Designing an Autonomous Underwater Robot. In Applications of Artificial Intelligence to Real-World Autonomous Mobile Robots: Papers from the 1992 Fall Symposium. AAAI Technical Report FS-92-02. Menlo Park, Calif.

Brutzman, Donald P. 1992b. NPS AUV Integrated Simulator. Master's thesis, Naval Postgraduate School, Monterey, California.

Brutzman, Donald P., and Compton, Mark A. 1991. AUV Research at the Naval Postgraduate School. *Sea Technology* 32(12): 35-40.

Brutzman, Donald P., and Reimers, Stephen. 1995. Internet Protocol over Seawater (IP/SW): Towards Interoperable Underwater Networks. Paper presented at the Ninth International Symposium on Unmanned Untethered Submersible Technology (UUST) 95,

University of New Hampshire, Durham, N. H., September 25-27. (ftp://taurus.cs. nps.navy.mil/pub/auv/ipoversw.ps)

Brutzman, Donald P.; Burns, Mike; Campbell, Mike; Davis, Duane; Healey, Tony; Holden, Mike; Leonhardt, Brad; Marco, Dave; McClarin, Dave; McGhee, Bob; and Whalen, Russ. 1996. NPS Phoenix AUV Software Integration and In-Water Testing. Paper presented at the IEEE Oceanic Engineering Society Conference AUV 96, Monterey, California, June 3-6. (ftp://taurus.cs.nps.navy.mil/pub/auv/auv96.ps)

Brutzman, Donald P.; Compton, Mark A.; and Kanayama, Yutaka. 1992. Autonomous Sonar Classification Using Expert Systems. Paper presented at the IEEE Oceanic Engineering Society Conference OCEANS 92, Newport, Rhode Island, 26-29 October. (ftp://taurus.cs.nps.navy.mil/pub/auv/oceans92.ps.Z)

Buhmann, J.; Burgard, W.; Cremers, A. B.; Fox, D.; Hofmann, T.; Schneider, F.; Strikos, J.; and Thrun, S. 1995. The Mobile Robot Rhino. *AI Magazine* 16(2): 31-38.

Burgard, W.; Fox, D.; and Hennig, D. 1997. Fast Grid-Based Position Tracking for Mobile Robots, 289-300. In *Proceedings of the Twenty-first German Conference on Artificial Intelligence.* Berlin: Springer Verlag.

Burgard, W.; Fox, D.; Hennig, D.; and Schmidt, T. 1996a. Estimating the Absolute Position of a Mobile Robot Using Position Probability Grids, 896. In *Proceedings of the Thirteenth National Conference on Artificial Intelligence.* Menlo Park, Calif.: AAAI Press.

Burgard, W.; Fox, D.; Hennig, D.; and Schmidt, T. 1996b. Position Tracking with Position Probability Grids. In *Proceedings of the First Euromicro Workshop on Advanced Mobile Robot,* Los Alamitos, Calif.: IEEE Computer Society Press.

Burns, Mike. 1996. An Experimental Evaluation and Modification of Simulator-Based Vehicle Control Software for the Phoenix Autonomous Underwater Vehicle (AUV). Master's thesis, Naval Postgraduate School, Monterey, Calif. (www.cs.nps.navy.mil/research/auv)

Byrnes, Ronald B. 1993. The Rational Behavior Model: A Multi-Paradigm, Tri-Level Software Architecture for the Control of Autonomous Vehicles. Ph.D. diss., Naval Postgraduate School, Monterey, Calif.

Byrnes, Ronald B.; Healey, Anthony J.; McGhee, Robert B.; Nelson, Michael L.; Kwak, Se-Hung; and Brutzman, Donald P. 1996. The Rational Behavior Software Architecture for Intelligent Ships. *Naval Engineers' Journal* 108(2): 43-55.

Congdon, Clare; Huber, Marcus; Kortenkamp, David; Konolige, Kurt; Myers, Karen; Saffiotti, Alexandro; and Ruspini, Enrique H. 1993. CARMEL Versus FLAKEY: A Comparison of Two Winners. *AI Magazine* 14(1): 49-57.

Campbell, Michael Scott. 1996. Real-Time Sonar Classification for Autonomous Underwater Vehicles. Master's thesis, Naval Postgraduate School, Monterey, Calif.

Cao, Y.; Fukunaga, A.; Kahng, A.; and Meng, F. 1995. Cooperative Mobile Robotics: Antecedents and Directions. Paper presented at the IEEE/RSJ International Conference on Intelligent Robots and Systems (IROS '95), Pittsburgh, Pennsylvania, August.

Carey, Rikk; Marrin, Chris; and Bell, Gavin. 1996. The Virtual Reality Modeling Language (VRML) Version 2. 0 Specification. International Standards Organization/International Electrotechnical Commission (ISO/IEC) draft standard 14772, August 4. (www.sdsc.edu/vrml)

Cassandra, A.; Kaelbling, L.; and Kurien, J. 1996. Acting Under Uncertainty: Discrete Bayesian Models for Mobile-Robot Navigation. In Planning with Incomplete Information for Robot Problems: Papers from the 1996 AAAI Spring Symposium. AAAI Technical Report SS-96-04, March. Menlo Park, Calif.

Cassandra, A.; Kaelbling, L.; and Littman, M. 1994. Acting Optimally in Partially Observable Stochastic Domains. In *Proceedings of the Twelfth National Conference on Artificial Intelligence*, 1023-1028. Menlo Park, Calif.: AAAI Press.

Cervantes-Perez, F. 1995. Visuomotor Coordination in Frogs and Toads. In *The Handbook of Brain Theory and Neural Networks*, ed. M. Arbib. Cambridge, Mass.: MIT Press.

Chen, C. X., and Trivedi, M. M. 1995. Task Planning and Action Coordination in Integrated Sensor-Based Robots. *IEEE Transactions on Systems, Man, and Cybernetics* 25(4): 569-591.

Chrisman, L. 1992. Reinforcement Learning with Perceptual Aliasing: The Perceptual Distinction Approach. In *Proceedings of the Tenth Annual Conference on Artificial Intelligence*, 183-188. Menlo Park, Calif.: AAAI Press.

Chung, K. L. 1960. *Markov Chains with Stationary Transition Probabilities.* Berlin: Springer Verlag.

Cohen, Charles, and Koss, Frank. 1992. A Comprehensive Study of Three-Object Triangulation. In *SPIE Mobile Robots VII*, ed. W. J. Wolfe and W. H. Chun, 95-106. Bellingham, Wash: Society of Photo-Optical Instrumentation Engineers.

Connell, Jonathan. 1992. SSS: A Hybrid Architecture Applied to Robot Navigation. In *Proceedings of the IEEE International Conference on Robotics and Automation*, 2719-2724. Los Alamitos, Calif.: IEEE Computer Society Press.

Connell, Jonathan. 1990. *Minimalist Mobile Robotics: A Colony-Style Architecture for an Artificial Creature.* Boston, Mass.: Academic Press.

Connell, Jonathan. 1989. *A Colony Architecture for an Artificial Creature.* Technical Report, 1151, Artificial Intelligence Laboratory, Massachusetts Institute of Technology, Cambridge, Mass.

Crisman, Jill D. 1992. Color Region Tracking for Vehicle Guidance. In *Active Vision,* ed. Andrew Blake and Alan Yuille. Cambridge, Mass.: The MIT Press.

Crowley, J. 1989. World Modeling and Position Estimation for a Mobile Robot Using Ultrasonic Ranging. In *Proceedings of the IEEE International Conference on Robotics and Automation*, 674-680. Los Alamitos, Calif.: IEEE Computer Society Press.

Curtin, Thomas B.; Bellingham, James G.; Catipovic, Josko; and Webb, Doug. 1993. Autonomous Oceanographic Sampling Networks. *Oceanography* 6: 86-94. (Additional information at web.mit.eduafs/athena/org/s/seagrant/www/auv.htm)

Daily, M. 1988. Autonomous Cross-Country Navigation with the Alv. In *Proceedings of the IEEE International Conference on Robotics and Automation*, 718-726. Los Alamitos, Calif.: IEEE Computer Society Press.

Davis, Duane 1996. Precision Maneuvering and Control of the Phoenix Autonomous Underwater Vehicle for Entering a Recovery Tube. Master's thesis, Naval Postgraduate School, Monterey, Calif. (www.cs.nps.navy.mil/research/auv).

Davis, Duane; Brutzman, D.; Leonhardt, B.; and McGhee, R. 1996. Operational Mission Planning and Mission Control for the Phoenix Autonomous Underwater Vehicle. *IEEE Journal of Oceanic Engineering.*

Dean, T. L., and Boddy, M. 1988. An Analysis of Time-Dependent Planning. In *Proceeding of Seventh National Conference on Artificial Intelligence*, 49–54. Menlo Park, Calif.: AAAI Press.

Dean, T. L. and Bonasso, R. Peter 1993. 1992 AAAI Robot Exhibition and Competition. *AI Magazine*, 14(4): 35-48.

Dean, T. L; Basye, K.; Chekaluk, R.; Hyun, S.; Lejter, M.; and Randazza, M. 1990. Coping with Uncertainty in a Control System for Navigation and Exploration. In *Proceedings of the Eighth National Conference on Artificial Intelligence*, 1010-1015. Menlo Park, Calif.: AAAI Press.

Dean, T. L; Kaelbling, L.; Kirman, J.; and Nicholson, A. 1993. Planning with Deadlines in Stochastic Domains. In *Proceedings of the Eleventh National Conference on Artificial Intelligence*, 574-579. Menlo Park, Calif.: AAAI Press.

Devijver, P. 1985. Baum's Forward Backward Algorithm Revisited. *Pattern Recognition Letters* 3(6): 369-373.

Dickmanns, E. D., and Graefe, V. 1988. Dynamic Monocular Machine Vision. *International Journal of Machine Vision and Applications*, 1: 223-240.

Donald, B. 1989. *Error Detection and Recovery in Robotics. Lecture Notes in Computer Science*, 336. Berlin: Springer-Verlag.

Drumheller, M. 1985. Mobile Robot Localization Using Sonar. Artificial Intelligence Laboratory Memo 826, Massachusetts Institute of Technology, Cambridge, Mass.

Du, F., and Brady, M. A 1994. Four Degree-of-Freedom Robot Head for Active Vision. *International Journal of Pattern Recognition and Artificial Intelligence* 8(6).

Du, Yu-feng. 1995. ALX: Autonomous Vehicle Guidance for Roadway Following and Obstacle Avoidance. Master's thesis, Department of Mechanical Engineering, University of Minnesota, Minneapolis, Minn.

Duda, R. O., and Hart, P. E. 1973. *Pattern Classification and Scene Analysis*. New York: Wiley.

Dudek, G.; Jenkin, M.; Milios, E.; and Wilkes, D. 1993. A Taxonomy for Swarm Robots. Paper presented at the IEEE/RSJ International Conference on Intelligent Robots and Systems (IROS-93), Yokohama, Japan.

Dugan, B., and Nourbakhsh, I. 1993. Vagabond: A Demonstration of Autonomous, Robust, Outdoor Navigation. In *Video Proceedings of the IEEE International Conference on Robotics and Automation*. Los Alamitos, Calif.: IEEE Computer Society Press.

Elfes, A. 1989. Using Occupancy Grids for Mobile Robot Perception and Navigation. *IEEE Computer* 22(6): 46-57.

Elfes, A. 1987. Sonar-Based Real-World Mapping and Navigation. *IEEE Transactions on Robotics and Automation* 3(3): 249–265.

Elsaessar, Chris, and Slack, Marc. 1994. Integrating Deliberative Planning in a Robot Architecture. In *Proceedings of the American Institute of Aeronautics and Astronautics /NASA Conference on Intelligent Robots in Field, Factory, Service, and Space (CIRFFSS '94)*, ed. Jon Erickson. NASA Conference Publication 3251. Houston, Tex: National Aeronautics and Space Administration.

Engelson, S., and McDermott, D. 1992. Error Correction in Mobile Robot Map Learning. In *Proceedings of the IEEE International Conference on Robotics and Automation*, 2555-2560. Los Alamitos, Calif.: IEEE Computer Society Press.

Erdmann, M. 1990. On Probabilistic Strategies for Robot Tasks. Technical Report, #1155, Artificial Intelligence Laboratory, Massachusetts Institute of Technology, Cambridge, Mass.

Fedor, C. 1993. TCX. *An Interprocess Communication System for Building Robotic Architectures: Programmer's Guide to Version 10.xx.* Pittsburgh, Penn.: Carnegie Mellon University.

Feng, L.; Borenstein, J.; and Everett, H. R. 1994. Where am I? Sensors and Methods for Autonomous Mobile Robot Positioning. Technical Report, UM-MEAM-94-12, Dept. of Computer Science, University of Michigan.

Firby, R. James. 1996. Modularity Issues in Reactive Planning. In Proceedings of the *Third International Conference on AI Planning Systems,* ed. Brian Drabble, 78-85. Menlo Park, Calif.: AAAI Press.

Firby, R. James 1995. The RAP Language Manual. Animate Agent Project Working Note AAP-6 Version 1, University of Chicago, Chicago, Ill.

Firby, R. James 1994a. The CRL Manual. Animate Agent Project Working Note AAP-3 Version 1, University of Chicago, Chicago, Ill.

Firby, R. James 1994b. Task Networks for Controlling Continuous Processes. In *Second International Conference on AI Planning Systems,* ed. Kristian Hammond, 49-54. Menlo Park, Calif.: AAAI Press.

Firby, R. James 1989. Adaptive Execution in Complex Dynamic Worlds. Technical Report YALEU/CSD/RR #672, Computer Science Department, Yale University.

Firby, R. James 1987. An Investigation Into Reactive Planning in Complex Domains. In *Proceedings of the Sixth National Conference on Artificial Intelligence,* 202-206. Menlo Park, Calif.: AAAI Press.

Firby, R. James, and Slack, Marc. 1995. Task Execution: Interfacing to Reactive Skill Networks. Paper presented at the 1995 AAAI Spring Symposium on Lessons Learned from Implemented Architectures for Physical Agents, March, Stanford, Calif.

Firby, R. James; Kahn, Roger E.; Prokopowicz, Peter N.; and Swain, Michael J. 1995. An Architecture for Vision and Action. In *Proceedings of the Fourteenth International Joint Conference on Artificial Intelligence,* 72-79. San Francisco: Morgan Kaufmann Publishers.

Firby, R. James; Prokopowicz, Peter N.; Swain, Michael J.; Kahn, Roger E.; and Franklin, David 1996. Programming CHIP for the IJCAI-95 Robot Competition. *AI Magazine* 17(1): 71-81.

Flagg, Marco. 1994. Submersible Computer for Divers, Autonomous Applications. *Sea Technology* 35(2): 33-37.

Foley, James D; van Dam, Andries; Feiner, Steven K.; and Hughes, John F. 1990. *Computer Graphics: Principles and Practice, Second Edition.* Reading, Mass.: Addison-Wesley.

Fortner, Brand. 1992. *The Data Handbook: A Guide to Understanding the Organization and Visualization of Technical Data.* Champaign, Ill.: Spyglass Inc.

Fossen, Thor I. 1994. *Guidance and Control of Ocean Vehicles.* Chichester, England: John Wiley & Sons.

Fox, D.; Burgard, W.; and Thrun, S. 1997. The Dynamic Window Approach to Collision Avoidance. *Ieee Robotics and Automation Magazine,* 4(1): 23-33.

Fox, D.; Burgard, W.; and Thrun S. 1996. Controlling Synchro-Drive Robots with the Dynamic Window Approach to Collision Avoidance. Paper presented at the IEEE/RSJ International Conference on Intelligent Robots and Systems (IROS-96), Osaka, Japan.

Fröhlinghaus, T., and Buhmann J. M. 1996a. Real-Time Phase-Based Stereo for a Mobile Robot. In *Proceedings of the First Euromicro Workshop on Advanced Mobile Robots*, Los Alamitos, Calif.: IEEE Computer Society Press.

Fröhlinghaus, T., and Buhmann J. M. 1996b. Regularizing Phase-Based Stereo. Paper presented at the Thirteenth International Conference on Pattern Recognition, Vienna, Austria.

Fukuda, T.; Nakagawa, S.; Kawauchi, Y.; and Buss, M. 1989. Structure Decision for Self Organising Robots Based on Cell Structures - CEBOT. In *Proceedings of the IEEE International Conference on Robotics and Automation*, 695-700. Los Alamitos, Calif.: IEEE Computer Society Press.

Garlich-Miller, M., and Donath, M. 1996. A Connectionist Approach to the Fusion of Three Dimensional, Sparse, Unordered Sensor Data. In *Proceedings of the Japan-USA Symposium on Flexible Automation*, ed. K. Stelson and F. Oba, 465-473. New York: The American Society of Mechanical Engineers.

Gat, Erann. 1997. ESL: A Language for Supporting Robust Plan Execution in Embedded Autonomous Agents. In *Proceedings of the IEEE Aerospace Conference*. Los Alamitos, Calif.: IEEE Computer Society Press.

Gat, Erann 1993. On the Role of Stored Internal State in the Control of Autonomous Mobile Robots. *AI Magazine* 14(1): 64-73

Gat, Erann 1992. Integrating Planning and Reacting in a Heterogeneous Asynchronous Architecture for Controlling Real-World Mobile Robots. In *Proceedings of the Tenth National Conference on Artificial Intelligence*, 809. Menlo Park, Calif.: AAAI Press.

Gat, Erann 1991a. ALFA: A Language for Programming Reactive Robotic Control Systems. In *Proceedings of the IEEE International Conference on Robotics and Automation*, 1116-1121. Los Alamitos, Calif.: IEEE Computer Society Press.

Gat, Erann 1991b. Reliable Goal-directed Reactive Control for Real-World Autonomous Mobile Robots. Ph.D. Diss., Dept. of Computer Science, Virginia Polytechnic Institute and State University.

Gat, Erann, and Dorais, Greg 1994. Robot Navigation by Conditional Sequencing. In *Proceedings of the IEEE International Conference on Robotics and Automation*, 1293-1299. Los Alamitos, Calif.: IEEE Computer Society Press.

Gat, Erann; Desai, Rajiv; Iviev, Robert; Loch, John; and Miller, David. 1994. Behavior Control for Robotic Exploration of Planetary Surfaces. *IEEE Transactions on Robotics and Automation* 10(4): 490-503.

Genesereth, M., and Nourbakhsh, I. 1993. Time-saving Tips for Problem Solving with Incomplete Information. In *Proceedings of the Eleventh National Conference on Artificial Intelligence*, 724-730. Menlo Park, Calif.: AAAI Press.

Georgeff, Michael P., and Ingrand, F. F. 1989. Decision-Making in an Embedded Reasoning System. In *Proceedings of the National Conference of Artificial Intelligence*, 972-978. Menlo Park, Calif.: AAAI Press.

Georgeff, Michael P., and Lanskey, Amy. 1987. Reactive Reasoning and Planning. In *Proceedings of the Sixth National Conference of Artificial Intelligence*, 677. Menlo Park, Calif.: AAAI Press.

Gibson, J. J. 1966. *The Senses Considered as Perceptual Systems*. Boston: Houghton-Mifflin.

Giralt, G.; Chatila, R.; and Vaisset, M. 1984. An Integrated Navigation and Motion Control System for Autonomous Multisensory Mobile Robots. In *First International Symposium on Robotics Research*, 191. Cambridge, Mass.: The MIT Press.

Gutierrez-Osuna, R., and Luo, R. 1996. LOLA: Probabilistic Navigation for Topological Maps. *AI Magazine* 17(1): 55-62.

Haigh, K., and Veloso, M. 1996. Interleaving Planning and Robot Execution for Asynchronous User Requests. Paper presented at the IEEE/RSJ International Conference on Intelligent Robots and Systems (IROS-96), Osaka, Japan.

Hannaford, B., and Lee, P. 1991. Hidden Markov Model Analysis of Force/Torque Information in Telemanipulation. *The International Journal of Robotics Research* 10(5): 528-539.

Harmon, S. Y. 1987. The Ground Surveillance Robot (GSR): An Autonomous Vehicle Designed To Transit Unknown Terrain. *IEEE Transactions on Robotics and Automation*, 3(3): 266-279.

Hartley, Ralph, and Pipitone, Frank. 1991. Experiments with the Subsumption Architecture. In *Proceedings of the IEEE International Conference on Robotics and Automation*, 1652-1658. Los Alamitos, Calif.: IEEE Computer Society Press.

Healey, A. J., and Lienard, D. 1993. Multivariable Sliding Mode Control for Autonomous Diving and Steering of Unmanned Underwater Vehicles. *IEEE Journal of Oceanic Engineering* 18(3): 327-339.

Healey, A. J.; Marco, R. B.; and McGhee, R. B. 1996. Autonomous Underwater Vehicle Control Coordination Using a Tri-Level Hybrid Software Architecture. In *Proceedings of the IEEE International Conference on Robotics and Automation*. Los Alamitos, Calif.: IEEE Computer Society Press.

Healey, A. J.; Marco, D. B.; McGhee, R. B.; Brutzman, D. P.; and Cristi, R. 1995. Evaluation of the NPS Phoenix Autonomous Underwater Vehicle Hybrid Control System. Paper presented at the American Controls Conference (ACC) 95, San Francisco, California, June.

Hennessey, M. P.; Shankwitz, C.; and Donath, M. 1995. Sensor Based Virtual Bumpers for Collision Avoidance: Configuration Issues. In *Collision Avoidance and Automated Traffic Management Sensors*, A. C. Chachich and M. J. deVries, eds., 48-59. Bellingham, Wash: Society of Photo-Optical Instrumentation Engineers.

Hinkel, R., and Knieriemen, T. 1988. Environment Perception with a Laser Radar in a Fast Moving Robot. Paper presented at the Symposium on Robot Control, Karlsruhe, Germany.

Hinkle, David; Kortenkamp, David; and Miller, David. 1996. 1995 Robot Competition and Exhibition. *AI Magazine* 17(1): 31-45.

Hoare, C. A. R. 1985. *Communication Sequential Processes.* London: Prentice Hall.

Hobbs, J. R.; Stickel, M.; Appelt, D.; and Martin, P. 1993. Interpretation as Abduction. *Artificial Intelligence* 63(1/2): 69-142.

Holden, Michael J. 1995. Ada Implementation of Concurrent Execution for Multiple Tasks in the Strategic and Tactical Levels of the Rational Behavior Model for the NPS AUV. Master's thesis, Naval Postgraduate School, Monterey, Calif.

Holliere, R. H. 1987. *Automated Guided Vehicles.* London: IFS.

Horswill, Ian 1995a. Analysis of Adaptation and Environment. *Artificial Intelligence* 75(1): 1-30.

Horswill, Ian. 1995b. Visual Routines and Visual Search. In *Proceedings of the Fourteenth International Joint Conference on Artificial Intelligence*, San Francisco, Calif.: Morgan Kaufmann Publishers.

Horswill, Ian 1994. Specialization of Perceptual Processes. Technical Report, AI TR-1511, Artificial Intelligence Lab, Massachusetts Institute of Technology.

Horswill, Ian 1993. Polly: A Vision-Based Artificial Agent. In *Proceedings of the Eleventh National Conference on Artificial Intelligence,* 824. Menlo Park, Calif.: AAAI Press.

Horswill, Ian, and Brooks, Rodney 1988. Situated Vision in a Dynamic Environment: Chasing Objects. In *Proceedings of the Seventh National Conference on Artificial Intelligence,* 796-801. Menlo Park, Calif.: AAAI Press.

Horswill, Ian, and Yamamoto, Masaki 1994. A $1000 Active Stereo Vision System. In *Proceedings of the IAPR/IEEE Workshop on Visual Behaviors,* ed., W. Martin. Los Alamitos, Calif.: IEEE Press.

Howard, R. A. 1960. *Dynamic Programming and Markov Processes.* Cambridge, Mass.: The MIT Press.

Hsu, J. 1990. Partial Planning with Incomplete Information. Paper presented at the AAAI Spring Symposium on Planning in Uncertain, Unpredictable, or Changing Environments, Stanford, Calif., March 27-29.

Hu, H. 1992. *Dynamic Planning and Real-time Control for a Mobile Robot.* Ph.D. diss., Department of Engineering Science, Oxford University.

Hu, H., and Brady, J. M. 1994. A Bayesian Approach to Real-Time Obstacle Avoidance for an Intelligent Mobile Robot. *The International Journal of Autonomous Robots* 1(1): 67-102.

Hu, H, and Brady, J. M. 1992. Planning with Uncertainty for a Mobile Robot. Paper presented at the Second International Conference on Automation, Robotics and Computer Vision, Singapore.

Hu, H.; Brady, J. M.; and Probert. P. J. 1993. Transputer Architecture for Sensor-Guided Control of Mobile Robots. Paper presented at the World Transputer Congress, Aachen, Germany.

Hu, H.; Brady, J. M.; Du, F.; and Probert, P. J. 1995. Distributed Real-Time Control of a Mobile Robot. *The International Journal of Intelligent Automation and Soft Computing* 1(1): 63-83.

Huang, X.; Ariki, Y.; and Jack, M. 1990. *Hidden Markov Models for Speech Recognition.* Edinburgh, Scotland: Edinburgh University Press.

Huber, Marcus J, and Durfee, E. 1996. An Initial Assessment of Plan Recognition-Based Coordination for Multi-Agent Teams. In *Proceedings of the Second International Conference on Multi-Agent Systems,* 126-133. Menlo Park, Calif.: AAAI Press.

Huber, Marcus J.; Bidlack, Clint; Mangis, Kevin; Kortenkamp, David; Baker, L. Douglas; Wu, Annie; and Weymouth, Terry. 1992. Computer Vision for CARMEL. In *SPIE Mobile Robots VII,* ed. W. J. Wolf and W. H. Chun, 144-155. Bellingham, Wash: Society of Photo-Optical Instrumentation Engineers.

Huttenlocher, Daniel P., and Rucklidge, W. J. 1992a. A Multi-Resolution Technique for Comparing Images Using the Hausdorff Distance. Technical Report, CUCS TR #92-1321, Department of Computer Science, Cornell University.

Huttenlocher, Daniel P.; Rucklidge, William J.; and Klanderman, Gregory A. 1992b. Comparing Images Using the Hausdorff Distance Under Translation. In *Proceedings of the IEEE Conference on Computer Vision and Pattern Recognition,* 654–656. Los Alamitos, Calif.: IEEE Computer Society Press.

Hwang, Y. K., and Ahuja, N. 1992. A Potential Field Approach to Path Planning. *IEEE Transactions on Robotics and Automation* 8(1): 23-32. HU

Iberall T., and Lyons, D. 1984. Towards Perceptual Robotics. Paper presented at the IEEE International Conference on Systems, Man and Cybernetics, Halifax, NS, Canada, Oct. 10-12.

IEEE Standard for Distributed Interactive Simulation (DIS)—Communication Service and Profiles. IEEE Standard P1278. New York: Institute of Electrical and Electronic Engineers. (www.sc.ist.ucf.edu/~STDS)

Ikeuchi, Katsushi, and Herbert, Martial. 1990. Task Oriented Vision. In *DARPA Image Understanding Workshop.* San Francisco: Morgan Kaufmann.

Jarvis, R. A., and Byrne, J. C. 1988. An Automated Guided Vehicle with Map Building and Path Finding Capabilities. *Fourth International Symposium on Robotics Research*, 498-504. Cambridge, Mass.: The MIT Press.

Jones, J. L. and Flynn, A. M. 1993. *Mobile Robots: Inspiration to Implementation.* Wellesley, Mass.: A. K. Peters.

Jossi, D., and Donath, M. 1995. Implementing Contact Tasks Involving Position Uncertainty with Impedance Controlled Robots. In *Proceedings of the IEEE International Conference on Systems, Man and Cybernetics, Vol. 2,* 1699-1704. New York: IEEE.

Kaelbling, Leslie Pack 1988. Goals as Parallel Program Specifications. In *Proceedings of the Sixth National Conference on Artificial Intelligence,* Menlo Park, Calif.: AAAI Press. I

Kaelbling, Leslie Pack 1987. REX: A Symbolic Language for the Design and Parallel Implementation of Embedded Systems. Paper presented at the AIAA Conference on Computers in Aerospace, Wakefield, Mass.

Kahn, Roger E., and Swain, Michael J. 1995. Understanding People Pointing: The Perseus System. In *International Symposium on Computer Vision,* 569-574. Los Alamitos, Calif.: IEEE Computer Society Press.

Kahn, Roger E.; Swain, Michael J.; and Firby, R. James. 1993. The Datacube Server. In Animate Agent Project Working Note AAP-2 Version 1, University of Chicago, Chicago, Ill.

Kambhampati, S., and Davis, L. S. 1986. Multiresolution Path Planning for Mobile Robot. *IEEE Transactions on Robotics and Automation* 2(3): 135-145.

Kanayama, Yutaka. 1995. Introduction to Motion Planning. In *CS4313 Lecture Notes,* Monterey, Calif.: Naval Postgraduate School.

Khatib, O. 1986. Real-Time Obstacle Avoidance for Manipulators and Mobile Robots. *The International Journal of Robotics Research* 5(1): 90-98.

Kirsh, David 1991. Today the Earwig, Tomorrow Man? *Artificial Intelligence* 47(1-3): 161-184.

Koenig, Sven 1991. Optimal Probabilistic and Decision-Theoretic Planning Using Markovian Decision Theory. Master's thesis, Computer Science Dept., University of California, Berkeley, Calif.

Koenig, Sven, and Simmons, R. 1996a. Passive Distance Learning for Robot Navigation. In *Proceedings of the Thirteenth International Conference on Machine Learning (ICML),* ed. L. Saitta, 266-274. San Francisco: Morgan Kaufmann Publishers.

Koenig, Sven, and Simmons, R. 1996b. Unsupervised Learning of Probabilistic Models for Robot Navigation. In *Proceedings of the IEEE International Conference on Robotics and Automation,* 2301-2308. Los Alamitos, Calif.: IEEE Computer Society Press.

Koenig, Sven; Goodwin, R.; and Simmons, R. 1996. Robot Navigation with Markov Models: A Framework for Path Planning and Learning with Limited Computational Resources. In *Reasoning with Uncertainty in Robotics, Volume 1093L*, Dorst, M. van Lambalgen, and R. Voorbraak, eds., 322-337. Berlin: Springer-Verlag.

Konolige, Kurt 1995. Erratic Competes with the Big Boys. *AI Magazine* 16(2): 61-67.

Konolige, Kurt 1994. Designing the 1993 Robot Competition. *AI Magazine* 15(1): 57-62.

Kortenkamp, David, and Weymouth, T. 1994. Topological Mapping for Mobile Robots Using a Combination of Sonar and Vision Sensing. In *Proceedings of the Twelfth National Conference on Artificial Intelligence*, 979-984. Menlo Park, Calif.: AAAI Press.

Kortenkamp, David; Nourbakhsh, Illah; and Hinkle, David. 1997. The 1996 AAAI Mobile Robot Competition and Exhibition. *AI Magazine*, 18(1): 25-32.

Kosaka, A. and Kak, A. C. 1992. Fast Vision-Guided Mobile Robot Navigation Using Model-Based Reasoning and Prediction of Uncertainties. *Computer Vision, Graphics, and Image Processing* 56(3).

Krantz, D.; Morris, T.; Donath, M.; and Johnson, D. 1996 . Watchdog Systems for Safety-Critical Vehicle Controls. Paper presented at the Third World Congress on Intelligent Transport Systems, Orlando, Fl, Oct. 14-18.

Kriegman, David J.; Triendl, Ernst; and Binford, Tomas O. 1987. A Mobile Robot: Sensing, Planning and Locomotion. In *Proceedings of the IEEE International Conference on Robotics and Automation*, 402-408. Los Alamitos, Calif.: IEEE Computer Society Press.

Krotkov, E. 1989. Mobile Robot Localization Using a Single Image. In *Proceedings of the IEEE International Conference on Robotics and Automation*, 978-983. Los Alamitos, Calif.: IEEE Computer Society Press.

Kuipers, Benjamin J., and Byun, Yung-Tai 1991. A Robot Exploration and Mapping Strategy Based on a Semantic Hierarchy of Spatial Representations. In *Robotics and Autonomous Systems* 8: 47-63.

Kuipers, Benjamin J. and Byun, Yung-Tai 1990. A Robot Exploration and Mapping Strategy Based on a Semantic Hierarchy of Spatial Representations. Technical Report, Department of Computer Science, University of Texas at Austin.

Kuipers, Benjamin J. and Byun, Yung-Tai 1988a. A Robust, Qualitative Method for Robot Spatial Learning. In *Proceedings of the Seventh National Conference on Artificial Intelligence*, 774-779. Menlo Park, Calif.: AAAI Press.

Kuipers, Benjamin J., and Byun, Yung-Tai 1988b. A Robust, Qualitative Approach to a Spatial Learning Mobile Robot. In *SPIE Advances in Intelligent Robotics Systems*. Bellingham, Wash: Society of Photo-Optical Instrumentation Engineers.

Kuipers, Benjamin J. and Byun, Yung-Tai 1987. A Qualitative Approach to Robot Exploration and Map-Learning. In *Proceedings of the IEEE Workshop on Spatial Reasoning and Multi-Sensor Fusion*, ed. A. Kak and S. Chen, 390-404. San Francisco: Morgan Kaufmann Publishers.

Latombe, J. C. 1991. *Robot Motion Planning*. Boston, Mass.: Kluwer Academic Publishers.

Lee, D. 1978. The Functions of Vision, *Modes of Perceiving and Processing Information*, ed. H. L. Pick, Jr. and E. Saltzman, 159-170. New York: John Wiley and Sons.

Lee, J.; Huber, M.; Durfee, E.; and Kenny, P. 1994. UM-PRS: An Implementation of the Procedural Reasoning System for Multirobot Applications. In *Proceedings of the American Institute of Aeronautics and Astronautics /NASA Conference on Intelligent Robots in Field, Factory, Service, and Space (CIRFFSS '94)*, ed. Jon Erickson, 842-849. NASA Conference Publication 3251. Houston, Tex: National Aeronautics and Space Administration.

Leonard, J. J., and Durrant-Whyte, H. F. 1992. *Directed Sonar Sensing for Mobile Robot Navigation*. Dortrecht, Holland: Kluwer Academic Publishers.

Leonard, J.J.; Durrant-Whyte, H. F.; and Cox, I. J. 1990. Dynamic Map Building for an Autonomous Mobile Robot. Paper presented at the IEEE/RSJ International Conference on Intelligent Robots and Systems (IROS-90).

Leonhardt, Bradley J. 1996. Mission Planning and Mission Control Software for the Phoenix Autonomous Underwater Vehicle (AUV). Master's thesis, Implementation and Experimental Study, Naval Postgraduate School. (www.cs.nps.navy.mil/research/auv.)

Lesperance, Y. and Levesque, H. J. 1995. Indexical Knowledge and Robot Action—A Logical Account. *Artificial Intelligence* 73(1/2): 69-116.

Levitt, Tod S., and Lawton, Daryl T. 1990. Qualitative Navigation for Mobile Robots. *Artificial Intelligence* 44(3): 305-361.

Littman, M. 1996. Algorithms for Sequential Decision Making. Ph.D. diss., Dept. of Computer Science, Brown University, Providence, R. I.

Littman, M.; Cassandra, A.; and Kaelbling, L. 1995. Learning Policies for Partially Observable Environments: Scaling Up. In *Proceedings of the International Conference on Machine Learning (ICML)*, ed. A. Prieditis and S. Russel, 362-370. San Francisco: Morgan Kaufmann Publishers.

Littman, M.; Dean, T.; and Kaelbling, L. 1995. On the Complexity of Solving Markov Decision Problems. In *Proceedings of the Annual Conference on Uncertainty in Artificial Intelligence (UAI)*, Ed. P. Besnard and S. Hanks, 394-402. San Francisco: Morgan Kaufmann Publishers.

Lorigo, Liana M. 1996. Visual Guided Obstacle Avoidance in Unstructured Environments. Master's thesis, Artificial Intelligence Laboratory, Massachusetts Institute of Technology, Cambridge, Mass.

Lozano-Perez, Tomas, and Wesley, Michael A. 1979. An Algorithm for Planning Collision-Free Paths Among Polyhedral Obstacles. *Communications of the ACM* 22(10): 560-570.

Macedonia, Michael R., and Brutzman, Donald P. 1994. MBone Provides Audio and Video Across the Internet. *IEEE Computer* 27(4): 30-36. (ftp://taurus.cs.nps.navy.mil/pub/i3la/mbone.html)

MacKenzie, D.; Cameron, J.; Arkin, R. 1995. Specification and Execution of Multiagent Missions. Paper presented at the IEEE/RSJ International Conference on Intelligent Robots and Systems (IROS-95), Pittsburgh, Penn., August.

Maes, Pattie 1990. Situated Agents Can Have Goals. *Robotics and Autonomous Systems* 6(1-2): 49-70.

Maes, Pattie; and Brooks, Rodney. 1990. Learning to Coordinate Behaviors. In *Proceedings of the Eighth National Conference on Artificial Intelligence,* 796. Menlo Park, Calif.: AAAI Press.

Marco, D. B., and Healey, A. J. 1996. Local-Area Navigation Using Sonar Feature Extraction and Model-Based Predictive Control. Paper presented at the IEEE Symposium on Autonomous Underwater Vehicle Technology, Monterey California, June 3-6.

Marco, D. B.; Healey, A. J.; and McGhee, R. B. 1996. Autonomous Underwater Vehicles: Hybrid Control of Mission and Motion. *Autonomous Robots* 3: 169-186.

Mataric, Maja J. 1994. Interaction and Intelligent Behavior. Technical Report, AI-TR-1495, Artificial Intelligence Laboratory, Massachusetts Institute of Technology.

Mataric, Maja J. 1992a. Minimizing Complexity in Controlling a Collection of Mobile Robots. In *Proceedings of the IEEE International Conference on Robotics and Automation,* 830-835. Los Alamitos, Calif.: IEEE Computer Society Press.

Mataric, Maja J. 1992b. Integration of Representation into Goal-Driven Behavior-Based Robots. *IEEE Transactions on Robotics and Automation* 8(3): 304-312.

Mataric, Maja J. 1990. Environment Learning Using a Distributed Representation. In *Proceedings of the IEEE International Conference on Robotics and Automation*, 402-406. Los Alamitos, Calif.: IEEE Computer Society Press.

Mataric, Maja J. 1997. Behavior-Based Control: Examples from Navigation, Learning, and Group Behavior. *Journal of Experimental and Theoretical Artificial Intelligence* 9(2-3): 323-336.

McCallum, R. A. 1995a. Instance-Based State Identification for Reinforcement Learning. In *Advances in Neural Information Processing Systems 7*, G. Tesauro, D. Touretzky, and T. Leen, eds., 377-384. Cambridge, Mass.: The MIT Press.

McCallum, R. A. 1995b. Instance-Based Utile Distinctions for Reinforcement Learning with Hidden State. In *Proceedings of the Twelfth International Conference on Machine Learning*, 387-395. San Francisco: Morgan Kaufmann Publishers.

McClarin, David W. 1996. Discrete Multi-Mode Kalman Filtering of Navigation Data for the Phoenix Autonomous Underwater Vehicle. Master's thesis, Naval Postgraduate School, Monterey, Calif.

McGillem, C. D., and Rappaport, T. S. 1988. Infrared Location System for Navigation of Autonomous Vehicles. In *Proceedings of the IEEE International Conference on Robotics and Automation*, 1236-1238. Los Alamitos, Calif.: IEEE Computer Society Press.

Miller, David P. 1994. The Long-Term Effects of Secondary Sensing. *AI Magazine* 15(1): 52-56.

Miller, David P.; Rajiv S. Desai, Erann Gat, Robert Ivlev and John Loch. 1991. Reactive Navigation through Rough Terrain: Experimental Results. In *Proceedings of the Tenth National Conference on Artificial Intelligence*, 823. Menlo Park, Calif.: AAAI Press.

Moore, A. W., and Atkeson, C. G. 1993. Prioritized Sweeping: Reinforcement Learning with Less Data and Less Time. *Machine Learning* 13: 103-130.

Moore, R. C. 1980. Reasoning About Knowledge and Action. Technical Note 191, Artificial Intelligence Center, SRI International, Menlo Park, Calif.

Moravec, Hans P. 1988. Sensor Fusion in Certainty Grids for Mobile Robots. *AI Magazine* 9(2): 61-74.

Moravec, Hans P. 1981. *Robot Rover Visual Navigation*. Ann Arbor, Mich.: UMI Research Press.

Moravec Hans P., and Elfes, Alberto E. 1985. High Resolution Maps From Wide Angle Sonar. In *Proceedings of the IEEE International Conference on Robotics and Automation*, 116-121. Los Alamitos, Calif.: IEEE Computer Society Press.

Moravec, Hans P. The Stanford Cart and the CMU Rover. *IEEE Proceedings* 71(7): 872-884. Piscataway N. J.: Institute of Electrical and Electronic Engineers, Inc.

Morellas, V.; Minners, J.; and Donath, M. 1995. Implementation of Real Time Spatial Mapping in Robotic Systems Through Self-Organizing Neural Networks. Paper presented at the IEEE/RSJ International Conference on Intelligent Robots and Systems ((IROS '95), Pittsburgh, Penn., August

Morrellas, V.; Morris, T.; Alexander, L.; and Donath, M. 1997. Preview Based Control of a Tractor Trailer Using DGPS for Preventing Road Departure Accidents. Paper presented at the IEEE Conference on Intelligent Transportation Systems. Boston, 9-12 November.

Murphy, Robin R. 1995. An Artificial Intelligence Approach to the 1994 AUVS Unmanned Ground Vehicle Competition. Paper presented at the IEEE International Conference on Systems, Man and Cybernetics, Vancouver, October 22-25.

Murphy, Robin R. 1996. Biological and Cognitive Foundations of Intelligent Sensor Fusion. *IEEE Transactions on Systems, Man, and Cybernetics* 26(1): 42-51.

Murphy, Robin R., and Arkin, R. C. 1992. SFX: An Architecture for Action-Oriented Sensor Fusion. Paper presented at the IEEE/RSJ International Conference on Intelligent Robots and Systems (IROS-92), Raleigh, N. C., 7-10 July.

Murphy, Robin R., and Mali, A. 1996. Lessons Learned in Integrating Sensing into Autonomous Mobile Robot Architectures. *Journal of Experimental and Theoretical Artificial Intelligence* 9(2): 191-209.

Murphy, Robin R.; Hoff, W.; Blitch, J.; Gough, V.; Hoffman, J.; Hawkins, D.; Krosley, R.; Lyon, T.; Mali, A.; MacMillan, J.; Warshawsky, S. 1995. Colorado School of Mines Behavioral Approach to the 1995 Unmanned Ground Vehicle Competition. Paper presented at the Mobile Robots X Conference, Philadelphia, Penn., 22-26 Oct.

Myers, K. L. 1996. A Procedural Knowledge Approach to Task-Level Control. In *Proceedings of the Third International Conference on AI Planning Systems,* ed. Brian Drabble, 158-165. Menlo Park, Calif.: AAAI Press.

Myers, K. L. 1993. User's Guide for the Procedural Reasoning System. Technical Note, SRI Artificial Intelligence Center, Menlo Park, Calif.

Myers K. L., and Konolige, K. 1992. Reasoning with Analogical Representations. In *Principles of Knowledge Representation and Reasoning: Proceedings of the Third International Conference (KR-92)*, B. Nebel, C. Rich, and W. Swartout, eds. San Mateo, Calif.: Morgan Kaufmann Publishers.

Neisser, U. 1989. Direct Perception and Recognition as Distinct Perceptual Systems. Paper Paper presented at the Cognitive Science Society Conference, August.

Neven, H., and Schöner, G. 1995. Dynamics Parametrically Controlled by Image Correlations Organize Robot Navigation. *Biological Cybernetics* 75: 293-307.

Niblack, W., and Petkovic, D. 1988. On Improving the Accuracy of the Hough Transform: Theory, Simulations, and Experiments. In *Proceedings of the IEEE Conference on Computer Vision and Pattern Recognition,* 574-579. Los Alamitos, Calif.: IEEE Computer Society Press.

Nilsson, Nils J. 1994. Teleo-Reactive Programs for Agent Control. *Journal of Artificial Intelligence Research* 1: 139-158.

Nilsson, Nils J. 1992. Toward Agent Programs with Circuit Semantics. Technical Report CS-TR-92-1412, Dept. of Computer Science, Stanford Univ., Stanford, Calif.

Nilsson, Nils J. 1982. *Principles of Artificial Intelligence*. Palo Alto, Calif.: Tioga Publishing.

Nilsson, Nils J. 1980. *Principles of Artificial Intelligence*. Palo Alto: Tioga Press.

Nilsson, Nils J. 1969. A Mobile Automaton: An Application of AI Techniques. In *Proceedings of the First International Joint Conference on Artificial Intelligence,* 509-520. San Francisco: Morgan Kaufmann Publishers.

Noreils, Fabrice R. 1990. Integrating Error Recovery in a Mobile Robot Control System. In *Proceedings of the IEEE International Conference on Robotics and Automation.* Los Alamitos, Calif.: IEEE Computer Society Press.

Noreils, Fabrice R., and Chatila, R. G. 1995. Plan Execution Monitoring and Control Architecture for Mobile Robots. *IEEE Transactions on Robotics and Automation* 11(2): 255-266.

Nourbakhsh, Illah, and Genesereth, M. 1996. Assumptive Planning and Execution: A Simple, Working Robot Architecture. *Autonomous Robots* 2(1): 49-67.

Nourbakhsh, Illah; Morse, Sarah; Becker, Craig; Balabanovic, Marko; Gat, Erann; Simmons, Reid; Goodridge, Steven; Potlapalli, Harsh; Hinkle, David; Jung, Ken; and Van-Vactor, David. 1993. The Winning Robots from the 1993 Robot Competition. *AI Magazine* 14(4): 51-62

Nourbakhsh, Illah; Powers, R.; and Birchfield, S. 1995. Dervish: An Office-Navigating Robot. *AI Magazine* 16(2): 53-60.

Olawsky, D.; Krebsbach, K.; and Gini, M. 1993. An Analysis of Sensor-Based Task Planning. Technical Report, #93-94, Univ. of Minnesota, Minneapolis, Minn.

Papadimitriou, C., and Tsitsiklis, J. 1987. The Complexity of Markov Decision Processes. *Mathematics of Operations Research* 12(3): 441-450.

Parker, L. 1993. Adaptive Action Selection for Cooperative Agent Teams. In *From Animals to Animats: Proceedings of the Second International Conference on the Simulation of Adaptive Behavior*, 442-450. Cambridge, Mass.: The MIT Press.

Parr, R., and Russell, S. 1995. Approximating Optimal Policies for Partially Observable Stochastic Domains. In *Proceedings of the Fourteenth International Joint Conference on Artificial Intelligence*, 1088-1094. San Francisco: Morgan Kaufmann Publishers.

Passini, Romedi. 1984. *Wayfinding in Architecture: Environmental Design Series, Volume 4*, New York: Van Norstrand Reinhold.

Payton, David W. 1986. An Architecture for Reflexive Autonomous Vehicle Control. In *Proceedings of the IEEE International Conference on Robotics and Automation*, 1838-1843. Los Alamitos, Calif.: IEEE Computer Society Press.

Payton, David; Rosenblatt, J. Kenneth, and Keirsey, David. 1990. Plan-Guided Reaction. *IEEE Transactions on Systems, Man and Cybernetics* 20(6): 1370-1382.

Pearl, J. 1988. *Probabilistic Reasoning in Intelligent Systems: Networks of Plausible Inference*. San Francisco: Morgan Kaufmann Publishers.

Pears, N. E., and Probert, P. J. 1993. An Optical Range Sensor for Mobile Robot Guidance. In *Proceedings of the IEEE International Conference on Robotics and Automation*. Los Alamitos, Calif.: IEEE Computer Society Press.

Pell, Barney et al. 1996. A Remote Agent Prototype for an Autonomous Spacecraft. In *Proceedings of the SPIE Conference on Optical Science, Engineering, and Instrumentation*, Bellingham, Wash: Society of Photo-Optical Instrumentation Engineers.

Pierce, D., and Kuipers, B. 1994. Learning to Explore and Build Maps. In *Proceedings of the Twelfth National Conference on Artificial Intelligence*, 1264-1271. Menlo Park, Calif.: AAAI Press.

Premi, S., and Besant, C. 1983. A Review of Various Vehicle Guidance Techniques That Can Be Used by Mobile Robots or Agvs. Paper Paper presented at the Second International Conference on Automated Guided Vehicle Systems, Stuttgart,Germany.

Preston, Howard; Holstein, J.; Otteson, J.; and Hoffman, P. 1995. Precursor System Analyses of Automated Highway Systems: Activity Area A - Urban and Rural AHS Analysis. In Battelle Transportation Systems Report FHWA-RD-95-043 (Reference 09529 AHS). Washington, D.C.: Government Printing Office.

Rabiner, L. R., and Juang, B. H. 1986. An Introduction to Hidden Markov Models. *IEEE ASSP Magazine* 3(1): 4-16, January.

Rabiner, L. R. 1990. A Tutorial on Hidden Markov Models and Selected Applications in Speech Recognition. In *Speech Recognition*, ed. A. Waibel and K. F. Lee. San Francisco: Morgan Kaufmann Publishers.

Rao, B. S. Y.; Durrant-Whyte, H. F.; and Sheen, J. A. 1993. A Fully Decentralized Multi-Sensor System for Tracking and Surveillance. *International Journal of Robotics Research* 1(12).

Rencken, W. D. 1993. Concurrent Localization and Map Building for Mobile Robots Using Ultrasonic Sensors. Paper presented at the IEEE/RSJ International Conference on Intelligent Robots and Systems (IROS-93), Yokohama, Japan.

Rivest, R. L., and Shapire R. E. 1993. Inference of Finite Automata Using Homing Sequences. *Information and Computation*. 103: 299-347.

Rosenblatt, J. Kenneth, and Payton, David W. 1989. A Fine-Grained Alternative to the Subsumption Architecture. Paper presented at the AAAI Spring Symposium on Robot Navigation, March. Stanford, Calif.

Rosenschein, Stanley J., and Kaelbling, Leslie Pack. 1986. The Synthesis of Machines with Provable Epistemic Properties. In *Proceedings of the Conference on Theoretical Aspects of Reasoning about Knowledge*, Joseph Halpern, ed., 83-98. San Francisco: Morgan Kaufmann Publishers.

Rumelhart, D. E.; Hinton, G. E.; and Williams, R. J. 1986. Learning Internal Representations by Error Propagation. In *Parallel Distributed Processing. Vol. I + II*, eds. D. E. Rumelhart and J. L. McClelland, 318-362. Cambridge, Mass.: The MIT Press.

Saffiotti, A. 1996. The Use of Fuzzy Logic for Autonomous Robot Navigation. *Soft Computing* 1(4).

Saffiotti, A. 1994. Pick-up What? In C. *Current Trends in AI Planning*, Backstrom and E. Sandewall, eds. Amsterdam: IOS Press.

Saffiotti, A., and Wesley, L. P. 1996. Perception-Based Self-Localization Using Fuzzy Locations. In *Reasoning with Uncertainty in Robotics: Lecture Notes in Artificial Intelligence 1093*, ed. L. Dorst, M. van Lambalgen, and F. Voorbraak, 368-385. Berlin: Springer-Verlag.

Saffiotti, A.; Konolige, K.; and Ruspini, E. H. 1995. A Multivalued-Logic Approach to Integrating Planning and Control. *Artificial Intelligence* 76(1/2): 481-526.

Saffiotti, A.; Ruspini, E. H.; and Konolige, K. 1993. Integrating Reactivity and Goal-Directedness in a Fuzzy Controller. In *Proceedings of the Second Fuzzy-IEEE Conference,*. New York: IEEE.

Sanger, T. D. 1988. Stereo Disparity Computation Using Gabor Filters. *Biological Cybernetics* 59: 405-418.

Sayers, Craig P.; Yoerger, Dana R.; Paul, Richard P.; and Lisiewicz, John S. 1996. A Manipulator Work Package for Teleoperation from Unmanned Untethered Vehicles—Current Feasibility and Future Applications. Paper presented at the International Advanced Robotics Programme (IARP) on Subsea Robotics, Toulon, France, March 27-29 (www. dsl.whoi.edu).

Schiele, B., and Crowley, J. 1994. A Comparison of Position Estimation Techniques Using Occupancy Grids. In *Proceedings of the IEEE International Conference on Robotics and Automation*, 1628-1634. Los Alamitos, Calif.: IEEE Computer Society Press.

Schneider, F. E. 1994. Sensor interpretation und Kartenerstellung für Mobile Roboter. Master's thesis, Dept. of Computer Science, University of Bonn.

Schoppers, Marcel. 1987. Universal Plans for Reactive Robots in Unpredictable Domains. In *Proceedings of the Tenth International Joint Conference on Artificial Intelligence* 1039-1046. San Francisco: Morgan Kaufmann Publishers.

Shank, Roger C. 1991. Where's the AI? *AI Magazine* 12(4): 38-49.

Shankwitz, C., and Donath, M. 1995. MIMIC Sensor Technology for Highway Applications: Potential and Challenges for the Future. In *Final Report, Minnesota Department of Transportation*, St. Paul, Minn.: Office of Research Administration, Minnesota Department of Transportation.

Shankwitz, C.; Donath, M.; Morellas, V.; and Johnson, D. Sensing and Control to Enhance the Safety of Heavy Vehicles. In *Proceedings of the World Congress on Intelligent Transport Systems.* Tokyo: Vertis.

Shen, W. -M. 1993. Learning Finite Automata Using Local Distinguishing Experiments. In *Proceedings of the Thirteenth International Joint Conference on Artificial Intelligence,* 1088-1093. Menlo Park, Calif.: AAAI Press.

Simmons, Reid G. 1996. The Curvature-Velocity Method for Local Obstacle Avoidance. In *Proceedings of the IEEE International Conference on Robotics and Automation,* 3375-3382. Los Alamitos, Calif.: IEEE Computer Society Press.

Simmons, Reid G. 1995. The 1994 AAAI Mobile Robot Competition and Exhibition. *AI Magazine* 16(2): 19-30.

Simmons, Reid G. 1994a. Becoming Increasingly Reliable. In *Proceedings of the International Conference on Artificial Intelligence Planning Systems (AIPS)*, ed. K. Hammond, 152-157. Menlo Park, Calif.: AAAI Press.

Simmons, R. G. 1994b. Structured Control for Autonomous Robots. *IEEE Transactions on Robotics and Automation* 10(1): 34-43.

Simmons, Reid G. 1990. An Architecture for Coordinating Planning, Sensing and Action. Paper presented at the DARPA Workshop on Innovative Approaches to Planning, Scheduling, and Control, San Diego, Calif., 5-8 Nov.

Simmons, Reid G., and Koenig, Sven 1995. Probabilistic Robot Navigation in Partially Observable Environments. In *Proceedings of the Fourteenth International Joint Conference on Artificial Intelligence,* 1080-1087. San Francisco: Morgan Kaufmann Publishers.

Simmons, Reid G.; Goodwin, R.; Haigh, K.; Koenig, S.; and O'Sullivan, J. 1997. A Layered Architecture for Office Delivery Robots. In *Proceedings of the International Conference on Autonomous Agents,* ed. W. L. Johnson, 245-252. New York: ACM Press.

Simmons, Reid G.; Lin, L.; and Fedor, C. 1990. Autonomous Task Control for Mobile Robots. Paper presented at the Fifth IEEE International Symposium on Intelligent Control, Philadelphia, Penn., Sept. 5-7.

Slack, M. 1993. Navigation Templates: Mediating Qualitative Guidance and Quantitative Control in Mobile Robots. *IEEE Transactions on Systems, Man, and Cybernetics* 23(2): 452-466.

Smith, R., and Cheeseman, P. 1986. On the Representation and Estimation of Spatial Uncertainty. *The International Journal of Robotics Research* 5(4): 56-68.

Smith, Samuel M., and Dunn, Stanley E. 1994. The Ocean Voyager II: An AUV Designed for Coastal Oceanography. Paper presented at the IEEE Oceanic Engineering Society Conference Autonomous Underwater Vehicles Conference (AUV-94), Cambridge, Massachusetts, July 19-20. (www.oe.fau.edu/AMS).

Sondick, E. 1978. The Optimal Control of Partially Observable Markov Processes Over the Infinite Horizon: Discounted Costs. *Operations Research* 26(2): 282-304.

Soldo, Monnett. 1990. Reactive and Preplanned Control in a Mobile Robot. In *Proceedings of the IEEE International Conference on Robotics and Automation*. Los Alamitos, Calif.: IEEE Computer Society Press.

Stentz, A. 1995. The Focused D* Algorithm for Real-Time Replanning. In *Proceedings of the Fourteenth International Joint Conference on Artificial Intelligence*. San Francisco: Morgan Kaufmann Publishers.

Stevens, Richard W. 1992. *Advanced Programming in the Unix Environment*. Reading, Mass.: Addison-Wesley.

Stewart, W. Kenneth. 1992. Visualization Resources and Strategies for Remote Subsea Exploration. *The Visual Computer* 8(5/6): 361-379.

Stolcke, A., and Omohundro, S. 1993. Hidden Markov Model Induction by Bayesian Model Merging. In *Advances in Neural Information Processing Systems 5*, ed. S. Hanson, J. Cowan, and C. Giles, 11-18. San Francisco: Morgan Kaufmann Publishers.

Strauss, Paul S., and Carey, Rikk. 1992. An Object-Oriented 3D Graphics Toolkit. *Computer Graphics* 26(2): 341-349.

Suchman, Lucy. 1987. *Plans and Situated Action*. New York: Cambridge University Press.

Sugihara, K. 1988. Some Location Problems for Robot Navigation Using a Single Camera. *Computer Vision, Graphics, and Image Processing* 42(3): 112-129.

Takahashi, O., and Schiling, R. J. 1989. Motion Planning in a Plane Using Generalized Voronoi Diagram. *IEEE Transactions on Robotics and Automation* 5(2): 143-150.

Tenenberg, J.; Karlsson, J.; and Whitehead, S. 1992. Learning Via Task Decomposition. In *Proceedings of the From Animals to Animats Conference*, ed. J. A. Meyer, H. Roitblat, and S. Wilson, 337-343. Cambridge, Mass.: The MIT Press.

Thalmann, Daniel. ed. 1990. *Scientific Visualization and Graphics Simulation*. Chichester, England: John Wiley & Sons.

Thau, Robert 1997. Learning Robust, Maintainable Maps. Dissertation Proposal, AI Laboratory, Massachusetts Institute of Technology, Cambridge, Mass., June.

Thrun, Sebastian (forthcoming). Learning Maps for Indoor Mobile Robot Navigation. *Artificial Intelligence*.

Thrun, Sebastian 1996. A Bayesian Approach to Landmark Discovery and Active Perception for Mobile Robot Navigation. Technical Report, CMU-CS-96-122, School of Computer Science, Carnegie Mellon University.

Thrun, Sebastian 1993. Exploration and Model Building in Mobile Robot Domains. In *Proceedings of the ICNN-93*, ed. E. Ruspini, 175-180. New York: IEEE Neural Network Council.

Thrun, Sebastian, and Bücken, A. 1996a. Integrating Grid-Based and Topological Maps for Mobile Robot Navigation. In *Proceedings of the Thirteenth National Conference on Artificial Intelligence*, 944. Menlo Park, Calif.: AAAI Press.

Thrun, Sebastian, and Bücken, A. 1996b. Learning Maps for Indoor Mobile Robot Navigation. Technical Report, CMU-CS-96-121, School of Computer Science, Carnegie Mellon University.

Torrance, M. C. 1994. Natural Communication with Robots. Master's thesis, Department of Electrical Engineering and Computer Science, Massachusetts Institute of Technology, Cambridge, Mass.

Torsiello, Kevin. 1994. Acoustic Positioning of the NPS Autonomous Underwater Vehicle (AUV II) During Hover Conditions. Engineer's thesis, Naval Postgraduate School. Monterey, Calif.

Tsumura, T. 1986. Survey of Automated Guided Vehicle in Japanese Factory. In *Proceedings of the IEEE International Conference on Robotics and Automation*, 1329-1334. Los Alamitos, Calif.: IEEE Computer Society Press.

Turk, Matthew A.; Morgenthaler, David G.; Gremban, Keith; and Marra, Martin. 1987. Video Road Following for the Autonomous Land Vehicle. In *Proceedings of the IEEE International Conference on Robotics and Automation*, 273-280. Los Alamitos, Calif.: IEEE Computer Society Press.

Ullman, Shimon. 1984. Visual Routines. *Cognition* 18: 97-159.

U. S. Army, Field Manual No 7-7J. Washington, D. C.: Department of the Army.

Van Dam, J. W. M.; Kröse, B. J. A.; and Groen, F. C. A. 1996. Neural Network Applications in Sensor Fusion for an Autonomous Mobile Robot. In *Reasong with Uncertainty in Robotics: Lecture Notes in Computer Science 1093*, ed. L. Dorst, M. van Lambalgen, and F. Voorbraak, 1-19. Berlin: Springer-Verlag.

Viterbi, A. 1967. Error Bounds for Convolutional Codes and an Asymptotically Optimum Decoding Algorithm. *IEEE Transactions on Information Theory* 13(2): 260-269.

Warren, C. W. 1989. Global Path Planning Using Artificial Potential Fields. In *Proceedings of the IEEE International Conference on Robotics and Automation*, 316-320. Los Alamitos, Calif.: IEEE Computer Society Press.

Wensel, D. J., and Seida, S. B. 1993. High Speed Extraction of Line Segment Features. *SPIE* 2064(January): 47-58.

Wilcox, W. H. 1987. A Vision System for a Mars Rover. In *Proceedings of SPIE Mobile Robots II*, 852. Bellingham, Wash: Society of Photo-Optical Instrumentation Engineers.

Yang, J.; Xu, Y.; and Chen, C. 1994. Hidden Markov Model Approach to Skill Learning and its Application to Telerobotics. *IEEE Transactions on Robotics and Automation* 10(5): 621-631.

Yeaple, Judith Anne. 1992. David Miller's Brainless Robot. *Popular Science* 241(6): 102.

Yen J., and Pfluger, N. 1992. A Fuzzy Logic Based Robot Navigation System. Paper presented at the AAAI Fall Symposium on Mobile Robot Navigation, Cambridge, Mass., Oct. 23-25.

Yuh, Junku 1995. *Underwater Robotic Vehicles: Design and Control.* Albuquerque, N. M.: TSI Press.

Zabih R., and Woodfill, J. 1994. Non-Parametric Local Transforms for Computing Visual Correspondence. Paper presented at the Third European Conference on Computer Vision, Stockholm, August.

Zucker, S. W. 1976. Region Growing: Childhood and Adolescence. *Computer Graphics and Image Processing* 5: 382–399.

Index